The Life and Times
of
Dillon Read

The Life and Times

of

Dillon Read

• BY •

ROBERT SOBEL

T·T

TRUMAN TALLEY BOOKS / DUTTON
NEW YORK

332.66
S67L

DUTTON
Published by the Penguin Group
Penguin Books USA Inc., 375 Hudson Street,
New York, New York 10014, U.S.A.
Penguin Books Ltd, 27 Wrights Lane,
London W8 5TZ, England
Penguin Books Australia Ltd, Ringwood,
Victoria, Australia
Penguin Books Canada Ltd, 2801 John Street,
Markham, Ontario, Canada L3R 1B4
Penguin Books (N.Z.) Ltd, 182–190 Wairau Road,
Auckland 10, New Zealand

Penguin Books Ltd, Registered Offices:
Harmondsworth, Middlesex, England

First published by Truman Talley Books/Dutton, an imprint of New American Library,
a division of Penguin Books USA Inc.

First Printing, May, 1991
10 9 8 7 6 5 4 3 2 1

Copyright © New American Library, a division of Penguin Books USA, Inc., 1991

LIBRARY OF CONGRESS CATALOGING IN PUBLICATION DATA
Sobel, Robert, 1931 Feb. 19–
    The life and times of Dillon Read / by Robert Sobel.
    p.   cm.
    Includes bibliographical references and index.
    ISBN 0-525-24959-1
    1. Dillon, Read & Co.—History.   2. Investment banking—United
States—History.   I. Title.
HG4930.S63   1991
332.66'0973—dc20   90-20013
                                                                    CIP

Printed in the United States of America
Set in Century Expanded
Designed by Eve L. Kirch

TP

Contents

Preface

While firms in the same industry may appear to share similar-
ities, the differences usually are more striking. Each likes
to consider itself unique, and more often than not, asserts that this
singularity is the mark of superiority. That this is so is not surprising; in this respect firms are like nations, which demonstrate
the same characteristics of broad similarity in outline yet remarkable particularity in detail. This history is an attempt to capture
both the general and the particular aspects of one firm in the
investment banking industry over time.

Dillon, Read & Co., Inc., is one of the oldest American investment banks, tracing its corporate antecedents back to 1832.*
Its development ever since has been generally related to the vi-
cissitudes of American finance, which is to say that as the nation's
financial needs evolved, so did the firm. Originating as a brokerage,
it helped raise funds for the Union cause during the Civil War,
and afterwards entered investment banking. By the end of the
century one of its leaders, William A. Read, was among the finan-

*For the sake of simplicity, the firm will be referred to henceforth as Dillon
Read.

vii

cial community's most respected bond experts. Even so, what first was Carpenter & Vermilye, then Vermilye & Co., and next William A. Read & Co. was not a major force in American finance. Rather, it was a handmaiden and supporting player in the drama, while the center stage was left to the likes of Jay Cooke and J. P. Morgan.

Dillon Read's position altered dramatically in the 1920s, when it became one of the more important American investment banks, at just the time New York was displacing London as the world's principal banking center. Its flowering was largely the work of Clarence Dillon, who in an almost serendipitous fashion had entered the firm just prior to World War I, and upon the death of Read assumed its leadership. He changed the firm's name to Dillon, Read & Co. in 1921, while rescuing Goodyear Tire and Rubber Company from a bankruptcy that might have caused a major financial panic.

Clarence Dillon was perhaps the most celebrated investment banker of the "Roaring Twenties," with reporters bestowing upon him the reputation of a fearless, high-flying, and resourceful financier. Much of this, as anyone familiar with the industry might suspect, was hyperbole; in fact, he was successful precisely because he was cautious and judicious, brilliant at calculating risk-reward ratios, and unwilling to enter a deal unless success was highly probable, if not virtually assured, and financed as much as possible by others.

With the advent of the Great Depression and a congressional investigation into investment banking, Dillon turned the firm's active management over to others. But even after his withdrawal from the day-to-day business, Dillon would continue to have a strong influence on the firm's policy, strategy, and "corporate culture" well into the modern age. His personal influence would wane in the mid-1970s, as he approached his death, which came in 1979 when he was ninety-six.

During the Depression the firm became one of Wall Street's more conservative banks. It was to remain so in the years that followed, even as it pioneered in financing techniques in such important fields as natural gas pipelines and petroleum. Prudence and solvency were in fact Dillon Read's hallmarks in the first two decades after World War II, when almost every Wall Street bank experienced growth and prosperity. When the business scene altered sharply in the late 1960s and 1970s, Dillon Read was slow to respond. As other Wall Street firms grew to enormous size and wealth by increasing their capital and by transforming themselves into multipurpose "financial supermarkets," or at least by branching into such new exotic areas as currency trading, conglomerate financing, and venture capital, Dillon Read remained traditional.

Dillon Read adhered steadfastly to Clarence Dillon's policy of "relationship" banking, in which the banker's principal service to a client is as an advisor, while firms that moved into the forefront of the industry in terms of size and profits did so by becoming more "transactional," moving from deal to deal rather then cultivating and ministering to all client requirements.

Dillon Read paid a price for this steady reliance on such traditional business, which it continued to conduct as a rather old-fashioned collegial partnership. Once a "special bracket firm," which ensured it a senior listing on major underwritings, Dillon Read became much smaller, known more for its leaders who served in Washington than for its banking operations—Secretary of Defense James Forrestal, Ambassador Paul Nitze, Presidential Assistant Peter Flanigan, and Secretaries of the Treasury C. Douglas Dillon and Nicholas Brady, the last of whom took command in 1971. It was respected, but not feared as a competitive force. Even so, the firm's earnings were quite good, its bankers well rewarded. Brady would later remark, "Having some basic principles is not only a pleasant way to live, but it is also profitable."[1]

This comfortable but perhaps old-fashioned way of operating changed in the 1980s, as the Dillon family relinquished control of the business and Brady and other partners began to encourage reforms. More formal managerial systems were required to do business in a more complex environment on a more efficient basis. Brady brought in John Birkelund, an investment banker with a venture capital background and strong managerial talents, who, while explicitly eschewing any thought of making Dillon Read a financial supermarket, led the firm into areas of specialized competence. More formal managerial systems were put in place. Today's Dillon Read is more entrepreneurial, less risk-averse, and more innovative.

Even so, it has not at all abandoned its traditional emphasis on relationship banking, but has and is adjusting skillfully to the ever-changing requirements of clients and markets. At the same time, overexpansion, bad management, and revelations of wrongdoing which have convulsed the financial community in recent years have reinforced Dillon Read's conservatism and high ethical standards.

Today, much as in Clarence Dillon's day, Dillon Read enjoys a reputation for conducting business with a selected group of clients with jewellike precison. "We believe as a general rule investment bankers are not what they were twenty years ago," said an officer at one of the firm's clients:[2]

> Twenty years ago investment bankers were considered confidants, really a member of the team, a member of the family, and you could call them and have trust that they would treat it in confidence, and that they would give you their candid opinion without concern for the almighty buck or whether or not they would be able to do the deal or not.

> I think, by and large, the investment banking community is no longer that—you can't do many things with most of the investment bankers that are out there today. There are still a few honest ones, dedicated to their clients, as opposed to dedicated to simple profits. We think Dillon Read's structure and their history and the philosophy comes closer to matching what we're looking for— and in investment banking what we have in the past, and are still looking for—than most of the others.

Works of this nature rarely are the product of a single person's efforts, and this is no exception. Dillon Read chief librarian Nancy Bowles was my prime contact at the firm, ferreting out information, arranging interviews, and acting as a sounding board for my ideas. Without her efforts and those of managing director John Haskell, who spearheaded this project, this history could not have come into being. It was they who in 1987 engaged me to write this history, through The Winthrop Group, Inc., under conditions which ensured I be given open access to all Dillon Read personnel and historical files, and a free hand to develop and present my own interpretations.

As is its practice in producing corporate histories, Winthrop asked that a committee be established to review the manuscript at critical stages for factual accuracy and substantive criticism. Its members included Dillon Read managing directors Haskell, Peter

---

Flanigan, David Niemiec, Ned Whitney, Richard Yancey, and John Mullin, along with George David Smith of Winthrop, who is also clinical professor of economics at New York University, and Thomas Huertas, a noted economic historian who now serves as a vice president of planning for Citicorp in Europe.

Mary E. Curry, a business historian who is a consultant at Winthrop, was an indefatigable and imaginative researcher whose abilities at ferreting out obscure materials proved positively uncanny. In addition she checked facts, verified sources, and performed any and all tasks required with skill and imagination. I benefited greatly from her efforts. Dan Jacoby went beyond the call of duty in providing research assistance, especially for the later chapters. Sally Brazil gathered the illustrations from several sources. George Smith read, edited, and criticized the manuscript, helped with interviews, and assisted in client relationships.

At the outset I assumed that few documents existed at the firm and I would have to struggle along with scraps of original materials, secondary sources, and interviews. Such had been the case in my earlier history of Salomon Brothers, and I knew of Vincent Carosso's similar experience in writing his history of Kidder Peabody. One day in late 1987, I asked Douglas Dillon whether he had any of his father's papers. He replied that there were none as far as he knew, but suggested I contact his sister, Mrs. Dorothy Eweson. This I did, and Mary Curry traveled to her Far Hills, New Jersey, home. There Mrs. Eweson showed her several filing cabinets filled with material, including Clarence Dillon's diary, an unfinished but detailed manuscript of a book dealing with his life and that of his wife, called "Anne's Story," and partners' meeting minutes for the late 1920s and early 1930s. Copies of letters, memoranda, and other papers for the 1920s and 1930s were filed there as well, along with documents relating to Dillon's most fabled deals and his preparation for testimony before the Pecora Committee in 1934.

As a body, the Clarence Dillon papers constitute one of the most important collections relating to the financial markets in those years. They inform many of the conclusions drawn regarding not only Clarence Dillon's activities but those of Wall Street as a whole in the years involved. Most historians' earlier judgments (including my own) regarding the financial history of this period will be challenged and modified by the rich contents of the Dillon papers, which provide a unique opportunity to follow the very thoughts of one of history's leading investment bankers almost as they occurred. I am eternally grateful to Mrs. Eweson for access to this historical treasure trove.

There are, of course, other documents and papers. In particular, the Ferdinand Eberstadt papers on deposit at Princeton University were a prime source for an understanding of Dillon Read's activities in Europe during the 1920s.

Unfortunately, the kinds of primary sources historians like best thin out for Dillon Read in the modern period. Part of the problem is that much of the documentation on recent events is necessarily proprietary. There is also a more generic problem with which all business historians are familiar. Institutions generate more paper than ever, but with less and less detail about the actual decision-making process; neither lawyers nor modern business practice encourage the creation and retention of such records. Then, too, while the invention of the telephone has done wonders for all aspects of our lives, it has cut down on the writing of letters and memoranda, to the detriment of the historian's work. Thus interviews with current and former Dillon Read personnel and public documents form a large part of the body of primary sources for the post–World War II period, augmented by understanding gained from viewing some key documents concerning the recent history that the firm has been good enough to share with me. It was requested by Dillon Read that specific citations of interviews with its employees not be made in footnotes, although the bibliography contains a complete listing of interviews. Where people have been quoted directly, the source is apparent in the text.

Finally, in addition to Dorothy Eweson, I am particularly grateful for the assistance provided by C. Douglas Dillon, August Belmont, and managing director Peter Flanigan, for their recollections of the firm in the late 1940s and 1950s. Managing Director James Brandi spoke with me about his father's career. Nicholas Brady, Arthur Treman, John Birkelund, and other Dillon Read directors shared their thoughts on the firm's development and philosophy, as did the many others who are listed in the interview section of the Bibliography.

—R.S.
September 1990

·1·

Carpenter & Vermilye

(1832–1861)

The origins of important undertakings, like the birth of infants who in the course of their development become consequential men and women, are often obscure. Only in retrospect do historians, biographers, journalists, and hagiographers attempt to locate the beginnings, and as is too often the case, they can find only scanty data and testimony.

Such is the situation presented in the case of Dillon, Read & Co.—or to be more precise, Carpenter & Vermilye, the original incarnation of the company, which appeared in New York City in 1832 to capitalize on investment opportunities during America's first industrial revolution.

At the time there existed a small commercial house registered in the name of Rufus Nevins, a respected businessman engaged in several pursuits. This firm had a modest office at 30 Wall Street, located at the southwest corner of Wall and William streets. Rufus Nevins was a member of the New York Stock & Exchange Board, but the firm actually was headed by his brother Richard, who had gone bankrupt several years earlier. Because of this Richard's designation could not be used, so his brothers Rufus and Russell backed him financially, while Rufus permitted his name to be used

1

as its head.[1] Russell, who had a brokerage office nearby at 42 Wall Street under the name of Nevins & Townsend, was one of the city's business and social leaders.

Washington Romeyn Vermilye was a clerk at the Rufus Nevins establishment. He came from a well-known, large, and distinguished family, so it is probable he arrived not only with credentials but the proper relationships. The Vermilyes had immigrated to the Netherlands, and since they were Huguenots it may have been they fled as a result of the persecution of Protestants which climaxed in the St. Bartholemew's Day Massacre of 1572.

According to one source, the family next took refuge in London.[2] In 1662 Isaac Vermilje (sometimes as Vermeille, Vermelje, and Vermuele) set out for the small settlement of New Amstel on the Delaware River. After a year there he left for the larger Dutch colony in New Amsterdam and settled in New Haarlem. Washington, who was born in 1810, was Isaac's great-great-great-great-grandson.[3]

Little is known of the occupations of most of Washington's ancestors. Several Vermilyes were soldiers, printers, and surveyors. Through land speculation, one of Washington's great-uncles, John, became fairly wealthy and passed down to his children what for those days was a fortune. Washington's grandfather was a builder and surveyor, and it would appear he too bequeathed something of an inheritance to his three children. His son William W. became a printer, with an establishment at Pine Street, not far from Wall. William had twelve children, of whom Washington was the sixth.[4]

Apparently the family was quite religious; two of Washington's brothers, Thomas and Robert, became ministers, and one of his sisters married a minister. Washington himself might have contemplated a religious calling; after what appears to have been slight schooling he found employment as clerk for the New York Bible Society. This didn't last long, and soon after he went to work for Nevins.

While not one of Wall Street's eminent houses, Nevins's establishment was respected. But not for long. He died in September 1831, and with this the firm might have dissolved. Yet it endured. Rufus and Russell Nevins were willing to see the business continue, and proposed that Vermilye and George Carpenter take charge of it. The revamped firm would start small, in a basement office at 42 Wall Street, next door to Rufus Nevins's more sizable quarters. It was down the street from New York Life Insurance Company in a narrow wooden building, situated between the Bank of America and the Merchants Bank, both of which were impressive marble-columned edifices.

Carpenter, who had some training in accounting, had arrived in New York from Connecticut some years earlier, and after working for a while at the Nevins establishment had gone into business on his own as an accountant. In the city directories of the period Vermilye listed himself as a broker. The two men accepted the Nevins's offer, and came together soon after, with the name changed to Carpenter & Vermilye. Carpenter was thirty-six years old and Vermilye twenty-two, which perhaps is why the names were in that order.[5]

Carpenter may have viewed Vermilye, who had the proper family connections and some capital, as a promising partner; Thomas E. Vermilye, on his way to becoming one of the city's most eminent clergymen, loaned his brother $1,000 to place in the firm.[6] Another brother, William M. Vermilye, joined the establishment, but left soon after to become a banker on his own. Jacob D. Vermilye, a younger brother, also entered banking, and he too may have participated in some of the dealings. Jacob later served as president of several banks, founded others, and eventually became involved with insurance companies as well.

This kind of affinity was quite routine in those years. Family firms, almost always partnerships, dominated the brokerage business. The brokers of this period, such as Carpenter & Vermilye, dealt in securities, lottery tickets (which were sold through agents by governments to raise funds and so avoid the hated taxes), and commercial paper.[7] Many brokers were characteristic "sedentary merchants," who engaged in diverse enterprises, prepared to invest in almost any kind of commercial venture from mortgages to land to insurance.[8] Some ran their own private securities auctions, charging fees to buyers and sellers, while others were members of the Stock & Exchange Board, which had been organized in 1792. Carpenter and Vermilye were not involved in this kind of business, since at the time of origination neither man was a board member.

It was a propitious time and place to enter the business. With a population of some 240,000, New York was America's largest city. Even before the opening of the Erie Canal it had been the leading commercial hub and fastest-growing manufacturing center, and now its development accelerated. "We are rapidly becoming the London of America," wrote businessman and charter member of the Stock & Exchange Board John Pintard in 1826. Pintard reflected upon the startling changes which had come about. "I myself am astonished & this city is the wonder of every stranger."[9]

New York was spreading northward at a rapid pace, its progress impeded only by such matters as fires, which were regular occurrences in a place where most structures were of wood and winter heat was provided by open hearths. In addition there was the occasional epidemic—a major cholera outbreak ravaged the town in 1832. It was a yeasty, bubbling place, where great wealth coexisted with wretched squalor. "The streets of New York are not to be perambulated with impunity by either the lame, or the blind, or the exquisitely sensitive in their olfactory nerves," cautioned John Duncan, a Scots visitor of the period.[10]

New Yorkers shrugged off all of this as the price paid for the new prosperity; they simply lacked time for such matters, though it was noted by some of the city's blue bloods. One of these, former Mayor Philip Hone, complained about the newcomers' lack of civility and the kinds of changes which were transforming his once pleasant town into a worldly city. He was also amazed at the financial costs of it all. Hone was able to sell several of his properties at sizable profits, only to see prices rise still further as the real estate market spiraled upward. "Everything in New York is at an exorbitant price. Rents have risen 50 percent. . . . Lots two miles from the City Hall are worth $8,000 or $10,000."[11] This was a princely sum in a period when $1,000 was a decent annual income for a well-to-do merchant.

In 1832 Wall Street was already the nation's most active financial community, having wrested that position from Philadelphia during the last years of the preceding decade. The Bank of New York, the Bank of Manhattan Company, the Merchants Bank, and the Bank of North America were there along with lesser institutions. Yet it hardly was a citadel of finance capitalism. Instead, the Wall Street neighborhood of the period resembled the typical midwestern downtown of a half-century later. Alongside the banks were such establishments as Baker's Tavern, A. Frumento's hair-dressing establishment, Richard Carlow's tailor shop, and other such places. There were six groceries between Hanover and Pearl streets along with several stables. Pigs, which constituted the municipal sanitation force, roamed the area at will, rutting through garbage and creating no inconsequential amount of filth of their own. There were scores of enormous, ferocious cats to control the rats which darted across the streets in broad daylight. Little wonder the rats thrived in the area; Wall Street had no sewers, but each house had a pit used for the purpose of sewage, which according to one source "the very opening of which is enough to breed the plague itself." Tucked in between the banks and shops were a number of modest two-story frame buildings, in which were housed some of the Street's brokers, loan contractors, and private bankers.[12]

The financial community which had sprung up in the Wall Street area had already become differentiated, in that several kinds of brokers and bankers existed, and their forms and functions were evolving rapidly. In such an environment a small firm like Carpenter & Vermilye, with the barest of connections, no hope of foreign business, and low capitalization, could hope for a modest place in the community.

Hardly anything is known of the kind of business transacted at Carpenter & Vermilye, but initially it probably was not in the private banking field, but rather brokerage. Apparently there was some business relationship between the Nevinses and the new firm. Russell Nevins proposed Carpenter for a seat on the Stock & Exchange Board, where he was admitted to membership on October 2, 1832.

There was nothing particularly outstanding about the business in the early years. Scores of other brokerage houses were mentioned in the newspapers of the 1830s, but not Carpenter & Vermilye. Vermilye had enough spare time to join the local militia as a private, and was sufficiently active to be promoted regularly, becoming a colonel in 1844.[13]

The partnership made it through the 1832 cholera outbreak and the fire that destroyed much of the city in 1835. In 1834 Vermilye married Elizabeth Lathrop, and the following year, when he was twenty-five years old, Elizabeth gave birth to the first of their children, Nehemiah. These changes in Washington's life, combined with Carpenter's Exchange membership, might have meant the brokerage business was doing well. It seems plausible, since activity on Wall Street in those years was intensifying.

The financial community experienced a major panic in 1837 which ushered in a four-year depression. The foreign business dried up, as state after state defaulted on bonds, with the British alone losing at least $130 million. The London *Times* probably spoke for thousands of investors when it wrote, "The people of the United States may be fully persuaded that there is a certain class of securities to which no abundance of money, however great, can give value, and that in this class their own securities stand preeminent." The Paris Rothschilds told Duff Green, the Jacksonian publisher, "You may tell your government that you have seen the man who is at the head of the finances of Europe, and that he has told you that they cannot borrow a dollar, not a dollar."[14]

Just about all the private banks suffered badly, and given its modest size and business, had Carpenter & Vermilye been in this field it almost certainly would have failed. As it was, it barely managed to endure. That the firm was in some financial distress may be seen in a complaint lodged against it in April by "Messrs. Dykers & Alstyne," who claimed Carpenter & Vermilye had failed to pay for twenty-five shares of a bank stock which had been delivered to them. The Board found for Dykers & Alstyne, and Carpenter & Vermilye agreed to make the payment.[15]

The hard times passed, and the partners appear to have done fairly well during the late 1840s. The reasons for whatever success they achieved probably had as much to do with larger economic and technological forces as with their own acumen. The creation of Adams Express in 1840, which started by carrying funds and then securities between Boston and New York, was followed by connections between other cities and the appearance of additional express companies. The subsequent development of the telegraph and its rapid spread throughout the Northeast caused many local securities markets to bow before the power of New York, and to a lesser extent, Boston and Philadelphia. By the mid-1850s there were over fifty telegraph companies in operation. In 1856 Western Union was formed and began absorbing smaller firms. Toward the end of the decade Wall Street was connected to every important

American city, and set most prices for them all, which made New York banks and brokers more attractive places to conduct business.[16]

Although local enterprises had markets for their securities made on regional exchanges, securities often were floated in New York or Boston.[17] The railroads in particular were growing rapidly in this period, as was public interest in them as investments. Never before had there been enterprises which required capital on such a scale as railroads, and opportunities were as broad-based as they were deep. By then there were more than forty railroad stocks traded at the Exchange. Information, transportation, and capital made New York the pivot of the nation's economy in this period, redounding to the benefit of the city's financial community. It would be inaccurate to say, however, that Wall Street was the dominant market, since the American financial markets were still quite dispersed. Rather, it was the largest.[18] Given the increased amount of business, it seems reasonable to assume Carpenter & Vermilye was able to attract additional brokerage clients.

In 1843 the firm moved to larger quarters at the 42 Wall Street address. When most brokerage houses operated out of offices in bank buildings or in cramped rooms elsewhere in the area, the size and location of Carpenter & Vermilye's chambers was another sign of its growing prosperity. Washington was sufficiently prosperous to apply for membership at the Stock & Exchange Board, which was granted on February 10, 1844.[19]

Carpenter was not particularly active at the firm after 1844, and it may have been that Washington sought out some help with the growing business. It was then that William Vermilye joined his brother in several ventures, perhaps in the area of underwriting, since he would have had access to such business. The later history of the firm indicates that William was perhaps a more astute businessman and banker than Washington, and his arrival in 1849 or 1850 augured well for the firm.

The business prospered. Washington purchased an uptown residence at West Fourteenth Street and by 1848 had a second office at 171 Greenwich Street, not far from his home.[20] Vermilye had property worth $14,000 in 1850, and two Irish female servants, all of which would have placed him squarely in the upper middle class, as would his Whiggish politics, colonelcy in the militia, and service on several Exchange committees. By then he had made his initial moves into investment banking, raising capital for and investing in several railroads, among them the Saratoga & Washington.[21] In other words, Washington Vermilye, now in his forties, had become part of the second tier of the New York Establishment.

Business improved during the prosperous early 1850s, when the combination of the California Gold Rush and intensified railroad creation resulted in prosperity, increased securities flotation, increased acitvity at the Stock & Exchange Board, and higher securities prices. Almost as many corporations were chartered in the 1850s as had been in the previous half-century, and many went to the securities markets for financing.[22] Commercial banking was also expanding, and nowhere more than in New York. In 1851 at least one new bank a month opened in the city. Fifteen more were added in the next two years, with a total capitalization of $16 million, much of it raised by the New York investment banks.[23]

The Europeans were slow to return as investors in American paper. As late as 1850 the Barings refused to purchase any rail securities except those issued by the B & O.[24] News of California gold revived interest, however, and by 1854 the foreigners were back in force. That year 26 percent of all American rail bonds were in the hands of foreigners, most of them English, and the Philadelphia & Reading and the Illinois Central were controlled by consortia of London investors. Even some American industrial stocks were purchased and traded on the London Exchange, with one of them, Norris Locomotive Works, a particular favorite. By 1856, there were some $1.5 billion worth of American securities outstanding, with railroad stocks and bonds accounting for more than half the amount. Foreign investors now owned $200 million of the total.[25]

During this period Carpenter & Vermilye continued as a brokerage house, and probably participated in additional underwritings, but never taking large positions. It was not a force in the international field, or at least it had no clients among the big London banks and insurance companies. The major newspapers carried stories of major brokerage houses and investment banks, and while there were some advertisements, none mentioned the Vermilye firm in news stories.

In 1857 the American markets were struck by the most brutal

panic until that time, caused by overspeculation and triggered by the failure of the Ohio Life Insurance Company. Yet in some respects it was a less serious debacle than that of 1837, and the aftereffects did not last long. Still, it seemed quite serious. Monitoring the situation from London, Karl Marx wrote gleefully to Friedrich Engels: "Despite my financial distress, I have not felt so cozy since 1848 [when the Revolution of 1848 was in full swing]." Marx went on to predict that the panic and depression might trigger a worldwide revolution. Engels, himself a perverse sort of capitalist, replied: "The general aspect of the Exchange here was most delicious in the past week. The fellows grow black in the face with rage at my suddenly rising good spirits."[26]

The financial community was badly damaged, as once again foreign funds dried up and then were repatriated. Almost half of the brokerage houses were wiped out; 985 merchants filed for bankruptcy, representing approximately $120 million. The Mining Exchange, at which were traded many of the speculative gold stocks, was shuttered. Some 30,000 or more in the city were fired from their jobs. *The New York Times* reacted to this news by wishing a Louis Napoleon Bonaparte would appear to put the unemployed to work rebuilding the city, as was then being done in Paris. As though in response, Mayor Fernando Wood suggested the unemployed be hired for that very reason, and paid in cornmeal, flour, and potatoes, in order to prevent starvation.[27] The depression ended soon after, however, as large-scale exports of southern cotton brought gold to America and restored confidence.

Carpenter & Vermilye survived; though now ill and shaken by the experience, the senior partner made plans for his final withdrawal from business. The coming of the Civil War in 1861, at which time Carpenter was sixty-five years old, was probably the date the firm dissolved. Carpenter remained in the city, where he died in 1872. Meanwhile, in a city directory for 1862–63 is found a new entry: Vermilye & Co., bankers, 44 Wall.[28]

· 2 ·

Vermilye & Co. in Transformation

(1862–1905)

That the Civil War was a major watershed in all aspects of American life need hardly be detailed. The conflict which began over differences regarding the nature of the Union and the institution of slavery ended with the federal government more dominant than ever before, and committed to ambitious development programs in such areas as banking, railroading, and industry. The United States once again had a strong national currency and bank system, a government committed to intervention in the economy, a high tariff, and a confident business community. Before 1861 one might argue credibly that perhaps America's future would be that of a Jeffersonian nation of small farmers and limited government. Yet even before the advance of urbanization, big business, and big government, there were signs that the dream of a bucolic Jeffersonian America was fading.

Government spending increased exponentially during the war. Federal expenditures rose from $66.5 million in 1861 to $1.3 billion in 1865. In this same period the national debt increased from $90.6 million to $2.7 billion. Some of the money needed to fight the war came from taxes and the issuance of more than a quarter of a billion dollars worth of paper money (greenbacks), fractional currency, and bank notes.[1] The rest came from borrowings, raised through the banking community. This was accomplished in such a way as to transform those small banks engaged in occasional underwritings for foreigners and a relative handful of local investors into impressive financial forces. These banks had to develop their distribution networks, join in syndicates to underwrite loans, and provide investment banking services to the expanding universe of industrial corporations, railroads, banks, and insurance companies.

Vermilye & Co. was a relatively minor force in 1862. Capitalizing upon opportunities such as these, within three years it became one of the nation's premier investment banks. The explanation for Vermilye's growth was the relationship it developed with Jay Cooke & Co., the Philadelphia investment bank which was the most original and powerful factor in the industry. Cooke became the mainspring of Union finance, the most important private financier the nation had yet seen.

Cooke came well prepared for the task. In 1842, at the age of twenty-one, he was a partner in the large and powerful E. W. Clark & Co. When Clark suspended operations due to losses in the 1857 panic, Cooke decided to go off on his own, doing so in a unique and singular fashion. Without bothering to establish a banking house, he approached several railroads which required capital and offered to raise funds through bond underwritings. He proposed to be compensated either by a commission or shares of common stock. At the same time, Cooke reorganized several defunct railroads and canals, taking shares and bonds in payment for services and selling them for profit once the enterprise was recognized as viable.

Convinced there was a sizable domestic market for such paper, Cooke created a force of commission salesmen which scoured the back country, selling the securities to country bankers, and eventually to almost anyone else considered a potential investor. Almost a century before the advent of Merrill Lynch's "People's Capitalism," Cooke argued that average Americans should own securities. By the time of Abraham Lincoln's election in 1860, Cooke was a combination investment banker-bond salesman-securities speculator. He was also better situated and experienced than anyone else to market large issues of securities. Yet Cooke could not do it alone; correspondent bankers in other cities, who knew their terrains, would be needed. Thus, he had to become a syndicator as well.[2]

On January 1, 1861, Cooke formed Jay Cooke & Co. In the early summer of that year he marketed a $3 million Pennsylvania state issue. He was able to locate buyers in every state in the Union, managing to do so by assembling and directing an army of 2,500 salesmen, including correspondents in other cities, supported by extensive advertising and public appeals to patriotism. In the process Cooke organized the nation's first major syndicate that transcended local bounds. Among the cooperating banks were Spencer, Vila & Co. of Boston and John Wills of Baltimore. Cooke had several New York agents, including Clark Dodge & Co., Fisk & Hatch, Livermore Clews & Co. (soon to become Henry Clews & Co.), and, in time, Vermilye & Co. as well.[3]

Cooke was one of the first to exploit systematically a sizable domestic market for capital that had been stimulated by the growth of the railroads. Others would soon follow, attracted by profits from participating in the wartime securities boom and later by the growth sparked by the expansion of railroads.

While many bankers were independent of group affiliations, there were two emerging communities of interest with many interrelationships, but often more significant differences, and these would endure well into the twentieth century. One was loosely known as the "Yankee bankers," usually though not always native-born, Anglo-Saxon Protestants who constituted such firms as Jay Cooke & Co., Drexel & Co., Kidder Peabody, Lee Higginson, and the antecedents of what would become J. P. Morgan & Co. Though not Anglo-Saxon, Vermilye & Co. belonged to this cluster. The other group was composed of German-Jewish bankers, whose strength and perseverance, as one scholar indicated, "rested largely on their access to European capital" and on "close family, ethnic, religious, and business ties, and the care they employed in conserving their capital and maintaining its liquidity." Members of this group were founders of such firms as Seligman & Co., Kuhn Loeb, Goldman Sachs, and August Belmont & Co. Most started as immigrant merchants or peddlers, although August Belmont had come to the United States in 1837 from Bavaria a full-fledged banker, as the representative of the House of Rothschild.[4]

While not as large or well known as several of the older banks, by the time the war began, Cooke was well connected with Anthony Drexel, the most renowned Philadelphia banker and a prominent Yankee, and through him, to Secretary of the Treasury Salmon Chase. In September 1861, Cooke was appointed Treasury agent to help sell Treasury debt issues. The initial distributions went well, though there was some trouble placing the bonds in New York, which was when and where his ties with Clews and Vermilye were strengthened. Cooke became one of the first non-Washington bankers to open an office there, doing so in February 1862, and he assiduously and successfully courted Chase and other prominent officials in the Lincoln government.

In this period all investment banks with correspondents outside their immediate region used the telegraph to communicate with one another. To prevent leaks, they created codes which were carefully guarded. Generally speaking, the more prominent the bank the more prominent the name it was assigned, so that frequent allusion would not be noted by a government censor. That year, Cooke devised a cipher for use in transmitting information about the progress of the war to agents in other cities. The code for August Belmont was Lincoln, and artillery was Drexel. All references to the "Secession Army" meant Vermilye & Co.—which also indicated that the name Vermilye appeared in most of the dispatches.[5]

Were it not for the war and the relationship the firm developed with Cooke, Vermilye & Co. might have remained a small, insignificant operation. Its successes weren't brought about by Washington Vermilye as much as by his brother William, who by then was a full partner. Most of Cooke's business with Vermilye & Co. was conducted with William Vermilye and Cornelius D. Wood, who was twenty-nine years old when the war began and an established and respected broker. It might have been Wood who brought about the Cooke relationship. Cooke expressed admiration for and confidence in both men on several occasions, and considered naming William Vermilye president of one of the banks he controlled.[6]

Still deeply concerned with military affairs, Washington Vermilye was by then a colonel in the Seventh New York Regiment, and as such one might have expected him to have entered the army once his unit was federalized. This was not so. Refusing to wait, Washington joined the Eighth Company as a private, served for three months, and then was discharged, returning to the firm in 1862.[7] Such a path to the military was not uncommon; ninety-day enlistments were possible that year, typically entered into by individuals who for patriotic reasons or for the sake of simple curiosity wanted a taste of battle. Washington's departure at that moment indicates that his presence at the firm was not vital, a further indication of his diminished importance there.

In early 1865, when it appeared the fighting had turned decisively in favor of the Union, the Treasury approached Cooke for another series of financings. Between February and July, Cooke organized several syndicates in America and Europe to place what for the time was a staggering $830 million worth of bonds in three tranches. The size of the issue indicates how important investment banking had become. The underwriting was a success. Were it not for the syndicates' ability to distribute the paper, the government might have been faced with technical bankruptcy.

Vermilye & Co. participated in all of Cooke's American offerings, taking on additional salesmen and clerks for the task. William Vermilye became a familiar figure at the Treasury, acting as emissary from Cooke to Chase, and afterwards to Chase's successor, William Fessenden. As for Washington, in addition to his tasks at the firm, he became president of the Greenwich Savings Bank and was named to the boards of several prominent insurance companies and banks, as well as to that of Western Union Telegraph. He prospered and moved into a higher level of society. Due to the success of the firm Washington was able to purchase a fine mansion in Englewood, New Jersey, where he spent an increasing amount of time.[8]

Vermilye & Co. now was recognized as one of the nation's more important securities houses, whose capital was about $1 million.[9] It still concentrated on distribution rather than direct underwritings. There is no record in the periodicals of the period of Vermilye & Co. ever taking a lead position; rather, it was content to remain one of Jay Cooke's most important allies in the city. For a while, when activity at the Gold Exchange surpassed that at New York Stock & Exchange Board, Vermilye & Co. became a significant factor in gold trading. False moves in this business would destroy several prominent Wall Street firms, but Vermilye & Co. was never threatened, probably because it acted as an agent and not as principal.[10]

The need to float government bonds became less pressing with the advent of peace in 1865. Along with others, Jay Cooke & Co. closed its Washington branch and turned elsewhere for business. New York was an obvious locale; why work through agents when by opening a relatively modest office in the Wall Street area the business could go directly to the firm? This was not as simple as it might appear. By then Vermilye & Co., Henry Clews & Co., and Fisk & Hatch had become strong enough to compete directly with Cooke should he sever relations with them.[11] Moreover, Cooke might have lacked the caliber of personnel to make the effort. H. C. Fahnestock, one of his New York correspondents, warned him against entering the city on his own unless he could employ someone "to compete with Crawford [Arthur Crawford of Clark Dodge & Co.] and [Cornelius] Wood, whom he considered the most accomplished brokers in New York."[12] William too continued to be well regarded. One contemporary referred to "Vermilye & Brother," which was what it was known as in some circles, the brothers of course being Washington and William, and indicates perhaps how the Street viewed the house.[13]

Vermilye & Co. was outgrowing its 44 Wall Street office. In the summer or early autumn of 1868 the firm took up new quarters in 16 Nassau Street at the corner of Pine, in the same building occupied by the Fourth National Bank.[14] Within two years it would expand into 18 Nassau Street as well. While other brokers either cut back or closed down after the war, Vermilye & Co. actually expanded, and hired more personnel.

Donald Mackay, twenty-five years old when he arrived in 1865, was one of the most important of the newcomers. Before the war he had clerked at his father's bank in Brooklyn, and then at a Wall Street brokerage house. Now Mackay became a confidential clerk at Vermilye & Co. The position was not as minor as the term implies. In this period confidential clerks were more akin to today's office managers, and it was not uncommon for them to be elevated to partnerships while continuing in that capacity. Washington Vermilye was impressed by Mackay's abilities, and he quickly rose to prominence at the firm. At Washington's urging, Mackay moved to Englewood, and the two men became important political and social leaders in that growing suburb.[15]

Other postwar arrivees included James A. Trowbridge, Latham Fish, and a son of the Vermilyes' clergyman brother, Thomas E.

Vermilye, Jr. Soon after, they were joined by George D. Mackay, Donald's half-brother, and Frederick K. Trowbridge, James's brother. William and Washington started to withdraw from day-to-day management of the firm, as Trowbridge and then the Mackays assumed increased responsibilities. Vermilye & Co. was experiencing the familiar generational change that occurs in all long-lived concerns.

Sometime in the late 1860s Wood became vice president of the Union Trust Company, one of Cooke's affiliated New York banks, and presumably devoted less time to Vermilye business. Others also left. Because of this the Vermilyes restructured the firm in 1870, taking in Donald Mackay, Trowbridge, and Fish as partners.[16]

That year Cooke received an important new assignment which involved Vermilye & Co. Interest rates had declined, so Cooke presented the government with a plan to refinance the national debt at significantly lower rates. Discussions dragged on, but Congress finally approved the flotation of $1.5 billion worth of securities at 4 to 5 percent interest, the proceeds of which would be used to redeem debts issued during the war.

Cooke won the award and immediately set about organizing a syndicate to market what remained of the first tranche of $200 million, most of which would be placed overseas. As expected, Vermilye & Co. handled a large share of the New York end of the business. There were ten American banks in the initial syndicate organized to market $10 million in gold bonds in the city. It included Jay Cooke & Co. (which by then had reopened its New York and Washington branches), with Vermilye & Co. responsible for $1 million of the offering.[17]

Cooke was also turning his attention to railroads. It was not a propitious move. Several of the more glamorous and promising lines had been poorly financed, in some cases due to poor management, in others the result of corrupt practices. Cooke himself was quite honest, but he dealt in the paper of railroads whose managements were, to say the least, suspect. These involvements, along with a struggle with the young J. P. Morgan in which Cooke lost some government business, left him in a weakened state.

There was a panic on Wall Street in 1869, caused by efforts to corner the gold market. Cooke was attempting to sell a large issue for Northern Pacific, employing the services of several of his old associates, among them Vermilye & Co. Given the disturbed nature of the markets the offering went slowly. By mid-1873 rumors circulated that Jay Cooke & Co. was illiquid. In addition it was generally believed the Northern Pacific owed Cooke $5.1 million, which it was unable to repay. He had gambled all on the underwritings and was close to failure.

On September 18, 1873, Jay Cooke & Co. shocked the financial community by shutting down. The news broke in New York, Washington, and Philadelphia, setting off a major financial panic. Rail issues fell sharply, prompting the failure of other brokerage houses and banks whose fates were tied to the railroads. Fisk & Hatch suspended, followed by nineteen other New York financial institutions and another dozen in Philadelphia. There were runs on banks known to have dealings with Cooke, including Union Trust, which suspended payments. The Exchange closed for ten days, an unprecedented move on its part.[18]

Some firms associated with Cooke, including Henry Clews & Co., were brought down.[19] Yet none of this affected Vermilye, or at least not to the point that there was any mention of its distress in the press of the period or memoirs written later on. This would seem to show the Vermilye brothers had no interest in Cooke's railroad schemes, or perhaps that they were satisfied to remain specialists in the government bond business.

That Vermilye & Co. did as well as it did bears some explanation, for by then railroads, especially the western lines, had become the focus of investment banking. The plausible explanation for Vermilye & Co.'s durability was its aforementioned conservatism. The Vermilyes had not chanced their own capital on underwritings, but rather acted as agents for others—including Cooke—who bore most of the risk and took for themselves most of the profits. And railroads, despite their enormous potential for profits, were highly uncertain investments.

Vermilye & Co. considered conservatism a positive good. Unlike many higher-flying firms of its day, it consistently rejected the possibilities of rapid growth for the security that came with prudent management and even avoidance of risks. According to Thomas E. Vermilye, this was the hallmark of the firm. With no little pride he told of the time he presented to a prominent Swiss bank his letter of credit, drawn on Vermilye & Co. One of the principals handled the matter and remarked, "I know the firm in New York very well, for I was in business near them in Wall Street. They are safe and reliable, but they might have been worth a great deal more money if they had been more venturesome." In relating the story, Vermilye said that his response was, "True, and might have gone into beggary, with injury to innocent parties." The clergyman, who told the story many years later, closed with the parable, "He that maketh haste to be rich shall not be innocent."[20] Finally, the author of Washington Vermilye's obituary wrote that "so thoroughly indeed was his business habits understood, that during the panic of 1873 not a suspicion of weakness was anywhere entertained with regard to his house."[21] It should be considered, however, that such accolades were quite the norm in tributes of the period. Yet in this case it might have been more precise an assessment than was to have been expected. Another contemporary, writing shortly before the panic, placed Vermilye & Co. among the "Leading Banking Houses" in the city, having this to say about it:[22]

> This is a very old and very successful house. It is one of the best types of old banking New York that can be found. On the street it is regarded as a conservative house—this is its peculiarity. Nothing rash, nothing novel, nothing untried, finds favor here. Slow and sure, is the motto that govern; careful and prudent, the repute. Content to earn the wealth it has sought, this house has rolled up a princely fortune, and has attained the highest rank among capitalists.

Thus, Vermilye & Co.—prudent, cautious, conservative—entered the ranks of the Street's foremost brokerage houses, capable of dealing as an equal with the likes of Lockwood & Co., J. & W. Seligman & Co., Clark Dodge & Co., Fisk & Hatch, Henry Groesbeck & Co., and Henry Clews & Co., which was reconstituted soon after its aforementioned failure.

Washington Vermilye died in 1876 at the age of sixty-six, and William followed two years later when he was seventy-seven years old. Jacob Vermilye, their youngest brother, was by then president of the Merchant's National Bank of New York and had only a passing interest in the firm. Lacking a competent Vermilye of the next generation, at this point leadership of the firm passed into the hands of Donald Mackay.

Mackay was to achieve an eminence in the brokerage community higher even than that of the Vermilyes. He was on many corporate boards, including the Merchant's National Bank and the Harriman National Bank, was selected for the NYSE's governing board, and in 1880 and 1881 served as the Exchange's president, an unpaid post usually bestowed on individuals the organization wanted to honor. Since in this period NYSE presidents tended to come from brokerage houses and not investment banks, the selection indicates that Vermilye & Co. was still primarily a brokerage, with investment banking functions in a secondary role by the 1880s.

While no records of Mackay's activities remain, it appears he was more growth-conscious than his predecessors. Mackay was able to bring in some important new business, and took the firm into new territory. Both the strategy and the style changed. During the 1870s and 1880s Vermilye & Co. was named fiscal agent for several railroads and trust companies and developed a correspondent relationship with Richardson, Hill & Co., one of the fastest-growing Boston brokerage houses, which may be attributed to Mackay's efforts.[23] Vermilye was one of the first investment banks to offer American Telephone & Telegraph bonds outside of New England. Shortly before the turn of the century Mackay opened a Boston office, a further indication of progress and the growth of the market for industrial securities. This was by no means atypical; by 1894 there were twenty-six NYSE members owning seats on the Boston Stock Exchange, and in 1901 more than a quarter of the NYSE members had branches outside the city.[24]

By then the partnership was being described as transacting "a general banking business, receiving the accounts of bankers, corporations, and individuals; securities are bought and sold on commission, a specialty being made of stocks and bonds for investment purposes, while railroad, city and municipal loans are negotiated."[25] The firm prospered, and more partners were added.

William Augustus Read, who became a partner in 1886, was one of these. Read had arrived at Vermilye & Co. in 1877, when he was nineteen years old and Donald Mackay was taking over as

leader. A native of Brooklyn, he had graduated from the Polytechnic Institute four years earlier, and probably had held a variety
of jobs before coming to Vermilye & Co. It seems unlikely that
Read initially would have performed any tasks beyond that of
messenger or clerk, which was the way most newcomers without
prior experience or connections started. He rose rapidly, however;
this too not unusual for a bright and aggressive individual.

Read concentrated on bonds, in time becoming known as one
of the most astute traders on the Street. In addition he was a
major innovator, devising complex funding schemes for Vermilye
& Co.'s growing list of clients. According to one account, "Many
features common in bond issues today were originated by him,"
which indicates Read was leading Vermilye into investment banking.[26] Among his innovations may have been the issuance of debentures rather than secured bonds in railroad financings, since
many railroads started to employ them in this period. Read also
excelled in placing bonds with institutions. He was not as adept
with smaller accounts, however, and was unable to attract much
in the way of trust accounts. Yet he was versatile. Read soon
became involved with underwritings and restructurings, and
brought a large volume of business to the firm. All of this would
explain the partnership, which came when he was only twenty-
eight years old.[27]

Years later financial writer Frank J. Williams commented on
Read's "wizardry in his skill with municipal bonds. There was
indeed a high order of intelligence."[28] Clarence Dillon, who worked
under Read for only a short period prior to his death, wrote:[29]

> He was an extraordinary man. His ability was widely respected,
> but he always had a more or less pugnacious attitude toward
> business rivals. To him, business was war, and I'm afraid he was
> right—though he may not have given of his great ability sufficient
> time to the winning of allies.

Read was quick to adapt to the ways of the financial community.
While not a member of the Street's aristocracy, he accepted its
values and traditions, and from the first signified an intention to
live by its rules and unspoken code. By accepting these he too
became accepted, and within a relatively short time Read was

invited to join the Downtown Association and Union League Club, was listed in the Social Register in 1893, and become part of the financial community social scene. He looked the part. As did the other prominent Wall Streeters, Read came to the office wearing a cutaway, together with a special touch: fresh violets in his buttonhole. He was fond of the opera and in later years became a member of the board of the Metropolitan. In addition, Read collected works of art, rare books, and sculpture at his residence at 4 East 62nd Street and later at his estate in Purchase, New York. He was, in essence, a proper Victorian who metamorphosed into an even more proper Edwardian.[30]

In 1890 Read executed a major coup. Acting for Vermilye, he joined with August Belmont & Co. to help underwrite a portion of what became a total of a $15 million offering for the newly organized National Cordage Company in the form of 8 percent cumulative preferred and common shares. Belmont and Vermilye were to handle the preferred segment of the offering, while the common went to management and others.

This was an important undertaking. National Cordage was an amalgamation of four of the nation's largest manufacturers of rope and twine. The money raised was to be used to recapitalize the company and complete the purchase of an additional ten concerns to solidify the firm's domination of the industry.[31]

This was Vermilye & Co.'s initial venture into a practice that was becoming fairly common at the larger, better-capitalized investment banks. Up to then the firm had been content to participate in underwritings as a middleman, going from deal to deal, hoping to perform capably and efficiently so as to obtain repeat business. With National Cordage Vermilye was to move into the area of assisting the company in structuring its operations, in the hope that by providing such services successfully it would obtain additional business. It was the kind of arrangement Kuhn Loeb had developed with the Pennsylvania Railroad, Morgan with the Chesapeake & Ohio, and Kidder Peabody with the Atchison, Topeka & Santa Fe. This was done as much to protect the banker as the firm; the banker wished to assure the firm's viability in order to retain those clients who purchased the shares or bonds because of their trust in his integrity.[32]

That Vermilye came in on the National Cordage deal was a

sign not only of enhanced reputation and power, but of Read's growing importance to the concern. Moreover, his ability to put the arrangement together was another sign of Read's ability to innovate, important for a bank whose reputation had been for solid performance in distribution, and not originality in investment banking.

While the underwriting was a success, National Cordage was not. Management continued its acquisitions program (without the assistance of Belmont and Vermilye) while its balance sheet became burdened with debt. It was in what amounted to a seasonal business, with binder twine accounting for four-fifths of its costs, and within a year both the economy and prices turned against the company. The firm declared bankruptcy in 1893, helping to set off one of the most severe financial panics in history. On May 1 National Cordage common sold at 52 and the preferred at 100; four days later, when bankruptcy was announced, the common collapsed to 20, the preferred to 67.[33]

While the National Cordage failure was painful and left bitter feelings, it did not reflect badly on Vermilye & Co., which by then had no direct or indirect connection with the ill-fated combine. Indeed, Vermilye came through the panic in good shape, and along the way underwent several restructurings, which can be traced through the partnership accords. This was not unique to the firm. The common practice for brokerage houses of the period was to enter into partnership agreements which ran for two or three years, with the understanding that they would be renewed upon expiration. The general rule was for shares to be allocated and reallocated as the relative importance and contributions of individual partners changed. Thus, it might have been that a partner who had a 13/100 share in distributed profits for a two-year period might have done very well, and been rewarded with an allocation of, say, 18/100 for the next period, the difference coming from a partner whose record had been less impressive.

The Vermilye accord of 1886, the first agreement of which direct evidence exists, was

for the purpose of carrying on in the City of New York, the business of banking, dealing in government securities and gold, and the purchase and sale upon commission of stocks and bonds,

and, in general, the like business theretofore conducted and carried on under the said name of Vermilye & Co., by a certain firm
composed of the said James A. Trowbridge, William A. Read,
Donald Mackay, Latham A. Fish, Frederick K. Trowbridge, and
George D. Mackay, which expired by limitation on or about the
31st day of March, 1886.

It was to run for two years, and on expiration the terms would be
reviewed and revised.[34]

We have no way of knowing what the shares were in 1886, but
it would appear that this time the Mackays and Trowbridges would
have received major portions. The partnership was revamped in
1888, 1890, 1892, 1893, 1896, and 1899, with new partners being
added (G. Trowbridge Hollister and Arthur S. Fairchild) and, presumably, the shares altered to reflect performance.

Donald Mackay and William Read seemed to complement each
other nicely, which doubtless was one reason for the firm's success.
Mackay was primarily involved with the retail side of the business
and developed a strong customer base, while Read concerned himself with syndication. The division of responsibilities could be seen
in that both of the Mackay brothers had NYSE seats, while Read,
who did not need one for his work, was never an exchange member.[35]

Read's tasks were the more difficult, since true to its tradition,
Vermilye & Co. continued to refuse to accept deposits from the
general public. This meant he had to draw upon the firm's capital,
participate in underwritings either as a manager or, if undertaking
distribution, knowing well in advance just how much could be
placed rapidly. Even so, Read was able to take the firm into the
upper reaches of the New York underwriting community, doing
so by his superb knowledge of the bond market and feel for bidding,
and the impression he made on the Street's more powerful bankers.

In 1894 Morgan underwrote a $6 million first collateral trust
issue for the Cleveland, Cincinnati, Chicago & St. Louis Railroad,
and included Vermilye and Drexel in its offering group. This
opened the path for future cooperation with several of the Street's
most prominent and distinguished houses.

Within two years Read was prepared to contest the giants for
business. In November 1896 New York City planned a $16 million
issue of 3½ percent gold bonds. Together with the London firm of

C. J. Hambro & Son, Morgan offered $104.71 for the entire issue. Bidding for Vermilye & Co., Read offered $104.59, and took the underwriting.[36]

Read had emerged as one of the very few bankers whose opinions were sought on debt financings of all kinds. As such, in 1896 he was brought in by the Baltimore & Ohio's reorganization committee, serving with such prominent members of the investment community as Howland Davis, Edward Bacon, and Henry Budge. Read worked for two years on this project, which linked Vermilye with Morgan, Kuhn Loeb, Hallgarten, and Belmont, a group which in 1898 took the large railroad out of bankruptcy. Read also joined a syndicate organized by E. H. Harriman which brought together three traction companies to form the Nassau Electric Railroad Company.[37]

By activities such as these Read took the leadership position at the firm from Mackay, and not only dominated its activities and brought in the most business, but was Vermilye & Co.'s spokesman to the financial community and the press. As such he was called upon to handle all kinds of relationships, from syndication to decisions to enter into affiliations with other investment houses. Before the end of the century, Vermilye had underwritten major loans for such railroads as the Atlantic Coast Line, the Wabash, and the Missouri Pacific.

In June 1901, Frederick Trowbridge gave notice of his intention to retire, and the following March his brothers James and Edwin did likewise. With this the Mackay brothers, Fish, Read, Hollister, and Fairchild reformed the partnership, and for reasons soon to be explored, this time the distribution of profits (or losses) and expenses is known:[38]

William A. Read	240/600
Donald Mackay	110/600
Latham A. Fish	85/600
G. Trowbridge Hollister	60/600
George D. Mackay	55/600
Arthur S. Fairchild	50/600

The relative shares indicate that Read was by far the most important individual at the firm, probably because profits from underwriting outstripped those from various forms of brokerage. The fact that the Trowbridges left together would suggest their departures had been sparked by a disagreement with either the Mackays or Read, or perhaps both.

Business was not particularly strong for some time. There were two underwritings in 1902, and the larger one, for $10.5 million raised for the Atlantic Coast Line Railroad, involved Vermilye & Co. as a comanager. The following year Vermilye had two underwritings for a total of $5.3 million, and another two in 1904, which came to $11.8 million. One of these was for the Philippine commonwealth, and marked Vermilye & Co.'s entry into the international field. It was a minor effort, however, the kind of placement banks such as Morgan and Kuhn Loeb were generally content to leave to the smaller houses.[39]

Perhaps it was the slow business that resulted in rancor at the firm, or it might have been something more personal. Whatever the cause, it appears that in May 1904 differences of opinion regarding the partners' relative positions caused a schism between Read and the others. Given Read's position and the practice of the period, it might very well have been that in the negotiations for the renewal of the partnership the following year Read had asked for an even larger share and was rebuffed. That the other partners realized dissolution was possible could be seen in their attempts to amend the articles of incorporation to provide means whereby the firm's name could be passed down to them if the firm was discontinued. Sensing what was being attempted, Read blocked this move. He then notified the others that he did not intend to renew the agreement, and that a liquidation of the firm would be necessary.

The other partners were willing to negotiate a settlement, but insisted that they be permitted to continue to operate under the Vermilye name, since among them they controlled a majority interest. The fact that Washington Vermilye had conferred the title to Donald Mackay, Fish, and James Trowbridge gave additional credence to their claims, as did an 1892 settlement for the name with the Vermilye heirs.

Read denied that this constituted a valid claim. Announcing he was prepared to bid for the title, he sued the others in state Supreme Court. Read's position was made public in a newspaper interview on February 9.[40]

Differences have arisen among the partners, and the present firm
will not be continued after March 31. The fact that the partnership
articles do not contain any provision that the firm name and goodwill are not assets to be distributed, appears conclusively from
the fact that some of the partners have brought suit to have such
a provision inserted in the articles. A suit has been commenced
by me to obtain an adjudication which will dispose of the whole
matter.

A short, closely followed legal battle ensued. That both parties
considered this a matter of great importance could be seen in the
attorneys retained by both sides. George Wickersham appeared
for Read and Alton B. Parker for the Mackays. Both were prominent members of the New York bar. Wickersham would go on to
serve as attorney general in the William Howard Taft Cabinet
while Parker, a former judge, had been the Democratic presidential
nominee the previous year.

While the lawyers battled it out, Read organized William A.
Read & Co. and the other partners united as Mackay & Co. Each
attempted to retain old clients, which prompted new charges. Read
alleged Mackay had falsely advertised his new company as a successor to Vermilye & Co., and when Mackay refused to alter the
wording of his circulars, Read obtained an injunction obliging him
to do so. All the while both new firms operated from the old offices
on Nassau Street. When a reporter arrived to interview both fac-
tions, Mackay airily informed him, "If you want to see Mr. Read,
he is sitting over in his corner conducting a solitary campaign."[41]

The case ended in a decision that neither Mackay or Read would
be able to use the Vermilye name. Judge Frederick Bischoff declared, "While my conclusion is that the plaintiff [Read] cannot
eventually succeed upon his prayer for a sale of the firm's name
to the highest bidder, still an injunction should issue to prevent
the defendants' [the Mackay group] unauthorized use of the name
as against the plaintiff after this partnership comes to an end."[42]

With the Mackays, Fish, Hollister, and F. W. Kendrick, manager of the Boston office, as partners, Mackay & Co. took quarters
at 14 Wall Street. In addition the firm would maintain its Boston
office. Read's new offices were to be at 25 Nassau Street, on the
first floor of the prestigious Equitable Life Assurance Society

Building, not far from the old Vermilye & Co. location, and next door to Belmont & Co., its closest associate.[43] There were to be two additional partners, Read's brother-in-law, Joseph H. Seaman, and Charles Hazard, the latter a member of the NYSE. Hazard had extensive brokerage experience, while Seaman, a Polytechnic of Brooklyn graduate like Read, had previously served as secretary to the president of Cromwell Steamship lines.[44] Furthermore, in 1905 Read announced the creation of a branch office in Boston to be managed by James Dean, and another in Baltimore under the supervision of Francis W. Smith. A third branch, in Chicago, would be managed by W.M.L. Fiske, who was to become an important figure at the firm for close to four decades. Like Read and Seaman, Fiske was a graduate of the Polytechnic Institute of Brooklyn and went on from there to Columbia University, from which he graduated in 1900. After traveling in Europe for two years he returned to New York and a post at Vermilye & Co. He had represented the firm in Chicago for three years when Read asked him to establish a headquarters operation in that city for William A. Read & Co.[45]

On April 1, 1905, there appeared the following notice in the city's press:[46]

Office of Vermilye & Co.
16 Nassau Street

The partnership existing under the name of VERMILYE & CO. expires this day by limitation.

All outstanding obligations will be liquidated by the former members of the firm at the above address.

VERMILYE & CO.

The notice might be seen as a way of signifying the end of what in its time had become one of Wall Street's most respected investment banks.

·3·

William A. Read & Co.

(1905–1916)

Shortly after being organized, William A. Read & Co. joined with Blair & Co. and William Salomon & Co. to market a $50 million 5 percent thirty-year bond issue for the newly restructured Western Pacific Railroad. Other major deals followed, as William A. Read & Co. swiftly established itself as a significant force in debt financings.[1] Even so, in this period the firm's personnel did not expand significantly. Read handled most of the work, with some assistance from Seaman. Hazard's primary tasks were taking care of the firm's smallish operation at the NYSE. That William A. Read & Co. could become a respected member of the Wall Street community with so few personnel was not unusual. Kidder Peabody and Kuhn Loeb each had a total staff, including secretaries, clerks, runners, and salesmen, of fewer than fifty, and there were some sole proprietorships with staffs of fewer than a half dozen.[2] Like them, William A. Read & Co. stayed small for two reasons. The fewer the partners, the greater their remuneration. More important, while expansion was relatively simple, contraction was not. From its inception, William A. Read prized smallness in the matter of staffing.

Business was good and getting better. From 1905 through 1907

William A. Read had six underwritings for a total of $17.2 million. Most of that sum—$10 million—was accounted for by a single issue of three-year notes for the Interborough Rapid Transit System of New York, in which William A. Read was a comanager. Four were for companies in New York State, one in New Jersey, and there was a $1 million offering for the Philippine government, indicating that Read was able to retain this small business from his days at Vermilye & Co.

In 1907 Wall Street was hit by another financial panic, the worst in the nation's history till then. Several of Wall Street's supposedly solid banks collapsed. William A. Read & Co. survived, and in the recovery that followed expanded its business once more. In 1908, as the nation recovered from the panic, William A. Read had thirty underwritings, raising close to half a billion dollars, with issues ranging from $200,000 for the Twin Cities Rapid Transit Company and associated firms to a comanaged $144.7 million for the Chicago & Northwestern Railway.[3]

William A. Read won some of the growing Canadian business, with eight small issues. The firm soon became known as the preeminent underwriter for Canadian government and railroad issues. This business, won in competition with some of the Street's largest firms, made Read a celebrity of sorts and marked his entry into the outermost fringes of the inner circle.[4]

There were personnel changes due to retirements. Hazard withdrew from the firm in 1909, which meant William A. Read no longer had representation at the NYSE. This was inconsequential; Read easily could have purchased another seat, but didn't bother to do so. By then the firm was concerned with underwriting and bond placement at large institutions to the exclusion of almost everything else. There were gaps in expertise, however. William A. Read lacked a dynamic sales force to place the issues it underwrote, and there was no one at the firm capable of bringing in large accounts. Other business was conducted through correspondent houses, but this was negligible.

Read's successes enabled him to expand operations beyond what had been the case during Vermilye & Co.'s last years. In 1908 he opened an office in London, obtaining representation in what then was the world's premier financial market. Nigel L. Campbell, a British banker, was taken on as manager, and three years later was elevated to a partnership, indicating that the business there was considerable. On April 1, 1909, William A. Read announced the elevation of three of its professionals to partner status. James Dean and W.M.L. Fiske, still in charge in Boston and Chicago respectively, were two of them, and John W. Horner, who had started as Read's assistant in New York, the third. The Dean and Fiske promotions were not made for reasons of longevity, but rather reflected the expansion of the bank's interests in those cities. In 1912 Roland L. Taylor was admitted to the firm as a partner in charge of the new Philadelphia office. Taylor previously had been president of the Philadelphia Trust Company and was one of the nation's most experienced industrial organizers. Among Taylor's creations had been Baldwin Locomotive and Midvale Steel, and presumably he intended to perform additional work along the same lines from the Philadelphia office.[5]

William A. Read & Co.'s expansion was also of a different order from that of Vermilye. The predecessor company had branches which executed policies with orders formulated in New York. William A. Read's regional offices had much more autonomy. Moreover, there was no centralized hiring policy; partners in the field had independence in such matters.

The underwritings continued to expand. There were twenty-two offerings in 1909, including a $150 million syndication for the Union Pacific and $120 million for the Lehigh Valley. William A. Read syndicated twenty-four issues the following year, and a like number in 1911. The firm concentrated on originating the underwriting and setting forth terms and rates, areas in which Read excelled. The firm had little interest in participating in selling the syndicates of others. Although on occasion it would do so, as noted, this was not an area of strength at the firm. Read would structure and assemble a deal, and then turn it over to firms with an interest in and ability at placement.[6]

In 1912, the same year he opened the Philadelphia office, Read was obliged to relocate due to the spectacular fire in the Equitable Building, which destroyed the structure. He found temporary quarters at 31 Pine Street, while seeking larger offices elsewhere in the neighborhood. Within a few months the firm moved to 28 Nassau Street.[7]

By the eve of World War I William A. Read had become one

of the Street's foremost bond houses. That it was not as prominent as some of the others was due largely to Read's insistence on conservative procedures, a legacy from his experiences at Vermilye. In writing to a new salesman in 1913, one partner described the company's business in this way:[8]

> We move along pretty cautiously in the projects that we take up:—do not go much into industrial enterprises—in fact, practically not at all. We do not want to be associated in promotions or underwritings, and we do not want to take on securities of properties which are not in operation. This, you will see, takes out a whole lot of work which would naturally devolve as among the duties of anyone working along the lines that have been suggested for you. We do not go on with business which I would not like to say was not good, and which I know other houses would be glad to go on with.

He added, however, "Another factor is that when we do make up our minds that an issue is good, we are perhaps apt to bid a little cautiously and we do not want to work for nothing."[9]

William A. Read was by no means one of Wall Street's leaders. In this period the investment banking community was dominated by six firms: Morgan, Kuhn Loeb, First National Bank, National City Bank, all of New York; and Kidder Peabody and Lee Higginson of Boston. They were interrelated; Kidder Peabody, Kuhn Loeb, and Morgan partners owned shares in National City.[10] Between 1907 and 1912 four firms—J. P. Morgan, Lee Higginson, Kidder Peabody, and Kuhn Loeb—handled $2.8 billion in underwritings, equivalent to 40 percent of the nation's total. The rest was divided among the several hundred other firms in New York and throughout the nation.[11]

Increasingly this business was being transacted by a new generation of bankers, who differed strikingly from their predecessors. Entry to a Wall Street career had changed from what it had been when Read arrived a quarter of a century earlier. In 1877 young men with ambition and little else could begin as runners, graduate to the cage, and then rise as rapidly as talent and opportunity permitted. This was still possible in the years immediately before World War I, but only at the small, young, and minor firms. J. P.

Morgan, Kuhn Loeb—and William A. Read—were looking for a different sort of person. By then the passport to Wall Street's investment banking elite was attendance at fashionable preparatory schools and Ivy League colleges. More often than not individuals with the proper social cachet would call upon a fellow fraternity member who through familial connections had obtained a post and, drawing upon past favors and old friendships, have the door opened for him. Once in the firm, the subsequent career path for a recruit was much as it had been earlier. The newcomer would undergo an apprenticeship of sorts and then, after seasoning, could hope for something better, and if all went well, eventually a partnership. Occasionally young men with excellent connections would enter as partners, usually placing capital in the firm when being admitted.

William Abbott Phillips, Worcester Academy '01, Harvard '05, went through the drill in the customary fashion. Upon graduation he obtained a post at William A. Read's Boston office, then headed by Charles Dean, himself a Harvard alumnus. Phillips began as a messenger, but within a year was on the road, selling bonds throughout New England. He did well; in 1909 Philips was transferred to New York, where he retailed bonds to large institutions.[12]

One day four years later, while in lower Manhattan, Phillips ran into Clarence Dillon, an old friend from Worcester and Harvard who had settled in Milwaukee. The two had kept in touch after graduation. In fact, they had met in Milwaukee a few months earlier, when Phillips tried to obtain some orders from Dillon's in-laws. Phillips spoke of his work at William A. Read and asked Dillon, "What are you doing nowadays?" Dillon replied that he was at loose ends. "You should get into the banking business," remarked Phillips, who offered to provide the means. "Come on over and meet Read. He is a man worth knowing."

They crossed the street, walked a few blocks, and entered the company's offices. "I never had less intention of becoming a banker than on that day," Dillon recalled later. "Banking meant less to me than most things, although I had a fairly thorough experience in business and knew something about investments. But Mr. Read seemed well-disposed."[13]

Read was at once impressed by Dillon. The two men chatted for a while, and then Read made the offer. "Why not take a desk here and look around for yourself? Then you can decide about being a banker." Dillon replied that he would have to discuss the matter with his wife. She was reluctant to leave the Midwest, but Read then responded by offering him a position at the Chicago office, which Dillon accepted, with a starting salary of $250 a month. A decade later Dillon recalled his sentiments at the time:[14]

> Banking as a business was wholly a new quantity. Before long I found myself interested, then enthusiastic. At that time the Read organization lacked adequate facilities for the distribution of its securities. So I devised a plan of distribution and talked it over with Mr. Read. He told me to go ahead, and that is where I started.

This is how the man who was to become the symbol of American finance capitalism in the second half of the 1920s, much as J. P. Morgan had been in the 1890s and Jay Cooke in the 1860s, entered the industry.

Dillon's path to Wall Street wasn't unfamiliar or terribly difficult. His father, Samuel Lapowski, was a Polish Jewish immigrant who arrived in America in 1868 and apparently immediately set out for San Antonio, Texas, where he opened a dry goods store.[15] There were other members of the family in America; a brother, Boleslaw, became a doctor and settled in New York City.

In this period Eastern Europeans of any religion or national origin often suffered from prejudice, and Lapowski doubtless felt some of the stings of bigotry. Like many of the more ambitious immigrants of the time, he was determined to assimilate into the American cultural mainstream as rapidly as possible, not only for himself, but for any children he might have. Around 1880 Lapowski met Bertha Steenbach, a Lutheran, the daughter of Swedish immigrants, whose family owned and operated several silver mines and owned land in Colorado and Texas. They married the following year. Clarence was born on September 27, 1882, and two daughters, Jeanie and Evelyn, followed. All were raised as Protestants.

Lapowski's business thrived, and he branched out into different areas, including banking, a natural expansion of the dry goods business. He would advance funds to ranchers and farmers to tide them over until they sold their cattle or crops, and he used part of the earnings from this activity to speculate in land in nearby Abilene, Texas, on which oil was discovered.[16] By then the family could afford some luxuries. To escape the brutally hot San Antonio summers the Lapowskis would vacation in New Hampshire or Maine. In this way Clarence was able to see more of the country than most boys his age.

Twice a year Lapowski would travel to New York on buying trips, occasionally taking Clarence with him. It was during one of these expeditions that his banker told Lapowski the boy should attend an eastern school, preferably one of the more prestigious ones in New England, and then go on to a fashionable college. Lapowski did not need much prodding. Like many immigrants who had prospered, he would have understood that such was the way to social acceptance in America.

As it happened, however, 1897 was a bad year for his business. Texas experienced a serious drought resulting in crop failures and the death of thousands of head of cattle. Due to this many farmers and ranchers who owed him money were unable to repay their loans.[17] Even so, Clarence was dispatched to Worcester Academy by his determined father. Lapowski had enrolled his elder daughter in a girl's school in Boston, and Clarence was able to visit her occasionally. In addition there were weekend trips to see his uncle in New York, who would take him to plays and show him the sights, which deeply impressed the boy. Clarence kept a diary in those years, in which he wrote about food, clothes, and friends, but little of classroom activities. He was bright and inquisitive, though not a particularly outstanding scholar—grades of D in Latin and French, A's in science, mathematics, and declamation, and more C's than B's. The school's newspaper notes Clarence's participation in a tennis tournament, debates, and school shows. He was president of a fraternity and selected to deliver the "Tree Oration."[18]

Worcester was one of the elite Yankee prep schools considered a way station to several Ivy League colleges, and Lapowski probably hoped to attend Harvard.[19] He failed the Latin portion of the Harvard entrance examination, and because of this entered the scientific school, where Latin was not required. At the end of the first year he retook the examination, failing once again. Even so, he was permitted to transfer to the college.[20]

Sometime in this period Samuel Lapowski decided to alter his surname to Dillon, which had been his mother's maiden name. The children also took the name, although Clarence would refer to himself as Clarence Lapowski Dillon, Clarence (Lapowski) Dillon, or simply C. L. Dillon throughout his college career.[21]

During the 1920s some Wall Streeters knew Dillon's father had been a Polish Jew, which may explain why Clarence's name was not on the roster of several exclusive clubs. Paul Nitze, a close Dillon friend, said Dillon never attempted to conceal his Jewish origins, though he did not consider himself a member of that religion. James Forrestal, who was Dillon's closest associate, concurred. William Read's son, Duncan, certainly thought him Jewish, although August Belmont, himself the descendant of the great nineteenth-century Jewish-American representative of the House of Rothschild, said he did not know. Lapowski had taken care to assimilate his family into the mainstream of American life. Clarence Dillon had of course changed his name, but he never went out of his way to deny the Lapowski connection, and afterwards belonged to several Polish interest groups. His church affiliation in those years, and later, was Episcopalian.[22]

At Harvard, as at Worcester, Dillon was not an outstanding student. While transparently intelligent, he demonstrated scant interest in his studies, although, significantly, he showed skills at and a liking for mathematics. He also developed a lifelong fascination with Napoleon; in later life Dillon would love all things French. At one point he attempted to win a place on the debating team, but failed to qualify. Dillon dabbled with painting and sketching, but not seriously. He was not to be a member of Porcellian, "Gas House," or A.D., though he did go out for and was accepted in the less-exclusive Institute of 1770.

Dillon enjoyed an expansive social life and had a wide circle of friends, to whom he was known as "Baron." According to one source, the term described his personality, dandyism, and rather "exotic" physical appearance, which was remarked upon also by the contemporary press. Dillon himself claimed that the sobriquet derived from his fascination with gambling, horse racing and trotting in particular, and the great pacer of the time, who was named "Baron Dillon."[23]

Those who knew him then say Dillon spent considerable time

and won substantial sums at cards. "He was a positive genius at poker," commented business writer John K. Winkler. "Often, when another player had raised him a few hundred, Dillon would expose his hand so all could see, and innocently ask, 'Do you think I am strong enough to call?' " The look on his opponents' surprised faces usually provided the answer. "In poker, Dillon's habit was to look them over in a nice, friendly, unworried fashion."[24]

In the Class of 1905 Dillon was part of a broad, cosmopolitan circle that would distinguish itself greatly in the next half-century. Ogden Mills, who became Secretary of the Treasury in the Hoover administration, graduated that year, as did Roger Baldwin, founder of the American Civil Liberties Union. Future diplomat Joseph Grew, Supreme Court Justice Felix Frankfurter, and Korea's President Syngman Rhee were on campus while Clarence was at Harvard. Franklin D. Roosevelt, who was the same age as Dillon, had graduated in 1904; from their future contacts it appears they had been at least acquaintances while students.[25]

One of Dillon's closest friends at Harvard was Armin A. Schlesinger, whose father, Ferdinand, had come to America from Germany in 1868 and settled in Milwaukee, where he became a manufacturer of mill machinery. From there Schlesinger expanded into iron mining and was president of several companies in that industry. During a visit to Cambridge the elder Schlesinger urged Dillon to relocate to Milwaukee, offering to help him find employment there, perhaps a new business in partnership with his son. Dillon accepted, and during the next three years the two men were associated at one of the Schlesinger companies, Newport Mining Co. and its subsidiary, the Milwaukee Coke & Coal Co.[26]

Dillon's arrival at Newport and Milwaukee Coke & Coal, like his subsequent appearance at William A. Read, was quite typical of the way he would operate throughout his business career. In Schlesinger and Phillips he had friends who became business associates as well. Throughout his life Dillon would have scores of associates, but only that close circle of friends acquired in college and his early years on Wall Street and in government. He prized friendship and family intensely. Later on Dillon would be known as one of the sharpest dealers on Wall Street, and would have his share of enemies. However, he had no former friends; these men would be with him as long as they lived.

Newport and Milwaukee Coke & Coal were straightforward

businesses which did not consume all of Dillon's energies. Because of this he could devote some time to the pleasures of Milwaukee society. Schlesinger was married soon after graduation, and through his wife Dillon was introduced to Anne McEldin Douglass. Her parents were George and Susan Dun Douglass. Susan Douglass's uncle had founded the credit reporting firm of R. G. Dun, at which her father and husband were employed.[27] Soon Anne and Clarence were engaged.

On a summer day in 1907, returning from visiting Anne at the Douglass's summer home in North Lake, Hartland, Wisconsin, Dillon waited for the Milwaukee train at the local station. The Pioneer Express came through, colliding with a St. Bernard dog, which was hurled through the air. The massive body struck Dillon, catapulting him against an iron post and fracturing his skull. For a few days his condition was critical. Dillon recuperated, but recovery was slow. For the rest of his life he would suffer occasionally from an inner ear malady caused by the misadventure, which subjected him to occasional bouts of vertigo and may have contributed to his volatile temperament.

Clarence and Anne married on February 4, 1908. After their honeymoon the Dillons returned to Milwaukee, where Clarence was told by his doctors he would be unable to work for at least a year. The railroad awarded him a settlement of $8,000 for the accident, and with this Clarence and Anne took off for an extended convalescence in Europe. He studied art, architecture, and cooking in Geneva and Paris.[28] Their first child, Clarence Douglas Dillon, was born in Geneva on August 21, 1909, which prompted consideration of a return to Milwaukee.

The Dillons did that in early 1910, by which time Clarence's headaches had subsided, and he was eager to find employment. His brother-in-law, George Douglass, had founded a firm he called the Milwaukee Machine Tool Company. Clarence purchased a half interest for $10,000, and became its president.[29] Orders picked up immediately; it appeared that Dillon was a superb salesman. Perhaps he was too good at it. He obtained a large order for lathes which the firm was unable to fill at the price quoted, and as a result Milwaukee Machine was in trouble. In 1913 the partners sold their company to Kearney & Trecker, and Dillon once again looked for something to do.[30]

Around this time the Dun heirs had a falling out, and Dillon went to New York to help arrange the liquidation of the Douglass holdings, which was when he met Phillips, and through him, William A. Read.

After a brief tutorial Dillon was dispatched to Chicago, to work as a bond salesman under the supervision of W.M.L. Fiske. He was a success from the first. Through friends in Milwaukee Dillon was able to obtain interviews with several prominent businessmen in the upper Midwest. One of these was William Horlick, president of Racine-based Horlick's Malted Milk, who after a discussion with Dillon gave him his portfolio to manage.[31]

This was early in 1914. Business was sluggish on Wall Street due to an economic slowdown, but even so Read felt his firm was not receiving its share of bond placements. The previous year the firm had participated in twenty-two underwritings which raised more than $77 million for its clients. But in 1914 William A. Read would take part in only fifteen underwritings, half of which derived from such familiar clients as the Canadians and New York City. New business simply wasn't arriving.

Read recognized the need for fresh blood. He perceived in Dillon uncommon qualities in the sales area, and wanted him in New York where he could try his hand at underwriting as well. Dillon protested that his successes with Horlick and the others resulted from having good contacts in the Midwest, which he lacked in New York. Read insisted, and the Dillons moved East early in 1914. Their first home was in Purchase, New York, not far from Read, who wanted Dillon as close to him as possible. The two would commute together back and forth to New York, discussing business and a wide variety of other subjects. Dillon became Read's protégé, and he quickly moved from sales to investment banking.[32]

Dillon wasn't given an assignment, but rather left on his own, with Read monitoring his activities from a distance. In March Dillon decided to attempt to arrange a $2 million offering for Schlesinger's Newport Mining. He traveled to Cleveland, purchased an issue of notes, and sold them to customers he had known there for a net profit of $100,000.[33] While this was impressive for a novice's initial showing, it was only a small portion of William A. Read's business.

In January 1914, when the bond market was dull because of a

business slowdown, New York State attempted to raise $51 million, with no takers. As a result there developed a large short position on the market, as speculators were convinced the prices would decline no matter what the offering bids. William A. Read joined with Kuhn Loeb and underwrote the issue successfully. In this instance Read made up the bid, conducted the negotiations with Kuhn Loeb and representatives of the city, and assigned to Dillon the task of distributing the issue.

It was a great success; all the bonds sold out in a matter of minutes. This led to panic among the shorts, who scrambled to cover their positions by purchasing the bonds from Kuhn Loeb and William A. Read. According to one account, "On the day of the sale the two telephone operators on the switchboard collapsed because of the pressure of incoming calls and the board actually did not operate for an hour or so." Not wishing to capitalize upon the distress of others, Read interviewed each of the short sellers, and in some cases would sell them the bonds at par rather than the premium to which they had risen.[34]

Read's actions restored confidence in the markets, and thus reinvigorated, prices stabilized. Several months later William A. Read united once again with Kuhn Loeb, this time to offer $65.9 million in New York City 4¼ percent bonds, and now the bond crowd declined to wager against his abilities at pricing such issues. "Wm. A. Read, with the poise of a man well-bred, independent, and equal, dignified and without fear, pitted his intellect against the great in Wall Street," wrote one contemporary. "He was free from the complexities of fear of the mighty or of subserviency. He fixed his gaze on the goal of buying securities for an ever-growing group of confident customers at the price of their merit and gave no heed to the politics of Wall Street."[35]

Soon after, Wall Street experienced another of several war scares that had disrupted markets during the past nine years. William A. Read was carrying a large inventory of bonds, which would have declined sharply in price in case of war, leading not only to large losses but to illiquidity, since the bonds had been purchased with borrowed money. As Dillon later recalled, he urged Read to cut back on the firm's position.

"He said, 'Why?' "

"There will be a war."

"They can't fight—not today, in an industrial world. They can't go to war."

Dillon agreed; he too couldn't see how they could, but he asked, "But who's going to back down?"

Read considered the question, but said little. The following day he approached Dillon, asked, "Who *is* going to back down?"

"That's what worried me."

"Well," Read replied, "I'm a little lame. Go ahead and liquidate the inventory."

At the time William A. Read owned $20 million in New York Central's 6 percent bonds which had been purchased with borrowed money. The entire position, along with others, was sold, leaving William A. Read almost completely liquid when the war finally erupted.[36]

The coming of war hardly caught Wall Street unaware. Yet the actual arrival of hostilities in the summer of 1914 did cause disruptions, resulting primarily from the recognition that major dislocations lay ahead. One of these was the British and French sales of their American investments to raise funds to pay for needed war materials. Another was intense pressure on Wall Street where the investment banking community was called upon to float Allied, and eventually American, bond issues.

The NYSE's initial reaction to the war was to close down for four months, the longest period during which there was no continuing auction market on the Street. This was done out of fear massive sell-offs would destroy not only the markets, but the liquidity of almost everyone involved with securities. Even so, this measure was the first indication of the new role Wall Street was to play in the world. All involved realized that apart from the temporarily skittish and those who were heavily margined, most of the selling would come from overseas, while the buyers would be Americans.[37]

The bond market also suffered in this period. Underwritings dried up, as both issuers and investors were skittish. After June 1914 to the end of the year, William A. Read had only one underwriting, a $660,000 issue for Victoria, British Columbia.

This is not to say that all on the Street suffered. Wartime demands were quick to be felt. This new atmosphere would enable Dillon to make his first fortune.

One evening in early 1915 Dillon dined with Waddell Catchings, an old Harvard friend then at Goldman Sachs, and J. P. Morgan banker Grayson Murphy. Morgan had organized a group to obtain supplies for the Allies. In effect, the bank had become the purchasing agent for the British government in the United States. They mentioned the pressing need for phenol, a substance used in the manufacture of TNT. Catchings and Murphy suggested that Dillon might be interested in developing an American source of the substance.[38]

Dillon mentioned the discussion to Read, who advised him not to invest his own money in such a venture. "Don't bother with a thing like that—you will lose everything you put in it," was the way Dillon recalled Read's warning. Dillon persisted, amassing facts and figures to show just how profitable the project might be. In so doing he demonstrated the approach which would characterize his activities after the war.

Before entering into any major project Dillon would undertake a research operation of some magnitude. In this case he learned all he could about the chemical industry, its possibilities and pitfalls, likely dangers, potential rewards, sources of supply and customers. This done, he attempted to put into place as many of the forces required, limiting the variables as much as possible, trying to see to it that these were of minor importance to the success of the enterprise as a whole.[39] The Dillon approach was perceivable first in this venture. It would recur with some frequency later on. Because of this, Dillon would reject many deals others thought highly promising. Of course, all of this was very much in the Vermilye and William A. Read tradition. In time Dillon would be seen as a major plunger, a speculator willing to assume major risks. As could be seen in scores of ventures addressed in the 1920s, the reality was quite different.

Having learned what he could about the business, Dillon contacted Armin Schlesinger and some other of his former associates at Newport Mining, presented them with a plan, and soon after formed a new firm to produce the needed phenol. Under the arrangement, Dillon would own 49 percent of the operation, the Newport executives the other 51 percent, and they would be in charge of running it. The project was under way by April, with Thomas Alva Edison taking benzol produced by Dillon and transforming it into phenol.[40]

The plant was a huge success. "By the end of 1915 we were

going great guns, and my monthy dividend was very substantial,"
wrote Dillon many years later. Since the operation had nothing to
do with William A. Read, the profits were all his. It went on this
way for more than two years. When the United States entered
World War I as a belligerent, Dillon and his partners turned the
plant over to the government so as not to benefit from war-related
orders. By then they had realized an enormous profit on their
relatively small investments.[41] More to the point, the episode convinced Dillon that he not only could function effectively as a banker
but had the makings of an industrialist as well. This too would be
significant after the war.

The investment picture on Wall Street brightened in 1915, but
business at William A. Read was below what it had been before
hostilities. The firm's largest underwriting that year was $11.5
million for Canadian Northern Railway, and the corporate business
didn't improve in 1916.

On April 1, 1916, Dillon became a partner at William A. Read.
He was thirty-three years old, and considered not only the critical
banker there but one of the brightest and most promising individuals in the financial industry. Informing a Harvard classmate of
the promotion, Dillon cracked, "This game is more fascinating than
no-limit stud poker," adding that he had just purchased a home in
Rye and joined a golf club.[42] As his name was added to the list of
partners, Read remarked to Joseph Seaman, "You see this new
name at the bottom? It will not be long before it is at the top."[43]

Read never returned to the office. He became feverish that
evening and died of pneumonia a week later at the age of fifty-
eight. Read left an estate of over $6 million, along with a major
collection of art and books.[44]

While the death was not sudden, it had been unanticipated.
The question at issue then was who would assume leadership of
the firm. Even though a junior partner, Dillon was a logical choice
for the position, since he was by far its most dynamic individual
and greatest producer. Without either Read or Dillon the firm
might not only have survived, but performed in a more than satisfactory fashion. Without both of them it probably would have
stagnated and eventually declined, as did so many other Wall
Street houses.

None of the other partners could match Dillon in accomplishments and promise.[45] Many years later Dillon claimed he waited until the others asked him to accept leadership and then, almost reluctantly, did so. On Wall Street, however, a different story made the rounds. According to this one, the partners sat around discussing the matter of succession, when Dillon rose, strode into Read's office, and took his seat, in this way assuming the presidency.[46]

This account rings true. From what we know of Dillon during the years that followed, that is the way he would have acted— swiftly and decisively—but in full knowledge the odds were strongly in his favor.

·4·

Dillon, Read & Co.

(1916–1921)

C larence Dillon was only thirty-three years old at the time of Read's death, and while highly respected still was an outsider, with less than three years' experience in the business, and little more than two of them in New York. Such matters did not concern him; Dillon never doubted his abilities. Later on he would tell an associate that one of his models was David, since he saw himself as the David from Texas who was to slay the Goliaths of Wall Street.[1] This is not to suggest that Dillon intended to disrupt the established power structure. Rather, he hoped to become part of it and transform William A. Read into one of Wall Street's powerhouses, the equal of any of the leaders.

Any firm recasting itself so dramatically was bound to be perceived as bold and adventuresome, but, while he often gave the impression of being so, neither adjective could rightfully be said to describe Clarence Dillon. In this period the press enjoyed publicizing "Young Napoleons," newcomers from the provinces who dazzle and astound. Reporters eagerly proclaimed him to be such a man. Yet the proper words to describe Dillon would be prudent, cautious, and circumspect. As will be seen, Dillon epitomized those

44

qualities, which already were present at William A. Read and before then, at Vermilye.

Decades later some would wonder how and when that venturesome investment bank of the 1920s became the very model of conservatism that it was perceived as being after World War II. The answer was that the spirit really hadn't changed. William A. Read and Clarence Dillon instilled the spirit there, as much as Thomas Watson, Sr., did for International Business Machines and Alfred Sloan for General Motors.

William A. Read & Co. was a strong firm; Dillon hoped to make it stronger still. Together with Phillips he soon raised sufficient funds to purchase Read's interest, and this increased his authority as leader. The firm's personnel remained the same. W. S. Charnley and Henry G. Riter III had arrived and were assigned to the Philadelphia office. The Read brothers arrived after the Armistice. Fiske was in Paris and in 1924 took charge of all European business.

Dean Mathey, Princeton '12, a tennis player of national reputation and Fiske's nephew, joined the firm as a salesman after graduation.[2] While a student Mathey served as a member of the editorial staff of the student newspaper, the *Daily Princetonian*. This was the beginning of a Princeton connection, an old school tie which would become important to Dillon Read over the years, as Mathey also did some of the recruiting for William A. Read. It was in this role that he came across James V. Forrestal, who was to become one of the firm's more important associates in the postwar period, and ultimately the president of Dillon Read.

Forrestal was born on February 15, 1892, in Matteawan, New York, then a town of some six thousand inhabitants. His parents were upper-middle-class Irish Catholic immigrants. Forrestal's father, also named James, was an itinerant worker who started a construction company in Matteawan, and in time became one of that town's wealthiest citizens and a major in the New York National Guard. His mother, Mary, had been a schoolteacher, and by then was mostly concerned with matters of family and church. Young James attended local parochial and public schools, all the while rejecting his mother's dream that he would enter the priesthood. He was a good student and, although short and slender, an aggressive athlete. Forrestal was also an apparently troubled person. Later, when he was a prominent public figure, reporters and analysts attempted to divine in him various underlying psychological disturbances which are beyond the capabilities of historians to fathom. There were reasons for such surmises, however, in his moodiness and occasionally inconsistent behavior, and of course in his eventual tragic suicide.

Forrestal attended Dartmouth for a year and then transferred to Princeton because he thought a degree from there more impressive. His classmates thought he came from a poor family, for while Forrestal's parents assisted him financially, he attempted to get by without any aid at all.

In those days Forrestal considered becoming a journalist. For the rest of his life he was interested in reportage and the written word, and he did have some experience as a reporter for a local newspaper. This caught the attention of Ferdinand Eberstadt, then editor of the *Daily Princetonian*, who asked him to join the staff as a cub reporter, which he did. In his senior year Forrestal was selected to be the newspaper's editor. The reason for this was his maturity, abilities at planning, and foresight. According to Eberstadt, he was serious and determined, and when others came up with ideas for articles, they often found Forrestal had already been promised the materials.[3]

The editorship was no minor post. Woodrow Wilson had been editor of the newspaper when he was a student in the 1870s, and other *Princetonian* editors of the period included John Foster Dulles and Thurman Arnold. Eberstadt had taken over from David Lawrence, who went on to become a well-known Washington columnist and founder of *U.S. News & World Report*.

The editorship rotated, and Forrestal stepped down in the second half of his senior year. Then, because of a dispute with a faculty member, Forrestal dropped out of school a mere six weeks before graduation in 1915, but remained in close contact with Eberstadt, who was known in his Princeton days as "King Eber," while Forrestal was dubbed "The Prince."[4]

It was not as though he lacked prospects. Mathey arrived on that recruitment trip shortly before Forrestal left. Knowing the school well, and having graduated less than three years earlier, he asked to meet the editor of the *Princetonian*. An employee of the firm later recalled a version of the meeting. "Mathey talked to Forrestal about coming to Read, and Forrestal was interested because he was about to face [the matter of selecting] a career and he was interested in anything. But he did not commit himself then." According to this source, "He wanted to make money and get underway" and perhaps thought prospects would be better in some other field.[5]

Forrestal's first job on leaving Princeton was at New Jersey Zinc, which as the name indicates was a metal smelter and fabricator. He quit after a short stay. Through the help of a fellow student and friend, Robert Christie, Forrestal obtained a position at the American Tobacco Company, which involved little more than wholesaling cigars and cigarettes in New York's East Side and hanging posters in local saloons.[6] He didn't like the work, and resigned to become a reporter for the *New York World*, a job he enjoyed enormously. The pay couldn't have been very high, and now that Forrestal knew more about investment banking, he realized he could do better in that field. He approached Mathey, who put him in touch with William Phillips, and in 1916 Forrestal started as a William A. Read bond salesman, the first in the newly opened Albany, New York, office, which included territories as far west as Buffalo. He proved a quick learner and a fine salesman, largely because of his aggressive approach to the business. At a time when such behavior was unusual, Forrestal would work long hours after the office closed to study individual securities and companies so as to have the information at the ready when needed. Before long he was assigned the task of recruiting others, and assembled a sales force which was one of the firm's best-producing units.[7]

Forrestal had arrived just when the boom caused by procurement for war was generating steam. The bond markets were flooded with calls for new financings. Early in 1915 the Allies asked for and received permission to float loans in America. After long negotiations they decided to attempt to sell a total of $500 million in bonds in several underwritings. The lead banks would be J. P. Morgan, which had a traditional relationship with the British and was the French government's official American bank, and Brown Brothers, originally of Baltimore, which had been conducting an international business for close to a century. Morgan organized a $10 million company, American Foreign Securities, to handle the underwritings. Once established, American Foreign sold additional bonds and used the proceeds to lend to foreign governments and companies.

Robert Bacon, who in addition to having been a Morgan partner also served as Secretary of State in the Theodore Roosevelt Administration and later on as ambassador to France, was appointed American Foreign's president. Dillon was named one of its directors, an indication of his standing in those years. William A. Read took $250,000 of the initial underwriting, while Dillon personally subscribed to $50,000 of the bonds. Under terms of its charter, American Foreign Securities "shall enter into a contract with the French Government whereby the Company will lend to the French Government the sum of $100,000,000 repayable July 31, 1919, and whereby the French Government will pledge with the Company in the United States as collateral security for the payment of the loan, securities having a value of approximately $120,000,000, calculated at quoted prices in existing markets, converted into dollars at prevailing rates of exchange between New York and Paris." The notes would be sold to yield 5¾ percent. The syndicate would receive ½ of 1 percent ($500,000) for services and another 2 percent ($2 million) as a commission. American Foreign sold 100,000 shares of $100 par value stock, of which Dillon was allotted 500 shares, which cost $50,000. His portion of the commission and fees came to $125,000.[8]

The second underwriting was for a $100 million three-year secured loan to France. William A. Read was a second bracket firm, along with Kidder Peabody, First National Bank, and Lee Higginson among others. Despite initial reluctance on the part of lenders, the issue was sold out. Other offerings followed. By December 1, almost $1.8 billion in bonds had been placed. During the neutrality years 1914–17 the total foreign loans raised on Wall Street came to almost $3 billion.[9]

Ordinarily such strong demand for goods and services would have resulted in inflation and higher bond yields. The cost of living did advance sharply. Increases in the consumer price index averaged 9 percent a year from 1914 to 1917. Even so, bond prices did not decline to offer higher yields, as they often would in such circumstances. The strong market resulted from the veritable flood of investment funds and gold to America, a good deal of which went to purchase American bonds, considered the safest in the world during such difficult times. Not only did British and French investors send their money to Wall Street, but the more than $200 million a year gold production in British mines in south and west Africa found its way to America. In 1915 and 1916 the United States absorbed over $1 billion in gold.[10]

America's entry into the war added to the demand for capital, which meant that the government too went to the markets. During the conflict the national debt rose from $1.3 billion to nearly $27 billion. There were four Liberty Loan drives and one Victory Loan, which together netted almost $21 billion. The rest of the capital requirements came from higher taxes (the income tax had become effective in 1913) and foreign investments.[11]

While the investment banking community prospered, its role in raising funds for the government was limited. Most of the loan campaigns were conducted by government agencies, which either sold bonds directly to the public through commercial banks or did so through dealers authorized to market government securities under the terms of the legislation establishing the Federal Reserve System. Since profit margins in this business were quite small, the larger firms tended to ignore it, leaving the business to obscure houses such as C. F. Childs & Co. and Salomon Brothers & Hutzler.[12]

This approach undermined the position of the old-line investment banks. Assertive newer ones and once-small operations had the opportunity to expand significantly if they grasped the meaning of the new dispensation and were bold and intelligent in reacting to it. None of this was apparent during the war, but many small and new firms were obtaining business and undergoing experiences which would enable them to play leadership roles in the postwar period. Wrote one student of the scene, "In the money market of the twenties, syndicates of relatively obscure or new houses could handle hundred million dollar issues without recourse to the old financial leaders."[13]

At least ten William A. Read executives, including William A. Read, Jr., enlisted in the armed forces when the United States entered the war in 1917. After some maneuvering, Forrestal managed to obtain a commission in the navy, and together with Read trained in naval aviation.[14]

Clarence Dillon tried to enlist, but several years earlier he had

been operated on and had lost a kidney, disqualifying him from
military service. Still, Dillon meant to serve in some capacity, and
through his connections was able to win the post of Bernard Baruch's assistant on the War Industries Board (WIB). Dillon was
one of three, the others being Herbert Bayard Swope, the city
editor for the *New York World*, and Harrison Williams, the owner
of a small tire company who would later become an important
utilities magnate.

The WIB was an outgrowth of the Council on National Defense, formed by President Wilson in 1916 to prepare the country
for possible entry into World War I. The council established the
WIB shortly after the Declaration of War on April 6, 1917.
Initially Baruch headed the raw materials section, and did not
become chairman until March 4 of the following year, when Dillon
joined him.

It was a difficult and complicated job. Baruch had to mold the
economy into a smoothly running, integrated operation. Clearly
such a task would have been impossible without an organizational
program and large-scale delegation of responsibilities, which was
where Dillon came in.

Baruch often remarked that his "flying executives" multiplied
his efforts threefold. Whenever a problem appeared he would assign it to one of the assistants, who would study the issue and
come back with recommendations.[15] That Baruch respected all
three was transparently clear. In his memoirs he characterized
Swope as "brilliant" and noted that Williams later would become
"a titan of the utility industry," while Dillon, "who already had
made a mark as one of the keenest minds in Wall Street," would
"make a much more impressive one after the war."[16] Dillon not
only served under "the Chief," but went with him to the Versailles
peace conference to assist him on the committee dealing with German reparations.[17]

In the process Dillon came into proximity with some of the
nation's most important businessmen. Among those serving on
WIB organizations were officers of such firms as the Southern
Railway, Westinghouse Electric and Manufacturing, International
Harvester, Buckeye Steel Castings, St. Joseph Lead, Illinois Steel,
Continental Can, and many more. Ten years later one journalist
put it this way:[18]

Capitalistic whales swam daily into the offices of the War Industries Board, spouting complaints and threats. They were received by the assistant to the chairman. They noticed that the latter was a relaxed, pipe–smoking young man. (Dillon had but recently permitted himself a pipe—the one dissipation in an otherwise rigidly regulated life.) Chairman Baruch's aide seemed to know a lot without saying much, but few of the mighty men of business had imagined enough to visualize in the tall, lean, dark young man a possible reincarnation of one of those silent, mocking, caftan-clad men of his blood who sat centuries ago in the chancelleries of Europe and ruled the world's trade routes.

The WIB experience was a watershed event for scores of young businessmen, creating a community of interests and shared experiences second in Dillon's case only to that of Harvard.[19]

For decades after the war Baruch and Dillon communicated regularly and cooperated on deals. Harrison Williams would be a close associate in many ventures during the 1920s and 1930s, and the two met socially as well. Williams helped pave the way for Armin Schlesinger to join the exclusive Sleepy Hollow Country Club, and in return Williams was included in underwritings for Schlesinger's companies.

In 1924 Williams created the North American Company, which by the end of the decade was one of the nation's largest utilities holding companies. Dillon handled much of the underwriting for the parent and component firms, as was the practice in obtaining the business without competitive bidding. Through Williams Dillon was able to make additional contacts, and he reciprocated by including Williams in lucrative underwritings.[20]

While at the WIB Dillon had met Joseph P. Cotton, Jr., who had been a partner at the law firm of Cravath, Henderson & DeGersdorff, which he had left in 1910 to organize his own firm, Spooner & Cotton. Cotton was a genial, humorous, tall, and handsome man, who bore some physical resemblance to Franklin D. Roosevelt. Despite a Harvard education, he affected a folksy attitude, complete with smoking a corncob pipe, even at formal occasions. This perhaps was done to put off adversaries, but not for long; Cotton was known as one of the cleverest lawyers on Wall Street.[21]

During the war Cotton served under Herbert Hoover at the Food Administration, which he left in 1918 to return to the practice of law. Within a year the firm was reconstituted as McAdoo, Cotton & Franklin, the senior partner being William G. McAdoo, Secretary of the Treasury in the Woodrow Wilson Administration and one of the nation's most prominent political leaders. George Franklin, a veteran Wall Street lawyer, was the third member. When McAdoo withdrew to return to California where he opened his own office and prepared to reenter politics, the firm was renamed Cotton and Franklin.[22]

Even before then, by virtue of their extensive political connections, McAdoo and Cotton had accumulated a striking list of corporate clients. The firm was instrumental in the creation of Radio Corporation of America, and brought together five major chemical companies into Allied Chemical and Dye. Soon it would become the leading New York law firm in the area of railroad and industrial reorganizations, the latter to be one of Dillon's major interests. As early as 1919 Cotton would work with Dillon on several minor financings. Until he left for Washington in 1929 to become Under Secretary of State, Cotton would be one of Dillon's most trusted attorneys.[23]

While shorn of many key executives, William A. Read prospered during the war. In 1917 the company managed a $60 million underwriting for the Pennsylvania Railroad, a $50 million issue for Bethlehem Steel, and a number of smaller ones for such clients as Wickwire Steel, Kansas City Terminal Railway, and the state of Idaho. The firm participated in the Liberty Loan drives, with Dillon named a member of the Committee on Distribution. He was not on the Central Committee, however, an honor bestowed upon the likes of Morgan, George Baker, Jacob Schiff, and Albert Wiggin, the giants of Wall Street.[24]

There were more than a score of small issues the following year for such firms as American Gas & Electric, the Wisconsin Central Railway, the city of Bayonne, New Jersey, and the state of California, none of which was for more than $2 million. One of the larger underwritings in 1918, which raised $5 million in 7-year notes, was for the Steel & Tube Company of America, a Schlesinger company which had recently been created out of several of the family's holdings.

Steel & Tube, then a significant factor in a specialized segment of the industry, was Dillon's most important client. In addition to raising funds for the company, he sought a merger partner for Schlesinger. One of these was Allied Chemical and Dye. Cotton was still Allied's attorney, and it was perhaps through him that Allied acquired an 18 percent interest in Steel & Tube.

Shortly after the completion of negotiations at Versailles, Dillon returned to America on the *Rotterdam*, rejoining the other William A. Read partners who had entered the service and now were back in the office. They encountered a transformed financial community, in a nation whose posture had been drastically modified. This was so due to a major alteration in the international balance of economic power. As it had been for a century, London had been the hub of world finance in 1914. Wall Streeters customarily began the day asking about securities prices and interest rates there, and their activities would be informed by such matters. By 1917 New York had assumed that role. At the time of President Woodrow Wilson's declaration of war on April 2, the *Manchester Guardian* editorialized:[25]

> European financiers would be well advised to face the fact that the war has radically transformed the relations between the United States and Europe. . . . The United States . . . by the end of this war will have wiped out most of its debt to foreign investors. It will have a currency of unimpeachable magnitude. The American bankers will have acquired the experience they have hitherto lacked in the international money market and all this strengthened financial fabric will rest upon an economic fabric which the war will have much expanded. It can hardly be doubted that under these circumstances, New York will enter the lists for the financial leadership of the world.

The writer proved prescient. From the position of a net debtor to the extent of more than $3.7 billion when the war began, the United States went to one of a net creditor by $5 billion in 1917. When President Wilson arrived in Versailles in January 1919, the American international investment position showed a balance of $6.4 billion.[26] The gross national product rose from $76.4 billion in 1918 to $84 billion in 1919 and then to $91.5 billion in 1920. As a result the labor shortage continued. Within six months more than 2 million servicemen had been discharged. The unemployment rate, which had been 1.4 percent when the war ended, remained at that level in 1919.

The economy declined once demands depending on reconversion and deferred spending were filled. The unemployment rate rose to 5.2 percent in 1920 and 11.7 percent in 1921, a year in which the GNP collapsed to $69.6 billion. The recession, one of the sharpest in American history, involved more than 30,000 bankruptcies and close to 500,000 farm foreclosures.[27]

The automobile and tire industries had been hard hit during the war. This was not so much because of the lack of demand as because of governmental controls. Citing the need for steel in the manufacture of a wide variety of military equipment, in early 1918 the WIB ordered the auto makers to produce only one-quarter as many cars in the last half of the year as they had delivered during 1917. The manufacturers had to cease production completely in 1919 to concentrate on military orders. As a result, automobile production declined from 1.7 million units in 1917 to 943,000 in 1918. The restrictions were lifted shortly after the Armistice, but the industry was badly shaken, and several small companies went into liquidation or were taken over by stronger units. The tire makers were even more severely impacted. On September 21, 1918, the Priorities Commission of the WIB placed rubber on the list of restricted products, and the manufacture of tires was limited to three-tenths of normal production.[28]

This situation created business for bankers, but initially little of consequence materialized at William A. Read. Shortly after returning from Europe Dillon concerned himself with several interesting possibilities. He monitored the automobile and tire industries as well as several others, realizing opportunities might soon be presented, and he prepared to act if and when they materialized.

There were some nibbles and business in 1919. Through Cotton, William A. Read entered into a relationship with Fisk Rubber, and the firm led a syndicate in a $15 million preferred stock underwriting for that mid-size tire manufacturer. For a while Dillon was engaged with Cotton and Williams in attempting a merger of Packard and Peerless which fell through.

William A. Read continued to concentrate on debt and to a lesser degree equity underwriting. In 1919 the firm participated in twenty-two syndicates which raised $90 million for clients, with $52 million in bonds and the rest in stocks. This was not a particularly striking showing for the transitional year, when many firms were raising funds for conversion programs. To appreciate what this meant, consider that the total American underwritings that year came in at $4.4 billion, meaning that William A. Read accounted for a trifle more than 2 percent of the domestic business.

There were some bright spots, however, in the form of new industrial clients such as Riordon Pulp & Paper, Wilson & Co., A. G. Spaulding, and Cutler-Hammer, and such utilities as American Gas & Electric, and Pacific Power & Light. As had been the case in 1918, one of the largest underwritings was for Steel & Tube, a $17.5 million issue of 7 percent cumulative preferred stock. It was a typical deal for the time, and so merits examination and comment on how business was transacted in those years.

Prior to the offering Dillon arranged a consolidation of the Schlesinger interests in Newport, Northwestern Iron, and Harrow Spring into Steel & Tube. The syndicate was to be led by William A. Read, Chase National, and Central Trust, and was open for bids on June 27.

This group, known as a "purchase syndicate," took the $100 par value stock at $90. The stock was then placed with a "managers' syndicate" at $92, which turned over the paper to a "selling syndicate" at $93. The selling syndicate then attempted to sell the shares as close to par as possible to the public and institutions. It was not unusual for the same firm serving as part of the purchase syndicate to give itself a role on one or both of the others, since it was in charge of such matters. The selling syndicate members received the most profit but also had the more difficult task, especially if an issue came to market at an unattractive price due to sluggish conditions.[29]

In this period each firm had its own style in syndication. Morgan would handle most of the distribution in purchase syndicates it headed, while Kuhn Loeb insisted that all members of the purchase syndicate play a role in selling the securities. Occasionally firms would permit their names to be used in the tombstone advertisements without participating, lending their prestige to obtain credibility and assuming a small amount of risk in return for a share in the profits. Other banks, including William A. Read, entered selling syndicates with some reluctance, while considering trading in the secondary market a derivative exercise, creating nothing of consequence, requiring risks out of proportion to rewards. Gradually William A. Read withdrew from trading, confining its activities in this area to management of a handful of small accounts, but not engaging in the practice for the firm's own account.

Clarence Dillon followed the Read practice. He wasn't especially interested in distribution, though Dillon Read later would establish a small retail business. Entering the distribution phase of the market meant purchasing bonds often without a clear, definite idea of to whom they would be sold. Purchasers of bonds often demanded the seller "make a market" in the paper, so they might be sold if that was suitable. Both distribution and market making required the commitment of capital, something Dillon shied from all of his life. Rather, his talents and those of the firm were best displayed in the kind of operation exemplifed by the Steel & Tube deal, namely the creation of a strategic plan, the marshaling of forces, and its implementation.

The purchase syndicate's profits ranged from 2.5 to 10 percent, and occasionally ran as high as 20 percent. As a result commercial banks devoted an increasing amount of time, energy, and capital to such business. *The New York Times* wrote that "the profits to be divided from underwriting have grown to such an extent that many banks of considerable reputation rely almost entirely on such profits for their income, letting the conventional banking business entirely alone." To this the *United States Investor* added that underwriting afforded bankers with "a pleasant occupation, involving no great risk and entailing the most exaggerated fees."[30]

To illustrate how this particular syndicate worked, consider that at the last minute Brown Brothers joined the Steel & Tube purchase syndicate. In the memorandum taking note of this Dillon wrote:[31]

> Brown Bros. & Co. have a $500,000 interest in the first syndicate. This is a closed transaction when the syndicate at 92 is made up. They then have a $1,000,000 interest in this syndicate at 92 which is a closed transaction when the 93 syndicate is made up; and they

have a $500,000 interest in the 93 syndicate, which is a separate transaction from its predecessors.

This meant Brown Brothers would have a $500,000 share in the purchase syndicate, a $1 million share in the managers' syndicate, and a $500,000 participation in the selling syndicate, which by then was the only one still open. It is possible William A. Read & Co. gave Brown Brothers a share in the first two syndicates in order to lure the bank into the selling syndicate, which in such times would have been the most difficult to assemble.

The underwriting, scheduled to run over a two month period, was set into motion in July. It began with the allocation of shares at the purchase syndicate price to individuals on William A. Read's "preferred list," who were allotted shares at what amounted to an insider price, and were virtually assured a riskless profit. Dillon withheld $1.5 million in Steel & Tube for those on his list. These individuals received shares at 92, and presumably would reciprocate by including Dillon and his colleagues on their preferred lists or in some other way. One of these, Otto Kahn of Kuhn Loeb, wanted a larger participation than was offered.[32] Dillon commented:

I explained to him that that offering at 92 was simply to our friends and his 100,000 was a liberal amount as we had given Sabin at the Guaranty only 100,000, Prosser only 50,000, Mitchell of National City Company only 50,000, etc. He said he would call me back and said in view of that would also like 250,000 at 93 and would withdraw it.

The actual placements began before the operation was set into motion, as Dillon contacted managers of fund accounts. In a diary entry for June 26 he wrote:

Saw Mr. Henry Evans and offered him Steel & Tube stock for the insurance companies. He took $300,000 worth; $150,000 for the Continental, $100,000 for Fidelity and $50,000 for American Eagle Fire Insurance Company. I told him I would give these companies an interest in the distributing syndicate and they could withdraw their stock.

As was the custom, Dillon placed Evans on his preferred list.[33]

I also told him that I would arrange a personal interest for him in our purchasing syndicate. I did not state the amount. I said that this was what I had discussed with him several days ago that I would like him personally to be interested in various businesses we were doing and should like to add his name to the few personal friends to whom I offer syndicate interests.

As it turned out, the shares were quite attractive. The Chatham & Phenix National Bank attempted to join the selling syndicate as soon as the issue was announced, and Dillon had to inform it the group was closed. On July 8 Kissell & Kinnicutt telephoned to say they would take $250,000 at 93 if permitted to have $100,000 at 92. Dillon agreed. He telephoned O. L. Gubelman to inform him he would be allotted $200,000 at 92 on taking $250,000 at 93. Hallgarten & Co. received $150,000 at 93.

Within a day the underwriting was almost complete, and Dillon now turned to other business.

This kind of deal and Dillon's actions were not at all uncommon among those investment banks which concentrated upon originating business and merchant banking, in which the banker took a direct interest in all of the aspects of the client's operations.

As can be seen, the profits from such undertakings could be large, with the partners having the advantage of taking the bonds at what amounted to wholesale prices and then selling them at retail. It was through participation in such deals that bankers earned most of their remuneration. In those years salaries were quite low. For the fiscal year beginning on May 15, 1919, and ending on May 15, 1920, for example, the firm paid total salaries of less than $60,000 to twenty-five individuals. Forrestal, who was one of the highest-salaried persons at the firm that year, received $5,083.33, and some were paid substantially less; Christie received $2,850. Compensation would derive mainly from bonuses and being given a percentage of profits and inclusion in deals.[34]

In 1920 William A. Read participated in twenty-two underwritings, nineteen in bonds and three in stocks, for a total of $198 million, almost 5 percent of the nation's $4 billion in underwritings. Even so, other than Canadian firms and Steel & Tube, there was not a single significant concern or government for which the firm was the lead banker. The firm's largest deal that year was as a second bracket participant in a $35 million Texas Company offering.

This was about to change; soon William A. Read would make an important breakthrough in clients, for the first time acting as the lead underwriter for one of America's largest and most visible industrial corporations. The firm made its mark as the lead investment banker in an underwriting for the Goodyear Tire & Rubber Company, which was born of tribulation.

Sales of both automobiles and tires had soared in 1919 and 1920. Manufacturers had responded by placing large orders for parts, and in the case of the tire manufacturers, fabric for casings and rubber. Few added to inventories as rapidly as did Goodyear, the largest, fastest-growing, and for years the most highly regarded factor in the industry. The company began in 1899 in a small factory which had formerly housed a strawboard operation. Business doubled each year in the span from 1908 through 1912. The company's revenues were $31 million in fiscal 1914; for fiscal 1918, the figure was $131.2 million, by which time Goodyear tires were on 60 percent of the nation's automobiles.[35]

Under the leadership of CEO Frank Seiberling, Goodyear had established such varied units as a cotton plantation in Arizona, a rubber plantation in Sumatra, and a factory to construct dirigibles in Akron, Ohio, as well as three additional facilities for the manufacture of tires. This program demanded heavy financing. Goodyear sold $17.5 million in common shares in 1916, and $26 million of preferred in 1917–18, both through Goldman Sachs. Anticipated postwar demand prompted Seiberling to construct another tire facility in California, and he sold $69 million in preferred for this project. Goldman Sachs acted as lead underwriter for this offering in a syndicate which included William A. Read & Co.[36]

All the while the company had relatively small cash reserves and a generally weak balance sheet. Difficulties in selling stock and bonds may have been the reason Seiberling established Goodyear Cotton Mills, Goodyear Tire & Rubber of California, Goodyear Textile Mills, and Goodyear Tire & Rubber of Canada in 1919 as separate entities. In this way they could stand on their own in the credit markets. Even so, in 1920 their bonds all were rated "B" by Moody's.

Inventory control, one of the most important parts of the business, seemed of no concern. In early 1920 Goodyear required 4,000 tons of rubber a month to produce tires and other items. The market price for rubber was $0.55 a pound, so a month's supply cost approximately $4.5 million. Cotton fabric was being used at the monthly rate of 1,200 tons at an average cost of $1.50, which came to another $4.5 million. Orders generally took four months to deliver, which meant that Goodyear had to maintain inventories to fill needs for at least that much time.

Seiberling did not consider the possibilities of an industry-wide slowdown, but behaved instead as though demand would continue at the current rate. Nor did he take into account the possibilities of drastic price changes. In January 1920, Goodyear had $36 million worth of rubber and fabric in its inventory.[37] The company's accountant would later testify:[38]

> Goodyear was well organized on the manufacturing side, the selling side and the general development of the business, and therefore it was able to take full advantage of favorable conditions; but it was weak as I see it on the side of control of purchases, control of finance and general control of accounts. Those are the weaknesses that become vital and fatal when you strike real adversity. They were unfortunate in being weak on that side when they struck a period of exceptional adversity which hit their particular industry particularly hard.

Commodity prices dropped sharply during the following months. The price of cotton fabric was cut in half, and rubber fell even further. Commitments for future deliveries of raw materials amounted to over $55 million, and were at prices about 50 percent above current quotations.[39] The result was huge inventory losses; Seiberling's accountants told him he would need a reserve of approximately $24 million in February to cover the excess costs of fabric alone, and even more for those of rubber. Goodyear had a net cash position of some $19 million. It was, therefore, teetering on the edge of insolvency.[40]

It couldn't have happened at a worse moment. Demand melted. Since the nation was in the midst of a depression, auto owners either drove on bald tires or simply put their cars on blocks to await the return of prosperity.

Seiberling could not maintain prices in the face of intensifying competition. By midyear he was selling tires at far below the costs of the raw materials that went into them. In March, Goodyear posted revenues of $20 million; by November they were down to $4.5 million. The company had operating losses of $13 million for the four months ending February 28, 1920. Losses for March and April came to another $5 million.[41] The situation worsened during the rest of the year. Tire production in April was 837,236; by December, it had plummeted to 117,865. Even so, Seiberling continued his generous dividend policy. In the year ended October 31, 1919, Goodyear paid $2.8 million on its preferred stock and $2.5 million on the common. For the next fiscal year, at the beginning of which conditions were poor and grew worse rapidly, the company disbursed $3.2 million in preferred dividends and $3.4 million on the common.[42]

Seiberling struggled to remain afloat. He was able to borrow $1 million by taking out mortgages on some western properties, and a settlement was worked out with some farmers who had contracted to sell their crops to Goodyear at a much higher price than the market demanded. A $500,000 policy on Seiberling's life, payable to Goodyear, was canceled. However, as investors soon realized, these were relatively insignificant moves. By October 1920, Goodyear preferred stock had declined from over 100 to 25, while the common shares, which once sold for more than 130, were under 10.[43] Knowing the end was near, Seiberling posted lookouts near the factory to spot court officials bearing bankruptcy papers and to report the news to headquarters.[44]

To complicate matters, Seiberling had to seek aid and perhaps protection at a time when Wall Street itself was in a precarious situation, with underwriters uncertain regarding their ability to market new offerings. In November 1920 he was able to negotiate a revolving line of credit of $25 million at an 8 percent rate through Goldman Sachs, with raw materials and finished goods as collateral. Over the next few months Goodyear drew down $18.8 million of this amount.

This was a stopgap measure, undertaken simply to buy time. It distressed Seiberling, since the credit line gave the bankers effective financial control of the company. Something of a more permanent nature, in the form of long-term financing, would be required if Goodyear were to remain viable and independent.

Waddell Catchings of Goldman Sachs contemplated $50 million in such financing, but doubted the market could support such an issue. Asked his opinion, Catchings thought receivership was inevitable.[45]

In this period it was not unusual for distressed firms to fall into the hands of a creditors' committee which would attempt a restructuring, keeping it out of receivership if possible but forcing it to declare bankruptcy if this was the only way the creditors could recover their debts. The company's attorneys would be brought in to protect its interests, and they in turn would solicit assistance from bankers who would be employed to raise funds required to repay the obligations. More often than not these took the form of high-yielding bonds, which were backed by specific assets.

Seiberling met with a group of his creditors, who quickly realized the situation was close to hopeless. Receivership seemed inevitable.

It was at this point—on December 28, 1920—that Seiberling retained Paul D. Cravath of what had become Cravath, Henderson, Leffingwell & DeGersdorff to serve as Goodyear's counsel. Cravath organized a team of associates which went over the books. He soon learned that Goodyear had creditors throughout the country, and that demands for payment were intensifying. Bankruptcy was imminent, which Cravath found troublesome, since he suspected that such a move would lead to a wave of other failures, perhaps panic. Failures of major firms had triggered financial collapses and even recessions in the past, so Cravath recognized that Goodyear's problems were of national concern.

There was some hope, however. "The Goodyear Company ought to be saved from a receivership and I think there is a fair chance of success," Cravath wrote to another of the company's attorneys. "It of course depends on the creditors. I hope they will be broad enough to carry the concern along until conditions change and the company can be financed."[46]

Cravath tried to interest Goldman Sachs in attempting a rescue operation, but was rebuffed. Guaranty Trust President Charles Sabin told Cravath it was willing to undertake a $2.5 million offering of first mortgage bonds, because the firm was "deeply interested in avoiding the shock that would result from the failure of the Goodyear Company," but this hardly sufficed.[47] For a few days it seemed that J. P. Morgan & Co. might agree to lead in a restructuring. Cravath invited Edward R. Stettinius of Morgan, Sabin of Guaranty Trust, James S. Alexander of National Bank of Commerce, Albert H. Wiggin of the Chase National, and Dillon to a conference to consider means of salvaging the situation at Goodyear. Stettinius thought it was an unpromising situation, not the kind of deal a firm with Morgan's reputation should undertake, and all the others except Dillon agreed.

Cravath convened a meeting of creditors on January 11, 1921. "If Goodyear goes down it will take some other important companies with it," he warned. "All of the rubber companies bought heavily in anticipation of continued business, and today these other companies can no longer rest in the shadow of Goodyear's financial troubles. They have troubles of their own. Serious troubles, as you men know."[48]

Several days later, at a meeting to which Dillon was not invited, Cravath asked advice regarding the next step, and "the suggestions were made by more than one conferee that Dillon, Read & Company would be the best bankers to secure, if we could secure them."[49]

Cotton attended the meeting as a representative of one of the creditors. He agreed with all present that what was most needed at that juncture was a leader who could arrange the restructuring. Cotton observed that Dillon was well equipped for the task, even though it was far more ambitious a project than any he had ever led. Dillon was sent for and given the opportunity to assume command of one of the largest and most complex workouts to that date.[50]

This came when Dillon had just achieved new symbolic prominence. In 1920 he was named senior partner, and on January 14 of the following year he altered the firm's name to Dillon, Read & Co. to signal what all on the Street knew was a fact; he had remade William A. Read & Co. in his own image. According to a story of the period Dillon rose at a partners' meeting and said, "Gentlemen, I have brought in 85 per cent of the business here and henceforth the name of the firm shall be Dillon, Read & Company. Those who do not like the arrangement can withdraw."[51]

Now the freshly renamed firm would be handed its first opportunity to distinguish itself. Dillon was presented with all of the needed documents and spoke briefly with several members of the committee. He asked for a few days to study the materials and think matters over.

As noted, Dillon abhorred risk, whenever possible operated on borrowed money, and was quick to anger at mechanical mistakes. He never entered a deal without initially investigating it thoroughly. Other bankers did the same, but not to the extent Dillon insisted upon. In the mid-1920s he would organize an "Industrial Department" at the firm to provide such information. In 1949 Karl Behr, who headed the department and was one of the firm's partners, testified on its role in the case of United States of America v. Henry S. Morgan et al.:[52]

> For instance, if we are going to finance a business the first thing that we want to do is find out about the industry; second, whether the business is a good business, and the main factors in finding that out are first the management, is the management up to date and able in all main categories. That means not only the president, but it means the sales manager and the plant manager—whether the plants are modern and whether they are operated efficiently so that their costs are proper. Their methods of selling are vital in any study of that kind, as to whether they are sound. Their methods of distribution and warehousing and so forth. That all is part of a study of a business for financing. Sometimes such a study has resulted in negativing a financing of a sizable business.

In keeping with traditional practice, Dillon made certain he would not be perceived as attempting to take a client from Goldman Sachs; such behavior was not tolerated in the investment banking community of the period. "We [do not] go to corporations and ask them to do business with us," Otto Kahn of Kuhn Loeb would later declare. "We hope that we have established a reputation which is our show window, which attracts customers. . . . I would not seek to take any client away from anybody."[53]

Once Dillon Read accepted a firm as client, it would attempt to become closely affiliated with its operations. In itself this was nothing new; as noted, J. P. Morgan and Kuhn Loeb among others had always placed representatives on the boards of their clients. Yet there was a difference. Such men were overseers to make certain the firm retained its creditworthiness and would report back to Morgan on actions taken, to which he might react positively or negatively. Dillon Read carried it a step further. Clarence Dillon always attempted to form close relationships with clients, which extended from financial advice to assisting in locating and taking on key personnel. In a 1928 speech before the partners, Behr said:[54]

> Our main function is perhaps that of maintaining contact with the companies we have financed. . . . Directorship work is supposed to function through this department and those directors who are from Dillon Read are supposed to inform this department of what is going on in each company they follow. We, on our part, have the duty of keeping each of our director representatives posted with regard to his particular company, its figures and any other matters of information of value to following its progress. Very often we ask a director to find out certain information for us.

In his later testimony in U.S. v. Morgan et al., Behr spoke of additional services to clients:[55]

> From time to time they [clients] would require personnel in the lower categories of their business, sometimes in higher categories: comptrollers, engineers, surveys to be made by engineering concerns, studies of their inventory situations, which were made even by ourselves at their request, our little organization; and there were innumerable detailed ordinary operating problems that a business would have within itself, a manufacturing business, that we were going into at the desire of the issuer, and not ourselves stepping in and saying, "We would like to tell you this and that."

This was what Dillon was to do at Goodyear. Dillon Read did not have an Industrial Department in those years; the firm was small, and resources sparse. He did what he could under the circumstances, starting with the financing, and making plans for managerial changes later on. In so acting Dillon developed the concept of utilizing new issues of high-yield bonds to salvage a company in such a way as would be employed by Wall Street investment banks in the 1970s and 1980s.[56]

During the next three days Dillon and Mathey developed their plan to save Goodyear. Then Dillon communicated with Cravath and presented him with a short memorandum outlining his approach to restructuring the debt. Negotiations and further discussions followed. By January 28 it was agreed that in order to provide Goodyear with much-needed working capital, Dillon Read would float $30 million of new 8 percent 20-year bonds. This was a time when high-grade corporates were yielding 5 percent. Another $27.5 million would be raised in the form of 8 percent ten-year debentures, half to repay bank loans and the rest to furnish additional working capital. To sweeten the debenture offering, for each $1,000 face value the purchaser would receive 10 shares of common stock. There would also be $30 million in 8 percent prior cumulative preference stock to take care of the claims of merchandise creditors.

The bonds and debentures were to be offered to the public below par, with the former callable at 120 and the latter at 110. Thus, their yields were higher than 8 percent and the owners stood to make a substantial capital gain. At one point it was suggested that the preference stock not contain provisions for accrual benefits. Probably because he felt the creditors would not accept it with these terms, Dillon said, "If that is done, I'll have nothing to do with the reorganization." The provision remained.[57]

Dillon was taking no chances that the offering would not be placed. He also proposed a sinking fund for the bonds, which would be retired at a rate of one-fortieth annually by purchase or redemption, so the owners of those bonds redeemed first would be paid at a rate of nearly 60 percent. This obviously was quite high, but it would take that kind of reward to attract investors. Goodyear common was selling for $5 and had a book value of *minus* $44 a share, and the preferred stock, issued at $100 little more than a year earlier, was selling at $25.[58]

Taking no chances on what remained a difficult market, Dillon agreed to float the $30 million bond issue only if the creditors' committee and the merchandisers' creditors' committee were able to place the other two issues.[59] Finally, the plan provided for the issuance of $10,000 in new management stock to be given to the three components—Dillon and the two committees—nominated to take control of and be responsible for the company. Needless to say, Seiberling was to be replaced as chief executive officer.[60]

Several Goodyear stockholders protested. Owners of the preferred stock issued in 1919 were irate, since their holdings would be worth less with those large new issues of bonds and debentures having first call on earnings. One shareholder, Lawrence Maxwell, alleged fraud and indicated that if the program was pursued to its conclusion he and others might organize a stockholders' committee to bring a legal action against the firm.

Meanwhile, Dillon informed Cravath he would organize a syndicate to distribute the bonds, "if the market has not changed for the worse and . . . no strikingly bad developments have come into the situation." Dillon Read and Goldman Sachs would head the underwriting group, with the latter having the largest share but Dillon Read receiving first mention in the tombstone advertisements. Others in the syndicate were to be National City, Lee Higginson, Halsey Stuart, Lehman Brothers, Guaranty Co., and White Weld.[61] It was a distinguished company, marking Dillon Read's debut as a major player on the Street. Dillon's memorandum concluded:[62]

> If the company and the creditors carry out the suggestions made, and I am able to assist by underwriting the First Mortgage Bonds, I propose that my compensation will be limited to 1% for forming the underwriting syndicate. I am in this situation purely by invitation and my interest is to be helpful. You will, of course, understand that at this stage I make no commitment in this business and that the company makes no commitment to me.

The shareholders' assent would be needed if the program was to be implemented, and Dillon scheduled a special meeting for that purpose for March 4. Goodyear's salesmen were pressed into service as proxy solicitors, and by the time of the meeting they had gathered support from two-thirds of the shares and creditors owning more than 75 percent of the debt. But this wasn't enough for approval; the creditor's committee correctly observed that without unanimous approval the reorganization could not carry. An adjournment was declared as Dillon, Cravath, and others attempted to whip the rebellious creditors into line. At first they failed. Several creditors filed suits to prevent the reorganization, with Cravath responding by obtaining legislation in Ohio to assert corporate rights to act in such a manner.

By the end of April most of the lawsuits had been dropped and more than 90 percent of the shareholder proxies had been obtained. Dillon now told Cravath he would proceed with the public underwriting once the resignations of the board members were submittted and the rest of the funds were in hand. When the market failed to absorb the debenture and preferred stock offerings, Dillon Read took a large portion of these, too. Blair & Co. and Hallgarten & Co. agreed to market two-thirds of the remaining $4.5 million of the other two issues if another bank would take the other $1.5 million. For a while it seemed the entire edifice would collapse since no one came forth, and Dillon had no intention of risking his firm's assets in this manner. Then John Sherwin, chairman of the Union Trust and one of the members of the bank creditors' committee, agreed to take $750,000 and R. C. Shaffner, president of the Chicago banking firm of A. G. Becker & Co., another creditor, took the remainder. So the deal was completed.

Part of the funds generated was used to pay off Goldman Sachs. Until the last of the bonds were redeemed, Dillon, Owen D. Young of General Electric who had strong connections with J. P. Morgan & Co., and John Sherwin were given the right to name a majority of Goodyear's board of directors and its management.

The reorganization plan was declared in force on May 9. Dillon Read had registered the $30 million offering on April 20 to expire two months later, and now the selling syndicate swung into action. The bonds were to be offered at 99. The purchase syndicate price was 90, the managers' syndicate price was 92, and the selling syndicate paid 94 plus accrued interest. Dillon Read's purchase syndicate profit came to $5.5 million, far less than the $12.5 million Goldman Sachs would take, but ahead of the others. In addition there was the syndicate's selling commission of 2 percent, and an additional commission of 1 percent.

Six years later Dillon claimed Dillon Read received $563,334 from Goodyear for all underwriting services during the period from 1921 to 1926, and an additional $252,002 for "profits and commissions." He later revealed that as part of the firm's compensation, it received an option to purchase 170,000 Goodyear shares at $1 a share. These options were still unexercised in February 1923, at which time Goodyear common was selling at $10. The profit on the options was $1.53 million.

Dillon's direction of his end of the deal was meticulously planned and flawlessly executed. There were great rewards, and minimal risks, a situation which would characterize many of his activities in this decade.

The underwriting was a success, and even before it was over Dillon ousted Seiberling and some other managers and replaced them with selections of his own. Onto the board came Armin Schlesinger, who served as Dillon's eyes and ears at the firm, to be followed by Dillon Read partners Karl Behr and W.M.L. Fiske. The new president was to be Edward G. Wilmer, a thirty-eight-year-old Milwaukee lawyer who, after working at Newport Mining, became counsel to the Schlesinger interests and in 1916 had been named vice president of Steel & Tube, Milwaukee Coke and Gas, and the Newport Company, for which he received a salary of $40,000 a year. This selection was not surprising; before agreeing to undertake the bailout Dillon had dispatched Wilmer to Goodyear's Akron facilities to make a feasibility study. He was, then, a close associate of Dillon and Schlesinger, who had no experience in the rubber and tire business, but understood the special situation at Goodyear.

Wilmer had no illusions regarding leading the firm on a day-to-day basis. Two of the Seiberling vice presidents, George Stadelman and Paul Litchfield, remained at their posts, and they had Wilmer's support in their actions as joint chief operating officers. "There is nothing wrong with Goodyear's manufacturing or sales," Wilmer told them. "The only problems are in finance. So I'll leave production and sales to you, and I'll see that you get the necessary funds."[63]

The circumstances of Wilmer's assignment were somewhat uncommon and require elaboration. Technically he did not work for Goodyear, but rather for the firm of Leonard Kennedy & Co., which was awarded a management contract by Dillon, Young, and Sherwin for $560,000 a year plus 5 percent of profits once these exceeded $10 million up to $20 million. In return for this payment Kennedy was to provide leadership for the firm. In addition to Wilmer, Loring R. Hoover, one of Harrison Williams's attorneys, arrived as a vice president, but in fact was more of a financial consultant and spent little time in Akron. Dillon later stated he "would not have sold the bonds if Kennedy & Company had not been in the management. By that I mean a management satisfactory to me."[64]

Dillon would later characterize Kennedy as controlling "a number of large enterprises supervised and conducted by a corps of highly trained and unusually capable executives, engineers, accountants and others of much experience and proved ability."[65] Yet Leonard Kennedy & Co. was a modest, unknown entity, with only four employees. It was later learned that before forming his company in 1920 with the assistance of Armin Schlesinger, Kennedy had been an officer of Ludlam Steel, a small company situated in Watervliet, New York, had served in the army, and before the war had worked for eight years at William A. Read & Co. as a clerk and then statistician-salesman. Kennedy had practically no experience in any industry other than steel, and currently none in the rubber industry.[66]

In 1988 Dorothy Dillon Eweson, Dillon's daughter, would characterize Kennedy as a "great friend" of the Dillons.[67] He also was a business associate. Forty-five percent of the stock in Leonard Kennedy & Co. was owned by the Nassau Corporation, which Dillon owned, and was later transferred to Anne Dillon.[68] The rest was owned by Schlesinger, Wilmer, and two other men affiliated with the Schlesinger interests.

For his work at Goodyear Wilmer was to receive a salary of $50,000 a year from Kennedy plus the use of a house purchased for him by Goodyear. The remainder of the $550,000, minus some other minor deductions for special assistance by Schlesinger company officials, went to Kennedy. The bulk of this money could have been transferred to Nassau, presumably accruing to the shareholders of that company, specifically Anne Dillon and the Schlesinger group.

Subsequent to the Goodyear contract, Kennedy received two additional assignments. One was for the leveling of sections of a small mountain known locally as Morro de Castillo in Rio de Janeiro to prepare it for the construction of housing, and the other was for harbor construction in Sicily. While Dillon Read did not underwrite loans for Italian cities and provinces in this period, it did float a $12 million loan for Rio de Janeiro in 1921 for this particular project. In testimony in 1933 partner Robert Hayward stated that the mayor of Rio asked Dillon Read to select a firm to do the work. Kennedy received the contract, said Hayward, "because we insisted that someone in whom we had confidence should do it."[69]

As was so often the situation with Dillon, Wilmer would be associated with him for life, going from one Dillon company to another, joining Dillon Read as a partner and then leaving, and being always involved with the Dillon interests on a personal as well as business basis.[70] Whenever there was a Dillon Read deal, one would find Dillon's friends as investors or participants, and they tended to come from three sources: Harvard and later on Princeton; Milwaukee; and former associates during the war. Just as Read had drawn upon Polytechnic Institute of Brooklyn for several of his associates, so Dillon felt most comfortable with those who had backgrounds similar to his. It was as though he had organized a repertory company in which the same actors appeared in different roles in different plays. Schlesinger, Baruch, Wilmer, Williams, and several others were in the Dillon circle. All profited from the relationship.[71] Traditionally these banks replied upon personal contacts for new business.

Wilmer's assumption of command at Goodyear was not the end of the Goodyear affair. The ousted Seiberling forces brought four lawsuits against the company, seeking to abrogate the contract and certain aspects of the bond and debenture placements. Dillon Read and Cravath bowed; the terms of the Kennedy contract were altered. They reduced the compensation to $250,000 a year, the Seiberling forces would be permitted five seats on the board, and some minor alterations were made in the bond structure.

More was to come. In 1926 the Seiberling brothers, together with other dissident shareholders, sued to recover from Dillon Read and Leonard Kennedy & Co. some $15 million of what they alleged were excessive profits derived from the reorganization and management of Goodyear. The suits were settled after eight months of maneuvering, in what has to be considered a defeat for Dillon Read. Under the terms of the agreement the management contract with Leonard Kennedy & Co. was terminated and Dillon Read paid all legal fees, which came to $2,225,000. In addition, Dillon Read agreed to forgo its commission on a future offering of $60 in 5 percent bonds, the proceeds of which were used to retire some of the higher yielding bonds and preferred stock issued in 1921.[72]

The lawsuits angered Dillon. Not only had his profits been cut,

GOODYEAR TIRE & RUBBER, 1917–1922
(figures in million of dollars)

Year	Gross Revenues	Interest Charges	Net Income	Surplus
1917	103.6	1.0	10.7	7.0
1918	122.7	1.0	9.3	4.6
1919	158.3	1.3	15.3	10.0
1920*	188.9	2.6	(2.0)	(8.6)
1921**	82.2	3.5	3.6	3.6
1922	102.9	4.8	4.4	4.4

* After inventory adjustment of $10 million.
** For ten months.
SOURCE: *Moody's Analysis of Investments, 1923*, p. 752.

but all could have been avoided with proper attention to details. At one point he suspected some problems existed and talked of them with one of his lawyers, who dismissed the matter as being a technicality with which Dillon need not concern himself. Moreover his attorneys had failed to take some perfunctory steps that could have obviated them. The Goodyear suits had a profound effect on Dillon. From then on he would distrust experts unwilling or unable to explain their activities in simple terms, and he insisted upon the most rigorous attention to details.[73]

Aided by a reviving economy, the Wilmer management went on to save the company. By November 30, 1921, it had cash items of $25 million, no short-term loans, and an assets-to-liabilities ratio of better than 11 to 1.[74] Dillon Read was in charge at Goodyear, having pulled off its first major coup in impressive style.

· 5 ·

The Business of Opportunity: At Home

(1921–1924)

G oodyear was not the only firm Clarence Dillon restructured in
the early 1920s. In October of 1922, Dillon, Read & Co., which
originally was a partnership, became a New York and Delaware
chartered joint stock association.[1] Eleven years later Dillon testified that the change was to avoid the same "complications incident
to settlement of Mr. Read's estate." He elaborated by adding: "This
structure had the advantage of permitting members to join the
association or retire from it by the purchase or sale of stock, thus
avoiding dissolution of the firm and the organization of a new firm
each time there was a change in membership, as is required in the
case of a partnership."[2]

Even so, the firm still referred to "the partners," and sent out
press releases in the years that followed referring to the admission
of new partners.[3] The change also meant that Dillon Read could
not be a member of the NYSE, since that institution would not
accept corporate members.

This was a period during which brokerage and trading would
grow exponentially, when commercial banks either expanded upon
their brokerage arms or created them. National City, Guaranty,
Bankers Trust, and others were becoming significant forces in this

73

and other areas of investment banking.[4] Dillon Read virtually ignored these activities, preferring instead to concentrate upon what it advertised as "the purchase and sale of new issues of securities."[5]

While his style and substance dazzled Wall Street in the 1920s and established Dillon Read as a major force, Dillon himself did not enter the inner circle. There was no single reason for this, but rather a combination of factors.

The Street's elite, still predominantly Protestant or German-Jewish, looked upon Dillon as an upstart. Dillon Read was staffed by Ivy Leaguers from Harvard and Princeton, but this did not alter matters much. Dillon was bold and resourceful, and in 1922 must have seemed more akin to those brash young men who arrived from the provinces during every bull market than a sober aristocrat. He had virtually no social contact with the Street's blue bloods; Dillon did not consort with either the Morgans or the Schiffs. He did not seek to become part of the financial community's Establishment. Dillon's daughter, Dorothy Dillon Eweson, referred to his solitary actions in an indirect fashion:[6]

> I know he used the Metropolitan Club in both New York and Washington if he wanted to be at a club, which was usually only to entertain some business person that he didn't want to bring home. Although he never brought work home, he also did not bring home business people except occasionally his own partners. But outside business people did not come to our house that I can remember, unless they were also sort of social friends of my mother's or her family.

This is not to suggest Dillon was unconcerned with such matters, or that he was something of a recluse. On the contrary, he had many friends and was deemed a brilliant conversationalist with a wide variety of interests. Rather, this was a period during which anti-Semitism remained strong and ever-present on Wall Street and the social world its denizens occupied, and it was generally known that Dillon had Jewish antecedents. That he never was a practicing Jew, and that his children were being raised as Protestants, was of no consequence.

This was a period in which "clubability" was a major attribute of members of what then and even now in some circles was known as "the white shoe crowd." Furthermore, membership on museum and charity boards was deemed almost an adjunct to business. Not for Clarence Dillon. Indeed, by mid-decade he was being referred to by some publications as "The Lone Wolf of Wall Street" and had become notorious for his occasionally blunt behavior in a world where traditions created a half-century earlier were still intact. This could be seen in Dillon's diary entry for June 23, 1919, when his greatest feats were yet to come:

> Saw Mr. J. P. Morgan and told him that I was not happy with the position our firm had in Dominion of Canada business that I would like a larger interest as I thought 4½% was not a proper interest for our firm. He said he entirely agreed with me and understood my feeling but that this was accepted by us in the previous syndicate and it would be very difficult to change now. I explained that I was ill at the time the other syndicate was formed or I should have taken this position then; whereupon he said he could increase it to 5% but did not think he could do more than that. I told him I was not any happier with 5% interest any more than a 4½% interest; whereupon he said he would leave it to me and I will do what I can but not be mad at me if I cannot do much better. I told him that if they really wanted us and needed us to help in this business we would be glad to do so but otherwise I would kick about the interest. He said well I do not want you to be unhappy about it and I will do more for you, if I can.

One simply didn't talk that way to the bearer of Wall Street's most distinguished name, and certainly this was not to have been expected from one who, after all, was still considered a newcomer. Yet Dillon's role at Goodyear had earned him the respect of the district. While the Goodyear rescue was all the more impressive for having been conducted during a period of economic distress, Dillon's abilities wouldn't be fully recognized until they could be displayed against a background of prosperity. During the rest of the decade, one of the most exciting in American business history, Dillon Read was involved in new areas of opportunity, and emerged as one of the Street's preeminent investment banks. This was accomplished through shrewd and bold dealings, superb salesmanship, originality, and Dillon's uncanny sense of timing and abilities at coordinating efforts of associates.

Due more to the workings of the economic cycle than any other factor, economic recovery began in late 1921. Business picked up as interest rates fell and inventories became depleted. The United States would soon experience the kind of growth the *Manchester Guardian* had predicted for it in 1917. By virtually any standard this was what one author called "the prosperity decade." With the exception of some farmers, coal miners, and textile workers, better times were known by virtually all social classes and sections of the country. Production and employment were high, and the average standard of living was rising.

The simple statistics present the most graphic image of a country in the midst of rapid change. During the 1920s American companies added $100 billion in new plant and equipment, much of it going into the transformation of the American factory. From 1919 to 1927 the number of electric motors in use rose from 9.2 million to 19.1 million, and the percentage of electric power machinery went from 31.7 percent to 49 percent. In this period the number of kilowatt-hours per capita rose from 425 to 860. By the end of the decade the United States generated more electricity than the rest of the world combined.[7]

The trade figures were equally striking; between 1922 and 1929 exports grew by 26 percent and imports by 16 percent. American businessmen had captured many overseas markets during the war when the Europeans couldn't service old customers. By and large these were retained, and in many cases the grip was strengthened. In addition the Europeans required immense capital investment for reconstruction of destroyed structures, and much of this was raised in the United States. Americans invested a good deal of their surplus capital overseas or made loans to foreigners; the nation's long-term overseas investments rose from $1.74 billion in 1912 to $7.47 billion in 1929, with 20 percent of the total in Latin America and almost all of the rest in Canada and Europe. The United States advanced a total of $10 billion to foreign nations and companies in the 1920s. All of this was accomplished with little in the way of inflation.[8] Even so, the recovery from the postwar recession was slow; in nominal terms the economic performance achieved in 1920 was not surpassed in most categories until mid-decade.

Not surprisingly, all of this economic growth and activity

sparked one of the most exciting bull markets in history. The hectic activity and sensational killings made by prominent speculators which were breathlessly reported in the press provided the bull market with publicity of the sort which made it appear the nation had become transfixed with the pursuit of paper profits. In fact relatively few Americans were involved in securities in any meaningful way. In 1929 there were 63 million Americans over the age of 25. That year member firms reported a total of slightly more than 1.5 million accounts, but that includes those who had more than one account and inactive ones. By the most generous interpretation, then, fewer than 2½ percent of Americans were "in the market." While there is no way to calculate just how many purchased shares on margin, it would appear from available evidence the figure ran between 500,000 and 750,000. This hardly gives the picture of a country gone stock market crazy.[9]

Even so, Wall Street was a more vital and pivotal arena than ever. As always, the primary function of the markets was to raise funds for businesses and governments. While government business declined in importance, the other segments expanded significantly. This was an age during which much of American big business was restructured, in what most scholars of the subject view as the second great merger wave (the first being 1894–1904).

There were three basic reasons for this development, which began at mid-decade and accelerated toward the end of the 1920s. In the first place, merger activities tend to accelerate when business conditions are good and corporations have excess cash. In such an atmosphere many companies find it more rewarding to grow through acquisitions and mergers than through expansion of existing facilities.[10] Another cause was the bull market, which heightened interest in securities, as higher prices and volatile activity made them superb vehicles for speculation. At such times, too, investment bankers find it relatively easy to distribute bonds and stocks to a willing clientele.[11] Finally, the nation was more comfortable with big business than it had been before the war. If the federal government did not always smile upon mergers and acquisitions, it at least adopted a more neutral stance. When it became apparent in 1915 that the nation could not gird for war while prosecuting large corporations, the government's antitrust crusade, which had been going on for more than a decade, ended.

After the war the courts seemed to sanction business expansion through acquisitions. In 1920, the Supreme Court decided in a 4–3 decision that United States Steel need not be dissolved, declaring sheer size alone was not an offense. Although it had attempted to monopolize the industry, U.S. Steel had failed to do so. The Justice Department then signaled it was willing to accede to further combinations in the steel industry, so long as U.S. Steel was not involved. In the following nine years Bethlehem absorbed Lackawanna, Midvale, Cambria, Pacific Coast, and the Southern California steel companies. Weirton, Great Lakes, and M. A. Hanna united to form National Steel. Republic added Donner, Bourne Fuller, and Central Alloy. American business took these moves as signals that as far as the Calvin Coolidge administration was concerned, the Sherman and Clayton antitrust acts were dead letters.

Consequently a great merger wave developed. From 1925 to 1929, thirty-seven new giant corporations were created absorbing assets of almost $5.4 billion, and in addition to these there were over 5,800 other mergers and acquisitions in this five-year period, all requiring the services of investment bankers.[12]

It was a period during which investment banks could parlay a proficiency in mergers and acquisitions as well as corporate restructurings into fortunes. As it happened, Dillon Read would capitalize upon these opportunities more effectively than any other house. Just as Dillon had performed astutely in the Goodyear workout during the postwar recession, so he would prove well suited by intelligence and temperament to succeed in the new expansionist phase.

The value of the firm's underwritings—more than $2.8 billion from 1919 to 1927—provides one of the measures of its growth.[13] It also serves as an indication of the company's position in the industry. In the same span of time American corporations issued $32.7 billion worth of securities.[14] Thus, Dillon Read accounted for slightly less than 9 percent of all underwritings, giving the firm an impressive but not dominant position in the industry. Yet throughout the decade it was generally considered one of the most profitable investment banks, with greater earnings than firms which were much larger and did a greater volume of business. As before, Dillon was not so much concerned with size as he was with

UNDERWRITINGS AND PARTICIPATIONS BY WILLIAM A.
READ & CO. AND DILLON, READ & CO. (1919–1927)

(figures in millions of dollars)

Year	Bonds	Stocks	Total
1919	53.0	37.0	90.0
1920	176.1	22.0	198.1
1921	323.1	—	323.1
1922	246.9	16.5	263.4
1923	164.4	63.7	228.1
1924	306.9	81.3	388.2
1925	393.7	118.7	512.4
1926	347.3	75.9	423.2
1927	393.7	44.8	438.5
			2,865.0

SOURCE: Dillon, Read & Co.

reputation and profitability, and he obtained both in large measure during these years.

Dillon Read proceeded on several fronts simultaneously. The firm became a significant factor in international finance, provided small investors with a means of profiting from its expertise and knowledge, and was one of the more important forces in corporate restructuring. Occasionally it was possible for Dillon Read to combine two or more of these operations.

Appropriately, the first of these opportunities came with Armin Schlesinger's Steel & Tube, and may be regarded as one of the key steel industry mergers which came in the wake of the United States v. United States Steel decision. We have seen how Dillon was seeking a merger partner for Steel & Tube in 1919. In May 1920 he attempted to arrange a deal whereby Semet-Solvay, the chemical company, would purchase an option on $5 million of the Schlesinger shares "at the then book value or appraised value."[15] Nothing came of this, but Steel & Tube did purchase a coke plant from Semet-Solvay, and the relationship between the two firms continued into the 1920s.

The postwar recession was difficult for the industry. By then there were twelve important steelmakers independent of U.S. Steel, ranging from Bethlehem, which had an annual capacity of 3.1 million tons, through Weirton, which poured 350,000 tons. Virtually all of them either posted sharply lower earnings or showed losses; Youngstown Sheet & Tube, for example, reported profits of $2.5 million in 1920, and a loss $2.7 million the following year. For 1921 Steel & Tube showed a loss of $2.6 million compared to 1920's profits of $6.3 million.

In December 1921, Theodore Chadbourne, who was backed by Kuhn Loeb, proposed merging five of these independents—Midvale (2.9 million tons), Lackawanna (1.8 million tons), Youngstown Sheet & Tube (1.5 million tons), Republic Iron (1.4 million tons), and Steel & Tube (900,000 tons)—along with several smaller entities, including Inland and Brier Hill, to form "North American Steel." One of the nation's more prominent attorneys, before the war Chadbourne had participated in the organization of International Motor Co., the predecessor of Mack Trucks. He understood the steel industry, having put together the components of what became Midvale Steel in 1915. Chadbourne now was prepared to move on to bigger things. This was the most ambitious undertaking of its kind since 1901, when J. P. Morgan had fashioned U.S. Steel. Had all seven acquiesced, the resulting firm would have been capitalized at around $750 million and become the second-largest entity in the industry.[16]

Schlesinger and Dillon agreed to participate in the mergers. Steel & Tube, Youngstown, and Inland were most committed to the combine, with the rest willing to come in only if granted premium prices for their shares.[17] Within two days all but these three had dropped out, and the survivors began a study of facilities, with each sending a team to inspect the others. On the basis of its study Inland opted to drop out, leaving Youngstown and Steel & Tube, which then continued bilateral negotiations.[18]

From the first Dillon was personally involved in these transactions, on April 15, 1922, telling a small group of insiders he and Schlesinger intended to form a $5.3 million pool "to take over Mr. Schlesinger's stock in the Steel & Tube Company," in preparation for a merger. Presumably this meant that those involved were receiving shares at prices which were bound to rise once the merger was announced or completed. In this way, Dillon would minimize his own financial exposure and risk.

Other companies were at work on deals. Bethlehem Steel's Eugene Grace had an agenda of his own, which included holding on to the industry position his firm had achieved during the war. In May he arranged for the purchase of Lackawanna, and hinted that other acquisitions were being discussed. Now the prices of steel stocks erupted, as rumors regarding the next purchase swept the Street. When on May 19 Youngstown announced its withdrawal from the Chadbourne venture and that it would "reserve its options," its price took off. Then came Midvale, while talk had it Inland would attempt to raid the larger Steel & Tube.[19]

Undeterred, Dillon proceeded with his plan. Of the total $5.3 million, Schlesinger had a $1.75 million stake, and $200,000 each went to Dillon and Harrison Williams, with Cotton down for $100,000. Two of Bernard Baruch's brothers, Sailing and Herman, were allotted $100,000 apiece, and Baruch suggested that Herman might go on the board of the merged company "if we wanted him." The price to the syndicate members was $10 a share, which approximated the market quote at the time. To sweeten the deal, Dillon Read underwrote an issue of 175,000 shares of preferred which netted the company $90 a share, resold it to distributors at 93, and apportioned some clients' shares at 96.[20]

In late June, at what turned out to be the top of the market for steel shares, Dillon Read arranged for the sale of Steel & Tube's assets to Youngstown for $33 million, making the new company the fifth largest in the industry. Youngstown would raise this amount through an offering of 6 percent bonds underwritten by a syndicate organized by Dillon Read. The company used $18.15 million of its new capital to redeem Steel & Tube's preferred stock at 110, providing those who had purchased the shares shortly before with a nice profit. This left approximately $15 in cash for each of the firm's 970,000 common shares. Before the merger talks Steel & Tube common was deemed a speculative holding by Moody's. It paid no dividend and was selling in the single-digit range. Thus, the profits to the pool members would be sizable.[21]

Throughout all of this Allied Chemical & Dye, which it will be recalled owned some 18 percent of Steel & Tube shares, protested that the price was too low. Allied alleged Dillon had acted wrongfully in the underwritings and pool operations. Dillon rejected these assertions out of hand. With Edward Wilmer and Schlesinger he considered the possibilities of Allied's winning its case, "and we all agreed that the suit was a ridiculous one. The Bill of Complaint was drawn with such utter disregard for facts and the affidavits entirely failed to in any way sustain the Bill of Complaint and we felt that there was a very good chance of the Court not only dismissing the case but probably reprimanding counsel for bringing such an action."[22]

On August 3, the Delaware Chancery Court found that Dillon, Dillon Read, and all others involved had not acted wrongfully. The Allied claims were rejected, though the facts were not disputed. The Allied counsel was not reprimanded, and the merger was permitted to stand.[23]

It remains to be noted that at the time Dillon Read did not consider itself a specialist in what generations later would be known as the "merger and acquisitions business." In those years investment bankers viewed themselves as generalists, prepared to take on virtually any kind of undertaking that came their way. The banker who was attempting to arrange a merger might at the same time be underwriting a bond or stock issue for another client, seeking merchant banking possibilities, or arranging the sale of debt for a municipality. When necessary, bankers would tailor-make financings for clients, usually without much consideration of whether or not they could prove a rubric for future undertakings. This was true not only for individual bankers but for investment banks themselves. Some of the larger ones would have partners known for one specialty or another, but even these were available for duties in related areas.

At no time, then and afterwards, did Dillon Read concentrate its corporate attention on any single project. While defending the Steel & Tube–Youngstown merger in March 1923, Dillon personally was working with or attempting to obtain business from such firms as Union Electric, Harbishaw Electric Cable, Standard Oil of California, North American Company, Willys-Overland, the Erie Railroad, A. O. Smith, Fisk Rubber, New York & Pennsylvania Paper, and the Kansas City Street Railway. That spring the firm was in the process of organizing a major new investment trust and considering the development of the Brazilian and Japanese economies and investments in Spain, all of which indicated the global reach of its interests. It was deeply involved with the restructuring at Goodyear, investing in Park Avenue real estate, and floating Wisconsin bonds.[24]

The initial underwriting of Commercial Investment Trust Corp., better known as C.I.T., was a typical deal. Founded in 1908, C.I.T. had grown into one of the nation's largest credit companies. By 1923 the company had receivables of $24 million, an increase of $8 million over what they had been the year before. Capital requirements were pressing, and given the firm's record and prospects, and in light of the strong stock market, management decided to attempt to sell its first issue of stock.

How and why C.I.T. selected Dillon Read to assist in its financings is unknown, but the firm was contacted, and in 1924 agreed to underwrite $3 million of 7 percent preferred stock at 98 with each share of preferred stock having the option to purchase 1⅓ shares of common at $30 per share. Also, there was an understanding at that time that the common shares would pay a dividend of $2.50. Dillon Read borrowed short-term money from several banks and paid C.I.T., while at the same time organizing its syndicates. As part of the understanding Dillon Read arranged for the listings of the issues on the NYSE.

With this Dillon Read became C.I.T.'s banker. Two members of the bank's inner circle, William Phillips and Wilmer, joined the company's board. Other underwritings followed. In April of 1925 Dillon Read marketed $10 million in notes for C.I.T. In November there was a 6½ percent preferred stock issue which included common stock purchase warrants. During the next fifty years Dillon Read would raise several billions of dollars for C.I.T., and much of the time one or more of its partners was a member of the company's board.[25]

The doubling in price of C.I.T. common in close to two years was an indication of the kind of market which had developed in this period. The upward move began in 1923, and gathered steam the following year. The securities markets responded with rallies when Coolidge was elected decisively over Democrat John W. Davis and Progressive Robert La Follette. While bonds did well, the performance of stocks was dazzling. The Dow Jones Industrials had closed at 103.89 the session preceding the election. On heavy volume it rose more than a point the following day. Within two weeks the index was over 110, and by the end of the year had added ten more points. In the same period the Dow Jones Railroad Index advanced from 89.53 to 99.50.

Dillon had suspected something like this would happen. On the morning following the election he met with Forrestal, who several years later recalled, "Mr. Dillon said, after reading the morning papers, that he thought the time was now opportune to begin the acquisition of common stocks."[26]

Some of the methods Dillon Read and other investment banks used in their flotations and deals differed strikingly from today's practices. Indeed, a good deal of what went for common procedure in the 1920s was to become illegal the following decade. Dillon and his colleagues were not dishonest, but rather operated well within the ethical boundaries of their era. For example, what at times was referred to as the two-price system flourished in the 1920s. We already have seen some indications of this in the way Dillon would reserve shares in deals for those on his preferred list. This was not at all unusual. Consider a 1927 underwriting of Johns-Manville which came to market at 79. Under the terms of the offering 400,000 shares were reserved, and sold to insiders at prices ranging from 47½ to 57½. As has been seen, this was the usual way bankers rewarded friends.[27] The entire J. P. Morgan underwriting for Alleghany Corporation was taken up by the firm for itself with 575,000 shares allocated to a group of 170 insiders, and none to the public. The price was $20 a share, and all knew it would go higher in the aftermarket. Among those in the preferred list were Charles E. Mitchell and Albert Wiggin, CEOs of the National City and Chase, two of the Street's most powerful banks. John W. Davis, who in addition to running for the presidency in 1924 was Morgan's personal banker, was down for 400 shares. Democratic National Committee Chairman John J. Rascob was allocated 2,000 shares, and in a bipartisan mood, the treasurer of the Republican National Committee, Joseph R. Nutt, was provided with 3,000. Former and future cabinet members Newton D. Baker, Charles Francis Adams, and William Woodin had shares, along with General John J. Pershing and Charles Lindbergh. Silas Strawn, former president of the American Bar Association, was on the list, as were a handful of leading bankers, who presumably returned the favor in their underwritings. The nexus between business and politics was evident, and more open and blatant then than it would be later on, when prominent Washington insiders would accept well-paid posts at Wall Street banks upon leaving office.[28]

Morgan made certain those involved understood the situation completely. In its letter to Woodin, the firm's secretary said:[29]

> You may have seen in the paper that we recently made a public offering of $35,000,000 Alleghany Corporation 15-year collateral trust convertible 5 per cent bonds, which went very well.
>
> In this connection the Guaranty Company . . . also sold privately, some of the common stock at $24 a share.
>
> We have kept for our own investment some of the common stock at a cost of $20 a share, and although we are making no offering of this stock, as it is not the class of security we wish to offer publicly, we are asking some of our close friends if they would like some of this stock at the same price as it is costing us, namely, $20 a share.
>
> I believe that the stock is selling in the market around $35 to $37 a share, which means very little, except that people wish to speculate.
>
> We are reserving for you 1,000 shares at $20 a share, if you would like to have it.
>
> There are no strings tied to this stock, so you can sell it whenever you wish. . . . We just want you to know that we were thinking of you in this connection and thought you might like to have a little of the stock at the same price we are paying for it. . . .

Little wonder politicians of both parties and many celebrities rushed to get on the lists.

These practices were hinted at in newspapers and radio programs; investors were aware that insiders were making huge profits. In addition, they knew the stock market was being manipulated. The newspapers featured lurid tales of speculators such as Jesse Livermore, Arthur Cutten, Mike Meehan, and Joe Kennedy, all of whom purportedly led powerful pools organized to push issues one way or the other. Rumors that one or another of these individuals was getting in or out of a stock could send it soaring or plummeting. Such information was beyond the grasp of small investors, who craved for some way to trade on the expertise of these men and others. Of course, they had no chance of working with any of the big players—certainly not with Dillon, who by then was being trumpeted in the press as an authentic financial genius.

Dillon was one of those who developed a means whereby small investors could profit from such intelligence. The vehicle was called an investment trust, an old concept utilized in the nineteenth century that would flourish again in the 1920s. Unlike mutual funds, they would not sell and redeem shares at asset value plus commissions; rather, they were pools of money provided to a manager, who was supposed to utilize his special expertise to purchase and sell bonds and shares.

Quite a few investment trusts were organized to participate in foreign securities. That this would be so was not surprising given the international scope of American investing in the 1920s. Shortly after defeating the Treaty of Versailles, Congress passed (and President Wilson signed) an amendment to the Federal Reserve Act known as "The Edge Act," which authorized the organization of domestic corporations for the purpose of engaging in international financial operations, either directly or through institutions chartered overseas. The drive overseas continued when the Republicans gained control of the White House. "We must give government cooperation to business," said President-elect Warren Harding. "We must protect American business at home, and we must aid and protect it abroad."[30] While most of these new investment trusts did not intend to function as Edge Act corporations, the legislation set the mood for international investment.[31]

The first internationally oriented investment trusts appeared soon after. The International Securities Trust of America, which was later transformed into the International Securities Corporation, came in 1920, and by 1927 was the nation's largest trust. Swedish-American Investment Corp., European Shares, German Credit & Investment, and First Federal Foreign Investments followed.[32]

Dillon Read entered the field in 1924 with its investment trust, named United States & Foreign Securities (US&FS). The name was chosen deliberately. Dillon Read was becoming a major force in international finance, and before the end of the decade was known as a prime conduit for foreigners seeking banks capable of floating their loans. A student of the subject wrote that US&FS "was an opportunity to let the public in on Dillon's investment brains."[33] This was one of the several reasons investors rushed to purchase shares.

The offering was handled through a syndicate composed of 380 participants, through which subscriptions to 250,000 shares of a first preferred allotment were received. These shares were taken by the syndicate at 96 and offered at 100, so the syndicate received $1 million for its services, out of which Dillon Read collected approximately $360,000.[34] In 1928 and 1929 Dillon Read sold 74,198 shares of the first preferred shares in addition to 120,552 common shares, for a profit of more than $6.8 million.[35]

Dillon Read purchased the entire issue of a second preferred stock for $5 million, and took 750,000 shares of common, for which it paid the nominal sum of $100,000. The company retained only 250,000 shares; the rest were distributed to the partners for 20 cents a share.[36] Dillon Read offered the public 250,000 shares of the $6 first preferred stock at 100, which brought in $25 million.[37] Purchasers of this issue received as a bonus one share of common for each of preferred, which of course came to 250,000 shares of common.

Under the terms of the offering the preferred shares had voting rights only if dividends on them were passed, which meant that unless and until that happened, Dillon Read would have complete control of the company. This was common practice during a period when Americans still were unaccustomed to purchasing stock and many insisted on dividends, being perfectly content to relinquish control to professional managers.[38]

That US&FS would have foreign securities in its portfolio was known at the time of the flotation. To assure potential investors they would both receive an opportunity to profit from Dillon Read's investment expertise and receive dividends, the company announced it intended to invest $2.7 million in the common shares of a new investment company, American and Continental Corporation, which according to the prospectus "is being formed for the purpose of financing industrial and commercial companies in Europe. . . . The American and Continental Corporation will begin its operations in Germany, where it has associated with a group of leading German banks." Another $2.5 million would be invested in securities of Brooklyn Edison, the Continental and Commercial Trust and Savings Bank of Chicago, General Electric, Central

Union Trust of New York, and First National Bank of New York. Dividends and interest from these holdings would contribute largely to the funds required for the $6 dividend on the US&FS first preferred.[39]

Investigating the creation of such trusts eight years later, the Securities and Exchange Commission (SEC), which didn't exist in 1929, concluded, "In short, the public furnished five-sixths of the capital and Dillon, Read & Company supplied one-sixth of the capital, subordinate to the other five-sixths, and received a three-fourths interest in the surplus profits."[40] Much was made of the disclosure that the partners were permitted to purchase shares for 20 cents, which they later sold for $50 or more. It should be noted, however, that in case the company did badly, the first preferred stockholders would have had initial call on all dividends, the second preferred whatever remained, and the common could get nothing. In other words, in some circumstances, Dillon Read could suffer more than those who purchased the preferred shares in 1924 or obtained them in the aftermarket. Moreover, the purchasers of preferred stock at the offering price received their share-for-share common without additional charge, so their profits on subsequent sales of the common were also sizable.

As it turned out Dillon Read did much better on its investment than did the public shareholders. The offering was made when the Dow Jones Industrials were at 102.6. On September 29, 1928, the Dow closed at 239.43, for an advance of 133 percent. In this span US&FS's assets rose by 76.4 percent. Those assets owned by the public were up by 23 percent, while Dillon Read's holdings were higher by 335 percent.[41]

US&FS was literally run as a sideline to Dillon Read's other operations, and in this period was domiciled in the Dillon Read offices. It had a total staff of seven, including secretaries and clerks, which was increased to nine in 1927 and thirteen the following year. Its chairman was Benjamin Joy, Harvard '05, a classmate of Phillips and Ralph Bollard, the latter an expert in trust management who became a partner in 1925.[42]

More important than fees and salaries, however, was the ability of Dillon Read to use US&FS as a customer for its underwritings, an accepted practice in this period. For example, five months before the US&FS offering, Dillon Read underwrote a $16 million common stock issue for Brooklyn Edison. As noted, the company told the press it intended to purchase Brooklyn Edison securities for the US&FS portfolio, and it might have been that these were "undigested" securities. On the other hand, Dillion Read had not underwritten securities for any of the other companies mentioned, so there were scant indications of what at a much later date would be considered conflicts of interest. In 1927, through a private sale, US&FS purchased $100,000 of a Louisiana Land & Exploration 7 percent bond issue along with 24,500 shares of common, at a time when that company's president, E. B. Tracy, was also president of US&FS. It might be argued Tracy was using his position at LL&E to benefit US&FS, or the other way around. In either case, this practice, routine in that decade, later on would be considered a conflict of interest, as would the purchase in 1929 of 12,500 shares of International Printing Ink Corporation from a trading account managed by Dillon Read. Apparently these were undigested securities from an underwriting conducted by the firm.[43]

While US&FS was Dillon Read's most important foray into the trust market, it was not the only one. The American and Continental Corporation, whose cosponsors in addition to Dillon Read were the French American Banking Corp. of New York, Kuhn Loeb, and the International Acceptance Bank, was capitalized at $25 million. During the succeeding two years, Dillon Read would act as lead underwriter for another fund, German Credit & Investment.[44]

On October 29, 1928, Dillon Read launched United States and International Securities (US&IS). Dillon Read sold 500,000 units consisting of 1 share of a $5 first preferred, 1 share of common, and 1 warrant to purchase an additional share of common at $25 for $100. It then used $10 million in profits accumulated in the US&FS treasury to purchase 100,000 shares of $5 second preferred, and 2.5 million shares of common.

For this underwriting Dillon Read received over $1 million in fees.[45] As a subsequent SEC memorandum commented:[46]

The creation of the subsidiary [US&IS] gave Dillon Read and Company, through its original investment of $5,100,000, control over combined assets as of October 31, 1928, in excess of $100,000,000 (parent company's net assets, September 30, 1928,

$52,950,000 plus subsidiary's capital $60,000,000, less $10,000,000 inter-company item). In short, the subsidiary provided a means to accelerate gains to the sponsor's original investment in the parent corporation. Hence, a gain of $1 in the assets of the subsidiary resulted in an 80 cent gain to the parent of which 60 cents accrued to the sponsor's investment.

What the SEC was talking about here was a form of pyramiding employed in the 1920s. Indeed, the US&FS-US&IS arrangement was one of the less complex and more straightforward of the decade. These merit some attention, since they would become important to Dillon Read later on.

There were other, more alarming pyramids in this period. Harrison Williams was CEO of the North American Company, which like other utility holding companies was highly pyramided. North American controlled ten companies, among them North American Edison, Union Electric Light & Power, St. Louis County Gas, Washington Railway & Electric, West Kentucky Coal, and Western Power. These in turn controlled other companies.[47] Among the North American Edison holdings were Cleveland Electric Illuminating, Milwaukee Electric Railway & Light, Wisconsin Electric Power, and Union Electric Light & Power. The subsidiaries had subsidiaries of their own. Union Electric's were Central Mississippi Valley Electric Properties, East St. Louis & Suburban, Mississippi River Power, and Union Electric Light & Power of Illinois. Some of these had subsidiaries—Central Mississippi Valley's was Keokuk Electric. Under the North American blanket were some 50 companies in a five-level pyramid. It was said that North American provided electricity to one-sixth of the country.[48]

The closest the Dillon Read trusts came to this kind of practice was the 1929 sale of 15,000 US&FS stock to US&IS, apparently in order to establish a loss for tax purposes.[49]

As with US&FS, Dillon Read sold US&IS securities from its trust accounts. Among the securities in which Dillon Read had a direct interest that were purchased by US&IS (often from a Dillon Read account, or securities from undigested underwritings) in the late 1920s were National Cash Register, Seaboard Airline Railway, Pennsylvania Railroad, Southern Pacific, St. Louis–San Francisco Railway, German Credit & Investment, and the Chicago, Rock

Island & Pacific Railway. The SEC would later conclude: "The fact that this account [called "the Railroad Joint Account"] which terminated November 12, 1929, resulted in the delivery to Dillon Read and Company and to the United States and International Securities Corporation of large blocks of unsold stocks, indicates that the Corporation was used to assist in financing the transaction."[50]

It is necessary to reiterate that such activities were commonplace in those years. They did not breach the ethical canons of the time. Nor were they in violation of any laws. When testifying about his activities with US&FS, Dillon appeared surprised when several inquisitors suggested he had behaved improperly. Asked by Senator James Couzens (R-Mich.) whether he had any second thoughts on the way he had performed with the US&FS underwriting, Dillon replied, "Yes, I do not think I should vary it, except that when I subscribe the junior money I might not have different classes of stock." Later on, when questioned on whether the public had been treated fairly in receiving so few shares of the common, he responded, "We could have taken 100 percent. We could have taken all that profit. We could have bought all the common stock for $5,000,000," all of which was undeniably true. This prompted Senator Alva Adams (D-Colo.) to remark, "Do you remember what Lord Clive said? 'When I consider my opportunities, I marvel at my moderation.' "[51]

None of this would have surfaced were it not for the 1929 stock market crash and subsequent developments which prompted the creation of the SEC and investigations that ran from 1933 through 1937. Until then US&FS was considered a well-managed, profitable enterprise which enabled small investors to draw upon the expertise of what had become one of the dominant forces in American finance.

· 6 ·

The Business of Opportunity: Abroad

(1921–1926)

In 1923 Irving Fisher, the most influential American economist of his time, wrote that Europe resembled an ailing man who couldn't be expected to repay debts, or in the case of Germany, make reparations.[1]

> The sick man after eight years, of course, must first repair his premises; he must acquire new tools for his trade, he must have raw materials. Therefore, for these things we must advance him credit, not altogether for his benefit, but for ours as creditors also, in order that we may put him on his feet and enable him to repay us.

There was only one important source of credit in the world: the United States, which would have to take the United Kingdom's place as the world banker and lender of last resort.

That the United States was bound to utilize its vast new wealth to enter world markets in a major way seemed inevitable. Some of its surplus capital would be used for foreign loans, which would be employed in part to purchase American goods, while increasing American influence abroad. Toward the end of the 1920s many scholars commented on this phenomenon which the *Manchester Guardian* in 1917 had predicted would happen and Fisher discussed six years later. Political scientist Max Winkler was one such analyst. "The most striking feature of American foreign trade," he wrote in 1928, "is the fact that our total foreign investments made within the past fourteen years together with our political loans to foreign governments almost exactly correspond to the aggregate excess of exports from the United States over imports into this country during the same period." To Winkler the lesson was clear enough: America's new role in the world benefitted everyone. "In other words, our foreign loans enabled foreign countries to absorb and to pay for our surplus production."[2]

These loans would originate on Wall Street, not in Washington, which is to say they would be generated by investment bankers and not governmental officials. Secretary of State Charles Evans Hughes made this abundantly clear in 1923 when he said, "It is not the policy of our Government to make loans to other governments, and the needed capital, if it is to be furnished at all, must be supplied by private organizations."[3]

Clarence Dillon shared his point of view. He had returned from Europe in 1919 with global ambitions. While on the *Rotterdam* he had been introduced to Henning Plaun, an official with the Landsman Bank of Copenhagen. Plaun spoke with him of his firm's organization of the Trans-Atlantic Company, which owned and managed the Russian-Asiatic Company, and that firm in turn had branches throughout Siberia and other parts of a Russia then in the midst of civil war. Trans-Atlantic controlled the Russian Trading Company, which in addition to its general trading business owned a salmon-canning operation in Vladivostok named the East Siberia Trading and Packing Company.

Dillon was drawn to Plaun, and for the rest of the year considered entering into a relationship with the Landsman Bank. He noted in his diary that "my idea is simply to get information regarding Russia and Siberia and their condition from these people who apparently have well established organizations there and it might later develop that they could be of some use to us in possible business out there."[4]

Nothing came of this foray into the murky terrain of Russian politics and business. As it turned out, it was all to the good; the

Soviets defeated the White armies, and the various Danish interests in Russia evaporated. Still, Dillon's appetite for foreign ventures had been whetted, and would remain strong throughout the decade.

Canada was an obvious target for more business. William A. Read had long been an important force in that country's financings, and continued to be so after the war. In 1920 the Canadian government called upon it to restructure the debts of the Canadian Northern and Grand Trunk railroads in preparation for their union as the Canadian National Railways. This had to be done in the trying market environment hitherto discussed. In October of that year the firm handled a $25 million underwriting for the Grand Trunk. Even though guaranteed by the Canadian government, the offering carried an unusually high 7 percent coupon. William A. Read had problems distributing the issue, and the fact that it did so successfully enhanced its reputation. As a result, another 7 percent $25 million issue, this in December for the Canadian Northern, was marketed with less difficulty. Reminiscing about that period, Forrestal commented, "It is again interesting in casting back to that time to recall that they were 7% bonds running twenty years and non-callable for fifteen years. There were a great many people who would not buy them then, and those of you who were in the organization will probably remember wrestling with a great number of recalcitrant investors who did not think that the guarantee of the Canadian Government written across each bond was a sufficient pledge of security to make the bond a good purchase."[5]

There were further Canadian railroad underwritings the following year, at 6½ and 6 percent, reflecting the earlier successful placements. A total of $112 million was placed by the firm in twelve months.[6]

The Canadian business would remain strong thoughout the decade, as Dillon Read and other American banks displaced their British rivals there. By 1929 Dillon Read was the most prominent investment bank on the Canadian scene. That year, in competition with British and other American and Canadian banks, it won a $40 million underwriting for the Canadian National Railways. In a 1929 article entitled "Decline and Fall of the British Empire Through Bad Money, Huge Debts, and the Great Interest Squeeze," one British columnist, with the byline "Arthurian," observed that during the past twenty years Dillon Read had raised over $1 billion for the Canadian railroad systems and another $568 million for Canadian provincial and municipal governments.[7]

> In being forced to specify thus invidiously, the firm of Dillon Read & Co., I must make amends by assuring investors, who may not know the firm, that it is a financial organization of the highest efficiency and probity, well versed in financial planning, and jealous to a degree of the interests of its lists of investors. It is, however, not its business to consider the survival of the British Empire, and it may soon be compelled to prefer that Canada should self-determine itself a part of the United States.

It was part of a pattern, repeated elsewhere in the world, especially in Latin America, where British bankers, once supreme, were elbowed aside by American counterparts. J. & W. Seligman dominated the market for Peruvian bonds. Kuhn Loeb had all of the considerable business of the Chilean Mortgage Bank. Hallgarten and Kissel/Kinnecutt were Colombia's bankers.[8]

As has been seen, in this period American banks would not seek to win clients from other banks, but this did not apply to contests with their foreign counterparts. So it developed that Morgan and National City dominated in Argentina, but Blair & Co. underwrote several issues. Colony Trust and Dillon Read underwrote Buenos Aires province issues, Blyth, Witter took some Buenos Aires city business, and Chase Securities cofinanced one national issue. National City underwrote securities for the state of Minas Gerais in Brazil, and Speyer & Co. was the sole lead underwriter for São Paulo. Hallgarten & Co. handled all of the business for the Colombian government, but there was no dominant force for that nation's Agricultural Mortgage Bank. Dillon Read underwrote a $3 million issue in 1926, but in the following year Hallgarten was lead banker for a $3 million issue and W. A. Harriman & Co. for a $5 million issue, and in 1927 and 1928 Harriman brought out $5 million issues. All of this was done smoothly, without ruffled feathers.[9]

In 1921 Dillon Read joined the English Rothschilds as Brazil's banker. Rothschild had been Brazil's banker since 1883, when it sold a government bond issue in London. It was a chancy business.

Even so, despite two suspensions during hard times, the Brazilians had always resumed payment of interest and principal, and so had a good credit rating. At the time of this underwriting Brazilian debt was selling close to par. The Rothschilds were attempting to convince the government it would have to offer a premium rate. While Rothschild and the Brazilians parried regarding terms, Dillon Read came in with a more attractive offer which won the underwriting. This was the first Brazilian federal offering of the post–World War I period, and established the firm as that government's banker. This was not an altogether new area for the company. The previous year it had underwritten a $7.5 million issue for Brazilian Traction.

As it happened the timing of the underwriting proved inopportune from a marketing point of view. J. P. Morgan had just completed arrangements for a $24 million offering for Chile, which came to the market the day before the Brazil loan was scheduled to appear. This temporarily satiated the demand for South American bonds. Dillon Read was obliged to offer the Brazil issue in two tranches of $25 million each, the first in May, the second in August, and both were successes.[10]

Other business followed. The firm placed the aforementioned $12 million bond offering for Rio de Janerio which resulted in the Leonard Kennedy contract. There were additional Brazilian underwritings in 1922, including a £2 million offering in London in May and several underwritten in cooperation with Blair and White Weld. During the mid-1920s Dillon Read was the prime foreign factor in the Brazilian capital market, raising more than $175 million in loans from 1921 through 1927.[11]

The concern with Latin America was part of an emerging pattern. Just as a century earlier British investors with surplus capital proferred loans to Americans, so Wall Street was seeking borrowers; the capital market was awash with American lenders seeking new opportunities. It didn't take long for the Latin American countries' leaders to realize that they were welcome on Wall Street. Indeed, it wasn't uncommon for one of them to request, say, a $10 million loan, only to be informed this was not enough, that he could have $15 million simply for the asking. Dillon Read became one of the leaders in this area, with special interests in Bolivia and Colombia as well as Brazil.

Even while cultivating the Latin American market, Dillon Read remained primarily concerned with Europe, which was both more familiar and more promising. A start was made in 1922 with leadership of a syndicate which handled a 125-million-guilder loan for the Netherlands government. It was an innovation, this being the first of a number of offerings in the United States set in the currency of the borrowing country. In 1924 Dillon Read helped arrange the purchase and subsequent resale in a public offering of Royal Dutch's 26 percent stake in Union Oil of California. As with several such deals, this resulted in Dillon Read becoming Union Oil's investment banker.[12]

Moves into Asia followed. In 1923 Dillon Read participated in a financing for Oriental Development Company, Ltd., the loan guaranteed by the Imperial Japanese Government. After the immigration law which contained a clause excluding the Japanese was signed, Dillon Read underwrote a $15 million offering for the Great Consolidated Electric Power Company. This was the first time a major Japanese utility had employed an American bank in its financings. In this period the firm managed or comanaged six financings aggregating $139 million for such firms as Tokyo Electric Light, Shinyetsu Electric Power, and Nippon Electric Power.[13]

Not all American bankers and businessmen were eager to send their capital abroad or underwrite such issues in those early postwar years. European currencies were weak, the French and British economies unsteady, Germany shattered. Russia was in the midst of civil war, with the Bolsheviks seeking to spread their revolution to other parts of the continent and world.[14]

Dillon had reason to believe that by working with Morgan and other banks he might obtain a fairly sizable portion of the total European business. He must have been encouraged by a 1919 meeting he attended with Morgan partners Henry Davison, Thomas Lamont, and Edward Stettinius, National City's Charles Mitchell, and representatives of Guaranty Trust and Bankers Trust "to discuss, in a general way, how we were going to handle the financing of Europe."[15] Davison wanted to "talk the matter over with a few of us and get our advice and views." What he had in mind was a $250 million investment trust company, in which William A. Read & Co. was to have a small stake—$1,125,000 in 3-year 5½ percent notes taken at 98 and $2,850,000 in 10-year 5½ percent bonds at 96¼. That with so small a participation Dillon was asked to offer his opinion indicates just how his reputation had grown in so short a period.[16] Even so, the larger banks hardly would grant him a greater source for this reason alone. Dillon would have to uncover some way to enter the markets with their assent, and finding the precise means to do so was one of his more difficult tasks.

Dillon Read had little reason to expect business in the United Kingdom and France. For generations the former country had been a special preserve of J. P. Morgan & Co., and that firm's leadership in obtaining loans during America's neutrality phase further cemented the strong bonds which already existed. The French were apprehensive of most foreign bankers, and while willing to work with some, preferred not giving too much business to any single concern. In the early 1920s Dillon Read managed only two French bond offerings, $22.8 million in 1921 for Lyons, Marseilles, and Bordeaux, and $10 million three years later for a steamship company.[17] Otherwise, Dillon Read had to settle for being included in some of the Morgan syndicates.

Dillon regarded Germany to be in quite a different category. While Morgan played a significant role in the reparations negotiations it was amenable to recognizing some other bank's preeminence there. While it is impossible to verify such matters, it is noteworthy that during the 1920s the Morgan interests conducted very little underwriting in Germany, while except for participation in the syndicates of others, Dillon Read was completely absent from the United Kingdom and had a minimal exposure to French government business.

This is not to suggest that Germany was to become a Dillon Read preserve. Other American firms, led by National City, became involved with the German market, offering Dillon Read substantial competition, and were also quite visible in France.[18]

The circumstances in Germany were complex, emotionally charged, but promising for American bankers seeking opportunities once the political situation stabilized. Germany had been devastated during the war, and the victorious French were intent on assuring that recovery was slow, and never to the point where Germany would again pose a military or industrial threat to its neighbors.

In 1921 the Allied Reparations Commission informed Germany it would have to pay $33 billion, in addition to Belgium's war debt.[19] According to a schedule presented later, $12.5 billion was to bear interest at 5 percent, with annual payments of $500 million plus 26 percent of the value of Germany's exports.

It was intended that the prostrate country would raise the initial sums through borrowings, but Germany had no international credit. Moreover, the economy was so weak that obtaining funds through substantial exports was out of the question. The result was reliance upon the printing press to obtain funds that might be exchanged for hard currencies, which then would be paid as reparations. Finally, there was a tremendous flight of capital out of the country, as those Germans with assets sought to preserve them from devaluation.

Germany did manage a first payment of $250 million in 1921, but was obliged to ask for a moratorium before the end of the year. One was granted, but the Allies refused to consider a request it be extended to 1925. In 1923, when payments were not made, French and Belgian troops occupied the Ruhr. Seventeen hundred square miles in area, the Ruhr was Germany's industrial heartland, without which economic recovery and financial viability would have been difficult if not impossible. Conflicts between the new German government and the French resulted in a shutdown of industry in the Ruhr. The Franco-Belgian rule resulted in the total disintegration of the German economy and finances; by September the mark was literally worth less than the paper on which it was printed.

The German crisis prompted a new meeting of the Reparations Commission, which appointed a group headed by American banker Charles Dawes to examine the matter of German payments. "The Dawes Plan," as it came to be known, provided for the evacuation of the Ruhr and annual reparations payments starting with $250 million and rising within four years to $625 million, with future payments adjusted to Germany's economic circumstances. Under the terms of the plan there would be created a new German central bank, which would have a fifty-year monopoly on the issuance of paper money. The bank's board was to be composed of seven Germans and seven foreigners. Germany would issue a new currency, the reichsmark, with a gold value of 23.8 American cents. To put

Germany in a position where it might better recover, there was also to be a foreign loan of $200 million.

J. P. Morgan played a key role in the creation and implementation of the Dawes Plan. Owen Young was a member of the Dawes group, and it was generally assumed that the Morgan bank would have a role to play in Germany.

In April 1924, the German government accepted the Dawes Plan, and the loan was floated in England and the United States, with a Morgan-led syndicate which included Dillon Read raising $110 million of the amount. The program went into operation on September 1, 1924. The last foreign troops left the Ruhr on July 31 of the following year, though they remained in the demilitarized Rhineland under terms of the Treaty of Versailles. That the American agent for the program was A. Parker Gilbert of J. P. Morgan was another indication of just how well positioned that firm was, and the difficulties others would have of competing with Morgan for overseas business. It should be noted, however, that in 1927 Dillon's representative in Europe wrote that he did not have great confidence in Gilbert's judgment and fairness and did not think Dillon would allow himself to be turned into simply a tax collector or executioner.[20]

The implementation of the Dawes Plan was taken as a sign that Europe was returning to normal, and that thenceforth business would be able to proceed in a far more stable atmosphere than had been the case for more than a decade.

Dillon Read now prepared to enter the German market in force. W.M.L. Fiske remained nominally in charge of operations, but now would be joined by a newcomer. Colonel James A. Logan, who previously had been the American observer at the Reparations Commission which helped write the Dawes Plan, now took prime responsibility for Dillon Read's European negotiations.[21] Intelligent and perceptive, Logan also had ideal connections. He was there to provide background information and expertise, and open doors which otherwise might have been closed to a banker who in those years did not have much of a reputation in Europe.

Dillon had some awareness of Germany from his vacations there before the war, and as has been seen, served with Baruch in Versailles on the commission that dealt with the reparations issue. In 1919 he had dispatched Ralph Bollard to Germany to make a study of the situation.[22] Dillon returned to Europe in the early 1920s and held conversations with his opposite numbers at several large banks, including J. Henry Shroder & Co., an important merchant bank with branches in New York and London, and the Hamburg-based Warburg Bank, headed by Max M. Warburg. As a result, Dillon Read became one of the first American banks to obtain German business after the war, and had some early successes. Together with the International Acceptance Bank, it handled a $2.5 million loan to the German dye industry.[23] The original intent of US&FS, organized the month following acceptance of the Dawes Plan, was to become involved in German securities. Certainly this was the case with American and Continental Corporation and German Credit & Investment; all of its sponsors either had or nourished ambitions for a larger European business following settlement of Franco-German differences. A contemporary observer wrote that "several important houses of issue, notably Dillon, Read and Company, have formed financing investment trusts for the purpose of acquiring foreign securities."[24]

The growing attitude that it now had become safe to invest in Germany was confirmed in October 1925, when at Foreign Minister Gustav Stresemann's suggestion representatives of the major European powers met in Locarno, a small town in Switzerland, and agreed that all future disputes would be settled through negotiations. Stresemann and Reich Finance Minister Rudolf Hilferding were among the most pro-American of the German leaders. Both mistrusted the French and British political leaders and preferred to ally Germany both politically and economically with the United States. One of the principal reasons Stresemann entered into the Locarno Pact was his conviction that the United States was becoming increasingly isolationist. The agreements, signed by the United Kingdom, France, Germany, Belgium, and Italy among others, seemed a guarantee of future peace. On his part, Stresemann pledged Germany would never attempt to seek revisions of the Treaty of Versailles through force. "The Spirit of Locarno" not only appeared to assure tranquility, but stimulated investment throughout central Europe.

If Germany could not have American political support, economic assistance would have to do. Speaking in 1924 during discussions leading up to the Dawes Plan, Stresemann told the Reichstag:[25]

"No European troubles" became the motto of every party in the
United States shortly after the war. "Never again will we intervene in European affairs." That attitude was disastrous to us, if
only for the reason that the United States are obviously best fitted
to play the part of the honest broker in the settlement of European
difficulties. They are too rich to be interested in the weakening
of Germany. They are far enough off to take an unprejudiced view.
I am sure, however, —and I would like to say this most emphat-
ically—that not only they, but all the other gentlemen who are
taking part in this inquiry, are equally animated by a spirit of
impartiality and are at one in their desire to settle the question
in a satisfactory manner.

While interested in Germany, the American bankers were cautious regarding commitments, investigating thoroughly before
seeking underwritings and investments. For all of 1924 the total
non-Dawes financings were only $10 million, and in the first four
months of 1925, the amount was only $58.5 million, most of which
was taken by private borrowers, only $8 million by public
corporations.[26]
    The key underwriting, the one that opened the floodgates, was
for August Thyssen-Hutte, the nation's largest pig iron producer,
which also owned mines turning out 10 percent of Germany's coal
and which exported 30 percent of its product, making it Germany's
leading earner of foreign currencies. Initially Thyssen negotiated
through a six-company coalition organized by the German-
American Securities Company, which approached Dillon Read asking for advice in obtaining a $100 million loan. Dillon agreed to
attempt to lead a syndicate whose commission would be 3 percent
of the gross, with 2 percent going to the industrialists involved in
setting up the deal.
    An underwriting of such magnitude would take time to put
together, and the companies had a pressing need for funds. To tide
the company over Dillon proposed a one-year $5 million loan, Dillon
Read receiving an option on the larger loan as part of its fee, and
in addition security for the loan in the form of finished goods.
    Dillon clearly was deliberate in this matter, knowing he was
entering unchartered territory. His hesitation caused the coalition
to crumble, upon which Dillon opened direct negotiations with

Thyssen. Now it was the Germans' turn to be reluctant, and they intimated they would look elsewhere. Dillon bowed, fearful of losing an opportunity to obtain not only new business but also prestige accruing to the American bank which opened the market. In early December 1924, he started to put together a syndicate to market a $15 million loan, either for a five- or fifteen-year term.[27]

On December 16, Dillon telephoned Charles Mitchell at National City to inquire whether he wanted to be included in the selling group. Dillon recorded that "[Mitchell] said he would be interested in a big way, but if it meant being the tail end of a big picture he would not be interested." In other words, National City would agree to take a large position in a small syndicate, but not a minor role in a larger group. "I [Dillon] said he was the only person I had talked to and that I should like the two of us to do the business together. He said he would be very glad to have his men look into it."[28]

This was the spine of the deal. In January 1925, Dillon Read and National City co-underwrote a $12 million 5-year 7 percent issue.[29] As it happened, it was a most difficult issue to market. The previous week Chase National had offered $10 million in bonds for Krupp, the giant industrial firm which had been the mainstay of Germany's munitions industry, which supposedly had been dismantled after the war. The morning of the underwriting a rumor swept the financial community that hundreds of cannon had been found at the works, and that the Allies were about to seize the installation and other German factories. The report proved false, but had the effect of unsettling matters. The Krupp issue still overhung the market when Dillon Read came out with the Thyssen loan. The firm's ability to organize a syndicate which placed it in the face of such difficulties did much to embellish its prestige in German industrial circles, and led to additional business.[30]

Dillon was quite certain he could handle whatever matters might arise concerning German financing in America, but he would need someone on the scene whose knowledge, intelligence, instincts, and diplomatic skills he could rely upon. Such an individual would have to know Europe, Germany in particular, possess the requisite cultural background along with experience in banking, and think along the same lines as others in his organization. There was no such person at Dillon Read, but through Cotton and Forrestal he located Ferdinand Eberstadt, who was brought into the picture and soon became a major player in Dillon's European business. At one point in the Thyssen negotiations, when the Germans insisted upon a quick determination, Dillon cabled that this was impossible due to the indisposition of his expert on German loans. Cologne banker Walter Barth, who headed the German team, referred to him as "this mysterious confidant." Undoubtedly, Eberstadt was the key figure in this negotiation.[31]

Short, wiry, intense, and vain, Eberstadt possessed an extraordinary capacity for work of a high order. As noted, he had known Forrestal while they were at Princeton. Eberstadt was considered one of the most prominent members of the Class of '13, and certainly the most active. In addition to his work at the *Daily Princetonian*, Eberstadt managed the varsity football team, earned a letter as a member of the wrestling team, and was elected to Phi Beta Kappa. "The King," as he was called, was voted by his classmates the most likely to succeed.[32]

After graduation Eberstadt spent a year in Europe studying politics and economics at the University of Berlin and the Sorbonne. That he went to Berlin may have been due to family connections. The Eberstadts were originally German, and Ferdinand's father, Edward Frederick, had emigrated to the United States in the 1870s. Eberstadts were sprinkled throughout central Europe, though some were also in England and France. One of Ferdinand's aunts had married Benedikt Bernard Kahn, and one of their many children, Otto Kahn, was to become head of Kuhn Loeb and a major financial force on Wall Street in the early 1900s. That these connections helped Eberstadt during the 1920s, when he became one of the most important American bankers operating in Europe, seems apparent.[33]

Upon his return to the United States in 1914 Eberstadt entered Columbia Law School, and while selected for the Law Review in his first year, wasn't particularly interested in the law. It was with a sense of relief that he took a leave of absence when the National Guard unit of which he was a member was called up to join General John Pershing's expedition to Mexico to capture Pancho Villa. He returned to Columbia in 1916, only to be recalled to the service the following year when the United States entered World War I. Eberstadt remained in Germany for almost a year after the Armistice to serve as a liaison between the German government and the Allied forces.

Arriving in the United States in 1919, Eberstadt learned that Columbia had decided that all law school seniors who had entered the service with passing grades would receive their diplomas without having to take their final examinations. In addition, New York had directed that all servicemen who had received their law diplomas and had been unable to take the bar examination because they were on active duty would be admitted to the bar on submitting an affidavit, and the United States attorney general made a similar ruling for the federal courts. This meant Eberstadt received both his diploma and bar membership simply by filing some papers.[34]

Eberstadt had clerked at Spooner & Cotton during the summer recess at law school. Now he was offered and accepted a position at what had become McAdoo, Cotton and Franklin. Eberstadt was immediately plunged into the creations of Radio Corporation of America and Allied Chemical & Dye, but the firm did not keep him on these assignments for long. In 1920 McAdoo, Cotton and Franklin dispatched Eberstadt to Germany to handle war claims for several clients. Other business along this line followed, and when McAdoo left the firm in March 1922 to enter California politics, Cotton made Eberstadt a partner, with responsibility for the firm's growing European business.[35] This brought him into close relationship with Dillon Read, by then one of Cotton and Franklin's more important clients, and especially with his old Princeton friend, James Forrestal.

It wasn't long before Eberstadt was seeking business for Dillon Read. In late 1924, for example, he was largely responsible for bringing Siemens & Halske into the Dillon Read circle. An initial $10 million in short-term bonds was floated early the following year, and in 1926 the reviving electric and telecommunications company sold another $24 million in bonds through the firm. Other German business delivered by Eberstadt in 1925 included a 7.5 million reichsmark offering for the Disconto-Gesellschaft, a major bank, and $3 million for the Rudolph Karstadt Company. In addition, Eberstadt may have had a hand in assisting Dillon Read with a $35 million Republic of Poland issue.[36]

Ever on the prowl, Eberstadt helped organize a syndicate to

purchase a half interest in the Deutsche Luxemburgische Company, originally part of the Hugo Stinnes industrial empire, which also owned eleven coal mines. Deutsche Luxemburgische, together with Siemens, Gelsinkirchen Mining, and Bochumerverein, comprised the Rheinelbe Union, the largest producer of coal, coke, and iron and steel in Germany. The price was $4 million. Not only was this a bargain, made possible by the still-shabby condition of the German economy, but the purchase provided Dillon Read with a presence in German affairs that assisted in other business.

This was the first of several Dillon Read investments in German companies, most of them made to obtain additional business. Soon after the firm took an interest in Disconto-Gesellschaft, and in January 1926 joined with the Amsterdam banking firm of Mendelssohn & Co. and several German banks to organize German Credit & Investment Corporation. Capitalized at $15 million, it proposed investing in promising situations in Germany, and in addition extended credits to firms there and in other parts of Europe on a short-term basis.[37]

The scope of Eberstadt's activities in this period was documented in Stresemann's diaries. On July 11, 1926, the German statesman wrote:[38]

Mr. Ferdinand Eberstadt . . . came to see me today. . . . He had just come from an interview with Herren Thyssen and Voegler [with] whom . . . he had negotiated a part of the new shares of the Steel Trust, and he could assure me that there had never been so favourable a market for German securities in the U.S.A. as there was today. Two years ago he had been only able to negotiate German investments at an interest rate of 10¼ per cent, but now shares bearing 6¾ per cent stood above par. There was only one difficulty in the way of negotiating German shares, and that was the existing uncertainty as to the final sum which Germany would have to provide by way of reparations.

To this Stresemann added, "Herr Eberstadt . . . thought he would be in a position to negotiate through his banking house in the next three or four years, one milliard [billion] dollars worth of these bonds, if Germany would undertake the payment of the interest and France stood security for it. Moreover, 300 million dollars' worth more were immediately negotiable."

The reasons for Eberstadt's conviction that this could be done rested in part on his new relationship with Dillon Read. Around then Dillon concluded that while Logan was well suited for his work, his lack of expertise in financial matters was troublesome. Someone else was needed in this area, and Eberstadt, who was devoting far more time and energy to the Dillon Read account than to all the others, was the obvious person for these tasks.

In late September of 1926 Dillon asked Eberstadt to join the bank as a partner, at a salary three times what he was receiving at Cotton and Franklin. In addition, there was further remuneration to be had through annual distributions and shares in deals. Eberstadt thought about it for a while, and then consulted with Cotton. The droll lawyer thought he should accept. "The investment banking business is the only business I know of where you can make money without either brains or capital, and I think you are well qualified on both sources," said Cotton. Whether stung by the remark or not, Eberstadt took Cotton's advice, and joined Dillon Read on February 4, 1926. He became a superb banker.[39] As Pike Sullivan, one of his later partners, remarked:[40]

> Eberstadt was driven by the sheer love of doing deals. The money was important, obviously; that was the underlying factor [but] . . . he had plenty of money and he certainly didn't have to worry about doing the next deal. I think it was a game he liked to play; it was fascinating to him.

Before he could become more deeply involved in European affairs, Eberstadt had to handle a problem on the domestic scene, the aforementioned Goodyear litigation. Working with Cotton, Eberstadt helped organize Dillon Read's defense. This out of the way, he sailed for Europe to report on conditions there and seek additional business, with the understanding he would return when his specific expertise was required. Eberstadt took quarters with Fiske at the Dillon Read offices at 39 rue Cambon in Paris, and for the next two years shuttled between there and the Hotel Adlon in Berlin.

After a short stay in Paris, Eberstadt set out for Germany and conversations with Stresemann regarding Dillon Read's willingness and suitability to finance the German debt and reparations payments. Stresemann, who had been impressed by Eberstadt in earlier meetings, was interested in maintaining the relationship.[41]

From Paris, Berlin, Weimar, and other points in Europe Eberstadt would dispatch long letters to 28 Nassau Street, sketching conversations he had with business and government movers and shakers, analyzing political and economic trends, and suggesting investment and underwriting strategies and tactics. One of the earlier letters came from Berlin on October 31, 1926. After delving into the possibilities of Franco-German cooperation, and noting indications of economic growth, Eberstadt reported on Dillon Read's chances of obtaining additional business, observing that there was a pretty general feeling among the influential industrialists and bankers that while Morgan would have to participate in the big German financing, Germany could not accept Morgan as its banker in view of the Morgan–Bank of England relationship. Eberstadt suggested there was no question Dillon Read was the only banking house that could challenge Morgan. He noted that by the end of 1926 Dillon Read would probably have issued over $100 million dollars of German industrial obligations, which had impressed observers in Berlin.[42]

How well did Eberstadt think the firm could do in Germany? In a November 1 postscript to the October 31 letter he reported on a dinner conversation with two officials from the state of Hesse. He said that it was possible for Dillon Read to handle at least $300 million of German bonds, doing so through a syndicate. The Germans appeared astonished, but Eberstadt assured them it could be accomplished given the proper political connections.

Three days later Eberstadt visited Stresemann, who continued to be interested in Dillon Read's ability to generate the kind of capital he talked about. When Eberstadt manifested interest in taking a major share of German borrowing to meet the Dawes Plan obligations, Stresemann asked how this could be done without cooperation with Wall Street's old elite.[43]

He [Stresemann] said, "I am extremely interested in that but let me ask you what are your relations with the Morgan group. Are they good, indifferent, or bad?" I said that it was clear to me that such an operation should be done in conjunction with and not in defiance of the Morgan group. He said, "Do you think they would do it jointly with you?" I said, "It depends on whether they have to, that is, on whether you insist." I told him that from the point of view of Germany I thought that they must insist even though Morgan participates in the financing that they have an independent banker and that this was the role in which we could be most useful to them.

In effect, Eberstadt was suggesting that Dillon Read be retained as Germany's exclusive banker, its liaison with Wall Street, representing its interests.

The conversation next turned to the matter of the government of Poland, which had recently become a Dillon Read client. Stresemann said he was "exasperated" with the lack of progress after a year and a half of negotiations with Polish officials, and told Eberstadt "so far as the standing of the house of Dillon Read was concerned in Germany he thought it would be a mistake for us to get out a Polish loan for some months." As it happened, Dillon Read did not underwrite another Polish issue for the rest of the decade and beyond, while the German business increased substantially.

Subsequent conversations with Stresemann later in the month concerned politics, the Dawes Plan, and always, the ability of Dillon Read to carry through on underwritings. All involved knew the success of the Dawes Plan was crucial to the fulfillment of all underwritings. Unless Germany made prompt and complete payments, or if that country didn't do so and the Allies accepted default, almost all of Germany's state and industrial bonds would collapse. Eberstadt had doubts that Germany could perform as promised. Writing to Robert Hayward in 1927, he suggested that Germany's major concern for the foreseeable future would be the payment of reparations, and he doubted that a nation of 70 million people would be willing to subordinate every governmental and industrial measure and activity to such payments. Eberstadt did not believe this would transpire, and felt the Dawes Plan would have to be amended so as to take this into consideration.[44]

Throughout this period one of Eberstadt's major concerns was to demonstrate to Dillon, and through him to American investors, the safety of the German issues. There was a definite logic to what they were doing, and a reason why Eberstadt was so concerned with German politics. The purpose of the private underwritings was to make Germany more productive; and if such were the case the country could more easily make the reparations payments. In a letter to Forrestal, he remarked that despite difficulties and problems with the Dawes Plan, Dillon Read should not be afraid to make "sound" loans to Germany. Eberstadt took the possibilities of a crisis involving the transfer of payments seriously, but thought that if one transpired, it would be managed so smoothly as to assure those involved of Germany's abilities to pay.[45]

Eberstadt proved not only masterful at obtaining business, but in this period was one of the soundest and most perceptive students of European affairs. Though Stresemann appreciated his qualities, Eberstadt had difficulties convincing some of his associates he could fulfill his pledges. For example, most German bankers perceived Dillon Read as inferior to Morgan. How could they rely so heavily upon so young and inexperienced a bank? Age and tradition were important in Europe, and Eberstadt knew it. "I told him of Vermilye & Co., etc.," wrote Eberstadt. Of course, a more current track record was important, too. "I also showed him some figures which I received from New York of the comparative issues in the last twenty months of J. P. Morgan, National City, Harris Forbes, and ourselves. The aggregate was about 818,000,000 against Morgan's 770,000,000." As for German financing, Dillon Read had $160 million, while runner-up Morgan had $110 million, which was represented by the Dawes Loan financing and nothing else. National City, in third place, had $79 million.[46]

Making progress was difficult. Competition was keen, and Eberstadt always had to keep in mind the possibilities of financial collapse. He wrote a year later to Hayward, by then resident partner in charge of foreign government financing, that he still felt optimistic on occasions, but that this was becoming less the case.[47]

Eberstadt performed his tasks well. While Dillon Read did not become Germany's de jure banker, the business expanded considerably. In 1926 there were underwritings for Berlin City Electric, Disconto-Gesellschaft, and Siemens. Almost all of these were conducted jointly with German banks, Schroder, Deutsche Bank, Dresdner, and Darmstaedtern.

In January 1926 Dillon Read sold a $25 million issue for Rhein-elbe Union, and in June came a $5 million financing for Thyssen. The most important German business that year was the creation of the Vereinigte Stahlwerke (United Steel Works). From the first Vereinigte Stahlwerke was intended to function as a cartel. One after another it assimilated Thyssen, Rheinelbe Union, Phoenix, and Rheinstahl, all with Dillon Read acting as lead underwriter and Eberstadt functioning as advisor. Heading a largely German syndicate, Dillon Read sold $30 million in 25-year 6½ percent bonds in late June 1926. A year later, again as syndicate manager, the firm sold another $30 million, this time in 20-year 6½ percent bonds, and in July came back with a $4,225,000 25-year 6½ percent bond.[48]

It was a remarkable accomplishment for a foreign bank; to appreciate this, consider how an American might have felt a generation earlier if the Deutsche Bank had financed U.S. Steel. Indeed, so preeminent was Dillon Read in German affairs that in 1927 it underwrote a $25 million 5-year issue for the Deutsche Bank. This was an unusual piece of business. As Forrestal later reminisced, "It was the first time, in the American market at least, that any bank in the world borrowed money over its own name. It was a departure from orthodox banking from our point of view, and caused a great deal of comment and a good deal of interest."[49] In addition, that year Dillon Read underwrote a 20-year, $30 million issue for the Vereinigte Stahlwerke. The following year saw a $15 million offering for Gelsinkirchen, a like amount for Karstadt, and a total of $20.6 million for several government entities in the Ruhr.

While dominant in Germany, Dillon Read was frustrated in France. On May 2, 1926, when he was embroiled in several important domestic projects and the firm's interests in Europe were well attended by others, Dillon traveled to Paris and remained there the entire month, meeting with businessmen, but, more important, government officials, including Premier Aristide Briand.

France was in the midst of a financial crisis. The franc had fallen to the value of two cents, higher taxes directed at restoring confidence not only failed but resulted in a large budget deficit, and to cap matters, there were insurrections against French rule in Morocco and Lebanon. The government could not float new bond issues, and it appeared there might even be a partial repudiation of the national debt. Unable to service its wartime inter-Allied debts, France's American investment bankers could not raise money for the country without first obtaining the requisite permission from the State Department.[50]

Dillon went to see if the crisis could be translated into business. It was a delicate task, for through its French affiliate, Morgan, Harjes & Co., Morgan was bound to learn of Dillon's discussions with Briand. He had to proceed cautiously. For this reason Dillon lunched with Lamont in late April 1926, and on that occasion offered details of his forthcoming European trip. Dillon assured the Morgan partner he would do nothing which might disturb their domestic relationship. Moreoever, he would keep Lamont informed of any significant developments in France. With this Dillon set off for Paris, where he began by conferring with Fiske and Logan.

Logan had a sophisticated knowledge of French politics and diplomacy, but lacked intimate information regarding that country's industry and financing. He was also unpopular with the Morgan representatives. Having devoted much effort to seeking new European corporate and municipal business, Logan had clashed with them repeatedly and had come to be viewed as the cutting edge of the growing Morgan–Dillon Read rivalry for new financings in these areas.

Because of the association with Lamont as well as Wall Street practices of the period, Dillon would say nothing negative to the French about Morgan, this not being necessary since Logan presumably had been doing so for months. For their part, the French obviously were hoping to find some kind of counterweight to Morgan, and were not above attempting to use Dillon as one of these. He seemed to understand this, and deftly sidestepped all such suggestions.

Dillon met with Briand on May 12.[51] Talk immediately turned to the question of loans, with Dillon carefully suggesting arrangements might be possible if the French had a definite proposal to make. Knowing Morgan, Harjes & Co. was one of the French government's leading bankers, Dillon wondered whether it would be possible to "broaden her group, and include Dillon, Read & Co. with the Morgans."

The Prime Minister replied that he had received such advice from Mr. Beringer and that in effect there was a general feeling of discontent in France, as well as in the Left elements generally throughout Europe, that Mr. Morgan's relations with the Bank of England were too intimate and that in effect it was Montague Norman and not Morgans who were guiding the European financial policies; that this criticism had been growing to somewhat an alarming extent and was fraught with possible serious consequences of a social order. He was therefore very glad to have this chance to talk to Mr. Dillon, and hoped that arrangements could be made whereby Mr. Dillon, on account of the independent position of his banking house, could join with the French present bankers in working out a solution of France's difficulties, that he had discussed this matter with the Finance Minister a number of times and that he would like very much to have Mr. Dillon meet the Finance Minister. . . .

The conference was arranged, with the French representatives assuring Dillon all was well insofar as governmental finances were concerned. The budget would be balanced, the franc strengthened, and the American Congress would agree to reduction in debt payments. They conceded, however, as Lamont had indicated, that $89 million of a $100 million loan obtained through Morgan two years earlier remained to defend the franc. This amount did not meet the government's needs; would Dillon Read be able to raise $150 million in short-term money, with the understanding the money would not be drawn upon until the $89 million was drained?

Mr. Dillon said that this put an entirely different aspect on the matter and that it put him in a most embarrassing position; that his understanding had been that what France wanted was for the House of Dillon, Read & Co. to join with the Morgans in the negotiations now under way. He said that he could not give credit nor make any offer independently but that if France felt it was desirable to have Dillon, Read & Co. with Morgans they should so inform Morgans. The Finance Minister said that that was what the French Government wanted and that he would further discuss the matter with the Prime Minister.

On May 19 Morgan Harjes partner Dean Jay told Dillon he had received a letter for him from Lamont, who was then vacationing in London. In this confidential "Dear Clarence" communication, dated May 14, Lamont told him of Morgan's activities in France, saying the government wanted a new loan to defend the franc. "As you know," he wrote, "they still have almost intact in New York the proceeds of the last loan which they are free to use, but seem reluctant to do so. I do not blame them, because to use it at this moment might seem like throwing good gold francs at the poor paper ones."

Lamont reminded Dillon, "We have done business for the French Government since Jack Morgan's grandfather in 1871 helped them finance the indemnity to Germany [following the Franco-Prussian War], and naturally people believe that when we undertake any operation for the Banque or Government, even though a private one, we must be satisfied that the situation is sound." Lamont went on to assert that after Morgan refused to consider a new loan unless specific guarantees were in place they had approached Kuhn Loeb's Mortimer Schiff, who replied that "he considered French Government business as our [Morgan's] particular responsibility." He didn't have to elaborate; Lamont expected as much from Dillon.[52]

This letter, which contained information Dillon already possessed, was significant in its thinly veiled suggestion that Morgan would be displeased by any attempt to break ranks on loans to France. In any case, from that point on Jay was included in the discussions, and apprised of developments.

On May 26, when it appeared certain he could hope for little from the French, Dillon wrote a "Dear Tom" letter to Lamont, responding to his letter of the fourteenth, telling of the meetings with Briand and the others. Included was a paper called "Exhibit D," a short version of the larger memorandum whose wording was changed to stress Dillon Read's fealty to Morgan. For example, there is this comment: "Mr. Dillon in reply to a request from M. Peret said that he had no suggestions to offer, as he would not under any conditions make any suggestions which might not be in accord with what Morgans or the Federal Reserve Bank was saying. . . ." The memo contained these words: "When we left, M. Briand and M. Peret stated that they understood our position, and that they realized our friendship for Morgan and our previous position in the business." It concluded with a reiteration of Dillon Read's original intent. "They respected the position which Mr. Dillon had taken in being unwilling to advance any suggestion under the circumstances, and that they would at once ask and urge

Morgans to invite Dillon, Read & Co. to cooperate with Morgans, and that they would advise the result of the request." In a cover letter Dillon assured Lamont he had "kept Dean fully informed."[53]

Paul Harjes of Morgan Harjes was called to the French Treasury a few days later and was asked whether it would be agreeable if Dillon Read were given a more prominent role in future underwritings.[54] Somewhat surprised, the banker asked if Morgan Harjes's work had been satisfactory. Jacques Robineau, governor of the Bank of France, told Harjes that while France felt grateful for what Morgan had done in the past, he should know that were it impossible for him to arrange this credit, it would be necessary for the French government to go elsewhere. Harjes replied that he presumed this referred to Dillon Read, and then suggested that as far as he knew, Dillon Read would not challenge Morgan Harjes's role in French financings. Robineau nonchalantly replied that his government could go "to Mr. Dillon or elsewhere."

This was a bluff; there were no other American bankers in the wings. However, the French would try to lure Dillon. On May 29 several Finance Ministry officials met with him to ascertain whether he would be interested in negotiating for the underwriting of a new loan for the Chemins de Fer de l'Etat and the Alsace-Lorraine Railway. There were also discussions of a loan for Paris, and a credit to the Bank of France to finance imports. Dillon Read might easily have had that business, but at great risk to the firm; not only was there Lamont's warning to consider, but given France's parlous circumstances, he was not certain such paper could be sold in America. So he continued to insist upon a larger role with Morgan, and was adamantly opposed to going any further than that.

The situation was resolved on June 1, when Morgan & Co. informed the Treasury it now understood "for the first time" that France wanted a large short-term credit to protect the franc, and was prepared to provide the funds. The reason for this change in stance is unknown. But soon after, Briand's office called Dillon to express his appreciation for his aid, "it being generally realized that he had been responsible for the French Government getting this credit, and there was general regret on account of past connections Mr. Dillon was not free to act alone, which position they thoroughly appreciated."

This was not the end of the affair. Dillon Read had kept faith with Morgan, but did not mean to give up entirely on French business. On his way back to New York Dillon stopped in London to meet with Lamont and Dwight Morrow, another Morgan partner, telling them that he felt free to make *indirect* loans to the French government, and that "if this was embarrassing to them it would be necessary for us to withdraw from their group." Lamont chose not to continue along this line of discussion, wheeling instead into Logan's activities, which he denounced bitterly. Dillon rejected assertions that Logan had behaved incorrectly.

> Turning from this question, Mr. Dillon stated that Logan probably would be talking to the French people about indirect methods of raising money, including the railroad bonds, which he mentioned specifically, that he wished it clearly understood that we construed the Morgan group as limited in its activities to the direct note of the Government of France—not a loan the proceeds of which might enure to the French Treasury as, for example, the Etat or the City Loan. Mr. Lamont stated that that was just the way they construed it.

The bankers then discussed German loans, with Dillon stating he considered Germany to be in quite a different category. He conceded Morgan dominance in France and the United Kingdom, but considered Germany his preserve. In a memorandum of the meeting, Eberstadt wrote:

> Mr. Dillon stated very clearly that we were interested in the German railroad bonds. There was a speech by Morrow along the lines of general policy of not playing on people's prejudices and acting toward keeping peace. He also stated that they had recommended a number of times against the sale of German bonds.

Morrow then returned to the question of France, but before the meeting ended Dillon had obtained his objectives. Dillon Read was included in Morgan foreign syndicates, and the two firms were coming to be seen as equals in power in some areas of the business. This did not mean Dillon Read abandoned France entirely. Rather, there would be no more attempts to win lead positions in syndicates.[55] Dillon would sail for America on June 8. Before leaving, he met with Montague Norman, and they discussed the meeting with Lamont and Morrow. On that occasion Dillon told the British banker that as a result of the exchange of views, "I felt probably the best thing to do was for us, in a perfectly friendly spirit, to withdraw from their French group." Dillon Read did open a larger Paris office in 1928, when it purchased a 12½ percent interest in Etablissements Kuhlmann, a company that controlled 80 percent of the country's chemical business.[56]

In the 1920s, then, Dillon Read emerged as the most powerful American banking presence for German industrial concerns, the major conduit for that country's securities into the United States, but remained a smallish player elsewhere in Europe. The German business made Dillon Read the third-largest American bank in the area of foreign flotations in terms of volume of issues, behind Morgan and National City but ahead of Kuhn Loeb and Seligman.[57] The firm had representatives on the board of Vereinigte Stahlwerke, which had become a dominant force in its industry, due largely to $70,225,000 in financing obtained through Dillon Read. In 1928 Eberstadt was able to explain to his United States–based associates just how significant the German accomplishments were by going over the roster of firms for which Dillon Read had become the investment banker:[58]

> We have in the iron, coal, and steel industry, the United Steel Works, which is approximately the size of Bethlehem Steel, and second only to the United States Steel Corporation. . . . In the electrical industry we took the Siemens, which recognizes as a rival only the United States General Electric. . . . In the banking field, we selected the Disconto and Deutsche Banks. Now, what do they correspond to in the United States? . . . The Disconto and the Deutsche Banks correspond to the First National and the National City.

This was no idle bravado. No less a figure than Leon Trotsky, the most authoritative Marxist theoretician in the world, considered Clarence Dillon the symbol of American financial imperialism. "Mr. Dillon's task is to buy out German metallurgical works as cheaply as possible," Trotsky wrote in 1928, responding to an article in a German magazine entitled "Dawes or Dillon, Which?"[59]

He needs a combination of coal and metal, he wants to create a
centralized European trust. He feels no compunction as regards
political geography. And I am even inclined to think he is ignorant
of it. And why should he be concerned with such trifles?

Dealings with the government continued strong. On December
17, 1929, when Germany was facing near-certain disaster, Dillon
received a communication from Hilferding sent via the Washington
embassy asking him to "open a credit to the extent of seventy-five
million dollars, to take effect immediately for the duration of six
or nine months." The government was "convinced," the letter went
on to say, "that the connection established between your house
and the Reich will continue and extend to other credit operations."[60] The attempt failed, in part due to the opposition of Reichs-
bank president Hjalmar Schact, who was unimpressed, saying
"Dillon Read [is] a second-class firm."[61] "The Dillon Read loan is
as good as dead," declared a Foreign Ministry official. "A direct
demand on the foreign market by the Reich government for either
long- or short-term funds is no longer a possibility."[62] With this,
Hilferding resigned, cutting one of the two major Dillon Read
connections to the government.

Such lingering attitudes were no doubt frustrating, and in any
case, Eberstadt was losing enthusiasm for the German business.
Stresemann had suffered a series of debilitating strokes in the late
1920s; Dillon Read's major sympathizer was on the wane, soon to
die. The Nazis and Communists seemed to be gaining power. Eberstadt longed to return home, which he did in the summer of 1928.
He arrived in the United States just as his services once again
were needed in New York on domestic business, as Dillon Read
was about to launch one of its most striking deals of the decade.

· 7 ·

The Wizard
of Wall Street, I

(1925–1928)

Dillon Read's Nassau Street offices were not those one might have expected to house Wall Street's fastest-rising investment bank. The entrance was unimpressive, the carpets and furniture old and worn, the elevators slow. Once past the small reception area one came into a large room. On one side were the partners' desks, and on the other, those of the salesmen. There was a conference room and, nearby, Clarence Dillon's private office. Salesmen were at some of the desks. In those years they were paid $8 a week plus a $350 drawing account, which was an advance against earnings. Commissions ran from ¼ to a full point on sales, a full point representing $10 a share.[1]

The firm was successful, exciting, and innovative during the early 1920s, but not a pacesetter. Then, in a period of two years— 1925 and 1926—it became a national and even global power, whose power in certain areas of investment banking was as great as any in the industry.

Several of the reasons for this celebrity, such as the European and Latin American deals, especially the creation of Vereinigte Stahlwerke, have already been discussed. The others included the takeover of Dodge Brothers, Inc., the world's third-largest auto-

119

mobile company, and the initial sale of National Cash Register (NCR) common stock. The Dodge purchase came in April 1925 and the NCR flotation in January 1926. These made headlines throughout the country, catapulting Dillon into the public eye, transforming him into a celebrity in the eyes of even those with little interest in Wall Street happenings.

In order to appreciate just what the Dodge Brothers acquisition meant to the general public as well as to the financial world, one must first understand the nature of the automobile business in the first quarter of the twentieth century. Not only did the industry grow impressively, but most of the founders of companies were still alive and active. Ford, Chevrolet, Durant, Jordan, Dodge, Chrysler, Graham, Willys, Cord, Leland, Olds, Packard, and Nash were not only automobiles, but human beings, read about in newspapers and magazines and seen in newsreels.[2] It also was a glamorous enterprise. The public was as fascinated with automobiles then as it would be with personal computers three generations later. Finally, it was an industry in flux. New companies were being formed, established ones faded and disappeared, and mergers and acquisitions were not only fairly common, but expected.

On July 7, 1914, Horace and John Dodge, formerly major suppliers of parts to Ford, established Dodge Brothers, Inc., which was capitalized at $5 million. Immediately the company was flooded with more than 22,000 applications for dealerships.[3] When asked how he thought the new Dodge cars would do when pitted against the Model T, John simply stared and observed, "Just think of all those Ford owners who will some day want an automobile."[4]

The Dodge cars proved sturdy and reliable and were well received. The company sold 45,000 of them in 1915, a year in which more than half a million Fords were purchased and the figure for the three-year-old Chevrolet was 13,292. The Dodges were so rugged that the following year the U.S. Army ordered three to use in General Pershing's Mexican expedition seeking to capture Pancho Villa. After one foray, Lieutenant George S. Patton, Jr., stated in his report to the War Department, "We couldn't have done it with horses. The motorcar is the modern war horse."[5] Sales rose to 71,000 the following year, and by 1919 were 106,000, against Ford's 820,000 and Chevrolet's 123,000.[6] In 1920 the company recorded sales of 145,389 cars which brought in revenues of $161 million and a net profit of $10.2 million.[7]

Glory was short-lived. The Dodge brothers died within eleven months of one another in 1920, with John going first. Horace was in poor condition, his ailments deepened by the depression he experienced during what remained of his life. He soon withdrew from active management, leaving this task to Frederick J. Haynes, Dodge's vice president and general manager.[8]

A Cornell University–trained engineer, Haynes had joined the Dodges while they were still in the bicycle business. He then apprenticed in autos at Franklin Motors Co. before returning to Dodge Brothers in 1912. Haynes was a proficient manager, the one person the Dodge widows truly trusted to run their business. His performance justified their confidence. Dodge's reputation was enhanced during his leadership, and the company became an even more powerful force within the industry, known for its superb dealership structure, modern factory, and dependable autos.[9]

Success created problems. The Dodge factory in Hamtramck was capable of turning out 1,100 cars during a nine-hour shift, or approximately 286,000 a year. Sales for 1925 came to 255,322, which meant that if the growth continued Haynes might soon have had to consider either a second shift or a factory expansion of some kind, or soon be faced with the unpleasant problem of allocating cars to dealers.

He procrastinated. This was not unexpected. Haynes was a prudent but unimaginative manager, and there was little innovation about the way he conducted business. At a time when General Motors was going over to annual model changes, Dodge improved its existing line rather than introduce new designs. Haynes agreed with Henry Ford in considering installment purchases imprudent; his dealers sold Dodges for cash.

While Haynes was sometimes criticized for being too timid, there really wasn't much he could do by way of change. According to one industry report, the company's management was overly conservative because as trustees for the estates the managers were obliged to hew to prudent practices. There was "the inevitable restraint on expansion and impairment of initiative inherent in operating a business in a fiduciary capacity where the primary obligation is conservation and initiative is retarded by legal technicalities and restrictions."[10]

This is not to say that Haynes maintained an altogether static posture. Dodge had a contract to supply the Graham Brothers

Truck Company with engines, snatching that business from Ford. On October 1, 1925, Dodge puchased a 51 percent interest in Graham, whose production of one hundred trucks a day moved to the Hamtramck facility, making it more crowded than ever. Now Dodge dealers offered Graham trucks, and these became one of the nation's leading utility vehicles. The Graham brothers moved into the Dodge organization, with Joseph becoming a vice president, Robert vice president and general sales manager, and Ray in charge of manufacturing. With this move it appeared that Dodge had solved its problem of locating a successor for Haynes.[11]

This was not quite the way the trustees and the Dodge survivors saw the situation. They knew and trusted Haynes; the Grahams were unknown qualities. Besides, they had no real interest in the business. The widows had remarried men preoccupied with the theater, and soon they were, too. None of the Dodge children cared much about business or cars, with one operating a small speedboat factory, another concerned with her stable of racehorses.[12]

The family appeared content to live on dividends, which Haynes obligingly provided. One year after Horace's death he declared a 160 percent payout, which came to $16 million. There was another $6 million dividend in 1922, $7 million in 1924, and $6 million in the first three months of 1925.[13] With all of this the company was quite solvent, though capital spending was low, and, given the need to expand production, lower dividends were likely in the future. Moreover, all of Dodge's expansion had been financed by retained earnings; the company had no debt. Had Haynes been younger the Dodges probably would have been content with the way matters were being handled. The Grahams were also known to be concerned with expansion, and this might have troubled the heirs, since growth was bound to be costly.

In February 1925, Haynes gave a committee acting on behalf of some Dodge officers and dealers an informal option to purchase the company, which was not exercised.[14] Then, at the suggestion of Bernard Baruch, the family agreed to meet with Charles Schwartz, a New York broker interested in arranging for the sale of the company. In this period Charles and his brother, Morton, were known as the "Golden Boys of Wall Street," as together with Baruch they conducted several daring and successful specula-

AMERICAN PASSENGER CAR PRODUCTION, 1920–1925

Year	Total (000s)	Chevrolet	Ford	Dodge	Dodge as % of total
1920	1,905	121,908	419,517	145,389	7.6
1921	1,468	61,717	903,814	92,476	6.3
1922	2,274	208,848	1,173,745	164,037	7.2
1923	3,624	415,814	1,817,891	179,505	5.0
1924	3,186	262,100	1,749,827	222,236	7.0
1925	3,735	444,671	1,643,295	255,322	6.8

SOURCE: *Historical Statistics of the United States*, p. 716; Heasley, *The Production Figure Book for U.S. Cars*, pp. 23, 33, 117, 149; New York Stock Exchange, Committee on Stock List, *Application of Dodge Brothers, Inc. 6% Gold Coupon Debenture, May 1, 1925; Moody's Manual of Investments, 1926*, p. 2050.

DODGE BROTHERS STATISTICS, 1921–1924
(figures in millions of dollars)

Year	Current Assets	Current Liabilities	Net Working Capital	Ratio
1921	22.3	6.5	15.8	3.45 to 1
1922	37.8	8.9	28.8	4.22 to 1
1923	48.1	12.5	35.6	3.86 to 1
1924	60.5	9.5	51.0	6.38 to 1

SOURCE: Dodge Brothers, Inc. *Chairman's Annual Report to Board of Directors, December 31, 1925*, p. 7.

tions. The son of a prominent New York banker, Charles was a courtly patrician who persuaded the widows to give him an option to purchase Dodge Brothers.[15] The firm clearly was on the block, with Schwartz having an inside track by virtue of his option.

At Baruch's suggestion Schwartz brought the option to Dillon, who agreed to pay him a finder's fee should it be exercised. Dillon Read, too, was no stranger to the automobile industry. As has been seen, in 1919 William A. Read & Co. had been engaged to develop a plan whereby Packard and Peerless would merge, and as a result of Dillon's experience with Goodyear had been consulted when it appeared Willys might fall into insolvency.[16] In anticipation of the successful conclusion of the deal, Schwartz organized and then placed his assets into a new firm, Multiple Cord Development

Corp., knowing that if a company received payment the tax consequences would be more favorable.

Not aware of the Schwartz option, J. P. Morgan & Co. dispatched representatives to Hamtramck. Morgan had some experience in the industry. After having initially rejected William C. Durant's request to back his International Motors (whose name was soon changed to General Motors), Morgan had a change of heart and had underwritten securities for several companies and later served as General Motors' investment banker.

Dillon's first impulse was to seek merger partners. He toyed with the idea of merging Dodge with Packard, Hudson, and Briggs Manufacturing to create a firm that would rival General Motors. He dropped this idea when the other companies showed no interest.[17]

By then the Street was being flooded with rumors regarding the possible sale of Dodge to some other automobile company. In mid-March, when gossip was being churned out at an accelerating pace, Haynes issued a statement to the press "that there are no negotiations pending with any one for the sale of Dodge Brothers."[18] This was technically the case, but even then Haynes knew Dodge's days as an independent entity were numbered.

Dillon Read opened discussions with the Dodge agents soon after, which prompted a Morgan protest. Morgan also wanted Dodge, presumably to bring it into the General Motors family. Discussions followed, concluding with agreements that both banks would submit bids, and leave it to the Dodge heirs to select the one they wanted.

The company's tangible assets were worth some $80 million, so any offer beyond that price would reflect the value placed on the name, goodwill, patents, dealer structure, and the like. It was the practice at the time to base the cash portion of bids for industrial companies on net assets. The bankers would ground the cash portion of the deal on liquidating value and issue bonds to cover other considerations. This approach was starting to change as the bull market roared ahead, but in 1925 many financial writers and analysts still argued an industrial stock was overpriced when it sold substantially over book value.

According to one source, Morgan offered $155 million, but only $65 million would be in cash, the rest in notes, to be paid serially at the rate of $10 million a year, without interest, evidently out of anticipated profits.[19] This was traditional; Morgan was offering less cash than the book value for the assets, with the remainder of its offer in paper. The Dillon Read bid was for $152 million, minus dividends paid since January 1, which worked out to $146 million, all in cash, which was approximately $66 million over book value.

Both proposals were quite conservative in the light of today's methods of valuation, but given the approach of the time the Dillon Read offer was spectacular. Easily the more attractive, it was accepted with alacrity. The formal contract for the purchase was signed on April 7 in a suite in Detroit's Book-Cadillac Hotel, with payment to be made on May 1.

In all probability General Motors' offer was not serious. General Motors doubtless would have purchased Dodge had it been able to do so at a bargain price, but Dodge would not have played an important role in the General Motors overall strategy, which was to position Pontiac, a successful offering, against Dodge in its market segment. Two months later Du Pont disclosed his thoughts on the subject to Thomas Cochran, the Morgan partner who had handled negotiations.[20]

> Now that the smoke of battle has blown away, I think we should all congratulate ourselves in not having been led to bid more for the Dodge properties. I am convinced that we "went the limit" in our bid. I figure—John Raskob agrees with me—that the reincorporation of Dodge would have to earn $2. to every dollar earned by our divisions in order to compete. That is quite a handicap, and I am glad it was not assumed by us.

The Dodge purchase was by far the largest cash deal till then in American history, and made headlines throughout the world. It wasn't over yet, however. Dillon Read now had little more than three weeks to raise what must have seemed a formidable amount to those who did not know how Clarence Dillon was structuring the financing.[21]

The firm did not command that kind of money. While there is no account regarding Dillon Read's finances in 1925, to judge from statistics available for other years its net cash position was probably between $5 million and $15 million.[22] Raising the funds requircd for the Dodge payment was not as difficult as might be imagined, however, when one considered that Dillon Read's offer was predicated on a belief that Dodge securities would fetch a good price.

Dillon Read expected to raise the necessary funds through a syndicate which made prior commitments to purchase all or most of the securities. In an internal memorandum dated March 16, 1925, when preparing an offer for the Dodge interests, the firm indicated how the deal would be organized, and who was to be rewarded. Indeed, the money required was already pledged when Dillon made his presentation.

Evidence exists that prior to that date the syndicate functioned as a blind pool, the members agreeing to take securities without knowing what they were, their prices, or marketability. There is support for this view in a memorandum prepared by a Dillon Read attorney.[23]

> The Managers "for the account of the Group" were vested with entire discretion to purchase the assets or stock and to dispose of the same in practically any manner deemed desirable by such Managers. The language of the Agreement vests in the Managers power to borrow money for account of the Group and with very wide discretion in the handling of the whole transaction.

That the Wall Street community knew what had happened could be seen in the June 5, 1925, issue of "The Bawl Street Journal," the annual spoof of its denizens. In a front-page article entitled "Cute Dodge Worked Over Long Distance—Dillon, Read & Company, Leading Blind Pool, Cop Large Auto Business for Public," there is this imaginary conversation:

> Mr. Hallgarten, this is Mr. Cohen, the fifth assistance [sic] manager of the Syndicate Department of Dillon, Read & Company. I have been asked to call you up to find whether you would be interested in going into a blind pool to purchase Dodge Brothers & Company. We don't know how much we are going to pay for it, but we are going to buy it, providing you and a few more like you come in on it. We are going to participate in a small way, and we expect to make 10% for you on the money you put up. Your risk will be nominal because we shall form a selling group im-

mediately to take the liability off your hands. Let us know in ten minutes, please.

This is pretty much the way such affairs were arranged and managed in this period. The underwriting was to be managed by Dillon Read and US&FS, which would head a group of 382 participants, including such familiar names as Armin Schlesinger, Edward Wilmer, Bernard Baruch, and all of the Dillon Read partners, who presumably made their commitments prior to March 16. The understanding revolved around the purchase syndicate, called "Managers" in the documents, and the selling syndicate, referred to as "Group," the former to underwrite the transaction, the latter to distribute its securities. The selling syndicate was Dillon Read itself, with a small interest going to US&FS.[24]

The selling syndicate agreed to remit 25 percent of the profits to the purchase syndicate, "until there is divided between the Group and the Managers' profits aggregating 5 percent upon the Group commitment (profits aggregating $7,300,000). Thereafter remaining profits to be divided 25 percent to the Group and 75 percent to the Managers." As for the division of the purchase syndicate's portion of the profits, US&FS was to receive 10 percent, Dillon Read 90 percent.

The selling syndicate organized a flotation of when, as, and if, or "temporary" stocks and bonds as they were sometimes known. The funds obtained from these underwritings would be used to pay the Dodge Brothers' owners. There was to be a $75 million 6 percent fifteen-year convertible debenture, 850,000 shares of 7 percent cumulative preferred stock, 1.5 million shares of Class "A" common, and 500,000 shares of Class "B" common. These securities were registered the following day, April 8, and turned over to the selling syndicate.

Units comprised of 100 shares of preferred and 100 of common were offered at $10,000, which raised $85 million. Add this to the $75 million in bonds sold at par. The issue sold out quickly and went to a premium. Afterwards it was learned the selling syndicate had placed the issue before it was formally offered. The shares went to a premium shortly after the public sale.[25]

Dillon Read received $74.25 million for the debentures, and

another $85 million came from the sale of the cumulative preferred stock. Thus, Dillon Read took in $159.25 million from the sale of Dodge securities, and paid the Dodge interests $146 million. The gross profit on the deal was $13.25 million. In addition, the purchase syndicate retained 367,500 shares of Class "A" nonvoting common shares, and 472,500 shares of Class "B" common, which had sole voting rights. The profit to Dillon Read itself, as member of both syndicates and after deductions, was $8.9 million in cash, 254,125 Class "A" shares, and 322,875 Class "B" shares. Had these shares been retained until the time Dillon Read sold Dodge, they would have been worth another $3.9 million for the "A" shares and $2.5 million for the "B" shares. Dillon Read would not keep all the profit. Multiple Cord Development Corp. was to receive a percentage of Dillon Read's proceeds. On December 10, 1924, Dillon Read sent a memo of understanding to Schwartz, confirming he was to receive "25 percent of our originating profit from the business." On May 5, Dillon Read received a receipt from Schwartz for $410,652, presumably partial payment for his services.[26]

It had been a riskless deal. As the Dillon Read attorney noted at the time, "It would be difficult to maintain the position that either Dillon, Read & Co. or the participants had any beneficial interest at the time of issue in the stock which had been sold in advance."[27] Dillon implied as much in 1934 when discussing his approach to the business. "If you had relied on houses like ourselves you probably would not have had the automobile industry in this country. We would not have risked it, and we would have taken it upon ourselves as a virtue."[28]

The Dodge transaction was a classic Clarence Dillon operation—bold, audacious, and carefully planned, with a minumum danger of failure and financial exposure. Dillon Read's investment had been time, effort, expenses, and most important, imagination.

The funds were released to the Dodge heirs in the form of a check for $146 million, which then was deposited to the accounts of the widows. Photographs of the checks appeared in newspapers and magazines throughout the world, usually to illustrate articles about Clarence Dillon.

The Dodge purchase certainly was a major coup primarily because of its size and the publicity it received. In all other respects, however, the Goodyear rescue was more complicated, difficult, and dangerous. Dillon Read acquired Dodge when both the auto company and the investment bank had credibility on the Street; it had rescued Goodyear when the firm was considered a secondary factor in the industry. This is not to suggest the Dodge purchase was inconsequential, but rather it was simpler, in most ways involved less risk.

That Dillon Read had bested J. P. Morgan & Co. captured the attention of the tabloid press, which dramatized what the newspapers considered a titanic struggle between the old warrior and the new challenger, which certainly wasn't the situation.[29] At the time of the sale Dodge had no investment banker, and so anyone seeking the business would not be breaching Wall Street practices. Dillon Read participated in Morgan syndicates before the Dodge purchase and afterwards as well.

Before turning to Dillon Read's attempts to operate the automobile company it would be useful to understand its business activities in the second half of the year.

The other important Dillon Read initial underwriting in this period was the conception and placement of the National Cash Register (NCR) equity issue. NCR was one of the nation's oldest business machine companies, founded by John H. Patterson who in 1884 purchased control of what then was a moribund outfit for $6,500. In shrewdly capitalizing upon developments in retailing and pioneering in salesmanship, Patterson made NCR the premium business machine company in America. By any standard the company was a huge success. There were problems, however. In his later years Patterson had become quite restrained, refusing to enter new areas in the expanding business machine industry. In 1921 NCR had sales of $29 million and profits of $2.8 million, and dominated the cash register business. Patterson was content to let it go at that.[30]

Patterson died the following year and nominally was succeeded by his son, Frederick, who together with his sister owned 51 percent of the company's stock; the rest was in the hands of relatives, friends, and associates. The firm's real leader, however, was its vice president, John H. Barringer, who was every bit as hard-driving as Patterson and eager to develop new markets and products. Even before Patterson's death he had ordered research into the creation of accounting machines, and the 2000 model, deemed the most advanced of its period, was ready for delivery in 1923. It met with widespread acceptance, and boosted sales and earnings. For 1925 NCR's profits were $7.8 million on sales of $40 million. In addition to having 85 percent of the world's cash register business, it was now a leading factor in an even faster-growing business.

NCR's performance and potential were well known on Wall Street. The company was regularly visited by investment bankers hoping to recapitalize the company and then sell its shares to the public. Frederick Patterson didn't seem interested, but in the winter of 1925 he started to stir. "If I could sell and still keep the management," he told Stanley Allyn, one of his officers, "I might be interested." Allyn replied, "Well, there ought to be a way to achieve that. The house of Dillon, Read recently set up a situation of that kind for the Goodyear people. Shall we sound them out?"[31]

Allyn contacted Dillon Read soon after. The bank was interested in the kind of arrangement Patterson wanted. Dillon dispatched Karl Behr and a group of accountants to NCR's Dayton headquarters. Behr opened an office at the plant, interviewed every important member of the management team twice, and pored over the records. NCR indeed was in excellent shape, in a financial as well as operational sense. The balance sheet was strong: $41 million in assets exclusive of patents and goodwill. There was no funded debt. After this thorough investigation Behr recommended making a bid for the underwriting.[32]

Dillon Read intended to recapitalize the company with 1.1 million shares of Class "A" common stock and 400,000 shares of Class "B," the latter having the right to elect a majority of the board of directors so long as the company paid a dividend of at least $3 a year on the common. This would enable Dillon Read to satisfy two constituencies: the Patterson interests would be assured of continued control, while potential investors would be all but granted the $3 payout. Dillon Read would purchase the entire issue of Class "A" stock, while the Class "B" would be distributed among the present owners. This part of the transaction was completed in late December 1925.[33]

On January 3 Dillon Read announced its intention to sell 1.1 million shares of NCR, with the Street forecasting that the price would be around $60, making it what then was the largest pure equity offering in American history. Immediately orders flowed into the company, not only from all over the United States, but Europe as well. Interest was heightened when rumors surfaced, quickly denied, that NCR intended using the proceeds of the sale to purchase the cash register business of Remington Arms.[34]

Dillon Read told reporters that one unusual aspect of the underwriting was that it would be submitted not only in the United States but in response to popular demand in Switzerland, the Netherlands, the United Kingdom, and Canada. The offering was made the following day and immediately sold out. The only surprise was the price: $50 instead of the expected $60. The stock opened for trading on a "when issued" basis at 52⅞, and the final distribution of the stock was made by Dillon Read at 54¼, the difference between the $50 and the distribution prices representing additional profit for the underwriter.[35]

A Dillon Read document of the period states that the purchase syndicate profit for the NCR restructuring was $851,739.53; the selling syndicate profit, $10,940.34; the total profit, $862,676.87.[36] Except for the Dodge operation, this was the firm's most lucrative single deal to that time. In addition, NCR was to become a Dillon Read client; later on Behr joined the board of directors, and there would be additional underwritings.

Some newspapers took note of the underwriting with front page stories. "Purchase of the NCR Company and the distribution of its securities to the public within a year after he had electrified the financial world by outbidding J. P. Morgan & Co. in a bitter struggle for the Dodge Brothers Automobile Company, has earned for Mr. Dillon, at 43, the sobriquet of 'The Wizard of Wall Street,' " was quite typical.[37] Writing that Dillon had become the very symbol of a triumphant and self-confident American finance, one journalist stated, "It seems that there is an inexhaustible supply of anecdotes of the lives of such Wall Street figures as Gould, Vanderbilt, Gates, Harriman, Schiff, and Morgan, and now a new figure has joined the long procession of men who have made Wall Street famous—Clarence Dillon."[38] That same year *The Magazine of Wall Street* asked, "Will Clarence Dillon capture the imagination of the public as did that titanic figure J. P. Morgan the elder, or that genius, E. H. Harriman?" and answered in the positive.[39] The *Hartford Daily Courant* put it this way:[40]

His firm, Dillon, Read & Co., in the decade he has been connected with it, has risen from an obscure position in the banking world to one of the most powerful financial institutions in Wall Street, ranked by many as second to the powerful house of Morgan. . . .

It has become a tradition in Wall Street that Dillon, Read & Co. always has something big in the works. With the National Cash Register deal still unfinished, Mr. Dillon is now quietly working on a merger of German steel companies and is also laying plans for the development of a powerful banking group to rival that organized by J. P. Morgan & Co. to assist in the sale and distribution of its new offerings.

The scope of Dillon's reputation may be gauged by several rumors which made their way through the Street during the 1925 Christmas season and appeared in the national and then world press in the last two days of the year and into 1926. One report was that Chase and Mechanics and Metals National Banks were discussing a merger. John McHugh, Mechanics and Metals' president, confirmed the stories. Then a second rumor surfaced, this one that Mechanics and Metal was also discussing a merger with three and possibly four other banks: Chatham Phenix, National Park, and Chemical were in the group, with Central Union Trust considering association. Furthermore, so it was claimed, Dillon was masterminding the second combination, which he would control, and use its assets to bankroll several deals larger even than the Dodge Brothers purchase.

Dillon was a director and a major stockholder of the National Park and had representation at Central Union. As it happened there was no substance to the second rumor, but it did cause the price of shares of the companies involved to rise substantially. The first story was correct, however; on April 12, 1926, Chase and Mechanics and Metals merged.[41] Three years later, with Dillon Read's participation, Chase also absorbed National Park.[42]

The significance of this episode—the merger which did not take place—was that it was so credible. Dillon Read was just about to complete the much publicized NCR flotation. That it would attempt to put together a bank which would be second in size only to National City seemed quite plausible and is yet another indication of the firm's standing in the mid-1920s.[43]

· 8 ·

The Wizard of Wall Street, II

(1925–1928)

That the Dillon, Read & Co. of the 1920s was quite unlike the William A. Read & Co. of 1916 is quite obvious. How could it be otherwise, considering the aforementioned changes in the business climate and the need to adjust to them? There were differences within the firm, too, and these merit consideration. For one thing, Read's acceptance of a relatively minor though profitable role had been supplanted by Clarence Dillon's ambitions for industry leadership. Under Read the firm had been willing to settle for second- and third-bracket positions in underwritings. Now Dillon insisted on being included in special bracket position, meaning it was listed in the first level of underwriters in advertisements. Not only did special bracket status contribute to the profits and earn subsequent underwritings, but it reinforced the firm's sense of well-being in the investment banking community. Indeed, Dillon aspired to be listed alone on the top of the tombstone advertisements, as syndicate manager. As sole manager Dillon Read would not have to share fees with any other bank. The firms which joined the syndicate would have to commit themselves for the sale of those shares they took, and risk their capital on the transaction. Thus the manager would have rewards but few risks, which was the way Dillon liked to operate.[1]

Even so, Dillon Read was still regarded as an upstart operation by the Establishment firms. As Robert Lovett of Brown Brothers, himself a banker in this period, asserted, "The old line houses stood aloof and apart from the Dillon Read operations. Dillon Read was ranked as aggressive, opportunistic, and flamboyant. It was something of a pirate ship, roaming the market for booty, indifferent to the orderly development of American industry."[2]

By its very nature investment banking is a service business, primarily concerned with raising money for clients by selling their securities to investors. In bankers like Dillon, Forrestal, and Eberstadt, Dillon Read had a team which excelled at obtaining clients, and in Phillips, Bollard, and others it had a cadre of excellent salesmen.

Forrestal clearly was the coming man. No one at the firm could match him in placements. When he arrived his salary had been $8 a week plus a $350 draw against commissions, which were 1 percent of total sales. In 1923 Forrestal was made a partner because, as columnist Arthur Krock later claimed, it was cheaper to give him a partnership than to pay that commission.[3]

Forrestal had more duties than the title indicates. In reality, he was in charge of syndicate operations. This meant he had responsibilities for negotiating or making bids on new issues, assembling the syndicate, and making certain the bonds and stocks were placed. In today's investment banks such functions are handled by scores of bankers. Forrestal did much of the work himself, assisted by clerks and two or three other bankers familiar with the operation and knowledgeable about potential customers. The day prior to major flotations Forrestal and the team would remain at work until well after the offices closed, sometimes sleeping on couches because they were so tired, or simply because they lacked time to go home before the markets opened. He had fashioned a large sales force which was considered one of the firm's more important assets, and enabled it to place those large underwritings of the period.[4] The story is told that one day, while Paul Nitze and Dillon were lunching, Forrestal entered the room excitedly to announce he had come up with a strategy to beat a competitor in a business deal, and would put his plan into action "the day after tomorrow." Dillon said he should do it the next day, and after a moment Forrestal replied he would do it tomorrow afternoon. What was wrong with the morning, Dillon wanted to know. "I'm getting married," was Forrestal's response.[5]

Forrestal clearly was the second most important figure at the firm, having earned that status through intelligence, perseverance, and application. He also excelled in developing appropriate financing vehicles for clients and obtaining and retaining new business. Dillon had come to look upon Forrestal as a younger version of himself. They had the same qualities, and, in addition, both were classic outsiders on the Wall Street scene who had obliged the Establishment to treat them with respect. From his beginnings at Dillon Read Forrestal had looked upon Dillon as a mentor and took it for granted the older man held him in high regard.[6]

By the late 1920s Dillon Read had some 750 personnel in offices throughout the country, many of whom were engaged in selling securities to the public.[7] Several branches, such as those in Boston, Philadelphia, Pittsburgh, and Chicago, were quite sizable. The office on Nassau Street in New York was one of the largest, with forty salesmen in 1929. Others, including the ones in Seattle, San Francisco, and Dallas, were much smaller. Many more, like the modest operation in Hempstead, Long Island, then a rural town, were nothing more than storefronts from which a few salesmen left each morning making calls on individuals, attempting to sell them bonds.

By then the salesmen were set on a different career track than the investment bankers. Typically an aspiring investment banker would start out as an office boy, while individuals recruited for sales entered a class of perhaps thirty to forty or so aspirants. When their brief education was over the new salesmen would be placed in an office, given a desk and telephone, and left pretty much on their own. The fortunate ones had friends and relatives to whom they might sell the Dillon Read underwritten securities, most of which were bonds. The others had to fend for themselves, making cold calls out of the telephone books, hoping for orders.[8]

Dillon Read's sales offices were quite unlike those of later generations, and not at all similar to full-line brokerages. The salesmen's primary task was the sale to the public of those Dillon Read-sponsored securities. Each day they would be informed of issues for which Dillon Read was a member of the selling group, and told of the allocation. They then would attempt to place these securities. To please a particularly good client who wanted non–Dillon Read securities they might attempt to make a purchase of them from another house, but this was unusual. Clients wishing to buy or sell stock could do so through Dillon Read, which utilized the services of NYSE members, most notably Dominick & Dominick, in the operation. The firm did not actively seek such accounts, however, and engaged in the brokerage business as a courtesy to those who were primarily interested in bonds.

In the 1920s bond buyers might have many brokers, each affiliated with an investment bank which participated in syndications, who would be called when the buyer learned of a particularly interesting new issue. Likewise, the Dillon Read salesmen were not interested in the secondary market, although they would make markets in old Dillon Read underwritten securities. Nonetheless a client wishing to purchase an old bond might have difficulties, and in such cases the spreads between the bids and asks usually were quite large.[9]

Salesmen were paid commissions, with the totals generally geared to volume. They were supported by information generated by the Industrial Department. "We were a source of information that anybody in our organization could reach to obtain existent information on any company that an investor or an investing client of theirs wished to know about," recalled Karl Behr.[10]

Due largely to the expansion prompted by the development of a retail business, the Dillon Read payroll went from $201,620 in 1922 to $534,090 in 1925. After making allowance for reserves, the net profits were divided among the partners according to shares, determined by Dillon himself, who allotted himself a 40 percent share. He decided what the others would receive based primarily upon his feelings regarding the individual's value to the firm and performance the previous year.[11]

Dillon Read wasn't involved with trading activities which would have required large amounts of capital, so there was little need to retain capital in the firm. Rather, its investment bankers structured deals and were able to borrow short term from a number of banks whenever funds were required. Dillon was also on the board of several banks, which may have provided him with loans when necessary. Among these were the Chase, Central Hanover, and Central Union. Douglas Dillon recalls, "They operated on borrowed money to clear these deals. They borrowed overnight, at the bank, and paid it [the loan] off two days later. The banks didn't ask for Dillon Read's bank statement, or anything like that. They just thought they were right. They knew my father had a lot of money. Most of them were that way."[12]

As noted, while the bankers' base pay was modest, sizable remuneration could be obtained from sharing in underwritings and other business.[13] The same was true for salesmen. A bond man could hope to make $5,000 or so on commissions, but there were some who were in the $10,000 range.[14]

Even so, investment bankers had no reason to envy the salesmen. They had other, often more rewarding sources of income. Partners participated in deals at wholesale and then could sell at retail; we have seen how they were able to purchase shares in US&FS at 20 cents and then sell them at enormous profits. There were other kinds of participation. Dillon Read was only one of the firms in a constellation. Eastern Corporation, which embraced Ashland Securities, was owned by the partners as a private investment affiliate. Apparently Eastern would be allotted securities from the choicer underwritings, which either would be retained and managed, or sold in the aftermarket; in this seven-year period Eastern had profits of $14.5 million, which presumably were divided according to shares. Other affiliates and their dates of organization included Plymouth Corp. (1922), German Credit & Investment Corp. (1926), New Eastern Corp. (1927), East 80th Street Corp. (1927), Pottersville Water Company (1927), the Bristol Corp. (1928), and Surrey Corp. (1928).[15] And of course there also were US&FS and US&IS. In Dillon's case, we have seen one of the operations of Nassau Corporation and Leonard Kennedy & Co. Whether or not there were others is not known.

There is no way of knowing even the approximate amounts of remuneration the top men at Dillon Read received in this decade. Considering their life-styles, and some information revealed in the next decade, it must have run into the millions for some, and for Dillon himself much more.

During the six years from 1922 to 1927, Dillon Read, by itself and without the subsidiaries, had a net profit of over $31 million.

DILLON, READ & CO., 1922–1927

Year	Net Profit
1922	$ 2,450,586
1923	1,149,815
1924	4,593,951
1925	12,295,281
1926	8,331,672
1927	2,346,299

SOURCE: "Dillon, Read & Company—1927 Earnings," document in the possession of Dorothy Dillon Eweson.

The firm's greatest growth was in the early part of the 1920s; its most profitable years were 1925 and 1926, the result of the Dodge Brothers and NCR deals among others.

In common with all investment banks in those pre–Securities and Exchange Commission years, Dillon Read kept spotty records. The federal government did not regulate the industry and New York State did little in this area, confining its attention to sporadic forays to unearth swindlers. The investment banks maintained records for tax and legal reasons, and all else was discarded.

Another reason for the lack of documents was the nature of the business and the way it was conducted. Anyone attempting to understand Dillon Read and other investment banks of the 1920s by assuming that they were companies with a definite structure, including lines of command and responsibilities, will be perplexed. Dillon Read was a collection of partners, each with generalized responsibilities, but also always aware of targets of opportunity. There was no hard-and-fast separation between domestic and foreign business or bonds and equities. Eberstadt was assigned to Europe, but he was called home when needs dictated. Dean Mathey had a special interest in the petroleum and natural gas industries, and generated much business there in during the interwar period. Harry Egly worked with Forrestal on syndications; after Dillon Read obtained an underwriting he would line up the firms which sold the securities to the public and institutions. Bob Christie was primarily concerned with domestic issues. Among his other assignments Bob Hayward handled the Brazilian business, and in addition had general responsibilities for running the office.[16] Dillon roamed the landscape seeking means to capitalize upon his expertise and reputation, and the same was true for Forrestal and most of the others. They would generate documents, but discard most of them when no longer necessary for ongoing business. There were rosters of underwritings, copies of tombstone advertisements, prospectuses, legal papers, and little else. Memoranda and like records which might offer insights into the way business was conducted are scarce.

Dillon kept a diary for several years and a business journal for others, which more resemble minutes of meetings than analysis of operations. That these survive, along with occasional memos, is more the consequence of happenstance and personality, as well as good fortune, than planning.

One untitled document which managed to elude the scrap heap is a memorandum from a partner, probably Dillon, regarding operations in 1927. The document asserts that two-thirds of the firm's gross profit of $7.7 million derived from repeat financings from established clients, and the other third from new customers. Half of all company profits came from underwritings for Canada, Latin America, Europe, and Japan. All but $137,532 came from bonds.

The profits from those syndicates which Dillon Read entered as participants were quite small. A minor bracket role in a Chicago, North West 4½s fetched the company commissions of only $85. Perhaps Dillon Read entered this syndicate either to obtain desired bonds for a client or a member of the firm, or as a courtesy. Or it might have been that the bonds couldn't be sold at the offering price and it had to be lowered in order to make the sales and clear the account. There was a $17.50 commission for a Chicago, Rock Island, and Pacific 4½s of 1952, $148 for a Massey Harris 5s of 1947, and a few additional ones in the triple-digit category. The largest profit from a participation was $58,622 from the State Mortgage Bank of Jugoslavia 7s of 1957, which was broken down to $57,213 from wholesale and $1,409 from retail operations. In all, Dillon Read was a member of ninety-three syndicates in which it was not the lead underwriter. For these it received commissions of $530,492, which averages to $5,704 each.

An internal document indicates Dillon Read was lead underwriter for thirty-three issues in 1927 on which the commissions were $3,457,145, for an average of $104,762. Some of the profits were small—$44 on a $5.5 million City of Genoa, Italy 5s of 1927 and $153 on the $7,650,000 Shinyetsu Electric Power 6½s of 1952, this probably due to weak markets and the need to sell the bonds at a discount. The largest profits on underwritings were $590,764 from a $41.5 million underwriting of 6½ percent 30-year bonds for Brazil, $564,758 on a 7 percent 31-year bond for Bolivia, and $358,395 on a 20-year 5½ percent General Cable bond issue. While a $30 million City of Milan underwriting in 1927 garnered prestige for the firm, the profits were only $115,901. According to this document, in the foreign field, Dillon Read earned $61,535 from Canadian business, $614,378 from Europe (with $319,804 from a single underwriting for United Steel Works), and $1,155,521 from Latin America, accounted for by those two previously cited issues. All of the rest, except for the Shinyetsu Electric Power issue, was domestic business. What is remarkable was that the firm did not report a loss on any of its undertakings. This doubtless was due in large part to Dillon's insistence that everything be in place before the deal was set into motion.

Yet in 1932, in testimony before a Senate committee looking into the sales of foreign bonds in the United States, Dillon provided statistics on the issues, including *gross* profits which differ from the figures in the internal document. According to this, some of the profits were quite sizable—$467,125 for a $25 million Brazil 8s of 1941 issued in 1921, $828,550 for a $35 million Poland 8s of 1950 issued in 1925, $551,872 for $30 million United Steel Works 6½s of 1951, and $539,308 for a $41.5 million Brazil 6½s of 1957. While the figures in the internal document approximate those provided Congress, there are differences, due presumably to different methods of calculating profits.[17]

Dodge Brothers did not require much by way of new financing in this period. After the initial underwritings Dillon Read sold an $8,250,000 note issue for the firm in April 1925. There was no need for additional capital. As noted, Dodge was highly solvent at the time of the sale, and the funds raised through the original recapitalization provided the company with ample financial resources. On the other hand, the company did not flourish as anticipated.

Dillon's original plan for Dodge was to utilize it as the core of a major new automobile company which in time would be larger than General Motors. To accomplish this would require mergers, and several candidates were considered—Hudson, Nash, and

SUMMARY OF DILLON, READ & CO., FOREIGN ISSUES,
1919–1931

Total Issued	$ 1,491,228,542
Total Outstanding, Jan. 1, 1931	1,189,653,300
Retired by Sinking Fund and Call	301,575,242
Amount Originally Placed Abroad	270,918,000
Segregation of Issues Outstanding	
Canada	499,376,300
Germany	252,701,000
Holland	115,000,000
France	22,779,300
Italy	32,304,200
Poland	27,300,000
South America	209,359,000
Japan	30,833,500
	1,189,653,300

SOURCE: United States, 72nd Cong., 1st Sess., Hearings before the Committee on Finance, United States Senate, January 4–7, 1932, "Sales of Foreign Bonds or Securities in the United States," p. 501.

Chrysler among them—but nothing came of these efforts. With this out of the way, Dillon set about running the firm through his own management.[18]

Dillon Read's management of Dodge during the next three years provides a near-classic case study on the limitations of financiers as general managers. Investment bankers of those years were generalists, often adept at analyzing a company but with little experience in running one. The best of them excelled at deal-structuring, and when one was completed they turned quickly to another, moving from deal to deal, underwriting to underwriting. Dillon had no difficulty switching from Dodge to Vereinigte Stahl-werke to NCR, from an underwriting in Brazil to a real estate investment in Manhattan. True, he might devote several months to the creation of understandings in Europe, but this was atypical.

Perhaps because of this investment bankers tended to treat industrial management as a by-product of financing, and not significant in itself and requiring quite a different set of talents and concerns. They appeared to believe that just as a good investment banker could handle a variety of underwritings in different industries and governments, so a capable manager might easily be transferred from one company or even industry to another. Speaking when Dodge was still a family company, a factory manager reflected on just what that meant.[19]

> If we had been obliged to get permission from a board of directors, from banking interests, or from outside stockholders, for the expenditure of the millions that we have put into new buildings, new machinery, and new processes, it [the expansion program] couldn't have been done. Things go smoothly when the actual owners are right in the factory, and are the most enthusiastic of all in having the best.

In the first months of Dillon Read control Dodge possessed strong professional management. Haynes remained until April 1926. Ray Graham became general manager, Robert Graham vice president and general sales manager, and Joseph Graham vice president in charge of manufacturing. They remained at Hamtramck for three months. The Grahams then sold their share of Graham Brothers Truck to Dodge, retired as the largest individual shareholders in Dodge other than Dillon Read, and a year later sold their stock and used the proceeds to purchase Paige-Detroit Motor Car, which they transformed into Graham-Paige Motors.[20]

Haynes's retirement and the Grahams's departure caught no one by surprise. The industry knew Dillon Read meant to install its own management at Dodge in the form of Edward Wilmer. The rescue of Goodyear was long completed by then, and Wilmer could easily be spared for another assignment. Before going to Hamtramck, however, he was rewarded for his efforts by being named a partner at Dillon Read, this being announced on April 20, 1925.[21] Thus, Wilmer went from law to industrial experience at the Schlesinger interests to the management of Goodyear, and now would combine leadership of Dodge Brothers with part-time work in investment banking.

On April 18 Wilmer addressed the Dillon Read sales organization on the subject of Dodge Brothers, and on this occasion indicated his ambitions for the firm. "I have had little to do with the motor industry," he confessed, before launching into an analysis of operations. As Wilmer saw it, the company's strengths lay in its dealer organization, modern plant, and reputation. That the facility was operating at close to capacity was a critical weakness. As Dodge sales expanded, either another shift would be needed or the firm would have to establish a second plant. Enlargement at Hamtramck would be troublesome, since the company did not own adjacent properties and these would be difficult and expensive to purchase.[22]

Wilmer's address, delivered a month before taking command, revealed his lack of a clear understanding of the situation at Dodge Brothers, and the automobile business in general.[23] He had no knowledge of automotive technology or the nature of markets, and a simplistic view of some major changes affecting the industry, such as the rise of installment purchases and annual model changes. Yet with Dillon's blessings he assumed full command. This was in sharp contrast to the approach at Goodyear, where at first he was content to leave management to George Stadelman and Paul Litchfield, while he concentrated on finances. Wilmer could call upon some of Dodge's remaining officers, including vice presidents A. T. Waterfall and A. Z. Mitchell. These were relatively junior officials, however, and lacked the authority Stadelman and Litchfield exercised at Goodyear.

Given this, Wilmer was bound to have difficulties and make missteps. For example, traditionally it cost Dodge Brothers approximately $100 more to construct its sedans than it cost Ford, and this was reflected in the prices, usually $100 or so higher than comparable Fords. A salesman by temperament, Dillon assumed that the celebrated Dodge dealerships might be able to extract a higher profit than that. This led him into profound error of judgment about the relative importance as well as the complexity of manufacturing operations in the automobile business. In his view, it was the dealers, not the managers of the assembly lines, who were the key element at Dodge. This perhaps was the reason why the following January management announced that henceforth two dealers would serve on the board of directors. It would also account for the new concentration on style and design, quite a change for the company.[24]

Under the old management all Dodges were powered by rugged and economical four-cylinder engines. Shortly after arriving Wilmer told his engineers he wanted to offer a six-cylinder model as soon as possible. At the same time designers were asked to create new, more streamlined bodies, the understanding being that Wilmer expected to have annual changes. He also notified the dealers that he intended to create a method by which they could offer customers the option of purchasing their cars on an installment basis. These changes, he thought, would enable Dodge to charge higher prices for its automobiles.[25]

Wilmer did not wait for the changes to alter the prices. They were quietly raised in 1926, and as a result sales sagged. He hastily reversed field and lowered prices. This led to record sales, but lower profits. Morale declined at the plant due to tinkering by management perceived to be amateur, so Wilmer resigned his Dillon Read partnership as of July 31 to devote himself full-time to the company. He conceded error during a January 1927 dealers' meeting. "The answer determined by your management at that time was greater volume, lower costs, lower prices, in fact drastic price reductions, lower margins for us, lower margins for you, and with that decision came a new strain upon you and a strain upon us for a restoration of legitimate margins because those same reductions went extremely far."[26]

New models geared at turning things around were introduced in late 1926. As expected, these were more stylish than the previous Dodges, but weren't up to the traditional Dodge quality insofar as engineering and workmanship were concerned. Prices were raised once again, as Wilmer thought he could recover costs in this way. The object was to position Dodge against Buick, not Ford and Chevrolet. The strategy didn't work. Moreover, the new models soon developed mechanical problems which surprised those who were accustomed to the reliable products for which the company had been so well known. Successful changes in design could not be rendered by fiat; more attention had to be paid to manufacturing systems.

Wilmer could not have blamed this for all of these troubles. In a good economic environment the new models might have been better received. There was an economic slump in 1927, however, and sales were down throughout much of the industry, with Dodge declining more sharply than most. Ford produced the last Model T on May 31 and then shut down for the rest of the year. Dodge was well situated to pick up at least some sales from Ford owners. As it happened, Chevrolet won much of this business, while the new General Motors entry, Pontiac, was taking sales from Dodge.

AMERICAN PASSENGER CAR PRODUCTION, 1925–1927
(auto company figures in thousands)

Year	Total	Chevrolet	Ford	Pontiac	Chrysler*	Dodge	Dodge as % of total
1925	3,735	445	1,643	—	132	260	6.8
1926	3,692	589	1,368	77	162	332	7.2
1927	2,937	1,750	356	135	182	205	7.0

* Company was known as Maxwell until 1927.

SOURCE: *Historical Statistics of the United States*, p. 716; Heasley, *The Production Figures for U.S. Cars*, pp. 23, 33, 36, 117, 149; *Moody's Manual of Investments*, 1928, p. 49.

To add to Wilmer's troubles, there was some grumbling in the dealerships. Financing arrangements were worked out with C.I.T., which as has been noted was a Dillon Read client.[27] Having operated without such sales devices for so long, and indoctrinated by the previous management on the dangers of such methods, the Dodge dealers did not feature this profitable business. Three out of four American automobiles were being purchased on the basis of installment payments in this period, while less than half the Dodges were taken that way. Alluding to the problems of 1926–27, Wilmer told his dealers:[28]

We all struggled for the recovery of legitimate margins. The high-pressure production into which we went, the high-pressure selling for which you organized and into which you went, the product difficulties that I say frankly you had and we had (some of them difficulties in design, others the result of poor workmanship), all bad enough, were further complicated by changes in executive personnel, by the problem of settling of this huge organization after the transition in ownership that I have told you—all serving to complicate a complicated year in a way I sincerely trust we may never again experience.

An indication of Dodge's plight was the change in its working capital: in its 1927 annual report the company restated the earlier figures. In the 1925 report the ratio of current assets to current liabilities for year-end 1924 was shown as a strong 6.38–1. This ratio was reported as 5.07 to 1 in the 1927 report. It was quite obvious that Dodge Brothers was in less than robust shape. The company's statistics told the story. Revenues rose in 1926 but

DODGE BROTHERS STATISTICS, 1924–1927
(all figures except earnings per share in millions of dollars)

Year	Sales	Profit	Earnings Per Share	Debt
1924	191.7	17.5	4.75	—
1925	216.8	22.6	6.84	59.5
1926	253.0	21.6	6.46	58.4
1927	173.6	14.8	1.55	57.3

SOURCE: *Moody's Industrial Manual, 1923–1928*, pp. 1274–75.

DODGE BROTHERS STATISTICS, 1924–1927
(figures in millions of dollars)

Year	Current Assets	Current Liabilities	Net Working Capital	Ratio
1924	60.5	11.9	48.6	5.07 to 1
1925	51.1	18.3	32.8	2.80 to 1
1926	49.6	12.7	36.8	3.89 to 1
1927	46.7	15.5	31.3	3.03 to 1

SOURCE: Dodge Brothers, Inc., *Chairman's Annual Report to Board of Directors, December 31, 1927*, p. 7.

profits declined as a result of management practices, and both fell in 1927.

On January 6, 1928, Clarence Dillon addressed his partners and salesmen on the general health of several companies in which the firm had an interest, including NCR, Goodyear, and Dodge Brothers. He attempted to portray a troubled situation as optimistically as he dared:[29]

When we went into the Dodge situation we realized at once that the line of cars would have to be redesigned, which was a stupendous undertaking. Not only did we have to build a new car, but we had to build a six-cylinder car—a new line of cars. Mr. Wilmer took that job in hand.

Mr. Ford, as you know, simply redesigned a four-cylinder car and shut down his plant for the better part of a year to do it. Mr. Wilmer kept Dodge running through a year when he not only redesigned a four-cylinder car from the ground up, but he brought out a six-cylinder car. They also rounded out the entire line of trucks by new six-cylinder products. Finally he brought out a new car which is a real innovation in automobile construction, and probably the most sensational thing of its kind that has been done in the motor industry in a good many years. He did all of those things and kept the Dodge plant running all the time, selling its product, paid his charges, both interest and preferred dividends, and added three or four millions of dollars to surplus while he was doing it.

I think that that is one of the most ousatnding industrial achievements that I know anything about. If any of you know about mechanics you can appreciate what problems Wilmer met in plant operation, all in one year, and keeping going and selling nearly 200,000 cars.

But in truth Dillon knew better. The new Dodges, hastily developed and poorly built, were priced at $1,500 (compared to $495 for the soon-to-be-released Ford Model A) and were not selling. The dealers were demoralized. Dillon realized he was in trouble; even then, he was attempting to sell Dodge Brothers.[30]

As with newcomers at any old institutions, neophytes at Dillon Read can count upon being told stories of how the company began, how it evolved, and tales of spectacular successes and failures. In time these are embellished to the point of distortion. While historians often can rectify misapprehensions, they should not overlook them, for in such beliefs can be found important aspects of the company's culture.

When they first arrived at Dillon Read, today's old-timers were told by Clarence Dillon's contemporaries of how he boldly played Walter Chrysler off against General Motors' Pierre Du Pont in selling Dodge Brothers. According to the story, Dillon had Chrysler in one hotel room and a General Motors' team in an adjoining one, and shuttled between them, obliging each to raise his bid for the valuable property.

It happened quite differently.

Rumors regarding additional Dillon Read activities in the automobile industry were fairly common by early 1926, and there may have been some grounds to them. In April Dillon and several associates traveled to Detroit for a series of meetings with auto executives, but nothing came of them.[31] In February 1927 there were reports of further consolidation in the industry, one of which being that Dillon Read was on the prowl, seeking to make Dodge the centerpiece of a much larger company. The old stories regarding Packard and Briggs were revived, while Studebaker and Essex figured in other reports. None had any basis in fact, and perhaps were floated by Dillon Read to create interest in the Dodge situation.[32]

There was a potential purchaser—Walter Chrysler, one of the industry's giants. In fact, General Motors CEO Alfred Sloan had suggested that Dillon contact Chrysler in this regard.[33]

Chrysler was fifty-two years old in 1927, and was arguably the industry's most dynamic figure. After a successful career in railroading he went to work at Buick as a combination engineer-production supervisor in 1911; the following year, when Charles Nash left the Buick presidency to take the same post at the parent company, General Motors, Chrysler replaced him. Soon after, Chrysler was made a vice president at General Motors, where he remained until he retired in 1920. After three months of retirement Chrysler went to Willys-Overland, then in deep financial trouble. While Dillon was discussing possible financial aid with John Willys, Chrysler was revamping operations, effecting economies while improving vehicle quality. It was due to Chrysler's success that Willys did not require Dillon's assistance in extricating itself from near-bankruptcy. Chrysler also demonstrated remarkable stamina and capacity for work. While accomplishing all of this he took on the assignment of saving the near-bankrupt Maxwell Motor Company. Together with his record at Buick, all this earned him the reputation as the foremost manager in the industry.

In this period James Cox Brady and his brother, Nicholas, had an important stake in and were on the board of Maxwell. They came from a wealthy and ambitious family. The Bradys' father, Anthony Nicholas, had been a tea merchant who entered the gas industry, went on to consolidate the transit lines in New York, Washington, and Philadelphia, and from there entered the electric generation business, in which he amassed a fortune estimated at $100 million. At one time or another Anthony Brady served as president of New York Edison, Consolidated Gas and Electric, and the Kings County Electric Light and Power Company. The Brady sons were also in the electric power business, with Nicholas serving as chairman of New York Edison and Brooklyn Edison.[34]

The brothers hit it off with Chrysler from the beginning, and it wasn't long before they were urging Chrysler to leave Willys and take over at Maxwell, which was close to failure. Maxwell had a poor reputation and an inventory of 26,000 unsold cars. Worried investment bankers owned $26 million in Maxwell notes.[35] Foreclosure was imminent.

The Bradys knew they couldn't match Chrysler's salary—he received $1 million a year just before leaving Buick, and a like amount at Willys. All they could offer was $100,000 a year plus options on a large block of stock. Chrysler accepted, on condition the Bradys advance the company $15 million, which they did. So in 1924 Chrysler became Maxwell's CEO. He made some changes on the autos in inventory to make them more attractive, lowered their prices drastically to clean out the inventory, and then set about producing his own cars.

One of his early changes was to design and bring out a new model, which he called the Chrysler. It was mechanically advanced, featuring the nation's first high-compression engine and hydraulic brakes. While smaller outside than the Buick it was larger inside, accelerated more rapidly, offered better fuel economy, and sold for the same price. The car was a success. In 1924 the company sold 29,000 Chryslers and 50,000 Maxwells. The Maxwells were dropped the following year; by 1927 the newly renamed Chrysler Corporation sold 182,000 automobiles and was the fifth-largest company in the industry.[36]

This expansion caused problems. Chrysler was turning out cars so rapidly that he had trouble obtaining some parts from suppliers. The Chrysler 50 in particular was selling very well, taking sales from Dodge among others, but other sales were being lost for this reason. Chrysler had been obliged to purchase all of his cast-iron parts in 1927, because he lacked a foundry. In addition he was paying premium prices for forged parts. Maxwell had purchased a plant from Chalmers in 1922, and three years later the Detroit property of the American Motor Body Company, but still lacked sufficient production capacity. Moreover, construction of a new facility would take time, and Chrysler did not want to face the kind of predicament that caused Ford to close down. In addition, he calculated that a new plant would cost $75 million, and he didn't have the money. Nor could it be borrowed easily; in that kind of market, with Chrysler's credit rating, he might have been able to sell 20-year bonds offering a yield of 6½ percent, which would infer interest charges of around $5 million a year.

Down the road was the Dodge plant—modern, efficient, and not being fully utilized, with a foundry and forge shop. Already Chrysler was purchasing parts from Dodge. A merger of Chrysler and Dodge would resolve problems for both companies. Dillon would be able to extricate himself from an unhappy situation, while Chrysler would have his additional capacity plus what remained one of the industry's brightest nameplates. Some of the Dodge models would directly compete with Chryslers, but this could be rectified by repositioning the Chryslers to compete with General Motors' Cadillac and LaSalle, while Dodge would go against Buick.[37]

Chrysler had met Dillon on several occasions, and through the industry grapevine knew he might be willing to sell the company. In addition they had some mutual friends and associates who might have brought them together. In the early 1920s Dillon had become increasingly friendly with the Brady brothers. In 1924 he had arbitrated a particularly delicate matter involving two of their trusts, for which the Bradys were grateful. Contacts between them continued, with Dillon purchasing shares in Brooklyn Edison and taking an interest in the firm.[38] It seems plausible the Bradys were involved in subsequent discussions.

According to Chrysler's account, Dillon approached him one day in early April 1928, and in the course of conversation asked if he was in the mood for "some trading."[39] "Hell, Clarence, I don't want your plant. What'll I do with it?" was Chrysler's response. Dillon must have known Chrysler wasn't sincere. That month Chrysler introduced the new six-cylinder De Soto as a lower-cost offering to go with the Chrysler. Dodge would fit in nicely with the kind of company Chrysler was creating—he was, in effect, attempting what Dillon had contemplated in 1925, which is to say create a firm larger than General Motors or Ford. Ironically, both men recognized that Chrysler and Dodge would make a good fit.

The conversation continued, after which Dillon left with nothing resolved. He returned a few days later, and at one point started to talk price. Chrysler rejected it, but indicated he might be interested "if it was a bargain." He then went on to suggest that the price would be lower in a few years. "When a big outfit like that starts slipping it can go down fast." Dillon rejected this.

"We're doing splendidly," he answered, "only I think your crowd could do better with it."

Dillon raised the issue again. One day toward the end of May, according to Chrysler, Dillon walked into his office and moaned, "Walter, bankers got no business trying to run a great big industrial enterprise. What do I know about making automobiles and selling them? That's your game. Why don't you take this Dodge business?" Chrysler said he then showed interest, always assuming the price was right.

Ten days later Chrysler and his aides closeted at the Ritz Hotel with Dillon and his team. There was no General Motors executive in the next suite. From the first Chrysler insisted on obtaining the assent of 90 percent of the Dodge shares for a takeover, since he did not want to be troubled by minority interests. Dillon concurred, and said he would take care of the matter. In the end it was agreed the bank would sell Dodge Brothers to Chrysler for par value of $170 million in Chrysler paper plus the assumption of the Dodge debt. One share of Chrysler common would be exchanged for each share of Dodge preferred, and 1 share of Chrysler would also be offered for 5 shares of Dodge "A" stock or 10 shares of Dodge "B" stock, which came to approximately 1.3 million shares. On July 17 Chrysler increased its authorized shares from 3.2 million shares to 6 million and made preparations to issue the new shares to the Dodge stockholders.[40]

There were some obstacles to concluding the sale. Obtaining the necessary 90 percent of the shares proved more difficult than imagined. As Dillon, Forrestal, Eberstadt, and others worked full time at obtaining proxies, Dillon Read was obliged to ask for an extension, which Chrysler rejected. On July 22 Dillon had 86 percent of the preferred stock, 76 percent of the Class "A" common, and all but a small fraction of 1 percent of the Class "B" stock.[41]

The Dodge shareholders met in Baltimore on Saturday, July 28, without knowing whether the full 90 percent was in hand. By then Dillon Read had entered the open market to make purchases. Under a plan engineered by Forrestal and Eberstadt, Dillon Read purchased the needed shares and simultaneously sold them short. It was a perfectly hedged position, which made little sense from an investment point of view. This was not an investment, however, but rather an attempt to win votes. Dillon Read obtained the shares needed to make up the 90 percent, and with this, the deal was completed. The agreement was concluded at 5:30 on the afternoon of Monday, July 30.[42]

The following morning Dillon came to Chrysler's hotel suite to smoke cigarettes with him and take care of some last-minute details. He told Chrysler that Wilmer was prepared to cooperate in every way and would remain on as long as needed. Chrysler thanked him for the courtesy but replied, "Hell, Clarence, our boys moved in last night."[43] Rumors had circulated that Wilmer would take a place on the restructured Chrysler board, but this did not transpire. Dillon was named to the Finance Committee, however. In this way Dillon left the automobile business, and Chrysler became a viable rival to General Motors.

Both Dillon and Chrysler might have claimed to have the better part of the deal. Dillon Read had made substantial profits from Dodge Brothers in addition to those from the sale. The firm was now divorced from an operation which gave it no small number of headaches. Wilmer returned as partner at Dillon Read, and would not be placed in another industrial management role. For that matter, this marked the end of Dillon's foray into merchant banking. Never again would he venture into this area.

Dillon Read had paid $146 million in cash for Dodge Brothers. It received paper which at the time had a market value of $160 million for the company three years later. This did not mean Dillon Read had a profit of $14 million. For one thing, the firm had extracted large profits on the original deal and more thereafter. Chrysler paid for the acquisition with freshly printed common stock, not cash. Now Dillon Read and the other Dodge shareholders would have to sell its shares in an increasingly difficult market. Available evidence indicates Dillon Read sold or distributed those shares rather quickly. As for Chrysler, its total capitalization rose from 3.1 million shares to 4.4 million. Dividends paid on the common in 1928 were $3.00 per share, so it would appear the payouts to the former Dodge shareholders would come down to $4 million, to which should be added the interest on the Dodge Brothers' debt, a $56.7 million issue maturing in 1940, which had to be assumed, this being another $3.4 million annually. So the cost to Chrysler came to around $7.5 million a year when incidentals and costs relating to transition were taken into consideration.

On this basis it was a bargain. Recall Walter Chrysler's thought that a new facility would have cost $75 million, which would have approximately $5 million a year in debt service charges. For $2 million more Chrysler obtained a completed, modern plant, a well-trained work force, a dealership network still considered one of the best in the business, and a nameplate he would be able to restore to its former luster. Finally, at the time of the purchase, Dodge had cash and equivalent items of $11.8 million (in its 1927 Annual Report Dodge had $25.4 million in cash and equivalents). The pre-Dodge Chrysler Corporation had assets of $103.9 million; with Dodge assets it rose to $226.8 million. Chrysler's revenues for 1927 were $172.3 million; consolidated figures with Dodge for 1928 would be $315.3 million. Chrysler now had the capacity to produce well over 700,000 cars a year to be sold by 1,200 dealers. With the purchase Chrysler became what Dodge had been when Dillon Read purchased it: the world's third-largest automobile company.[44]

What neither Dillon nor Chrysler could have known, of course, was that the economy would peak in early 1929. The signs were there to be seen, analyzed, and acted upon, but few were able to interpret them in any meaningful manner. The rate of consumer spending was declining. It had advanced at a pace of 7.4 percent in 1927–28, and slowed to an unpropitious 1.5 percent in 1928–29. Business inventories more than tripled in 1929, while residential construction slowed. Industrial production started to weaken and unemployment to rise. In August the Federal Reserve Board raised the discount rate to 6 percent. All the elements for a recession were in place. President Hoover recognized them, and was prepared to act. He had expected a thunderstorm, and instead found himself in a typhoon.[45]

The stock market, we know now, peaked in September and then crashed in October. There would be some recovery in the markets, but the underlying economy was weak, and by 1931 there was little doubt the nation was in serious trouble. The slide into the Great Depression was under way.

At the time of the purchase most industry analysts thought Chrysler had overpaid for the company, that he had been out-maneuvered by Dillon.[46] Chrysler disagreed then, as he did six years later, when he still felt the need to defend the purchase.

"Downtown, in New York, in 1928, the consensus was: Chrysler's bought a lemon." This was not so, he claimed. "Buying the Dodge was one of the soundest acts of my life."[47] To this Clarence Dillon might have added that while buying Dodge was one of his more fortunate acts in the 1920s, selling the company was a close second. As a division of Chrysler, Dodge would not surpass its 1926 sales record until 1938.

· 9 ·

Denouement

(1929-1932)

Clarence Dillon greatly admired Ferdinand Eberstadt, perhaps because they were so alike. "Eberstadt enjoys the hunt," wrote one contemporary. "His eyes take on the intense look of a man in the midst of an absorbing game."[1]

Eberstadt had been displeased with his status and compensation at the firm ever since he and Forrestal had played so critical a role in the sale of Dodge to Chrysler. Dillon had increased their partnership interests in 1927, but while Forrestal had a 10 percent interest Eberstadt's was only 3 percent of profits and he felt that in the light of his successes he deserved at least 10 percent. Frustrated, Eberstadt had all but decided to leave and strike out on his own.

Eberstadt rightfully concluded that his reputation was such that clients would not be difficult to secure. If Forrestal joined him, however, they would possess the foundation for a major contender which might drain important underwriting business from Dillon Read. Uniting the two rising stars of Wall Street as it would, the new firm would be assured of instant success. There were also indications that several others at Dillon Read, also discouraged with their circumstances, including Bob Christie, might join them.

155

Eberstadt discussed the matter with Forrestal, who was under-standably reluctant to abandon what amounted to the number-two position at the firm.

By then Forrestal and Eberstadt had become even closer than before. Each probably recognized he possessed qualities absent in the other. As Charles Murphy, a journalist of the period who knew both men quite well, put it:[2]

> Eberstadt's relationship with Forrestal was, in many ways, a balance of opposite qualities. Eberstadt was brilliant, quick of thought and assertive. . . . Forrestal was intuitive, hesitant, re-served and assailed privately by doubts and misgivings. However, separately and together, Eberstadt and Forrestal towered above the senior financial leaders of their day.

Forrestal had become increasingly important to Dillon, who though only forty-eight years old in 1928, was beginning to show signs of becoming somewhat bored with investment banking. With the Brady brothers' assistance, Dillon had purchased land in Far Hills, New Jersey, where he created a magnificent estate adjacent to their residences and named it Dunwalke. There Dillon spent long weekends dabbling in farming, cattle raising, painting, and other pursuits. If Dillon withdrew from the day-to-day operations at Dillon Read, Forrestal would be his likely replacement, to hold power until Douglas Dillon was prepared to assume command.

By summer Eberstadt was growing more impatient for a sub-stantial increase in his partnership share. That autumn he dis-cussed the matter with Dillon, pointing out to the penny just how much business he had brought to Dillon Read, for which he de-served a larger share of the profits. The assignment of shares was a touchy issue at Dillon Read. Dean Mathey, who was as close to Dillon as most, later remarked:[3]

> Eber was a very tough and uncompromising person and very difficult to work with [but] if you think Eber was tough, you should have known Clarence Dillon. He was probably . . . the meanest man that ever lived as far as we [the partners] were concerned. To this day, I don't know whether he cheated us at the end of the year in divvying up the pie. He just called you in and told you what you were going to get with no rhyme, reason, or calcula-tions—very arbitrary.

Dillon refused to budge on the compensation issue, and according to Mathey, he fired Eberstadt on the spot.[4]

After a long vacation, Eberstadt was invited by Owen Young to join his team involved in renegotiating the German reparations payments, which resulted in the Young Plan of 1929. From there he went on to manage the New York branch of Otis and Co., Cleveland financier Cyrus Eaton's investment bank.[5] This hardly proved a fitting launching pad for his new career, however. The firm would come close to insolvency within less than three years, a casualty of the Great Crash and Depression.

Ostensibly Eberstadt had left Dillon Read because he was unhappy with his share of the profits, but the departure might have come because the profits themselves had declined considerably. As has been seen, profits in 1925 had been $12.3 million and fell to $8.3 million in 1926 and $2.3 million in 1927. By the spring of 1928, when Eberstadt had started to discuss leaving the firm, it was already evident there would be another dip that year. It would be reasonable to assume that due to his efforts Eberstadt's percentage of the compensation fund for 1927 doubled. Even so, this would mean that because of sharply lower earnings he would have received less than half the 1927 amount. Since there were fewer underwritings and deals, his receipts from this end of the business also would have been smaller. Of course it would have been even less had he remained.

Signs of problems on Wall Street surfaced in the spring of 1929, but this was not unusual; rarely is the financial sky cloudless. Indeed, Wall Street experienced a strong summer rally, after which prices started to decline. In September they fell at a disturbing rate. The dreaded word "panic" was now appearing in the newspapers. Yet that month $1.6 billion in underwritings came to market, of which $1 billion was in common stock. The equity sold that month was almost twice that of any *year* before 1928.

The decline quickened as September wore on and continued into October. Now the newspapers issued alerts, but they seemed more puzzled than troubled regarding the sell-offs.

It was a panic, a purely stock market panic, of a new brand. . . . It came when money was 5 percent, with a plethora of funds available for lending purposes, normal inventories, corporations flush with surplus money, sound industrial conditions, and so on.

> It is because of the fact that the slump was due to the market itself that the storm has left no wreckage except marginal traders forced to sell at a loss.

Such was the view of the *Wall Street Journal*, set down in editorial form, regarding the market's performance on Monday, October 28, 1929, when on a volume of 9.2 million shares the Dow closed at 260.64, down 38.33 points for the session. The following day, "Black Tuesday," the index would close at 230.07, for a loss of 30.57 points on what for the times was a record 16.4 million shares. The Dow Utilities declined by 12.65 points to 74.31, another record. The Rails gave up 8.35 points, ending at 147.06. The Dow Bonds slid fractionally to 93.13, off by 0.55 point, a large move for that index. To understand the magnitude of the September-October sell-off, consider that one month earlier the Industrials had been at 347.17, the Utilities at 141.71, the Rails at 175.88, and Bonds at 92.18.

In those years "prudent investors" still did not hold industrial stocks in high esteem. Utilities were regarded as being more dependable, but so many of them were involved in holding companies that skittish speculators sold them too. The Rails performed comparatively better, in large part because they hadn't fully participated in the Great Bull Market, and so were not viewed as being overvalued. There was virtually no alarm in the bond markets. It was a panic, to be sure, but the owners of prime railroad stocks and bonds might have felt somewhat smug, reflecting that what goes up rapidly occasionally collapses just as fast.

After the crash it appeared reasonable to presume investors would be attracted by the safety afforded by bonds. There were indications that this was so. More bonds came to market in December than in October.[6] Indeed, there would be a sharp increase in domestic bond underwritings in 1930. During the first five months of the year new bond issues averaged $643 million per month, which was more than the same periods in 1928 and 1929. The foreign bond business, which declined sharply in 1929 due to the beginnings of signs of default, also rallied.[7]

One might have expected Dillon Read to perform fairly well, if not prosper, in this kind of market. Its retail operations concentrated in bonds; the firm had never been very concerned with

NEW SECURITIES OFFERINGS, 1926–1930
(figures in millions of dollars)

	1926	1927	1928	1929	1930
Total New Issues	6,344	7,791	8,114	10,183	7,023
Corporate Debt	2,666	3,182	2,385	2,078	2,980
Municipal Bonds	1,344	1,475	1,379	1,418	1,434
Foreign Bonds	1,156	1,573	1,325	763	1,020
Pfd. Stock	509	874	1,149	1,517	412
Common Stock	578	600	1,812	4,407	1,091
Other	91	87	64	0	87
Common as % of Total	9	8	22	43	16

SOURCE: United States, Department of Commerce, *Survey of Current Business*, February 1938, pp. 16–19.

equities and still was not a member of the NYSE or any other exchange. Indeed, with minor exceptions Dillon Read would remain essentially a bond house for the next half-century. The domestic bond business did hold up. For the rest of the year Dillon Read's major problems would come in two areas: US&FS and the foreign bond underwritings.

On October 24 US&FS common closed at 44¼; it was half that price six days later, and would decline into the single digits in the months ahead.[8] Even so, by merely surviving US&FS did better than most investment trusts. Others in the group experienced similar sell-offs, and many would not exist four years later. Moreover, US&FS managed to outperform the popular averages in the period from inception to June 30, 1933. In that stretch its assets declined by 28 percent, while the Dow Industrials and Railroads were down by 47 percent and 65 percent respectively.[9]

Except for Canadian issues demand for foreign debt deteriorated sharply in 1930. After the first half of the year, European offerings had difficulty attracting buyers, while there was a decided decline in interest for Latin American debt. Revolutions in Chile and Argentina prompted Moody's to lower its bond ratings, and troubles in Brazil, Bolivia, and Venezuela led the rating agency to rate their federal debts low, as well. This came as no surprise to investors, who had sold them into a declining market months be-

MOODY'S RATINGS FOR SELECTED FOREIGN
GOVERNMENT BOND ISSUES

Country	1929	1930	1931	1932	1933
Argentina	Aa	Aa	A	Baa	Baa
Bolivia	Baa	Ba	B	B	Caa
Brazil	Baa	Ba	B	B	B
Canada	Aaa	Aaa	Aa	Aa	Aa
Chile	A	A	B	B	Caa
France	Aa	Aa	Aa	Aa	Aa
Germany	Aa	Aa	Baa	Baa	Baa
Venezuela	Baa	Ba	Baa	Baa	Baa

SOURCE: Wigmore, *The Crash and Its Aftermath* (Westport, Conn., 1985), pp. 596–97.

NEW ISSUES OF LONG-TERM DEBT,
UNITED STATES, 1929–1932
(millions of dollars)

	1929	1930	1931	1932
Domestic Total	9,420	6,004	2,860	1,165
Corporate	8,002	4,483	1,551	325
Municipal	1,418	1,434	1,235	762
Foreign Corporate	637	461	213	0
Foreign Government	120	448	41	26
Total	757	909	254	26

SOURCE: Wigmore, *The Crash and Its Aftermath* (Westport, Conn. 1985), p. 668.

fore. Many of those bonds Dillon Read had offered at par were well below 50 by late 1930.[10]

There was a wave of repudiations starting with Bolivia in January 1931. Peru defaulted in May, followed by Chile in July. Brazil defaulted in October.[11] In March Bolivian, Chilean, and Peruvian bonds were selling under 8. Practically all South American issuers except Argentina eventually defaulted in these years.[12]

Dillon Read had started to retreat from the markets long before most of the other investment banks. The bare statistics present the picture of a firm withdrawing as though anticipating problems. The peak of its activity came in 1925. This was the year of the Dodge purchase, the negotiations with NCR, Eberstadt's procurement of the 7.5 million reichsmark offering for the Disconto-

UNDERWRITINGS BY DILLON, READ & CO., 1925–1928

(figures in millions of dollars)

Year	Bonds	Stocks	Total
1925	393.7	118.8	512.5
1926	347.3	75.9	423.2
1927	393.7	44.8	438.5
1928	152.8	140.2	293.0

SOURCE: "Amounts of Issues by Dillon, Read & Co. and predecessor by years," memo prepared for congressional investigation, 1933, in Dillon Read files.

Gesellshaft, the $35 million Republic of Poland issue, and the purchase of a half interest in the Deutsche Luxemburgische Co. From 1921 through 1925 the number and amount of new issues underwritten by Dillon Read had increased in the same proportion as the total volume of new securities offerings in the United States. In 1919 Dillon Read accounted for 2 percent of all capital issues underwritten in the United States; in 1925, the year of the Dodge deal, the Dillon Read share was 7 percent. Profits were almost triple what they had been in 1924.

Activity declined afterwards, with 1928 being the slowest year since 1923, which many date as the beginning of the bull market. By 1928 the firm's share of total American underwritings had declined to below 3 percent, the lowest since 1919.[13] Dillon Read handled sixteen bond underwritings in 1928 and thirteen for equities, for a total of twenty-nine; in 1925 the figures had been forty-four for bonds and ten for equities, totaling fifty-four.

This is not to suggest that Dillon Read was deliberately turning away from bonds and toward the more fashionable stocks. Rather, the firm's corporate clients probably wanted to sell shares rather than debt since investor demand was so strong. In such matters investment bankers follow the markets rather than lead them. Even so, Dillon Read was not as strong a participant in the market as it had been at mid-decade.

Was this because Dillon anticipated problems ahead and was retrenching in preparation for them? In 1933 Dillon Read attributed its post–1925 policy "in no small measure to the careful examination applied to prospective issues by our organization and our rejection of many of the proposals for new financing presented to us."[14] One company legend has Dillon ordering his partners that spring to cut back on activities and personnel, and then taking off for his annual summer vacation. When he returned in the autumn and saw that the cutbacks had not been made, Dillon abruptly ordered his partners to fire every third person.[15] Another is that Dean Mathey, chairman of the Princeton investment committee, moved the portfolio out of stocks and into bonds in 1928, because he feared a sharp sell-off.[16]

One demonstration of the making of this legend is supplied by Paul Nitze. The last hire Dillon made prior to the Crash, Nitze recalled a conversation on this subject almost sixty years after the event.

Upon graduating from Harvard in 1929 with a degree in history, economics, and literature, Nitze took a post as accountant at Container Corporation of America. From there he went to the Chicago banking firm of Bacon-Whipple & Co. After a brief stay at the home office Nitze was dispatched to Germany to see if there were better values there than in the United States.

Knowing of Dillon Read's activities in Germany, through a mutual friend Nitze obtained a letter of introduction to Clarence Dillon. They met in early summer, and on that occasion Nitze asked Dillon to provide him with letters to German bankers. Dillon was interested in the young man's activities, gave him the letters, and suggested they remain in contact.

Nitze returned to New York in early September, and stopped by the Dillon Read office to discuss his impressions and say that he had written that report on the German situation. Dillon asked to see it, and Nitze provided a draft. The report recommended against German investments, not because of economic reasons, but because of the uncertain political climate. Dillon read it overnight and telephoned Nitze, inviting him for a weekend in Dunwalke.

Driving through New Jersey, Nitze recalled asking Dillon if he thought the market decline an omen of hard times ahead.

"No. I don't. I don't think it portends that at all."

Nitze said, "Well, what do you think it indicates?"

Dillon thought for a few minutes and replied, "I think it presages the end of an era."

By this Dillon meant that what lay ahead was not merely a period of retrenchment, after which affairs would be conducted as before. Rather, the world was in for a major overhauling of institutions.[17]

There would be not a recession, but a depression of greater magnitude than anything we had seen before. Today, and in fact since the Civil War, Wall Street has had more power than Washington. This is true for those of us in Wall Street today. But after the depression that's coming, we will not have such power. Some other people will be the group in power. And that's why I refer to it as an end of an era.

Whatever his private thoughts, Dillon's actions in late 1929 were those of a prudent businessman cutting back on commitments before what he might have thought a normal correction of an overheated market, and the prelude to utter disintegration. For example, there were no mass firings, and the significant elimination of positions started in 1930, not 1929. As will be seen, Dillon did not dispose of his retail operation until late 1933, and this would have been the first to go if he had any belief in catastrophe.

Dillon probably was confident the boom would continue, but he assumed a more defensive stance. At the end of 1927 the firm owned $14.9 million in securities in addition to those in the syndication accounts. By the end of 1928 the amount had fallen to $8.8 million.[18] Dillon Read was in good shape to weather a decline on the magnitude of earlier ones such as those of 1873, 1907, and the bad times of 1920–21.

There is striking evidence that the long-term significance of the crash dawned slowly on the Dillon Read partners. Minutes survive of partner meetings in 1929.[19] These present a unique picture of a group of investment bankers who were prepared for a sell-off a few days before it occurred, but had little inkling of the deeper message of the September decline which carried into October. Perhaps because as noted the bond business was relatively unaffected, in the first weeks after the crash they went about their business as they had earlier.

With Dillon absent, Forrestal chaired the early autumn meetings. Requests were arriving from other investment banks wanting to purchase additional shares of a new offering for US&FS. Most were rejected due to strong demand. There were underwritings to consider for Germany and Brazil, arrangements to sell Consolidated Cigar to United Cigar, and other like business.

Upon Dillon's return on September 26 there was a burst of activity, ranging from an underwriting of an issue of Royal Dutch bonds to a deal with the Texas Company to raise $60–$75 million for a petroleum pipeline to the possibilites of obtaining a rayon concession in the U.S.S.R. Dillon was present for meetings in early October, at one of which note was taken that Paul Shields planned to organize a new brokerage house and had invited Dillon Read to take a share in it. The reply, "We would have no interest in such a firm," was duly noted in the minutes.[20]

On October 7 the partners decided not to participate in a pool in Chrysler stock being organized by Goldman Sachs, but were willing to "go along in a small way if a pool is formed [for Union Oil of California]." The following day they rejected the opportunity to underwrite an issue for Bankers' Commercial Securities. Soon thereafter the firm showed interest in underwritings for C.I.T. Financial, May Department Stores, and the Simmons Company. So it went in those weeks prior to the crash.

On October 21, with the Dow Industrials closing at 320.91, the partners, with Dillon and Forrestal absent, adopted a rule requiring a payment of 25 percent against all purchases made by new accounts. Dillon was there the following day, opening with an announcement suggesting he saw troubles ahead. "Mr. Dillon stated that he wished to remind the meeting of the policy of keeping capital of the firm liquid and not using it for investment purposes except in rare instances." On October 24, Black Thursday, when at one point the market was down almost 33 points, the partners discussed some coming business in ways to indicate a willingness to make new commitments, and the same was so the following day.

The first direct indication the partners were distressed appeared on October 31, when the Dow closed at 258.47. "Mr. [Henry] Riter stated he considered it necessary that the retail sales department be authorized to make definitely reassuring statements regarding U.S. & F.S. and U.S. & I.S. and he proposed to discuss this matter with Mr. Dillon."

The markets were closed on November 1, but nonetheless the partners met. Dillon expressed appreciation for Christie's efforts in handling the firm's call loan accounts during the "recent break in the market." From this it might be assumed Dillon Read had less trouble in this regard than many investment banks, but it also might have referred to the creation of a pool of undigested stocks

By the 1860s, Washington Romeyn Vermilye was accepted as part of the
New York "Establishment," and was one of the city's more prominent
bankers. *(Courtesy of the New York Stock Exchange Archives.)*

George Carpenter, the senior partner
of Carpenter & Vermilye, conducted
brokerage activities for the firm. He
died in 1872. *(Courtesy of the New
York Stock Exchange Archives.)*

Donald Mackay, who arrived at
Vermilye & Co. in 1865, became the
dominant force at the firm in the
1880s, and served as president of
the New York Stock Exchange.
*(Courtesy of the New York Stock
Exchange Archives.)*

The Nassau Street headquarters of Vermilye & Co. sometime in the late nineteenth century. *(Courtesy of Chase Manhattan Bank Archives.)*

The Equitable Building, which housed William A. Read & Co., was destroyed by fire in 1912. Read would soon relocate to 28 Nassau Street. *(Courtesy of The Equitable Life Assurance Society Archives.)*

William A. Read was one of the more innovative investment bankers of his time. Beginning his career at Vermilye & Co. in 1877, he became the leading partner by the end of the nineteenth century. In 1905, after differences with some partners, Vermilye & Co. was dissolved and Read established his own firm. *(Courtesy of Duncan H. Read.)*

Clarence Dillon, undated,
probably in the early 1920s.
(*Courtesy of the Bettmann
Archive.*)

Clarence Dillon in his Nassau Street office in the late 1920s.
(*Courtesy of Dorothy Dillon Eweson.*)

The mature Clarence Dillon, as shown in the portrait in the Dillon Read boardroom.

Leonard Kennedy, whose firm worked closely with Dillon Read and the Schlesinger interests in the Goodyear Tire & Rubber Company reorganization. Kennedy was a very close personal friend to Dillon as well as a key business ally. *(Courtesy of Dorothy Dillon Eweson.)*

Armin A. Schlesinger, Clarence Dillon's friend at Harvard College, was responsible for bringing Dillon to Milwaukee, where he worked for Schlesinger's father at the Newport Mining Company. The professional association between Dillon and the Schlesinger family interests would endure for years to come. *(Courtesy of Dorothy Dillon Eweson.)*

F. A. Seiberling, who built the Goodyear Tire & Rubber Company,
stepped down after Dillon Read's reorganization of his company
in 1921.   *(Courtesy of Goodyear Tire & Rubber Company.)*

Edward G. Wilmer (second row, center) was installed as head of Goodyear Tire &
Rubber Company at the behest of Dillon Read, through its business ally, Leonard
Kennedy & Co. He is shown here with Goodyear managers in 1921.   *(Courtesy
of Goodyear Tire & Rubber Company.)*

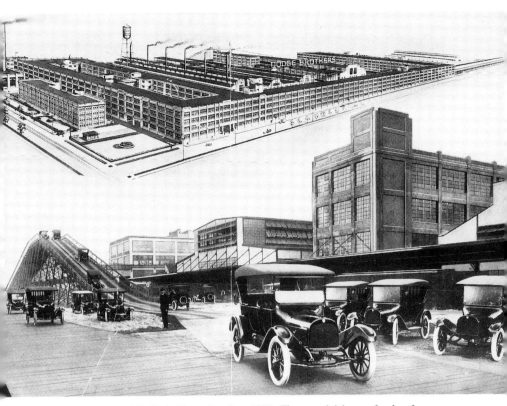

The Dodge Brothers Works in Detroit, *circa* 1925. The acquisition and sale of Dodge was one of Clarence Dillon's greatest coups as an investment banker.

The check for $146 million drawn by Dillon Read in 1925 to pay for the acquisition of Dodge Brothers, Inc. At the time, it was the largest cash deal in the history of American business.

Ferdinand Eberstadt, one of many Dillon Read partners to have been educated at Princeton University, is shown here as a student, *circa* 1913. Eberstadt was instrumental in helping establish Dillon Read's business in Europe, particularly in Germany. *(Courtesy of John Payne.)*

Gustav Stresemann, the German foreign minister with whom Ferdinand Eberstadt negotiated terms for financing Germany's debt and reparations payments in 1926–27. *(Courtesy of the Bettmann Archive.)*

Walter Chrysler, one of the leading figures in the early years of the automobile industry, purchased Dodge from Dillon Read in 1928.

W.M.L. Fiske, a partner in the firm since the days of William A. Read, represented Dillon Read in Europe from the 1920s to the 1940s. *(Courtesy of Patricia H. Zabalaga.)*

(Left) Ferdinand Pecora, the nemesis of Wall Street, posing for news photographers on October 2, 1933, the day before Dillon Read partners would be called to testify before the Senate Subcommittee of the Senate Banking Committee. Pecora was the special counsel for the hearings that came to bear his name. *(Right)* Pecora with Senator Carter Glass, the cosponsor of the Glass-Steagall Banking Act, in 1933. *(Courtesy of the Bettmann Archive.)*

Dillon Read principals C. Douglas Dillon, Robert E. Christie, Jr., Paul Nitze, and Clarence Dillon leaving the second day's proceedings of the Pecora Hearings, October 4, 1933. *(Courtesy of the Bettmann Archive.)*

Dillon Read's James V. Forrestal (right) and Paul M. Strieffler (left), who served as president of the Dillon Read–controlled Beekman Company, flanking Forrestal's lawyer, Bernard Knollenberg, at the Pecora Hearings, October 14, 1933. *(Courtesy of the Bettmann Archive.)*

James V. Forrestal was Clarence Dillon's alter ego during the 1920s and 1930s. In reality, he led the firm in the latter decade, though Clarence Dillon did not consent to his being named president until 1938. *(Courtesy of Princeton University Library. Papers of Ferdinand Eberstadt.)*

Charles S. McCain succeeded Forrestal as head of Dillon Read from 1939 through 1951, during a difficult period for both the firm and the industry. *(Courtesy of Chase Manhattan Bank Archives.)*

Dillon Read partners at a partners' dinner during the 1940s. From left to right are Paul Nitze, William Draper, James Forrestal, William Phillips, Harry Egly, Edward Bigelow, and Karl Behr. *(Courtesy of Dorothy Dillon Eweson.)*

Dillon Read partners at a partners' dinner during the late 1940s. From left to right are C. Douglas Dillon, William Phillips, Frederic Brandi, Charles Kock, Wilbur Dubois, and Thomas Troxell. *(Courtesy of Dorothy Dillon Eweson.)*

German-born Frederic Brandi became chairman of Dillon Read in 1952 and served into 1971. *(Photo by Kelsey Cape Cod Studio.)*

August Belmont, the bearer of one of the most distinguished names in investment banking, was deemed one of the most astute experts in the field of petroleum financing. *(Courtesy of August Belmont.)*

The Big Inch Pipe Line bending toward New York at Phoenixville, Pennsylvania. *(Courtesy of the Bettmann Archive.)*

One of many successful public works for which Dillon Read arranged financing in the postwar era was the Triborough Bridge, shown here in the 1930s. *(Courtesy of the New York City Municipal Archives.)*

Judge Harold Medina presided over the antitrust case *U.S. v. Henry S. Morgan, et al.*, one of the most extensive investigations into the investment banking industry in history. Though the case was dismissed in September 1953, and though the charges against Dillon Read were relatively minor, the matter hung like a cloud over the firm after the case was filed in 1947. *(Courtesy of the Bettmann Archive.)*

Peter M. Flanigan, one of many Dillon Read bankers to go into public service, is shown here with President Richard M. Nixon, for whom Flanigan served as an assistant from 1969 to 1972. After a stint as director of the Council on International Economic Policy, he returned to Dillon Read in 1975.

Frederic H. Brandi talks with John H. F. Haskell, Jr., in the Dillon Read office at 46 William Street in 1969. Haskell had been Dillon Read's representative in Europe during the early 1960s, as the firm began to reestablish its presence abroad. *(Courtesy of Victor Milt.)*

TWA President Charles C. Tillinghast stands over a model of a supersonic jetliner alongside his chief financial officer, James J. Kerley, and Dillon Read bankers Frederic H. Brandi and Arthur L. Wadsworth. Dillon Read assisted TWA in completing what was then (December 1967) the largest one-package debt financing in history. *(A New York Times photograph.)*

Nicholas F. Brady, though titled as managing director in 1978, had been CEO of Dillon Read since 1971. On his right is Arthur B. Treman, Jr., who was second in command until 1981. Brady would accept an interim appointment as U.S. Senator for New Jersey in 1981 before returning to Dillon Read as its chairman in 1983.

Lorenzo D. Weisman, who has headed the London office since the early 1980s, started his Dillon Read career in New York in 1973. *(Courtesy of Ric Gemmell.)*

C. Douglas Dillon, former Secretary of the Treasury and managing director of Dillon Read, shown in his office in 1978.

In 1980, Dillon Read sold part of its equity to Skandinaviska Enskilda Banken, and a year later, Bechtel Corporation purchased controlling interest. Enskilda's Marcus Wallenberg and Bechtel's George P. Schultz joined the board. Here they are shown (left to right) with C. Douglas Dillon, John P. Birkelund (who had recently joined Dillon Read as its new president), and Nicholas F. Brady in 1981. *(Courtesy of Dana L. Duke.)*

John P. Birkelund and Nicholas F. Brady, cochairmen of Dillon Read, shown in 1987. Birkelund, cofounder of New Court Securities, had come to Dillon Read in 1981 as its chief operating officer, and would lead the firm through an important transition in strategy and structure. Brady would leave Dillon Read in 1988 to become secretary of the treasury in the Reagan and Bush administrations. *(Courtesy of William Taufic.)*

which were placed to US&FS, which would cause the firm some embarrassment later on.[21]

On November 4, Christie raised the issue of whether the firm should consider selling its large block of Chrysler stock. The partners agreed this should not be done, but the entire meeting for November 7 was devoted to "a thorough discussion of all inventories and commitments."

As the year drew to an end Dillon Read assumed an increasingly cautious stance. The toiletries concern of Ed Pinaud approached the bank in November asking it to underwrite an issue. The offer was rejected "on account of present conditions." On November 19 Ralph Bollard informed Dillon he intended to terminate the employment of a staff worker "because I felt it most essential we do everything possible to cut non-essential overhead and that for the time being at least we could get along without Bell's services." The previous day Mathey had declined an offer from Eberstadt to participate in an underwriting that Otis & Co. was handling for Glenn L. Martin Co. On November 27, with the Dow at 238.95 after a brief but strong rally, Duncan Read informed the partners that Dillon wanted to start liquidating remaining positions in May Department Stores, Chrysler, and C.I.T. Furthermore, in the future employee margin accounts would not be permitted.

If the firm was cautious and wary of the markets, this was not reflected in its investment portfolio, which was composed largely of shares in companies for which it conducted business. The securities in the Syndicate Department's portfolio comprised stocks undigested after underwritings and were in the process of being sold after underwritings. (See tables, p. 166.)

Dillon Read was never in serious trouble during this period. The firm's balance sheet at the end of 1929 survives. It shows assets of $78.1 million, with a net worth of $14.7 million. Dillon Read had cash and equivalent items of $28.5 million. It presents the image of a conservative, liquid firm well positioned to survive in difficult times.[22]

The firm's 1929 corporate income tax return shows a reported total profit of $4.2 million, more than half of which was derived from "dealings in securities," $1.3 million from "interest on bank deposits, notes, mortgages, and corporate bonds," and $383 thou-

LARGEST HOLDINGS IN INVESTMENT PORTFOLIO,
DECEMBER 31, 1929

Security	Value
Chrysler Corporation	$833,995
General Printing Ink	728,100
General Realty & Utilities	250,000
Sun Ray Oil	225,475
Warner Co.	217,710
German Credit & Investment	124,500
National Cash Register	98,350
International Printing Ink	80,000
Louisiana Land & Exploration	79,500
General Cable	54,000

SOURCE: January 1, 1930, "Dillon, Read & Co. and Surrey Corporation," document in possession of Dorothy Dillon Eweson.

LARGEST HOLDINGS IN SYNDICATE PORTFOLIO,
DECEMBER 31, 1929

Security	Value
May Department Stores	$988,876
Commercial Investment Trust	521,092
General Printing Ink	314,735
US&FS	240,000
Seaboard Air Line	201,960
Globe Underwriters Exchange	191,900
Doehler Die Casting	82,500
International Printing Ink	65,790
Pennsylvania Bankshares	50,220
Bethlehem Steel	47,375

SOURCE: January 1, 1930, "Dillon, Read & Co. and Surrey Corporation," document in possession of Dorothy Dillon Eweson.

sand from dividends. Officers' compensation that year was $291 thousand, rents another $313 thousand, and salaries and wages, $2.9 million. The company reported a net loss of $2,818, and so was hardly in distress.[23]

By the early 1930s the deepening pessimism on Wall Street was palpable, as President Herbert Hoover struggled to bring the nation out of the Depression. There were fewer meetings at Dillon Read, and at these fewer deals to be discussed. Increasingly partners would present propositions, and the decision would be "not to bid" on them. The foreign business was particularly hard-hit. Here are a few samples from the 1930 minutes:

January 20. Mr. Hayward asked if a Polish loan could be sold at this time. It was felt this was not possible.

January 21. Mr. Willcox reported that Harris, Forbes & Co. have withdrawn from our group [to underwrite issues for Siemens & Halske and the German government].

January 24. Mr. Bollard reported that three participants in the common stock underwriting syndicate have not taken up their stock. Mr. Bollard is to discuss with Mr. Dillon the question of our bringing suit as Syndicate managers.

January 28. Mr. Willcox said that Field, Glore & Co. and the International Acceptance Bank withdrew last week from this account [Siemens & Halske].

March 10. The Guaranty Company told us that they have dissolved their group on this [State of Bremen] business.

April 14. Mr. Riter said that we had sold ourselves out of our commitments in Kreuger & Toll except for our interest in the trading account which, at the present time, was not long any stock.

May 1. Mr. Behr reviewed the present situation [at Rossman Corporation]. The company is not paying interest on its debentures today and unless something is worked out, the company will go into receivership.

That month the firm suffered one of its largest losses for the period. Chase Securities, which was having a rocky spell, formed a trading account in the stock of Chase National, and Dillon Read, along with J. & W. Seligman, joined as partners. They started out with 90,000 shares, worth almost $15 million. Three months later there were 70,000 shares in the account, valued at approximately $13 million.[24]

On June 20 the partners, with Dillon absent, considered the possibility of underwriting a $10 million 5-year issue for Berlin Gas & Water. Upon being sent a copy of the minutes, Dillon scrawled on the memo: "Understand me. Have no commitment. This market may possibly get worse and offering be inadvisable."

In April the firm was informed that the rooms it was renting in the Wadsworth Building were required by another tenant, and Dillon Read might have to move to another floor. On April 11 Christie informed Dillon he had canceled all leases in the Wadsworth Building, "and I am not taking any additional space." It was not a good year for the company; Dillon Read's capital declined by $2.8 million to $12.1 million.[25] Even so, it remained in better shape than most investment banks.

By then the economy was crumbling. Two sets of figures illustrate the situation starkly. The gross national product, which in 1929 had been $103.1 billion, declined to $58 billion in 1932. In 1929 1.5 million Americans were unemployed, this being 3.2 percent of the civilian labor force. By 1932 there were 12.1 million unemployed, which was 24.1 percent of the labor force.[26]

Contrary to legend, the Wall Street sky was not filled with brokers and clients leaping from windows. Nonetheless, business was wretched. A NYSE seat changed hands at $625,000 shortly before the Crash; one could be had for $68,000 in 1932, with no takers, one measure of how Wall Street's value depreciated. Another is the startling statistic which showed that the value of all shares listed on the NYSE had declined from $90 billion to under $16 billion from September 1, 1929, to July 1, 1932.[27]

The industrial equities markets had captured the public's attention, as virtually all stocks performed poorly. The Dow Industrials declined from a 1929 peak of 381.17 to a 1932 low of 41.22, the Utilities from 144.61 to 13.23, and the Rails went from 189.11 to 16.53. In 1929 a record 1.1 billion shares were traded at the NYSE; the figure for 1932 was 425.2 million shares.

Bonds did much better—at least until major defaults began in 1931. The Dow Bonds peaked at 96.32 in January of 1929, drifted, but then recovered; in September 1930 the index rose to 97.68 before settling back. Then bonds started downward, collapsing to 87.01 a year later. In May 1932, the index stood at 66.30. By the end of the year, half the approximately $50 billion in new securities underwritten in the postwar decade would be worthless.[28]

The record for those issues Dillon Read had underwritten was better than might have been expected. Of the $2.7 billion in bonds represented by 353 offerings the firm had taken to market during the 1920s, only two had defaulted in the decade, and one of these subsequently paid off arrearages. Four additional issues defaulted in 1930, all of them domestic, with face values of $3.4 million.

The floodgates opened in 1931, when seventeen issues with face values of $134.8 million defaulted, of which five were foreign, all Bolivian and Brazilian. There were another seventeen failures in 1932, these with face values of $69.4 million, six foreign, all of which, except an issue of the Deutsche Bank, being South American. This came to 6.3 percent of the firm's bond underwritings to that time, a record far superior to those of most investment banks.[29]

Unsurprisingly, the brokerage and investment banking industries, which came through the crash virtually intact, suffered badly thereafter as business dried up and inventories declined sharply in value.

Kidder, Peabody failed in March 1931. The firm reappeared soon after, but all the top personnel were gone, with only the name remaining.[30] Others followed: Pynchon & Co. and West & Co. closed within days of one another in April. The old and distinguished bond house of Kountze Brothers suspended operations, as did Palmer & Co., a more speculative concern. Otis & Co, where Eberstadt was in charge, consigned its brokerage business to E. A. Pierce & Co. and concentrated on investment banking. Chase Securities merged with Harris Forbes, and closed down eighteen of its seventy offices. Bankers Trust, Manhattan Trust, and Chemical Bank suspended operations at their securities affiliates.[31]

Dillon Read came out of the maelstrom with fewer problems than most, but it hardly was in robust health. In the years which followed the firm would continue to shrink. The Pittsburgh office was shuttered on November 5, 1930. On November 24, 1933, Henry Riter would depart for the purpose of forming Riter & Co., which took over all of Dillon Read's retail offices, including the Boston, Philadelphia, and Chicago offices. Joining him were several associates, but no other partner. When asked about the move, Riter said they quite simply weren't making much money at Dillon Read, because there were so few underwritings. One of Riter & Co.'s partners was Aubrey S. Whiteley, a member of the NYSE. Functioning as a typical brokerage house, Riter hoped to do a retail

DILLON READ BALANCE SHEETS, 1927–1931
(figures in millions of dollars)

December 31,	1927	1928	1929	1930	1931
Assets					
Cash	8.0	2.6	15.5	3.2	1.1
Call loans receivable	13.3	13.7	12.2	2.7	1.2
Other loans receivable	0.4	4.5	0.8	3.3	0.5
Securities owned	14.9	8.8	3.8	6.3	6.5
Syndicate securities	11.9	19.5	28.4	10.0	5.1
Debit balance	10.2	9.6	6.2	2.7	2.3
Misc. assets	0.2	0.6	0.3	0.3	0.1
Assets held for coupon payments and redemptions	3.5	22.5	10.9	11.4	9.0
Total*	62.4	81.8	78.1	39.9	25.8
Liabilities					
Credit balances	44.7	32.3	33.5	9.5	3.6
Loans payable	0.9	—	—	—	—
Syndicate liabilities	1.3	11.3	18.4	6.7	3.5
Reserves for taxes	0.8	1.0	0.2	—	—
Misc. liabilities	1.0	0.6	0.3	0.1	0.2
Deposits for coupon payments and redemptions	3.5	22.5	10.9	11.4	9.0
Capital accounts	10.3	14.1	14.7	12.1	9.3
Total*	62.5	81.8	78.1	39.8	25.6

* Assets do not equal liabilities due to effects of rounding.

SOURCE: "Schedule, Answers to Question No. 14," in *Stock Exchange Practices*.

business in stocks and bonds.[32] He left Dillon Read on good terms with everyone there, and Dillon loaned him $100,000 to help get the new firm started.[33]

By then all of the other branches had been shuttered, and the personnel, including partners, were down to around fifty. Dillon Read would not have more than eighty employees until well after World War II.

Whatever his private doubts and anxieties, Dillon appeared fairly confident when discussing world and national problems. In

UNDERWRITINGS BY DILLON, READ & CO.
1928–1932
(figures in millions of dollars)

Year	Bonds	Stocks	Total
1929	224.6	77.3	301.9
1930	247.7	0.2	247.9
1931	146.5	3.0	149.5
1932	36.2	0.5	36.7

SOURCE: "Amounts of Issues by Dillon, Read & Co. and Predecessor Firms," in Dillon Read files.

a widely covered speech before the American Club in Paris on May 13, 1932, he noted that the workings of the business cycle meant economic declines were inevitable. Each recovery took the economy higher than the previous peak, however, and he was confident this would be the case again. Specifically Dillon called for such conventional measures as a balanced budget, the working out of a new German reparations program, and the funding of short-term credits with long-term financing to take pressures off the financial markets, all of which were standard Republican fare that season.

Toward the end of his talk Dillon observed there was a huge amount of frozen credit in the world.[34]

> Today creditors everywhere want to be paid, and when paid that capital lies idle. In most cases credits are frozen because payment is desired, but when confidence returns creditors will not want to be paid, paradoxical as that may sound, for they no longer want to hoard their capital but will want to reinvest it, and much of what is today frozen credit will again become gilt edge.

A year later Dillon's concept would surface in a different version, when incoming President Franklin D. Roosevelt would tell a demoralized nation the only thing it had to fear was fear itself.

·10·

Pecora

(1933–1934)

During the Great Depression Dillon Read adjusted to adverse circumstances as best it could. Always cautious despite its reputation, the firm became even more deliberate, the partners more than ever concerned with preserving their personal worth. By late 1932 Dillon Read had all but completed its transition to a more modest status in keeping with the sharply altered circumstances in the capital markets. The balance sheet for December 31, 1932, indicates the impact the Depression had upon the firm. Net assets had fallen to $20.3 million from the $78.1 million they had been three years earlier.[1] From this one figure it is possible to appreciate just how severely the erosion of business had affected the firm.

The Crash had set off a flurry of activity in Washington. Before the end of the year six bills to regulate corporate finance and the securities markets had been introduced in Congress, only to die as Wall Street appeared to revive and contain the damage. The measures resurfaced as the markets turned downward.

President Hoover had received reports that major Democratic speculators were attempting to unsettle the markets and so discredit his administration, and so was amenable to an investigation.[2]

172

In late 1931 Senator John G. Townsend, Jr. (R-Del.), a member of the Banking and Currency Committee, introduced a motion calling for an investigation of bear raids. Hoover supported the call, but when it came out of the Senate the resolution also directed the committee, or one of its subcommittees, "to make a thorough and complete investigation" of other practices as well.[3]

A start was when the Senate Committee on Finance investigated the flotation of foreign bonds in the United States. This was a poorly attended and followed investigation, which attracted little newspaper attention until Senator Hiram Johnson (R-Calif.) revealed that the investment banking firm of J. & W. Seligman had bribed the son of Peru's president to obtain the award of underwriting contracts.[4] This created a stir and prompted additional demands for investigation.

Clarence Dillon appeared to testify on the firm's activities, and sensing he had struck a rich lode, Johnson inquired whether Dillon Read had paid a bribe to obtain the Milan underwriting, which Dillon denied. Dillon also rejected assertions that these were necessary to obtain business. "We negotiated with governments direct," he told Johnson. "We declined to make bids for loans."[5]

The Johnson hearings received sufficient attention as to lead to further calls for another, broader investigation. In the face of opposition from several of Wall Street's leading figures, led by Thomas Lamont, Hoover came out in favor of the wide-ranging probe of financial dealings.

On April 11, 1932, the Senate Banking Committee established a special subcommittee to conduct an investigation into stock exchange practices. Its chairman was Senator Peter Norbeck (R-S.D.), a frequent and vocal critic of big business, who nonetheless made it more than apparent that he knew little and cared less about finance. Despite his political affiliation Norbeck was no friend of the administration, belonging as he did to a cadre of populist midwestern reformers the press had dubbed "the sons of the wild jackass," who had bedeviled Coolidge and now did the same for Hoover.

The first witness was Richard A. Whitney, the NYSE's acting president, who simply denied the Exchange was anything less than a "perfect instrument." A compulsive gambler who within five years would resign from his position as head of the Exchange for having embezzled from its pension fund, Whitney himself was far from perfect. At this time, however, as broker for the House of Morgan, Whitney was viewed as one of the financial community's most important spokesmen. As expected, he denied that widespread wrongdoing existed. His testimony was followed by those of a slew of speculators, who verified that stocks could be rigged and pools existed, none of which could have been surprising to anyone who had followed the markets in the late 1920s.

The questioning was led by temporary chief counsel Claude Branch, and it immediately became apparent that Branch knew even less than the senator about the matters at hand. Under his direction the hearings foundered. For a while the subcommittee employed the services of William Gray, who did somewhat better, but he, too lacked a firm grasp of the issues. Even so, Gray was able to demonstrate that several investment banks had organized blind pools and had maintained preferred lists which enriched several prominent individuals.

Searching for a qualified counsel during the summer recess, Norbeck offered the post to Harold Ickes, Samuel Untermyer, and Samuel Seabury. Ickes was a crusty, single-minded foe of "The Interests," and Untermyer was famous for his role in the 1912 Pujo Investigation, an earlier investigation of Wall Street, while Seabury had recently probed the administration of New York Mayor Jimmy Walker, which led to his resignation. All turned the job down, so Gray continued on, unmasking the frauds of Swedish match king Ivar Kreuger, deceptions by the investment banking firm of Lee Higginson, and the problems of Goldman Sachs Trading Company, a major investment trust.

After the sweeping Democratic victory at the polls that November, Norbeck stepped up his campaign to locate an acceptable counsel. For a few days he thought he had found one in Irving Ben Cooper, one of Seabury's assistants. Cooper promptly asked Norbeck to sign five hundred blank subpoenas, which the senator refused to do. He resigned, telling the press that Norbeck wanted someone to "sit on the lid."[6]

Norbeck next consulted with Senator Duncan U. Fletcher (D-Fla.), who was due to take over the Banking Committee chairmanship and that of the subcommittee, to determine his choice for the post. Among those Fletcher mentioned was Bainbridge Colby, who had been Woodrow Wilson's Secretary of State. Colby wasn't interested, but he recommended the fifty-one-year-old Ferdinand Pecora, with whom he had worked during the 1912 presidential campaign. Fletcher passed on his name to Norbeck, who offered Pecora the $2,750-a-year post. Pecora accepted on January 24, three weeks before the hearings were scheduled to be resumed.

As it turned out, by virtue of his background and temperament Pecora was close to ideal for the position. He was born in Sicily and arrived in America when he was four years old. After considering and then rejecting the notion of entering the priesthood, Pecora attended college until he was obliged to leave due to his father's injury and incapacitation. A series of unpromising jobs followed, until he managed to obtain a post as clerk in a law firm. Pecora attended law school as a part-time evening student, graduated in 1906, and was admitted to the bar five years later.

Pecora entered politics in 1912 as a Bull Moose Progressive but, impressed by Woodrow Wilson, he switched to the Democrats in 1916. As a reward for his activities in the mayoralty campaign that year, he was named assistant district attorney of New York County. As such, Pecora specialized in prosecuting securities fraud cases. After failing to win the Democratic party's nomination for district attorney in 1930, he opened his own law office. Bored with the work, he was delighted to accept Fletcher's offer.

That Pecora craved elective office was known to all in New York politics. Just as Charles Evans Hughes had used his position as chief counsel during the Armstrong investigations of the New York insurance industry as a springboard from which to launch his gubernatorial bid in 1907, so Pecora might do the same and seek some designation in the 1934 New York City contests.

Pecora assembled a capable staff which included Max Lowenthal, a muckraking attorney skilled in deciphering corporate records, and financial journalist John T. Flynn. Together they scoured the subpoenaed documents until the hearings reconvened under Fletcher's leadership.

No reformer, the seventy-four-year-old senator nonetheless was sufficiently astute to appreciate the partisan advantage which might be gained from such a hearing, and recognized in Pecora a prosecutor of unusual commitment and talent. In addition to Fletcher the subcommittee was made up of Townsend, Norbeck,

Alben Barkley (D-Ky.), Edward Costigan (R-Col.), James Couzens (R-Mich.), and Carter Glass (D-Va.).[7]

The hearings resumed on February 15. After peeling away the many layers of Samuel Insull's utilities empire, Pecora turned to Halsey Stuart, which organized syndicates to support the prices of Insull stocks. Then he moved on to National City Bank, which was headed by Charles E. Mitchell, one of the most prominent financiers of the decade. In 1902 the Comptroller of the Currency had ruled that national banks could not underwrite equities and had limited rights with bonds. To get around this the banks organized securities affiliates, which engaged in bond underwritings. Mitchell had led National City into the securities field, making it the nation's largest investment bank. Then, in 1927, the McFadden Act gave the Comptroller of the Currency the right to permit the affiliates to underwrite stocks, and National City entered this area as well. This made Mitchell a major power in American finance. His successes prompted others to follow, to the point where the investment affiliates were becoming major forces in the distribution of securities and were entering underwriting in strength, troubling traditional investment banks, including Dillon Read.

Pecora sought to demonstrate that Mitchell had engaged in shady practices. He did not succeed particularly well in this segment of the questioning, but performed better when he turned to Mitchell's personal finances. Mitchell had received a salary of over $1 million in 1929, and through incurring a capital loss on the sale of National City shares to his wife, evaded paying income taxes. Mitchell's testimony prompted Senator Burton K. Wheeler (D-Mont.) to exclaim, "The best way to restore confidence is to take these crooked presidents out of banks and treat them the same way they treated Al Capone when Capone avoided payment of his tax," while Senator Couzens added, "These unreasonable salaries and bonuses lead to unsound banking and the sale of securities."[8] This resulted in Mitchell's humiliating resignation from the bank, a Justice Department investigation, and a subsequent indictment on tax charges.[9]

This sensational development preceded testimony from J. P. Morgan partners. Morgan's chief counsel, John W. Davis, recommended that the banker refuse to cooperate or appear, since the questioning went beyond the scope of the subcommittee's mandate under its enabling resolution. Pecora asked Fletcher for a revised resolution, received one, and now Davis informed the Morgan partners they had to testify.

If Mitchell was one of the most commanding bankers of the decade, the house of Morgan was the very symbol of finance capitalism. This time Pecora unearthed nothing consequential; the firm was powerful, influential, and resourceful, but had violated no laws. Later on Pecora would concede that "the investigation of the Morgan firm elicited no such disclosures of glaring abuses" as he found with National City and several other banks, while Morgan complained about the ungentlemanly treatment he had received from the committee. "Pecora," he said, "has the manner and the manners of a prosecuting attorney."[10]

Pecora did disclose Morgan's preferred lists, and revealed the roster of famous individuals involved in the Alleghany underwriting. Such activities as setting up what amounted to a two-price system, with insiders receiving preferential treatment, seemed unconscionable in the aftermath of the market collapse and in the midst of the Great Depression, when bankers had become the scapegoat for the nation's ailments. Heroes during the bull market, the bankers were now cast as villains or worse. When Morgan partner George Whitney claimed nothing was expected in return from those in the preferred lists, a bemused Senator Couzens remarked dryly, "I never heard of anything so altruistic in my life."[11]

Over the years Pecora had learned the value of publicity, having received his share of it while an assistant district attorney. During the hearings he would attempt to provide at least one "shocker" a day for newspapermen to feature in their stories. He took good care of the press, and the reporters reciprocated. So it was that *The New York Times* condemned what it called the "gross impropriety" of the Morgan bank, and wrote of "the small arts of petty traders," and other newspapers were equally indignant, and would remain so throughout the hearings.[12]

What really angered those who followed the testimony in the press was the fact Morgan had not paid personal income taxes in 1931 and 1932. Indeed, taken together, the Morgan partners paid a total of less than $50,000 in taxes for 1930, and none at all in 1931.[13] Pecora insinuated this was illegal, which was not the case. In this way the press concentrated on personal abuses, seemingly ignoring the more important matters of Wall Street structure and investment banking practices.

After similar evidence was elicited from partners and officers at other investment banks the subcommittee adjourned for the summer. Pecora announced that the first witnesses the following October would be from Dillon Read.

Pecora emerged from his first session a coming leader in the reform movement. "I looked with astonishment at this man who, through the intricate mazes of banking, syndicates, market deals, chicanery of all sorts, and in a field new to him, never forgot a name, never made an error in a figure, and never lost his temper," wrote John Flynn of his chief a year later.[14] Yet there was another side to the man. Pecora proved a consummate actor and politician, orchestrating the hearings and playing upon the emotions of the public and the cravings of reporters for sensational stories. Reviewing the record from the perspective of 1969, John Brooks evaluated Pecora in a more balanced fashion:[15]

> He painted his adversary as black as he could, and as black as the angry and frustrated country wanted him to. In this manner and in others, he overstated the case. . . . The coin was turned; the irrational business worship of 1929 had become its equally irrational opposite; and Pecora, three-quarters righteous tribune of the people, was one-quarter demagogic inquisitor.

Meanwhile, during what came to be known as the "Hundred Days," Congress passed and President Roosevelt signed a veritable flood of recovery and reform legislation. Some of the measures were introduced, passed both houses of Congress, and ratified in one day. On several occasions the legislators learned of the contents of bills not from the official record but by reading about them in the newspapers. As was to have been expected, some of the measures concerned the investment banking industry.

In a March 29 message to Congress, Roosevelt asked for laws based on "the ancient truth that those who manage banks, corporations, and other agencies handling or using other people's money are trustees acting for others."[16] From this came the Securities Act (sometimes called the Truth-in-Securities Act), passed and signed on May 27, requiring among other things full disclosure in the issuance of new securities. It was followed on June 16 by the Glass-Steagall Banking Act, which divorced investment and commercial banking, making illegal operations such as those in which Mitchell had engaged.

There was talk of more to come, especially if the Pecora hearings provided more revelations regarding the perceived abuses of the industry. Already those closest to Roosevelt were discussing the need for federal regulation of the securities industry and for the creation of a permanent commission to make certain such malefactors could never again manipulate markets to their own ends.

The subcommittee reconvened on October 3, but the preparations for the testimony began much earlier. In June Pecora's assistants subpoenaed Dillon Read for documents. Staff personnel traveled to New York to look through the firm's files. Tens of thousands of documents were photostated, indexed, and packed into cases. These then were placed into two large vans, each with guards, driven to Washington, and unloaded in the offices Pecora had rented for the investigation. Together with his assistants, he pored over the papers prior to calling the first Dillon Read witness, Clarence Dillon himself, who was informed that the initial inquiry would be on the subject of US&FS and US&IS.[17]

Dillon and his partners read the earlier testimony for hints of what might be asked, and consulted with attorneys regarding the firm's practices over the past dozen years. Eberstadt was called in for advice, and under his guidance several Dillon Read assistants put the financial affairs of the partners in order, so as to offer as small a target for Pecora as possible. On June 14 Eberstadt sent a memorandum on the subject to Forrestal. Journalist David Lawrence was in his office that day, and Eberstadt asked him what areas he believed might be covered. Lawrence replied he thought they would be profits and influence accruing from the directorships of corporations and banks, investment trusts, and foreign loans, among others. Lawrence also cautioned against engaging anyone publicly to deal with the press on behalf of the firm. Rather, one of the partners should be given the task, and Lawrence thought Dillon the best for the task. The newspaperman suggested there be many dress rehearsals with harsh cross-examinations. In his opinion the most important element was the mood and attitude of the witnesses, which was to be patient, polite, good-humored, and frank under all circumstances.[18]

Dillon Read called in the most talented experts available. Ivy

Lee, the nation's premier public relations man, who had helped alter John D. Rockefeller's negative image by having him dispense dimes to children, was the most important of these. Lee realized that Pecora's challenge was as much a function of show business and politics as anything else, and set out to stymie the counsel at every turn. Working under Lee and Bob Christie, the staff drew up position papers, commissioned studies, and did an altogether thorough job of formulating responses to just about any question that might be asked. Particular attention was paid to the foreign underwritings, as Christie and Lee appeared to believe that in light of revelations at the Johnson hearings, Pecora would concentrate on that aspect of Dillon Read's business.[19]

Clarence Dillon was sworn in on the first day, with the press expecting some of the fireworks witnessed the previous spring. Writing in the *New York World Telegram*, Thomas L. Stokes referred to Dillon as the "enigmatic miracle man of the frenzied foreign bond era." He thought "it . . . somewhat painful for Mr. Dillon, that shrewd, brilliant man about whom legends have grown, to project his tall, lean figure and quizzical face under the spotlight of a Senate investigation." In the same vein, John O'Donnell and Doris Fleeson, Stokes's counterparts on the *New York Daily News*, wrote of "Manhattan's lean, black-eyed, soft-spoken Clarence Dillon, skilled juggler of millions in the Wall Street whoopee days before the crash," and "the tanned and healthy looking Dillon, who handled more money in the dizzy decade than did the late J. Pierpont Morgan at any similar time in his career."[20]

Dillon spoke from a prepared text, in which he defended the underwriting and operations of US&FS and US&IS. He then was interrogated by the senators and Pecora about US&FS. For several hours Pecora and Couzens explored with him the structure and flotation of US&FS, and they continued along the same path the following morning. They went over the same kind of material discussed with previous witnesses regarding commissions, profits, and preferred lists. It was learned that six directors of US&FS received allocations of from 100 to 500 second preferred shares at the underwriting, which, as has been noted, they obtained at 20 cents a share.[21] George Wickersham, who had been Attorney General in the William Howard Taft Administration, and afterwards became a Wall Street lawyer, was on the allocation list for 100 shares of second preferred; his was the only "big name" on the roster. Pecora noted that on an investment of $5 million, Dillon Read obtained control of US&FS and US&IS, which were capitalized at $90 million, to which Dillon replied, laconically, "That's right."[22]

Pecora suggested that Dillon Read did not provide sufficient timely information about its underwritings, but this did not strike sparks. Dillon had little difficulty answering questions, and when he needed additional information he would turn to his counsel, George S. Franklin, and Christie, who sat directly behind him prepared with the materials.

Because he was unable to respond to some of the more technical questions, Dillon stepped down after more than two hours of testimony, and Christie took his place. The interrogation continued, with Christie noting that the Dillon Read partners who had purchased US&FS shares sold for an average price of $56 a share in 1928–29.[23]

Pecora pursued the matter throughout the rest of the morning, sensing he had provided the headline for the next day. So he had. As Pecora must have known they would, the newspapers referred to the operation as a pool, and concentrated on that 20-cent price and Dillon Read's profits. For example, the *Washington Herald* headline that evening was "Dillon 'Pool' Made a Profit of $6,819,270." "Stock Bought for 20 Cents and Sold for $56, Pecora Asserts" *(Washington Evening Star)*; "Wall Street Banker Says Firm Paid 20 cents a Share" *(New York Sun)*; "Dillon Read Co. Paid 20 Cents for $72 Stock" *(Brooklyn Daily Eagle)*; "Dillon Co. Sold Bargain Stock to Wickersham" *(New York World Telegram)*; "Senate Quiz Reveals Stock Bought for 20 Cents Soared to $72 a Share" *(New York Evening Post)*.[24] The editorial in the *Christian Science Monitor* the following day encapsulated the general tone:[25]

The examination by a Senate Committee of Dillon, Read & Co., the third private bank to disclose its operations to public gaze, yields an unpleasant story about the investment trusts, those mushroom growths of the boom period. . . . The evidence shows that eleven members of the firm took profits of $6,819,270 on the sale of common stock of an important investment trust founded by Dillon, Read & Co., for which they paid $24,110. . . . In the years when the sky was the limit, the financial columns teemed with feature stories on how John Doe of Squeedunk had multiplied several hundred times an original outlay of $100 in an investment trust.

Unfortunately for John Doe, the profit was all on paper. In the tale unfolded to the senatorial committee, most of the members of the firm cashed in on their winnings. They not only got rich, but they got out.

It seems that members of the press objected to Dillon Read's having made money, yet there was nothing illegal or unethical about any of the firm's activities in US&FS. In the increasingly hostile climate for business, few bothered to point this out. One who did so was Forrest Davis, a columnist for the *New York World Telegram*, who observed that the first day's hearing "was productive of nothing detrimental to Dillon, Read." Davis went on to suggest that "the whole inquiry into that firm's practices will establish no evidence of wrongdoing. The opinion hereabouts is that the firm is in the clear."[26] Whether because of pressures or a sincere rethinking of the matter, Davis reversed himself the following day. "Yesterday I accepted advices regarded as entirely trustworthy that Dillon, Read & Co. would be able to establish innocence of bad faith in dealing with the public. Perhaps the conclusion was too hasty."[27]

Clarence Dillon came off rather better. Two days earlier the newspapers hinted at "sensational evidence" to be revealed.[28] There was none of this from him. That day several of the newspapers commented favorably on his testimony.[29]

Despite a constant battering from committee counsel and members, Mr. Dillon kept his serene disposition, answering all questions and producing all documents called for. The desire to cooperate evidently had been so marked even before the public hearing that Ferdinand Pecora, counsel for the committee, who has had trouble with some firms, informed the committee at the outset that his investigators had received the utmost consideration and had obtained all the data required.

Pecora continued the questioning along these lines the following day, clearly believing the US&FS situation to be the major point, which it proved to be at least insofar as the press was concerned. Once again, Pecora's instincts were correct. He repeatedly attempted to have Christie characterize the operation as a pool. Christie, who had recently been elected president of the Investment Bankers' Association of America and as such was considered an industry spokesman, was able to assay this difficulty skillfully, prepared as he was for the questions. When unable to lead Christie into making concessions on the matter, Pecora showed irritation for the first and only time. He again asked Christie if one operation didn't strike him as "nothing more or less than a pool." Christie turned to another partner for information, at which Pecora broke in, "Is it necessary for you to confer with your associate to answer that?"

Senator Glass thought this uncalled for. "The witness is entitled to confer with his associate if he wants to," he said. "It doesn't show on the record every time you confer with your associates, Mr. Pecora." To this Pecora shot back, "I must insist that the position of counsel and witness are not analogous. I need all the help I can get from my associates and any one else." More of this interplay followed, and in the end Glass turned to Christie, and assured him he could talk to anyone whenever he wanted to.[30] There would be more squabbles between Glass and Pecora during the hearings.

While the press concentrated on Dillon Read there were two other stories brewing which soon would transcend the partners' testimony. Then, on the morning of October 6, former Secretary of War Patrick Hurley threw a bombshell into the investigations. For several weeks Pecora's agents had been attempting to serve a subpoena to utilities magnate Howard Hopson, senior vice president of Associated Gas and Electric, the nation's largest utilities holding company believed as highly leveraged as any in the field. Always Hopson had eluded them, and rumor had it he was preparing to flee the country. Acting as Hopson's attorney, Hurley told the subcommittee his client was prepared to appear and submit all of his records for investigation. The news appeared to eclipse and perhaps shorten the Dillon Read testimony, which in any event already had appeared to demonstrate the main thrust of Pecora's argument, that Wall Streeters were grasping and unprincipled.

Ernest Tracy, president of US&FS and US&IS, had been

scheduled to testify that morning. He was told to wait, while those subcommittee members present interrogated Hurley and Charles Travis, counsel for Associated Gas & Electric. Pecora's attempts to compare Associated with the Insull companies provoked Hurley to charge the counsel with seeking to damage the investors in what he claimed was a legitimate enterprise which had violated no laws. It was a good season for businessman-bashing, and Pecora was benefiting from it, but he increasingly appeared more prosecutor than fact finder.

Whatever followed would appear tame after the byplay between the fiery and flamboyant Hurley and Pecora. So it was. At one point Pecora employed the phrase, "I imagine it was done that way," to which Glass snapped, "My understanding is a little superior to your imagination." Visibly irritated, Pecora stated he had not sought the assignment, and his salary of $225 a month was hardly an incentive. Glass responded he did not assume Pecora was there for the salary. "Far from it," he said, apparently alluding to Pecora's political ambitions.[31] In between all of this Tracy was questioned about syndicate operations, adding nothing new. The big stories in the press that day and the following morning were about Hopson, Glass, and Pecora, not Dillon Read.

There was some substance behind Glass's retort. In this period Pecora was negotiating with the New York Democratic leadership for a place on the municipal ticket in the 1934 elections. Pecora now informed the press he would run for the office of New York district attorney. This would not interfere with his work on the subcommittee, Pecora assured them, adding he intended to devote weekends to the campaign until the end of the year, and if the investigation had not been completed by the end of the year, would submit his resignation.[32]

From that point on Glass and several other senators seemed somewhat distrustful of their counsel. On learning of the Pecora announcement, Senator Glass said:

I wish Mr. Pecora success in his candidacy for District Attorney. I think he is an aggressive man and possesses a talent for that sort of work. I have no enmity toward Mr. Pecora. My only purpose had been to make the investigation a Senate investigation and not a Pecora investigation.

Glass then added, "I do not think it is right that Mr. Pecora should continue as counsel in charge of this investigation while he is seeking political office in New York, and I believe when the matter is presented to the committee it will take the view that it is not right for Mr. Pecora to continue."[33]

Morgan, who later complained that Pecora treated him like a horse thief, sent his congratulations. The next day when Pecora entered the room, Dillon rose to shake his hand, and with a smile wished him luck.[34] Couzens was irate. "I don't want this hearing to end with a mere exchange of flowers," he snorted.[35]

All involved seemed to assume that from that point on Pecora's actions would be monitored as closely as were their own by individuals wondering whether he was pursuing malefactors or a political agenda. Strikingly, it didn't happen. None of the reporters covering the hearing so much as hinted that Pecora might be using the hearings to advance his career.

(Pecora failed to win election the following year, and instead accepted an appointment to the new Securities and Exchange Commission. He later accepted appointment to the New York Supreme Court, but his political ambitions remained unslaked. In 1950 Pecora ran as a Fusion candidate for the New York mayoralty, and once again failed to achieve his objective.)

Taken together, the Hopson and Pecora items made anything else which might be revealed in the Dillon Read testimony an afterthought. That this would be so might be seen in the absence from the October 5 session of Senators Barkley, Costigan, Couzens, Glass, and Townsend. Glass would not return, telling reporters, "I'm tired of making this hearing interesting," implying this was all Pecora was seeking to do.[36] By then there were only four or five senators present, and occasionally not even that many. Further interest in the Dillon Read section of the hearings was evaporating.

On October 9 the subcommittee delved into Dillon Read's South American underwritings, especially the defaulted Bolivian issues. Under different circumstances this might have been a touchy issue, but the senators and Pecora didn't seem to think so. They returned again and again to the US&FS and US&IS situations, while the press seemed to be far more concerned with the forthcoming Hopson testimony. Tracy conceded that Dillon Read had engaged in transactions to avoid taxes. "You created a loss to offset profits?" asked Couzens, to which Tracy replied, "That's right."[37]

Pecora next turned to the matter of whether Dillon Read used the trusts as what the press characterized as a dumping ground for undigested securities. Tracy said that on several occasions US&FS's board decided to purchase certain stocks and bonds, and Dillon Read had them to offer; it was as simple as that.

Tracy appeared somewhat disingenuous, but Pecora couldn't get him to budge on this matter or concede wrongdoing. This was a matter that troubled Ivy Lee when preparing the partners for the hearings, and he feared it would prove more embarrassing than anything else which might be discussed. Perhaps Pecora's mind was on other matters—Hopson, his political objectives, the conflict with Glass. Whatever it was, he failed to dig as deeply into this subject as he might have done.[38]

Forrestal testified on October 13, and admitted having avoided $95,000 in United States income taxes by transferring some securities to a Canadian company he owned (Beekman Co. Ltd.) and then selling them. "Naturally I had a desire to pay the minimun taxes which I could legally," he said. It was soon learned Beekman paid no taxes from 1930 to 1932, and in 1933 paid only $6,000, conceding the latter payment was made because he knew he would be testifying before the committee.[39] Pecora was harsh with Forrestal, who was the only Dillon Read witness attacked on personal, as distinct from business, grounds.

Then Dillon reappeared, commenting on exhibits, defending the firm's practices, offering an analysis of the economy, and finally stating his sympathy for market regulation, in particular the notion of a Securities and Exchange Commission then being considered by drafters of the Securities Exchange Act.[40] Dillon went on at length regarding the need to restore public confidence in the securities industry, saying this was crucial, because so many refundings would be required in the coming years. Senator Couzens brushed this aside.[41]

So in other words, you expect to secure public confidence; as I understand, that is necessary before all of this refinancing can be done, and you expect to secure public confidence after disclosures made here with respect to Dillon Read's investigation of handling not only foreign loans but domestic sales. I think if you are still of that viewpoint, after all of this testimony, you are very gravely in error as to the return of public confidence and you will have a continued difficulty, if not almost an impossibility of accomplishment, of a refund of these securities you say have to be refunded.

In other words, I just cannot conceive of public confidence being returned in investment houses after the disclosure of Dillon, Read & Co. and after the investigation of these foreign securities and these domestic securities, as was particularly disclosed with respect to the investment trusts.

To which Dillon could only reply, "I am sorry, Senator Couzens, you feel that way."

Hayward appeared to discuss foreign business, indicating just how profitable it had become, and here again the senators and Pecora did not dig as much as they might have done. Nor did the press delve into the matter, or feature it in the next day's stories. The hearings were almost over, and interest was turning to other issues.

Hayward testified that Dillon Read's first Brazilian loan was for $50 million. It was taken at 90 and sold to the public between 97 and 98½, yielding a profit of over $700,000. A 1927 Bolivian loan was bought at 90 and sold at 98½, with Dillon Read's profit approximately $575,000. Hayward also revealed the operations of Leonard Kennedy, after which Kennedy testified. Had Pecora devoted more attention to Hayward and Kennedy he might have delved into those areas which concerned Lee, especially the Latin American underwritings. Once again his mind appeared to be elsewhere. In late afternoon Hopson took the stand, and the following day's headlines. This was the last session of testimony for Dillon Read.

The hearings continued, but interest dwindled after the Hopson testimony. In practical terms the Pecora investigation was over, although its official end occurred on May 4, 1934.

Taken as a whole and to put it in its best light, the Pecora investigation can be viewed as a combination of an educational experience for the American public and a necessary prelude for passage of the Securities Exchange Act, to which Pecora and Flynn contributed. The most vivid memory of the entire experience was the widely publicized publicity picture of a midget who sat on

J. P. Morgan's lap after his testimony. In the end the subcommittee proved to have produced more smoke than fire. Charles Mitchell was the only witness found guilty of violations of law. Dillon Read came off better than any of the other investment banks examined. Still, the hearings had resulted in a black eye for the industry and contributed, for better or worse, to the climate for regulatory reform.

Practices and ethics change; the Crash and its aftermath saw to that. Even so, the bankers were found culpable in a striking version of retroactive indignation. Joseph Kennedy, father of the future President and one of the decade's most audacious plungers, thought the investigations showed that nearly all the important people in finance were unethical. Yet this was not truly the case. Dillon, Mitchell, Morgan, and the rest acted within the bounds of the Wall Street ethics of their time. To a later generation, angered by insider trading, for example, it might come as a surprise that in the 1920s such practices not only were legal but considered ethical as well. So were preferential treatment of clients and the rest.

It remains to note that even before the hearings business had forfeited whatever remained of its reservoir of goodwill, embodied in Calvin Coolidge's adage that the business of America was business. A nation in the midst of its worst economic disaster in history searched for its causes and came up with the business community, Wall Street in particular. A later generation would cast doubt on the nexus between the Great Crash and the Depression, but not this one. Now would be the time for retribution, revenge, and reform. More than any other development in the period, the Pecora hearings created the mood in Washington and the rest of the nation for regulatory legislation. Finally, the hearings, along with the regulatory legislation passed in 1933 and 1934, provided a clear signal that Wall Street's days of independence were over, that the presence of Washington would be felt there increasingly in the years to come.[42]

The unmasked activities of the investment bankers appeared shocking to many outside the business. But the relish and self-righteousness of those who had once engaged in the same activities but who were now publicly condemning their exposed colleagues was, to say the least, hypocritical. Joseph Kennedy wrote, "The belief that those in control of the corporate life of America were motivated by honesty and ideals of honorable conduct was completely shattered."[43] He soon would be named to head the Securities and Exchange Commission (SEC), enforcing rules to prohibit the very kind of behavior he had once profitably engaged in with some panache and skill.

It was left to the iconoclastic Governor Huey Long of Louisiana to offer what was one of the most perceptive assessments of the hearings. Taking note of the nature of the criticism and moralizing, Long said, "First we prod them, kick them, poke them, and make sure they're dead. Then, once we're sure of that, we all shout together, 'Let's go after them,' and we do."[44]

·11·

The Lean Years

(1934–1939)

Truly fortunate are those individuals who appear when and where their particular aptitudes are in demand. There are many whose latent talents go unappreciated only because the time and circumstances are not suited to exploit them. Clarence Dillon was among the more favored in this regard. His personality and abilities were ideally suited to the Wall Street scene of the 1920s, which was when he made his fortune and reputation in the investment banking community. As the Great Depression deepened Dillon's deal-making skills were less in demand. He sensed this was so, and was prepared to step aside gracefully.

He might have done so in any event. Dillon had been rudely shocked and dismayed by the treatment he received from the Pecora Committee. Convinced that he and his firm had done no wrong, Dillon deeply resented having to submit to the kind of interrogation he had received from Pecora and Couzens, and the occasionally disrespectful way he was treated by a segment of the press. In a different age, for instance the 1870s or 1980s, men in Dillon's position would have to come to terms with such treatment almost as a matter of routine, but not in his time. It was the most difficult period the bankers would ever experience. No other generation of investment bankers had ever soared so high only to fall so low. Yet many of them had prospered during the Great Bull Market and came through the Crash with only a few ruffled feathers. These would retire to lives of travel, entertainment, hobbies, and dilettantism. Others remained in the business and did what they could to eke out livings in trying circumstances. A small number of investment bankers assayed a migration to different industries, attempting to adapt skills learned on Wall Street to insurance, manufacturing, and other enterprises. Relatively few entered government service; Wall Street was strongly conservative, and there was little room for bankers in the Roosevelt Administration, even had they agreed with his New Deal policies, which most did not.

In addition to the traditional laissez-faire Republicanism of Wall Street, there were two other reasons for this antipathy, one economic, the other emotional. There was a palpable fear on the Street that New Deal spending programs would lead to hyperinflation of the kind Germany suffered from after World War I. The raw statistics were disturbing to a generation accustomed to budget surpluses, minimum government, and regular tax cuts. From 1920 through 1929 the federal budgets showed a surplus of $7.1 billion. The surplus was $737 million in 1930. Then, in 1931, there was what for the times was a large deficit, $462 million, followed by a $2.7 billion deficit in 1932. During that year's presidential campaign Franklin Roosevelt had promised to balance the budget through cutbacks in government spending. The 1933 deficit was $2.6 billion, as FDR actually did spend less in his first year in office than Hoover had in 1932. In 1934, however, as the New Deal programs rolled into operation, disbursements advanced from $4.6 billion to $6.6 billion, and the deficit came to $3.6 billion.[1]

Because large deficits traditionally were accompanied by inflation, concerns about depression alternated with worries regarding price increases. This anxiety over the prospects of one extreme or the other kept the markets in an unsettled condition, making long-term financing difficult. The bond sector languished, while the stock market entered the most prolonged slump in its history. Well into the recovery stimulated by the Second World War there lingered a mordant fear of another collapse, a concern which surfaced whenever the market underwent a correction, and never fully disappeared. This was one important reason for the continuing moribund state of investment banking. The lack of confidence in their futures felt by the vast majority of the nation's businessmen was bound to adversely affect all parts of the economy. Cutbacks and retrenchment were the order of the day.

As for the more emotional antipathy to the New Deal, a majority of the industry's leaders judged Roosevelt and some of those around him radical, possibly socialistic. Though many reform-minded bankers and others on Wall Street supported legislation which separated banking from the securities industry and resulted in the creation of the SEC and the National Association of Securities Dealers, they remained uncomfortable about the prospect of outside control. Others were more resolute in their opposition to regulation of any kind, looking upon New Deal securities legislation as rank interference with natural economic law as set forth in the eighteenth century by Adam Smith and refined by generations of classical economists. Albert Wiggin, CEO of the Chase National, spoke of the "God-given" market system, while Richard Whitney asserted, "If a market place for securities is to fulfill its function in the economic order of things, it must fairly and honestly permit the forces of supply and demand to determine prices."[2]

In the face of the federal presence in their backyards some bankers contented themselves with merely grumbling, while others called for the return of conservative government in 1936. A number of them joined the American Liberty League, organized by Al Smith Democrats, to deny Roosevelt his legislative desires and a second term.

Among the pro–New Deal bankers was, of course, Joseph Kennedy, a New England Democrat and an early Roosevelt supporter. Dillon Read's James Forrestal, who recognized reforms would be necessary if the Street were to survive, was another Democrat who supported much of the New Deal. As had been seen, Clarence Dillon, too, acknowledged the need for change, and accepted the Securities Act and the concept of an SEC. Throughout the Depression he spoke of the need for the creation of an atmosphere in which the refinancing of the debt and the creation of additional liquidity would bring about an economic revival. Trust was needed, and if the SEC could provide it, then it would serve an important function.

Though they outwardly expressed fear and outrage, the bankers must have been surprised and pleased by the relative mildness of the government's program. Indeed, one program provided them with a role in the reform and recovery effort. On June 16, 1933, a month after endorsing the SEC, Roosevelt signed the National Industrial Recovery Act, which established the National Recovery Administration (NRA) as the prime vehicle in his program. The NRA was the most ambitious attempt by an American government to regulate the peacetime economy. The antitrust laws were to be suspended, and companies encouraged—even prodded—into working in harmony with one another. Competition was to be replaced by cooperation. At a time when many businessmen feared marketplace pressures, the NRA seemed at least temporarily acceptable. Among the provisions of Title I of the Act was a section requiring all industries to decide upon a code of fair conduct. Dillon Read's Robert Christie, who headed the Investment Bankers' Association, selected a committee to draw up a code, and after lengthy hearings and discussions, in March came up with a document which was accepted and went into effect on April 23, 1934.

The new code was in harmony with the spirit of the SEC, insofar as it mandated fuller disclosure, outlawed preferred lists, required underwriters to disclose spreads, and provided for closer supervision of sales efforts. The Investment Bankers' Association had long attempted to oblige its members to adopt higher standards. "It is hoped," said Christie, the code "will mark the birth of a new epoch in American investment banking, in which the best traditions of the business will govern."[3] Compliance was complete, and for a few months at least this one aspect of the New Deal was popular on the Street. Then, in May 1935, the Supreme Court found the NRA unconstitutional. Even so, the reforms were maintained, though Kennedy, who was to depart the SEC four months later, feared the old ways would return once the crisis atmosphere lifted.[4]

The Securities Act and the SEC were another matter. There was little sign of acceptance of them in the summer of 1934, as Kennedy roamed Wall Street, attempting on the one hand to assure the bankers he was not intent on destroying them and on the other trying to persuade his fellow commissioners of the need to restore confidence in the banking community. He did all possible to ease the transition to regulation. The SEC's attorneys replaced the initial reporting forms with simpler ones and asked the advice of several of the Street's leaders as to how they might proceed, receiving little by way of encouragement. Utterly frustrated, in March 1935 Kennedy blasted the community as being "cowardly and unmanly and un-American [in blaming] the government for its own lack of courage and enterprise."[5]

What particularly riled Kennedy was his suspicion that Wall Street's Establishment had organized an informal "strike of capital," hoping perhaps that the freezing of underwritings would compel Roosevelt to back down on his reform agenda. That activity had declined was obvious: in the month of July 1934, a normal one for the times, new securities registrations came to $113 million. By January 1935, the figure was a minuscule $11 million.

If there was a strike it was broken in March, and thereafter business picked up. Even so, there would be no true recovery until 1936, by which time it appeared the Depression was ending. This short interlude was followed by another reversal, which further demoralized the Street and led many to believe they might never again experience prosperity. Having said this, it remains to be noted that while Dillon Read had only six lead underwritings that raised a total of $130 million, the partners' payouts were generous for the time. We know Forrestal would have a 29 percent interest in 1938, and given the practices of the period, probably had around the same percentage in 1935, when his payout came to $175,000. Roland Taylor received $50,000, Ralph Bollard $40,000, and William Draper, $30,000, among others.[6]

Given the Pecora revelations and the general mood in Washington and Wall Street, it seemed government would continue to impose its will upon the industry to the point where finance would become nationalized. That would mean an end to securities-based capitalism, and its replacement by some form of fascism or socialism. Thus, the political environment was hardly conducive to recovery.

The full measure of the decline in activity could be seen in the aggregate statistics. From 1920 to 1930, Wall Street had underwritten $9.3 billion in securities, of which $7.5 billion represented new capital, the rest refinancings. In contrast, from 1930 to 1939, the banks procured $4.5 billion for business and governments, and of this amount only $2.2 billion represented new capital.[7]

When compared with other investment banks of the period,

NEW CORPORATE SECURITIES, 1926–1939
(figures in millions of dollars)

Year	Bonds and Notes	Preferred Stock	Common Stock
1926	3,354	543	677
1927	4,769	1,054	684
1928	3,439	1,397	2,094
1929	2,620	1,695	5,062
1930	3,431	421	1,105
1931	2,028	148	195
1932	620	10	13
1933	227	15	137
1934	456	3	31
1935	2,225	86	22
1936	4,029	271	272
1937	1,618	406	285
1938	2,044	86	25
1939	1,979	98	87

SOURCE: United States, *Historical Statistics of the United States* (1975), II, 1005–6.

Dillon Read was neither overly timid nor unimaginative. Indeed, if anything the firm demonstrated more imagination and creativity in the 1930s than even during the turbulent 1920s. This was not surprising; during hard times investment banks were obliged to innovate, and the years of the Great Depression were no exception.

Dillon Read endured by adapting creatively. It did not thrive, however. Wesley Stanger, Jr., a Dillon Read salesman at the time, recalls how dismal the situation had become:[8]

Dillon occupied the corner office at the 28 Nassau Street office. There was an open room beyond with many rolltop desks where the partners are supposed to sit, but there also were small offices where they went to work. One day Dillon came out of his office and asked, "Where's all the partners?" Well, nobody seemed to know where they were. It turned out they were in those small offices. Dillon called a partners meeting and he apparently said, "Listen, times are tough. Clients come, and they want to see people at work. Starting Monday morning I'm going to sit in the front desk there, and Forrestal you sit behind me and Phillips you sit here, and Mathey you sit here and Barnes you sit here. I want the people to see who's running the business."

The Depression environment haunted Dillon, who after 1934 became most concerned that the firm simply survive. He steered clear of anything which might invite government investigation, traveled more to Europe, and began preparing the way for his son's accession to leadership. Only fifty-two years old in 1934, he hardly was about to retire in the conventional sense of the term. Yet he was losing much of his taste for direct participation in the business scene, now that it had been so diminished.[9] As early as 1930 Dillon had rented separate offices at 124 Broadway, and though he often went to the Nassau Street offices for conferences, he was away much of the time.[10] In the mid-1930s he took a suite at 40 Wall Street, across the street from Dillon Read, from which he ran US&FS.

Dillon also developed new outside interests. In 1934, on the recommendation of the Rothschilds, he purchased the famed 104-acre estate Château Haut-Brion, which produced some of the world's most acclaimed wines. The acquisition was not made as an investment, however, but as his son later recalled, a project "that would be something to keep him busy. It was not a good business, but an amusing thing."[11]

Perhaps Haut-Brion also served as a welcome distraction when the Pecora Committee was troubling him. From then on, however, the vineyards occupied a good deal of his thought and consideration.[12] Other French investments would follow, including interests in Baccarat Glass and several Paris hotels. Dillon also took up bridge, and serially devoted himself to several hobbies—collecting prints, raising cattle, and keeping vegetable gardens, among others. The weekends at Dunwalke lengthened. Dillon was not as much semiretired as he was engaged in discovering new interests and reawakening old ones. Dillon was deeply concerned with finance when the business was exciting and fast-moving; he was less interested when Wall Street fell into a torpor.

The Depression was part of the reason for the Wall Street slump, but in addition the federal government, through the Reconstruction Finance Corporation (RFC) and other instruments, had itself become a financier of private companies. As a Harriman Ripley partner testified in 1941, "There can be little doubt that . . . a great part of the function of what in an economic sense is investment banking is now being conducted by government."[13]

As the basic outlines of the New Deal emerged, it became obvious that public spending on construction would expand, not only to endow the nation with needed bridges, roads, and other infrastructure improvements, but with jobs as well. Federal expenditures on construction rose from $318 million in 1932 to $985 million in 1934, and then to $1.2 billion in 1936.[14] The Public Works Administration (PWA), established under Title II of the NRA, was mandated to spend $3.3 billion in two years on various projects throughout the nation, with the understanding the funds would be allocated indirectly, through cooperation with local and state governmental agencies. These sprouted in every state, which competed with one another for ventures.

The PWA endorsed the issuance of bonds based upon revenues received by the builder—payments for water and electric service, rents, and in the case of bridges and tunnels, toll. Revenue bond financing, said the agency, is "not only sound in theory but . . . in its application may well result in the long run in a more equitable distribution of the charges for municipal services." By the end of 1936 the PWA had purchased or agreed to purchase securities of municipalities or local government agencies of $550 million, of which revenue bonds accounted for $250 million.[15] Some of these bonds were held by the PWA, while others were resold to the public, usually to insurance companies and other institutions.

One of these agencies, the Triborough Bridge Authority, organized by the state of New York, was granted the right to issue its own bonds based upon anticipated toll revenues, and soon won a $9 million federal grant and a $35 million loan from the PWA for the purpose of contructing the Triborough Bridge.[16] This was a revolutionary concept which had never before been attempted.

Robert Moses, who headed the Authority, was a flamboyant individual but a prudent fiscal agent. Soon it became evident that the bonds issued by the Triborough were backed by substantial cash flows, and so were perhaps even safer than general obligation bonds. Moses was courted by several banking firms, one of which was Dillon Read. The firm won its initial public underwriting in 1937 by developing new techniques to provide savings for the issuer.

Such ventures gave rise to new questions which demanded answers. For example, how was an investor to know how much revenue might be generated by a facility such as a bridge, and how might the underwriter assure him the interest would be paid? In those instances where revenue bonds had been issued to construct bridges the underwriter would base his calculations on the fares paid to the ferry boats that the bridges would replace, considering the traffic on the bridge would approximate that for the ferries. Moreover, such revenue bonds were still uncommon. Investors had been accustomed to considering bonds as having a first lien on total revenues. Now they were asked to contemplate purchasing bonds on which interest would not be paid unless earned. The concept seemed quite risky, especially when the economy was in such poor shape.

Dillon Read, which was granted the underwriting, based its projections for the Triborough on the concept of "induced traffic," believing the superior replacement not only would obtain the ferry traffic, but new users as well. As it turned out, the concept of induced traffic proved sound and has been utilized by investors ever since. This was one of several key innovations generated by Dillon Read in those harsh times.

Another was Dillon Read's development of what were then called "open end" bond offerings by municipalities and governmental entities, whereby the issuing authorities had the right to sell additional revenue bonds based on expanded earnings. It made sense, since one might expect the bridge's revenues to increase along with recovery and growing familiarity. This approach won the approbation of Moses, who was able to save substantial underwriting fees. (This concept may be considered the forerunner of today's shelf registration of bonds.)

Dillon Read sold $53 million in bonds in 1937 for the Triborough in two offerings, and in 1940, when the firm was a major factor in New York financing, another $98.5 million was raised in the same fashion.[17] Other bridge business followed.

In 1939 Dillon Read underwrote a $71 million California Toll Bridge Authority issue. Dillon Read's work in California involved helping finance the Oakland Bay Bridge. Potential purchasers were reluctant to commit funds. Finally Dillon partners Jack Fowler and Bob Christie convinced an insurance company to write policies on the bonds, in effect guaranteeing them. This opened the way for other revenue bond offerings. Dillon Read went on to become one of the leading banks in this area in the 1950s and 1960s.

All of this was done with Clarence Dillon's knowledge but not direct participation. His withdrawal from day-to-day affairs was ambiguous. Dillon remained both the real and nominal head of the firm, even as Forrestal took over its operations, briefing the salesmen each morning, occasionally joined by William Phillips. At the end of the day Forrestal would send out a memo to Dillon summing up the session's activities and laying out the schedule for the next day. There would be daily telephone calls to the office and occasional visits, but the latter were increasingly infrequent. Even so, there was no doubt who still exercised ultimate control over policy. "His [Dillon's] influence never dimmed," partner John Magrane told an interviewer more than forty years later.[18]

> His authority never weakened. His shadow lay over everything, including Forrestal's precincts. His strength issued from more than his chairmanship or his vast wealth. It was in the power of his mind. His knowledge.
>
> No other banker knew as much as he did about the subtle and pervasive value of money in all human affairs. The appreciation of money underlay even his hobbies. Stained glass windows, cattle and the wines of France—all drew him into considerable investments. But as he pondered the move into a new interest, he first exhausted the knowledge available about the past and prospective values of the field. He was an expert in many areas.

Even so, there was a change in titles; while remaining senior partner, in 1938 Dillon consented to have Forrestal named president of Dillon Read.

Dillon's continuing influence over policy is significant. With few exceptions, such as the Triborough Bridge financings, he guided the firm into restrained paths. Some who did not know the Clarence Dillon of the 1920s assume the shocks of 1929–33 had completely transformed his way of conducting business. This was not as obvious as it seemed. The picture of Clarence Dillon as a bold risktaker, for example, does not square with the evidence, which shows him to have been a most judicious individual during the Great Bull Market, always asssuring himself the rewards justified the risks, and then minimizing exposure to risk even further. The circumspect banker of the 1930s was to a large degree prefigured in the previous decade. This was not obvious in the 1920s, when Dillon's prudence was overlooked or simply not acknowledged. The change was a matter of degree, not kind. During the Great Bull Market Dillon Read had been the subject of scores of articles and Dillon was a Wall Street superstar. There was a perception that Dillon Read was a brash operation prepared to challenge the Establishment, a characterization which as has been demonstrated was far from being so, but nonetheless persisted due to Dillon's flamboyance. After the Crash, the man and his firm presented increasingly low profiles, avoiding publicity and shunning the public glare. In keeping with this policy, Dillon Read halted all advertising except for tombstone announcements, and would not advertise again until 1953.[19] The firm had become in the public mind the quintessential "Establishment Bank," taking on a reputation which endures to this day.

The new age of prudence was evidenced by the rise to prominence of Wilbur DuBois. DuBois had arrived in the late 1920s and quickly became an important figure in directing the mechanical aspects of underwriting. Dillon had always been meticulous in the drafting and presentation of what went for prospectuses in those pre–SEC days. Now that the SEC was a presence on the Street, he became even more intent on following regulations to the letter, and in DuBois found a person with those same inclinations.

Charged with making certain that due diligence was followed and all of the regulations obeyed, DuBois became one of Dillon's major means of keeping informed of happenings at the firm. DuBois was commissioned with the task of preserving the Dillon interests and reporting on developments he thought might imperil them. John Haskell, who arrived at the firm in 1958, was initially placed under DuBois's guidance. He recalled:

Wilbur DuBois was in charge of the investment banking department, so he knew every deal; he would assign both the partner or the vice president and the associate to each deal; he would review the work product. DuBois was really the quality control center. Every document; every contract; every engagement that we had would go through his office and he'd look at it very, very carefully. DuBois insisted that we do that as part of our due diligence, and I guess it was to protect Mr. Dillon as well as to do what was considered the proper way of doing business in those days.

Many years later a journalist who clearly conducted research with company cooperation wrote, "Described by a family friend as a 'dominating person,' he [Dillon] imposed a stringent code of honor that went well beyond federal regulations, and he enforced it by employing an 'ogre schoolmaster type' to scrutinize each bit of business and veto anything below standard."[20]

Obsessed with details, DuBois had difficulties delegating work to others, and when he did they would be closely supervised. With some reluctance he took annual vacations, and while he was gone, Dillon Read's attorneys would send partners and associates to pass judgment on prospectuses and other documents which might lead to troubles if drawn improperly. Though DuBois was by no means proficient at sales or obtaining new business, formerly a sine qua non of seniority, he nonetheless was made a vice president in 1938.

This was only one indication of the enhanced conservatism at Nassau Street. Another, more substantial one, was a reluctance to be associated with any but other special bracket firms and a handful of other highly respected banks. Dillon Read now rejected more business than before, and all in the office knew that to fail in an undertaking due to the assumption of more risk than Dillon thought wise would have dire implications and could imperil careers.

Thus, Dillon put a second imprint on his firm. In the 1920s he had led the partners into ventures which despite their limited risks dazzled admiring onlookers. During the next decade he transformed Dillon Read into a house known for high-quality client relations, specialized abilities in a variety of businesses, traditional behavior, and a reluctance to adapt to and accept innovation.

The amplified conservatism of the period also could be seen in the way the firm met change. The official transfer of leadership from Dillon to Forrestal in 1938 prompted the framing of a new partnership agreement. As one Dillon Read managing director recalls, under its terms there was to be a minimum fixed amount retained at all times in the Compensation Fund. Whatever profits the firm had at the end of the year would be divided in such a way that the owners, meaning Dillon and his family, would receive 33⅓ percent, with the other 66⅔ going into the fund, to be divided among the partners according to perceived performance. The percentages would be changed regularly to reflect the contribution the partner had made to the firm the previous period. It should be noted, however, that there often was very little left for bonuses after all of the expenses were covered. In some years, however, the partners received bonuses in the form of stock in Louisiana Land & Exploration, a Dillon Read-financed company some of whose shares were in the bank's portfolio. Moreover, those large profits from participation in deals vanished. Not only were there fewer of these to enter, but in the risk-averse atmosphere of the times the partners preferred keeping their assets in safe, conservative securities and properties.

By then the industry's structure had been as sharply altered as were the rules and regulations under which it operated. The playing field had changed, and so had the players. Under the terms of the Glass-Steagall Banking Act the major commerical banks and their investment affiliates separated. Each took a slightly different path. Most of the J. P. Morgan & Co. partners opted to remain in commercial banking, but a few believed there was a future for them in investment banking. In July 1935, several partners, including J. Pierpont's son Henry S. Morgan, decided to form an investment bank. Two months later they united with Drexel & Co. to form Morgan Stanley & Co. This firm was destined to retain almost all of the Morgan investment banking business. For instance, when Walter S. Gifford, president of AT&T, met with former Morgan partner Harold Stanley, he inquired as to the truth of rumors that Stanley and Henry S. Morgan were forming the investment bank. On learning they were, Gifford replied, "That solves my problem." Morgan Stanley's initial underwriting, brought to market in October, was for $43.7 million in bonds for AT&T.[21]

Other commercial banks spawned similar offspring. The investment affiliates of Chase National and First National of Boston came together to form First Boston. Harriman Ripley was created through the union of National City Company and Brown Brothers Harriman. There were others, of course, but these were the more important of the newcomers, which together with the older investment houses of Dillon Read, Kuhn Loeb, Smith Barney, and Blyth, become the most prominent investment banks of the New Deal era.[22]

The creation of new investment banks took place in an era of declining competitiveness. In line with the more cautious atmo-

DISTRIBUTION OF UNDERWRITINGS, 1934–1939
(amounts in millions of dollars)

Firm	Bonds	Preferred Stock	Common Stock	All
Morgan Stanley	2,014	88	39	2,142
First Boston	937	49	—	986
Dillon Read	573	99	8	680
Kuhn Loeb	596	2	20	618
Smith Barney	354	94	24	472
Blyth	337	38	13	389
14 Other New York Firms	1,557	279	134	1,970
18 Firms Outside of New York	1,000	51	63	1,114
All Other Firms	421	260	181	862
	7,790	961	483	9,233

SOURCE: United States, 76th Cong., 2nd sess., Temporary National Economic Committee, *Investigation of Concentration of Economic Power* (Washington, D.C., 1940), pt. 24, p. 12991.

sphere on Wall Street, and with the new mood of intra-industry cooperation encouraged by the government, there arose a consensus that competitive bidding on underwritings was harmful to all concerned. Despite protests from regional investment bankers, the inclination on Wall Street in the second half of the 1930s was decidedly in the direction of private and away from competitive bidding.

As it happened, Dillon Read remained a major force in the bond underwriting field, in third place behind the newcomers Morgan Stanley and First Boston. Dillon Read had 7.4 percent of the total bond underwritings by dollar volume, and a like percentage of total underwritings in the six years from 1934 to 1939.

Otherwise, none of the restructuring in the wake of the Glass-Steagall Banking Act affected the firm. Dillon Read had engaged in some minor private banking, and this was discontinued, and of course it had never been involved with commercial banking. While affected by the workings of the Securities Act and the Securities and Exchange Commission, the fact that the firm was not a member

DILLON READ'S PARTICIPATION IN
SYNDICATES, 1934–1939
(figures are percents of total dollar underwriting)

Lead Underwriter	Dillon Read Share
Morgan Stanley	2.5
Blyth	1.8
Mellon Securities	0.9
Kuhn Loeb	0.7
First Boston	0.7
Harriman Ripley	0.5
Smith Barney	—

SOURCE: Temporary National Economic Committee, *Investigation of Concentration of Economic Power* (Washington, D.C., 1940), pt. 24, pp. 13001–4.

of any exchange meant it did not have to be directly concerned about the revamping of the markets. As previously noted, the retail business had been disposed of when Riter & Co. was established, and Dillon Read was able to maintain a lean profile.

Business was quite slow, with some months going by without a single underwriting. As part of the cutbacks Dillon Read no longer showed much interest in accepting roles in the syndicates of others, and usually shied from distribution, preferring instead to manage underwritings and then structure selling syndicates. Dillon Read was willing to permit others larger shares in its syndicates than it took in those of other banks.

In this slack period underwritings were few and far between. Records for 1937, for example, show that the firm had five underwritings that year, totaling $158 million. All were conducted as head of a syndicate; in the unassertive 1930s few houses dared go it alone on even the smallest issue. In one underwriting Dillon Read assembled a group of six firms to bring to market a $10 million 15-year 3½ percent convertible debenture for Union Oil.

Such slow business meant remuneration was far below that of the 1920s. While no detailed record of partner compensation exists for much of this period, in 1938 the House of Representatives Ways and Means Committee released a roster of the most highly remunerated Americans for 1936. These figures were for total re-

PARTICIPATION BY OTHERS IN DILLON READ SELLING SYNDICATES, 1934–1939

(figures are percents of total dollar underwriting)

Participant	Share
Dillon Read	23.3
First Boston	5.9
Harriman Ripley	4.5
Blyth	4.3
Smith Barney	3.5
Kuhn Loeb	3.4
Mellon Securities	2.4
Morgan Stanley	1.1

SOURCE: Temporary National Economic Committee, *Investigation of Concentration of Economic Power* (Washington, D.C., 1940), pt. 24, p. 13003.

TOTAL UNITED STATES CORPORATE UNDERWRITINGS, 1934–1940

(millions of dollars)

Year	Aggregate Corporate Bond and Note Financing	Private Placements	Percentage of Aggregate Privately Placed
1934 (est.)	456	115	25.2
1935	2,117	335	15.8
1936	4,026	287	7.1
1937	1,673	285	17.0
1938	2,043	802	39.3
1939	1,871	818	43.7
1940 (est.)	2,300	1,300	56.5

SOURCE: Temporary National Economic Committee, *Monograph No. 37, Savings, Investment, and National Income* (Washington, D.C., 1940), p. 63.

ceipts, including bonuses, profit sharing, commissions, etc. The highest-paid person that year was General Motors president Alfred Sloan, Jr., who received $561,311 and netted $165,342 after taxes. Of the thirty-five who grossed over $250,000, fourteen were in show business. Chairman Winthrop Aldrich of Chase was the highest-paid banker at $175,000. Forrestal topped the roster of investment bankers, with a gross of $146,200 and a net of $72,166.

It is not known what Forrestal's share of the compensation fund had been that year, but it would be 29 percent in 1938, and probably wasn't too much lower in 1936. Other than Dillon, no other Dillon Read executive drew as much as $50,000.[23] Even when the much higher purchasing power of the dollar at the bottom of the Depression is taken into account, it would appear investment banking no longer was the lucrative enterprise it had been in the 1920s.

In this period Dillon Read's partners garnered some new business. The most striking and important was in the natural gas transmission field. This was not a completely new industry; gas had been known and used in the nineteenth century, but most of what was used for illumination was generated locally from coal.

Large new fields of natural gas were discovered in the 1920s and early 1930s, which resulted in sharply lower prices and increased usage. The nation produced 776 billion cubic feet in 1922, which grew to 1,979 billion in 1930. After a period of Depression-induced decline, the figure rose to 2,225 billion cubic feet in 1936, when for the first time sales of natural gas surpassed those of coal gas.[24]

One of the major problems facing the industry was the transportation of the gas from the southwestern fields to consumers in the North and upper Midwest. The first long-distance all-welded pipeline was a 217-mile project of the Magnolia Gas Company of Dallas, which ran from northern Louisiana to Beaumont, Texas, and was completed in 1925. This project, like others undertaken in the 1920s and early 1930s, was financed locally. Some were constructed by producers, but increasingly they were undertaken by new companies, not originally in the gas discovery business, which intended to purchase gas from producers and sell it at higher prices to consumers. The thousand-mile, twenty-four-inch-diameter line, running from the Texas Panhandle to Chicago, was laid by one of these new firms, the Natural Gas Pipeline Company, in 1931. The financing for this project was arranged by Dillon Read prior to the financial collapse of that year.[25]

A lower level of demand, combined with scarcity of capital, soon brought a virtual end to construction. The successful underwriting of a natural gas pipeline issue during the early Depression years would have been difficult, since the market was poor for virtually all new issues, particularly for a young firm in an untested industry. Then, in 1935, Dillon Read arranged what was the first significant private placement of a pipeline company's bonds, $16 million for Northern Natural Gas, all of which were sold to insurance companies. It was the firm's initial financing in this industry, which was to become a significant source of business in the future.[26]

This was a key undertaking, setting the tone and creating the pattern for most that followed. Dillon Read started out with two sets of contracts: those for the supply of natural gas from producers, and others for the purchase of the commodity from consumers and wholesalers. Thus, the market was there, and the price established, and this assured purchasers of bonds of their worth. The only risk was that the contract would be abrogated, which in these cases did not seem likely. In addition to the contracts, the bondholder held what amounted to a mortgage on the properties themselves.

On the surface this would appear to have been a secure deal, but recall that this was in 1935, a year during which most businesses were suspect. That Dillon Read was able to act so creatively under such trying circumstances was as impressive an accomplishment in its way as the Triborough Bridge financing.

The firm was not so fortunate overseas, as its foreign business dwindled in the early 1930s and was completely cut off in World War II. While there were no new underwritings, and would be none until after the war, there was some work in restructurings and refinancings. This was not wholly unexpected in the light of the bond failures of the 1931–34 period and the political problems in Europe.

Dillon Read's most important observers overseas were W.M.L. Fiske, Colonel Logan, F. Y. Steiner, Seymour Weller (who was Dillon's nephew), and, for a brief period, Charles Kock. All were decidedly gloomy regarding the outlook on the Continent. Steiner was particularly negative on Germany, a country in which Dillon Read had minor concern after the departure of Eberstadt and Stresemann's death. He reported that under Hitler the nation was rearming at a rapid pace. Steiner, understandably but as it turned out incorrectly, thought Hitler's military spending would weaken the German economy. "If one is able, as I was when in Berlin last week, to have a look at Germany from within, one can really not understand why there is so much panic in the world about Germany's force," Steiner wrote to Dillon on November 30, 1937. "The country, while running full force in a production which is largely devoted to non-productive ends, is quite obviously getting poorer and poorer by the day."[27] That Steiner would have come to this conclusion perhaps had been influenced by the replacement of Hjalmar Schacht by Walther Funk as Minister of Economics on November 24. Schacht had warned that military spending was harming the German economy, and if continued would bring on a revival of the kind of inflation that had crippled the nation in the early 1920s. Some in the West considered that Funk would prove more pliable, spending would indeed rise, and the economy soon would be in ruins.[28]

While Steiner did not presume to offer advice, his message in this and other communications was quite clear: Germany was no place for American investment, and Siemens & Halske and United Steel Works remained the sole Dillon Read clients in the country after Hitler seized power. The closest Steiner would come to offering recommendations was to suggest that American securities appeared more attractive than before due to the gloomy outlook for Europe. Steiner wrote:[29]

> With all these prevailing uncertainties about the value of the various currencies and with gold as the way out not considered as a solution by most, the investor all over the world will have no other choice than to go into equities again. This may not mean for a time to come that Europe will buy American shares as indiscriminately as they have done before because they will find it hard to forget how little the New York market was technically prepared to withstand a downward movement.

The business continued for a while longer. In a December 1937 report on current developments, Fiske sketched activities. The firm was converting the South American business of Armour & Co. to English ownership, and arranging the placement of an issue of Armour's preferred stock in Europe. There were refinancings of loans for the Danish government, Siemens & Halske, and United Steel Works, and the refunding of issues for the city of Bergen, Norway, and the Alpine-Montan Co. Dillon Read was also helping to recapitalize the Franco-Yugoslavian firm of La Dalmatienne. New financings were being discussed for a wide variety of companies, including the French Line, the Dutch arms firm of Fokker, Petrole de Gironde (a Texas Co. affiliate). Together with the investment banks of Mendelssohn & Co., Amsterdam, and the Nederlandsche Handel Maatschappij, Dillon Read was attempting to introduce American securities on the Amsterdam Stock Exchange.[30]

Dillon not only monitored such foreign business, but kept in touch with clients through his trips abroad each summer. Always a traveler, Dillon now spent more time overseas. Together with his wife he would leave for Paris in early April and remain at an apartment he owned on rue Barbet-de-Jouy on the Left Bank, remaining there until late July, conducting business, maintaining contacts, and attempting to gauge political developments. As a consequence, Dillon became one of the nation's best-informed individuals on European affairs.

Dillon's rich and varied social life afforded him opportunities to learn what headline-capturing figures were thinking and saying. He regularly met with some of the leading political figures in France, the United Kingdom, Italy, and Spain, who shared with him thoughts on what was happening in their countries. In a series of what seems to have been notes on conversations that took place in 1939, Dillon set down his opinions of Francisco Franco, Henri Pétain, Pierre Laval, Paul Reynaud, Édouard Daladier, Arthur Balfour, and others. He wrote that if war erupted in Europe, American foreign trade would evaporate, forcing the United States to sell to the Allies. In an entry for February 24, 1939, Dillon sketched what he heard at a cocktail party attended by several prominent world figures:[31]

> She (Wally) [the Duchess of Windsor] against English said they were liars and hypocrites—Royal family just didn't know what a war was all about—thought they would always have 6 white horses—Duke only one who saw things as they were—but he still thought of England as a constitutional monarchy but was getting over that—Duke when we were alone talked like child—asked Laval foolish questions—Duke anti-semitic Nazi leanings.

By then, probably as a result of conversations and meetings such as these, Dillon was considering closing down all European operations. He was not surprised by the outbreak of World War

II in 1939. Unlike his activities in 1918–19, however, Dillon was not to play a direct role in this conflict. His expertise and connections were too valuable for the American government to ignore. In September 1939, President Roosevelt asked him to drop in at the White House for a discussion of world conditions, and he was requested to convey to Prime Minister Winston Churchill the President's assurance that he would assist the British in any way possible, given the strong isolationist impulse then present in the United States.[32]

Dillon Read's final abandonment of Europe was precipitous. Germany attacked Poland on September 1, 1939. Two days later the United Kingdom and France declared war on Germany. Soon after, Dillon ordered his London representative, E. I. Treasure, to shutter the office there, which he did. Soon after, Treasure notified Dillon that he had written to Weller telling him to do the same in Paris.[33] By then Fiske, Steiner, and the others had left, with Weller the sole remaining Dillon Read representative.

Treasure need not have written; Dillon had cabled Weller to take his family and leave France by the first available ship. Weller refused to do so, saying he loved France and intended to remain, even if the Germans successfully invaded the country. Years later Weller would tell John Haskell, who became the Dillon Read representative in Europe, what happened. With the Germans at the gates of Paris, Dillon sent another telegraph, calling Weller a "damn fool," but adding that since he was staying anyway, he should go to Haut-Brion and take care of his interests there, as well as watching out for the hotels and other investments. This Weller did, writing of Haut-Brion's activities, local gossip, and other matters in a series of "Dear Uncle Baron" letters.

By then Dillon Read's domestic operations had contracted and the firm had become quite small, with only a score or so of professionals and as many secretaries, clerks, and support staff. There had been a depletion of personnel by attrition. Christie and Hayward died within two months of each other in 1934, less than a year after the Pecora hearings. Bermingham retired in 1933, William Charnley in 1934, and Phillips in 1935. In 1938 Henry Egly resigned to accept a position with the Securities and Exchange Commission.

Newcomers took their places, the most prominent being

C. Douglas Dillon, Clarence's only son. After his birth in Switzerland in 1909, Douglas and his sister, Dorothy, had been raised in several homes in the New York area and, eventually, at the Dillons' Far Hills, New Jersey, home. Douglas was an intelligent child; the Dillons hired a private tutor for him, and he was able to read before his fourth birthday. He attended several private schools, with the greatest impression coming from Pine Lodge in Lakehurst, New Jersey. While there he was a schoolmate of the Rockefeller boys—Laurance, Nelson, and John III. Douglas then, predictably, attended prep school at Groton, and graduated second in his class, and then, equally predictably, went from there to Harvard.

Unlike his father, Douglas was serious about his studies. He did help manage the freshman and varsity football teams, and played squash and tennis. He had no real interest in finance. Douglas majored in American history and literature, never taking a course in economics. Like many sons of famous and accomplished men who are expected to enter "the family business," Douglas appears to have quietly begun to turn against the idea when still young. Whether or not Douglas would have entered investment banking at all were he not the son of Clarence Dillon is problematical. That he would join the firm was simply taken for granted. Clarence was intent that Dillon Read be headed by a Dillon, something he drilled into his son. Under different circumstances Douglas might have become a writer, a patron of the arts, possibly a teacher. Instead he developed an interest in politics and foreign affairs, and art, and as will be seen, would have a distinguished public career. In the 1930s, however, he was impelled into the financial arena.

Douglas married three months before graduation, and after a honeymoon trip to Europe returned home to begin his Wall Street career. Clarence purchased a NYSE seat for him in 1931, and Douglas worked at Dillon Read, where he functioned as a liaison betweeen the staff there and his father. Every morning Douglas would arrive at the US&FS offices, discuss matters with his father, and then walk over to the Dillon Read offices to learn what was happening there. Douglas would then return to US&FS and report to his father. In 1936 he joined US&FS and US&IS, of which he became president.[34]

Through divided interests and lack of opportunity rather than lack of talent and ability, Douglas did not have a particularly celebrated career during the decade. His father was always there, of course, alternately pushing and pulling. The pressure was intense, but toward the end of the decade Douglas took a more significant role at the bank. He learned to put together deals. The most important of these in this period came in 1940, when Douglas handled the sensitive task of organizing American Viscose Corporation from a subsidiary of the British firm of Courtaulds Ltd. This was a major undertaking for the times, and an indication of what he might have accomplished in a more fortuitous period of investment banking.

American Viscose was the world's leading producer of rayon, with assets of approximately $100 million, and represented a sizable part of the estimated $900 million of direct British investment in the United States which was being liquidated to provide funds to purchase arms for the United Kingdom.

In this instance Dillon Read co-underwrote the purchase with Morgan Stanley, and together the two firms organized a syndicate which included some of Wall Street's largest and most prestigious banks. Under the terms of the underwriting, the British government was to receive $40 million in cash, with additional payments made out of the proceeds of the sale of assets to American investors. From a financial standpoint, it was one of the largest deals seen since 1933, the first of several in which British assets were sold to Americans. It was in this transaction that Douglas demonstrated his innate qualities of diplomacy, which would serve him so well in his public career later on.[35]

Meanwhile, others were also rising in the firm to take the place of departed partners. Arthur (Ted) Wadsworth arrived in 1935 after receiving his degree from the University of Wisconsin and then the Harvard Graduate School of Business, and soon was perceived as a coming man. Paul Nitze was promoted to what would have been a partnership under the old dispensation, but was called a "vice presidency" and "membership" in 1937, a time during which the economy declined sharply and business was generally bad. The following year, when both the economy and business improved, Dillon Read advanced seven additional men to that status, one of whom was Frederic Brandi.

Brandi, who was to become the dominant force at Dillon Read after World War II, was born in Germany in the city of Essen in 1905. Frederic's father apprenticed as a coal miner and worked his way up to the point where he managed a consortium of coal mines owned by United Steel Works. Brandi studied accounting at the University of Hamburg and spent a year in England, so he had command of the English language.

In the summer of 1926 Germany was well on the road to economic recovery, but Brandi, who was then twenty-one years old, had concluded that given all of the country's problems he really could not have much of a career there. America was the place to be. Several of his English-speaking German friends had emigrated, and some wrote of the opportunities they had found on Wall Street. Against his father's wishes, he decided to join them.

Given the family connections, Brandi had no difficulty obtaining letters of recommendation, and considering Dillon Read's interests in Germany and at United Steel Works, it is not surprising that one of these letters was to that firm. "For six weeks I looked around," Brandi later recalled, "and one day I found the position I wanted."[36] It was at Dillon Read, where he would remain for his entire career.

Dillon was willing to give him a job, but Brandi's education and experience could not be immediately applied to any company operation. Clearly his knowledge of Germany and the German language would be of value, but Brandi had to learn more about the United States, the financial markets, and banking before he could be of much use. Because of this the only work he could obtain was in the mail room, as a runner and clerk. It was the sort of training which was quite common in those days. Brandi spent about nine months there, learning what he could and waiting until he could move into something better paying and more interesting.

Brandi's break came when he was asked to translate a letter Dillon had received from a German businessman. Dillon was taken by the young man, even though he did not present the image of a typical investment banker. Brandi was rather stout and spoke English with a slight accent—as he did six or seven other languages. He was urbane, well read, and informed on a wide variety of subjects having little or nothing to do with business. So when he complained that he was tired of working in the back room, the best Dillon could come up with was a role in the syndication of railroad equipment and related securities.

This work was fairly straightforward, much of it involving calculating yields to maturity and arranging for the printing of schedules and distributions. After a year and a half of studying and operating in this rather stolid and uncomplicated market, Brandi expanded into electric utilities. He also was instrumental in helping to obtain the Northern Natural Gas underwriting, a significant piece of business, and thereafter worked in that area and petroleum as well. By then Brandi had captured Forrestal's attention and interest, and in addition worked with Dean Mathey on several of his deals. Mathey had become the firm's specialist in oil and natural gas, and he introduced Brandi to these fields, in particular to operations at Louisiana Land & Exploration and Amerada, two firms for which Dillon Read served as banker. Mathey and Forrestal acted as Brandi's mentors in this period, and may have been supportive in helping him obtain his vice presidency.

There were clear indications the utilities business would soon become extremely significant for the firm. Thus, Brandi was fortunate in coming to the utilities, natural gas, and, indirectly, petroleum businesses when they were poised for growth.

The Pecora investigations had focused attention on the electric utilities, such as the pyramiding practiced by men like Samuel Insull and Howard Hopson. While Congress had concentrated on passage of the Securities Exchange Act in 1934, it was quite clear that additional laws would be forthcoming to curb or force the dismantling of the utilities holdings companies.

The Public Utilities Holding Company Act of 1935 was one of the most far-ranging pieces of regulatory legislation passed during the New Deal, in that it resulted in the reshaping of an entire industry. The key portion, Section 11, was the so-called death sentence provision, which empowered the SEC to limit each holding company "to a single integrated public utility system," meaning those gigantic operations would be dismantled. In recognition of the enormity of the work involved, this part of the Act was not to become operational until after January 1, 1938. Other sections of the law gave the SEC additional regulatory power over the industry.

Recall the intricacy of those utilities holding complexes of the late 1920s—the Insull, Hopson, and Williams empires, which in the aggregate owned or controlled the bulk of the nation's operating companies. All these and others were to be dissolved, recreating the industry, and in the process providing a great deal of work for the investment banking community. Aware of the possibility and considering it an unwholesome situation, Congress passed the Chandler Act in June 1938, which placed some limitations on the powers of investment bankers in reorganizations of publicly owned corporations.[37]

From the first it was obvious the industry would fight the law in the courts and in the press. The prime assault revolved around the matter of constitutionality. By then Roosevelt had nominated and Congress had approved enough justices so that the Supreme Court moved away from its former conservative bias toward big business. Of the 280 cases filed under terms of the Act, the companies were able to win only 2.[38]

As anticipated, the breakup of the utilities empires resulted in business for the investment banks. Not only would their assistance be needed in the divestitures and restructurings, but the newly independent entities would have to be refinanced. While Dillon Read was not the leader in this area, it was able to garner a good share of the business for several of the companies.

Practically all of the firm's utilities underwritings were for Harrison Williams's North American or its subsidiaries. In the early 1930s there had been offerings for Union Electric, Cleveland Electric Illuminating, and Potomac Electric Power. In 1939 North American itself sold a bond and a preferred issue with a face value of $104.8 million. In the three years from 1939 to 1941, North American accounted for more than three out of every four of the firm's lead underwritings.[39]

Were it not for this, Dillon Read doubtless would have become a smaller bank than it was. Additional underwritings were scarce, and when the opportunity for them arose, Dillon Read was as apprehensive as the others in conducting dealings with clients.

Even when there was business, remuneration was quite low. In 1939 Dillon Read represented Fisk Rubber in negotiations for its sale to United States Rubber. The consultations were delicate, extended over several months, and occupied much of Behr and Wadsworth's time and effort. The fee, agreed upon in advance, was $25,000 if the takeover failed, and $50,000 if it succeeded. Even taking the purchasing power of the dollar into consideration, this hardly was a lucrative deal. The merger did take place, so presumably Dillon Read received the $50,000 fee.[40]

Testimony before the Temporary National Economic Committee (TNEC) in 1939 revealed just how business was transacted in the Depression, the power of the corporations seeking funds and the diminished strength of the banks scraping for whatever scarce business existed.

The TNEC was established in 1938 to conduct a study of the American economy, still in depression, to discover the causes of the malaise and to generate a series of recommendations. The Roosevelt Administration appeared to believe that the roots of the poor economic performance lay in the unwillingness of big business, Wall Street included, to accept the reforms legislated earlier in the decade. More specifically, several prominent New Dealers were convinced that conspiracies to create and maintain monopolies were at the heart of the problem.

The prime case in which Dillon Read was involved was that of Shell Union Oil, which was part of the Royal Dutch–Shell group run from London. In 1935 Hayden Stone and Lee Higginson were the firm's investment bankers. Unhappy with the relationship that summer Shell/Union approached other bankers, among them Lazard Frères and Brown Brothers Harriman, asking them to bid on a forthcoming $50–$60 million issue, the proceeds to be used to retire higher coupon debt issued earlier. "I would say that Shell/Union did not go around soliciting different proposals," the firm's treasurer testified, "rather bankers offered proposals as to what might be done to meet Shell/Union's situation, all of which we were glad to consider and compare."[41] George Whitney of J. P. Morgan elaborated by saying it was not an unusual situation. Forrestal was later quoted as saying bankers were ethical when they obtained business, which is to say they insisted on keeping would-be poachers away from their clients, but they became "unethical and lousy" when they lost it, and would do just about everything in their power—within limits—to win clients.[42]

Following that dictum, in this particular case Dillon Read hoped to bring to market what was then to be a $50 million issue at 97, which provided the underwriter and distributor with the three-point spread, for a gross profit of $1.5 million. Dillon Read's pro-

posal was unsatisfactory; on November 1 it appeared that Shell/
Union would grant the business to Lee Higginson and Hayden
Stone, with Lehman Brothers the runner-up followed by Lazard
Frères.[43] On learning of this Dillon backed down, and on January
13, 1936, telephoned Shell/Union to say he was prepared to take
the offering with a smaller spread. With this concession Dillon Read
reentered the competition.

Additional discussions followed, the upshot being that Dillon
Read and Lee Higginson were selected as joint managers. They
would arrange the syndication, but not necessarily be part of the
selling syndicate. It was further agreed the issue would be a $60
million 15-year 3½ percent debenture, which would be offered to
the public at 99.[44]

The markets then turned soft, so it might have seemed the
underwriters would have difficulties distributing the bonds. In the
light of this, on March 6 Dillon Read attempted to induce Shell/
Union to reduce the price to 96½, which would have meant the
syndicators would receive $300,000 more from the offering, or al-
ternatively offer them at a lower price and higher yield. This was
declined, but Dillon Read accepted the old terms, and in addition
agreed to waive the customary management fee of ⅛ of 1 percent.
The group then proceeded with the underwriting, which as feared
went slowly, with only half the issue taken the first day.[45]

That Dillon Read was prepared to make such concessions, which
would have been unusual in the late 1920s, indicates just how far
the firm was prepared to go in meeting client demands in the mid-
1930s. As it was, the attempts at renegotiation disturbed Shell/
Union. Moreover, the inability of the syndicate to distribute the
bonds more smoothly meant that future Shell/Union offerings
might have difficulties being marketed. In all, Shell/Union was not
particularly pleased with the effort.

As was to have been expected, Dillon Read hoped this Shell/
Union underwriting would result in additional business. This was
so despite Shell/Union's continued independence and the general
feeling the initial underwriting had been less than a complete success.[46] When in early 1937 Shell/Union decided to attempt to refund
another of its older issues with lower yield paper, it turned once
again to Dillon Read, though probably with a degree more wariness
than previously had been the case.

The issue in question was a $40 million 15-year 3½ percent

debenture to be offered at 101. The proceeds were to be used in part to refund a $34,350,000 5½ percent preferred stock which Shell/Union intended to call at par. In addition, the company intended to offer 500,000 shares of 4½ percent no par cumulative convertible preferred stock to holders of an old 6 percent preference issue on the basis of one new share plus $2 for each old one, with the terms of the conversion up for discussion prior to the offering. The common shareholders were to be given the right to subscribe to the new issue at 103. Negotiations with Dillon Read commenced in January 1937, with simultaneous discussions being held with Hayden Stone, Lee Higginson, and others. It was soon agreed that these three firms, together with Lehman, would handle the refinancing, with Mathey the Dillon Read representative.

According to an agreement of March 16, Dillon Read was to be the lead underwriter with 40 percent of the deal, the rest going to the others. But once again Dillon Read attempted to alter the conditions subsequent to the agreement. After consultation with the group, Mathey informed Shell/Union the group proposed to take a 4½ percent convertible preferred to market with different stipulations. It would be convertible the first 2½ years at 35, and the next 2½ years at 40, which would have made the issue more attractive than Shell/Union thought necessary. Shell/Union's CEO R.G.A. van der Woude told his board he had "informed them this was very disappointing and no use pursuing further unless they can change their views." He added, however, that the New York bond market was weak, indicating the bankers' position was not unreasonable, and the following day cabled, "Referring to my cable 24 [of March 16] consider we should give Dillon group every opportunity of revising their offer and propose to set time limit say 10 days," adding that lacking substantial concessions, he was prepared to approach Kuhn Loeb, Morgan, and others.[47]

Nothing happened for more than a month. On May 11, 1937, a correspondent at Halsey Stuart's New York office wrote to Harold L. Stuart in Chicago regarding the financing: "I understand Morgan Stanley are working on a good size bond deal for Shell Union Oil. I further understand that Dillon Read, who handled the last issue, made such a botch of it, the Company will have nothing further to do with them." Perhaps this was putting the matter too harshly, but the fact remains that Morgan Stanley did get the business, and for the rest of the decade Dillon Read did not conduct business with Shell/Union.

The TNEC's investigators wanted to learn the relationship of the investment bankers to one another in this transaction. Peter Nehemkis, the committee's special counsel for this portion of the investigation, probed to discover whether Dillon Read, Morgan Stanley, and the others had colluded in any way. Had Dillon Read "cleared" matters with Lee Higginson before talking with Shell/Union, and was the same done with Morgan Stanley later on? While denying this had happened, Mathey conceded that Perry Hall of Morgan Stanley had had a conversation with Forrestal on the matter.[48]

> He said that the Shell people had approached them and wished them to be their permanent bankers and he just thought as a matter of courtesy they should tell us about it, and wanted to know how we felt about it. We said we weren't very happy about it, there was no idea it wasn't cleared one way or the other, it was a courtesy call, they asked us how we felt about it. We said we weren't very pleased with it.

The matter was dropped soon after. Nothing of consequence came out of the TNEC hearings insofar as Wall Street was concerned.

The interrogation of the investment bankers had begun in December 1939, shortly after the outbreak of World War II in Europe. The examination of the Shell/Union financing was conducted only days after Roosevelt had submitted his 1940 $8.4 billion budget, with $1.8 billion of the amount for national defense. The great debate over just who was responsible for the 1929 crash and the Depression had ended, and along with it the impulses which had guided the New Deal. The TNEC investigations proved to be the last gasp of New Deal reformism. Within months, principals of Dillon Read would be among the many businessmen whose activities had been criticized by the TNEC to go to Washington, where they would work for the administration in the growing emergency.

·12·

Revival and
Rehabilitation

(1939–1948)

Clarence Dillon had monitored the worsening European situation with care and concern, and spoke occasionally with administration leaders and foreign officials of his apprehensions. In May of 1940, perhaps after his White House visit, he analyzed the world situation in a discussion with Paul Nitze.

At the time Dillon was less concerned than most regarding the failure of France to halt the German advance. He had no doubt the United States would play a role in the war, perhaps as a belligerent, certainly as a supplier of goods to the Allies. "The war will be fought with modern weapons," Nitze recalls him having said. "So in a sense the balance will be decided between what the Ruhr produces and what Detroit can produce. Detroit will produce more." Nitze then moved on to a more immediate matter. If France fell, could the United Kingdom prevent a trans-Channel invasion?[1]

Dillon was sure Britain would survive. They would control the Channel. The fleet would be the decisive force, so long as the French fleet was kept out of German hands. It was essential that the French fleet be destroyed. In my presence he telephoned [Lord] Beaverbrook [Britain's most influential publisher] in London, to urge him to bring his influence to bear immediately inside the British Government toward a decision that the French fleet be attacked and sunk forthwith. Where the survival of a nation is at stake, he said, the higher needs of preserving a civilization overcome scruples.

By then Roosevelt's mobilization effort had swung into action. The momentum accelerated with the launching of Hitler's blitzkrieg and the subsequent fall of France. In May 1940 the President asked Congress for an additional $1.3 billion for defense; in June he obtained $1.8 billion. The Navy received $1.5 billion for new ships and personnel, and Chief of Naval Operations Admiral Harold Stark requested $4 billion more to create a two-ocean force. So massive an enterprise required financial and managerial talents, and into Washington came a steady stream of businessmen with the requisite skills.

Just as it had been fashionable to castigate the "fat cats" of Wall Street in the 1930s, so it became commonplace in time of war to praise those businessmen who were directing "the Arsenal of Democracy." Wall Street had contributed brainpower to the Wilson Administration in 1917. So it would for Roosevelt when, as he put it, "Dr. New Deal" was replaced by "Dr. Win-the-War." Indeed, many of those who left for Washington and the armed services in 1939–42 did not expect to return to the wasteland that Wall Street had become in the 1930s.

Roosevelt told Paul Shields that he had come to the conclusion it was necessary to build a more solid foundation for his support in the United States, particularly on Wall Street. He thought the time had come to build a bridge between Washington and Wall Street.

As a result the financial industry became one of the prime sources for government talent searches, providing a share of executives disproportionate to its numbers. W. Averell Harriman and Robert Lovett of Brown Brothers Harriman were two of the more distinguished and prominent of these. In light of its already diminished size, Dillon Read's contributions to government and the armed forces were greater than most. To no one's surprise, Colonel William Draper's commission was activated in June 1940, and he joined the Army General Staff. Former SEC Chairman and now

Supreme Court Justice William O. Douglas along with Tom Corcoran, a Roosevelt advisor who once had been associated with a law firm which handled some of Dillon Read's business, urged Roosevelt to bring James Forrestal into the government. Forrestal arrived in Washington to become one of Roosevelt's "secret six" special administrative assistants, whose pay was set at $10,000 a year.

Forrestal asked Nitze's advice about whether to accept. Nitze asked, "Jim, if you were to go down to Washington, do you think you could do a good job?" Forrestal thought it over, and replied, "Well, I think I thoroughly understand Wall Street, but I know nothing about Washington. I'm not at all sure that I could do it." So Nitze asked, "What if you go down there and you find it doesn't work. What will you do next?" Forrestal thought he would then return to Dillon Read. Nitze indicated this all but settled the matter. "Well that wouldn't be so bad, would it?" Forrestal agreed. Then Nitze added the clincher. "Suppose that you turn it down, would you ever have a feeling of regret that you didn't give yourself a chance to see what you could do in a wider field than Wall Street?" Forrestal said, "Well, I think I always would have that feeling." I said, "You answered your own question. If it doesn't work, you don't lose much. If you don't take it, you'll lose quite a lot." So, he went.[2]

Initially Forrestal was involved in liaison work concerned with Latin American relations, a delicate matter in light of the pro-German sympathies of some governments. That work proved temporary. In August Forrestal became Under Secretary of the Navy and was given broad responsibilities and authority to create a two-ocean Navy.[3]

Forrestal soon recruited other present and former Dillon Read executives to help him. The first of these was Nitze, who initially served as his assistant, followed by Douglas Dillon, who eventually assisted Forrestal in the creation of the Office of Strategic Services. Forrestal also enlisted Ferdinand Eberstadt, who became one of the key figures in the mobilization effort. Ted Wadsworth left for service with the War Production Board, and afterwards, with Forrestal's aid, entered the Navy.

What was good for the country was not necessarily good for Dillon Read, as the exodus of so many of its key men in the face of a business revival posed serious problems of client development and leadership. Clarence Dillon was still across the street at US&FS, and as had been the case under Forrestal, still exercised control. Forrestal had to be replaced, of course, and Dillon's selection was Charles S. McCain, who had been with the company for only a year.

This change in management was no doubt meant to be a temporary expedient. Surely Forrestal's assignments in Washington would be of a transient nature, though of course no one was certain how long and in which capacities he would be needed. As it turned out, Forrestal was to become one of the most important figures in the government. In 1944, he became Secretary of the Navy, and in 1947 was selected to be the first Secretary of Defense. He never returned to Dillon Read. Instead this brilliant but, as it turned out, fragile man came to an unhappy end. After the war, Forrestal grew despondent and increasingly subject to bouts of depression. He resigned in 1949 and committed suicide on May 22, 1949, while hospitalized.[4]

McCain was little more than a caretaker. He was not involved to any great extent in underwritings or sales. Nor did he structure deals or innovate in any meaningful way. McCain was well remunerated; in 1939 he received a base salary of $50,000, a lavish sum by Dillon Read standards. (That year Draper and Bollard, two veterans, each received $12,000, as did Brandi and several others.) Yet McCain had only a 5 percent share in the compensation fund, which was not increased when he became president and was far lower than most of the others (Forrestal's share in his last year at the firm was $27^{78}/100$ percent).[5] Such treatment would make it appear that in this respect McCain was more a hired manager than a partner in the old sense of the term.[6]

McCain's accession was symbolic of Dillon Read's circumstances. He was an amiable man, capable of managing the firm, but not of performing in the dazzling fashion Dillon had demonstrated in the 1920s. Nor did he possess Forrestal's far-ranging knowledge of investment banking, sophistication, and imagination. By some measures McCain wasn't even an investment banker. Rather, he had had a career in commercial banking and utilities management. However, McCain did possess that singular characteristic which recommended so many individuals for positions within the Dillon Read galaxy: he was a friend and associate of Clarence Dillon, and as such a member of the board of United States & Foreign Securities. McCain served on many other boards as well, and so was in a position to help bring in new business.

McCain was fifty-six years old at the time, only two years younger than Dillon, apparently in his prime but as it turned out with most of his career behind him. Born in Pine Bluff, Arkansas, and raised in Little Rock, he came from a poor family and worked at a local bank while in high school to obtain pocket money. After graduation McCain attended Erskine College in South Carolina for a year, and while there decided he wanted a career in commercial banking, and had little chance of getting far without a degree from a more prestigious institution. So he worked for a year to obtain funds, applied and was admitted to Yale, and worked his way through school. Upon graduation in 1904 McCain went back to Arkansas to become a cashier in a bank in Prescott. When the bank burned down he took a similar post in a McGehee, Arkansas, bank. It wasn't much; McGehee had a population of one hundred or so. Young and hardly experienced, McCain returned to Prescott two months later, and within two years had opened two banks. The success of these prompted him to seek a larger canvas, and he traveled to Little Rock, entered banking there, and soon became president of the Bankers Trust Company of that city.[7]

McCain moved to New York in 1926 to accept the vice presidency of the National Park Bank, where he met Dillon, who was a member of the board. Recall that in 1926 Dillon was rumored to be attempting to create a huge banking complex which would include National Park, and three years later did help merge National Park into Chase. When unification came about McCain moved over to Chase to become its president, and in 1930 chairman of the board, making him one of the nation's most prominent commercial bankers. Some spoke of his having gone from what may well have been the nation's smallest bank to its largest in a quarter of a century.[8]

McCain was very much an instrument of the Rockefellers, who controlled the bank. As such he testified before the Pecora Committee, agreeing that basic reforms were needed and investment banks should be licensed and regulated.[9] His chairmanship at Chase did not last long. Realizing that his was little more than an interim appointment and believing commercial banking didn't have much of a future in the 1930s, McCain moved on to the presidency of United Light & Power, a Chicago-based holding company in which the Field family of Chicago had an interest, and for which Dillon Read was banker. (Nitze was on United Light & Power's board of directors.) While not in the same league as North American, United was a sizable operation; in 1939 its subsidiaries served 3.7 million customers. McCain also became president of three of United's subsidiaries, and it was then that he started collecting directorships. He left United Light when its relationship to Dillon Read was under SEC investigation.

McCain took the helm of Dillon Read at an opportune moment for the firm. Seldom has an economy revived as rapidly as did that of the United States during the early years of World War II. Unemployment declined from 17.2 percent in 1939 to 1.2 percent in 1944, the last full year of war. In the same period the gross national product rose from $90.5 billion to $210.1 billion.[10] The Great Depression was over in such industries as steel, coal, clothing, railroading, foodstuffs—in fact, virtually every form of manufacturing and services. As long as the conflict continued, shortages, not gluts, were the problem. The Works Progress Administration, criticized by conservatives for having engaged in "make work" projects, was quietly phased out in 1943, when it had become apparent that finding workers, not creating jobs, would concern businesses for the duration of the conflict. The military effort accomplished what eight years of the New Deal had not— it ended the Great Depression.

As had been the case during World War I, the investment banks helped the government raise funds. In addition, there were increased underwritings for firms involved in the defense effort, as well as continued refinancings and restructurings. Along with other investment banks, Dillon Read restructured its various clients' financings so as to adjust to requirements of the war-inspired Revenue Act of 1942. The new tax code also prodded Dillon Read to make another change in its structure. On January 1, 1942, the firm became a partnership once again.

Still smarting from the bruises of the Great Depression, most companies utilized their new profits to repay debt and retire their bonds while selling stock. Some repurchased their own common

SELECTED STATISTICS, 1939–1945

Year	G.N.P. (billions)	Unemployment (percent)	Personal Savings (billions)	National Debt (billions)
1939	$ 90.5	17.2	$ 5.49	$ 40.4
1940	99.7	14.6	6.31	43.0
1941	124.5	9.9	10.89	49.0
1942	157.9	4.7	34.55	72.4
1943	191.6	1.9	37.67	136.7
1944	210.1	1.2	40.96	201.0
1945	211.9	1.9	37.15	258.7

SOURCE: United States, *Historical Statistics of the United States* (1975), I, 135, 224, 262; II, 1117.

stock so as to lower their capitalizations. When requiring funds, they tended to borrow directly from the government, where they could obtain lower interest rates and faster decisions and were not troubled by undigested securities, as might have been the case on Wall Street. Government construction of defense plants and their leasebacks to private concerns were commonplace, as were low-interest-rate loans to finance specific defense-related projects. Federal expenditures were $34 billion in 1942, and in 1943, $79.4 billion. The figure expanded to $95 billion in 1944, and then rose slightly to $98.4 billion in 1945. The bulk of the money went to finance the war effort, and a large portion was used to purchase equipment from American corporations.

As a result many corporations were extremely liquid. In 1939, for example, nonfinancial corporations had $10.9 billion in cash items; in 1944, the figure was $23 billion. Total current assets of the corporations went from $54.6 billion to $98.8 billion in the same period, while current liabilities rose to only $53.3 billion from $30 billion.[11]

This meant that fewer securities flotations would be required, and there would be less business for the investment banks. While the situation was not as melancholy as had been the case during the Depression years, underwritings were scarce. From 1940 to 1944 less than one-third of all new capital required by American corporations was raised through the issuance of securities. In 1941 some $301 million worth of new equity was sold by the investment bankers in the form of seventy-six offerings; during 1942 only $80.7 million of equity was floated by twenty-three companies, with half the amount accounted for by four issues of public utility preferred stock. Bond sales were also in decline; in 1941, $2.1 billion in bonds were sold, and in 1942, $1.2 billion.[12] The result was a shrinkage of debt, which left the nation's businesses more solvent after the war than they had ever been before, but meant the investment community would not experience the kind of prosperity such activity might suggest.

The combination of a high level of activity in American industry and the continued depressed situation in many parts of the investment sector led to a further hemorrhaging of talent from the industry. As personnel departed managers found it difficult to attract replacements. For example, in 1928 17 percent of Harvard Business School's graduates entered the investment field. Only 4.4 percent went to Wall Street in 1940, and a survey of the 1941 class indicated the figure had fallen below 2 percent.[13] Despite these problems, Dillon Read's underwriting business continued to improve during the war, as the firm concentrated its efforts on utilities, petroleum and natural gas, and governments.

Significantly, a good deal of the firm's new business was for equities. Dillon Read had always considered itself a bond house and continued to do so, but now it was perfectly willing to adjust to new market conditions. Of the twelve corporate issues Dillon Read underwrote in 1940, five were for common stock, due to awakening interest in this segment of the market. More immediately important was the growing attraction of equity in the face of higher taxes on interest during the war.

For 1941 there were twelve underwritings, virtually all for petroleum companies or utilities emerging from the North American complex, and of these five were common stock. The following year Dillon Read managed or comanaged eleven issues with the same mix; four were for Southwestern Public Service in the form of bonds, notes, and common and preferred stock. Nineteen forty-three was one of Dillon Read's busiest years since the beginning of the Great Depression. That year it handled nineteen underwritings, all but one of which was for equities. The firm helped bring Radio Keith Orpheum out of bankruptcy, and became more involved with the industrial sector, numbering among its clients

DILLON READ UNDERWRITINGS OF
REGISTERED ISSUES, 1938–1946
(figures in millions of dollars)

Year	Managerships	Rank	Participations	Rank
1938	161.7	3	42.7	10
1939	220.3	1	47.0	6
1940	181.3	3	64.9	4
1941	235.1	1	39.7	6
1942	66.7	2	14.8	8
1943	20.4	12	12.7	22
1944	132.0	6	21.8	29
1945	247.7	4	78.8	11
1946	190.3	1	58.5	17

SOURCE: Justice Department material prepared for use in United States v. Henry S. Morgan et al.

Ingersoll Rand, New Jersey Zinc, and Riegel Paper. The expansion continued into 1944, when there were twelve issues, and as before they were concentrated in the utilities and petroleum and natural gas sectors, with equities accounting for the same amount of business as debts.

The end of the war in 1945, combined with industrial plans for reconversion, translated into an active new issues market. Industrial corporations were becoming the darlings of Wall Street, as the nation converted to peacetime production. Dillon Read handled twenty-six issues, including offerings for such companies as Allied Chemical, Celanese, Colgate-Palmolive-Peet, General Mills, and Goodrich. Still, Dillon Read's main business remained in utilities and petroleum-related paper, most of which, however, were now equities.[14]

These opportunities came when a long generational change at Dillon Read, which had begun in the 1930s, was moving toward completion. W.M.L. Fiske, who had opened William A. Read's Chicago office in 1906 and had a long career at the firm, died in 1940, as did Roland Tayler in 1943. Dean Mathey retired in 1945 and Ralph Bollard in 1946. Karl Behr died in 1949, and Edward Bigelow retired two years later.

Newcomers arrived to take their places. By then the firm had acquired the services of a banker who would prove one of its most important figures in the next two decades, and who was instrumental in bringing to fruition Dillon Read's most impressive undertaking since the Crash. This was August Belmont IV, the bearer of one of the Street's most distinguished names. The offspring of his illustrious nineteenth-century namesake, Belmont was himself a seasoned financier, although he didn't start out that way.

The first August Belmont of financial importance arrived in New York in 1837 to represent the Rothschild interests in the United States, where he organized August Belmont & Co. One of his sons, named August Jr., became head of the firm on his father's death in 1890, and among his other activities worked with Vermilye & Co. and then William A. Read & Co. on the financing of New York City's transportation complex. The younger Belmont also financed and had a substantial stake in the Cape Cod Canal, which provided users with a saving of seventy miles on the Boston to New York run and was completed in 1914 at a cost of $12 million. Like his father, August had a lifelong love of horses, and was one of America's leading equestrians. He had three sons, one of whom, August III, was admitted to the family firm in 1910 and died in 1919 at the age of thirty-seven, leaving, along with a firm in the process of decline, a widow, two daughters, and one son, August IV, who was born in 1908.[15]

August Belmont & Co. was then headed by August III's brother, Morgan Belmont, who was trying to settle his grandfather's estate. It was deeply in debt, with the major asset the interest in the Cape Cod Canal, which had been taken over by the government during World War I. While hardly impoverished, the Belmonts were by no means a wealthy family at the time of August III's death. His father was still alive; the elder Belmont would die in 1924, when August Belmont & Co. was moribund. That same year Morgan sold the canal to the government. This revived the family fortunes, but little of the money went to young August IV.

August attended St. Mark's and from there went on to Harvard, where he was one of Douglas Dillon's classmates. Joining the family firm was never much of an option. "It didn't amount to much," August recalled. Morgan offered to sell the firm to his nephew. "Do you want the name or don't you want it?" he asked. August replied, "Listen, Morgan, if I wanted to run a firm called August

Belmont & Company I don't think you could stop me. I wouldn't have to buy that name. So you go ahead and liquidate it."[16] The firm lingered on for a few more years, however, finally passing from the scene in the early 1930s.

Rather than enter the deteriorating August Belmont & Co., August took a position as a runner at the investment bank of Bonbright & Co. at a salary of $50 a week. Bonbright survived the Depression and so did Belmont, even as employment at Bonbright fell from over eight hundred to thirty-three. In this period he rose along the traditional career path, working in all parts of the firm, then settling in at the syndication department. Belmont came to specialize in the utilities underwritings and restructurings which so occupied investment banks in those years.[17] He had a reputation of being a rapid and efficient worker, and occasionally impatient with those unable to keep pace with him.

Throughout this period Belmont maintained close relations with Douglas Dillon, who after he arrived at Dillon Read talked with him about taking a position there. Belmont resisted, since business at Bonbright was improving. After passage of the Public Utilities Holding Company Act of 1935, the firm became more deeply involved with utilities restructurings. It acquired the role of investment bank for Electric Bond & Share and United Gas Corporation, and other lucrative business. Bonbright assigned several related transactions to Belmont, who was dispatched to Texas where he worked out arrangements to restructure some key properties. As a result of this work he was named a vice president and director in 1939.

As noted, Dillon Read also garnered part of this business, which was handled by Nitze, and in 1940 the two men devoted a considerable part of their time to the workouts. Then Nitze departed to join Forrestal in Washington. Soon after, Belmont wrote to Forrestal offering his services, which were accepted, and he became Forrestal's special assistant. His work brought Belmont into contact once again with Douglas Dillon, and both men worked initially in the procurement area. Belmont joined the Navy soon after the United States entered the war, emerging as a lieutenant commander in late 1945. Douglas Dillon left the service soon after the end of the war, to assume the post of Dillon Read chairman. Once again he invited Belmont to join Dillon Read as a vice president, and this time Belmont accepted. Within months Belmont was involved with one of the most important deals in the firm's history.

As expected, government contracts were canceled when the fighting ended, and Washington hurried to divest itself of businesses it had accumulated during the war. Many highly liquid corporations required few underwritings, but there was business to be had in the restructuring area. The most significant operation of the period involved the privatization of one of the government's most important business creations of the wartime period, the so-called Big Inch and Little Big Inch pipelines.

The pipeline deal was one of the largest, most complicated, and delicate any Wall Street firm had managed in a generation. It originated in a government decision to construct several pipelines from the southwestern oil fields to the industrial Midwest and East. Planning began in the summer of 1941, when the United States was ostensibly neutral but in fact was aiding the Allies with munitions and other war-related items. It became a more pressing matter after the United States became a belligerent. Pipelines were necessary to save tanker space at a time when German submarines prowled the coastal sea-lanes seeking targets of opportunity. When the project was being planned there was no way of knowing the total cost, but an initial $60 million would be required for just the first phase of what eventually would be known as the "Big Inch," which was to run from Longview, Texas, to Linden, New Jersey. A second line, the "Little Big Inch," was also projected.[18]

For a while there was talk of an industry-wide consortium which would design and construct the pipeline. The Cole Act, which was passed and signed into law in 1941, anticipated that this would occur, and provided means whereby private interests could apply for the right of eminent domain in obtaining required land and become entitled to federal aid. Once the United States entered the war the concept of private construction and ownership was rejected, since the government had concluded that private enterprise could not have raised funds for so vast an operation or obtained necessary clearances. Moreover, the construction company would have to wend its way through the Washington bureaucracy in order to obtain priority treatment for the estimated 137,500 tons of steel the project would require. It was decided that the Reconstruction

Finance Corporation would finance construction, and in the end it provided $77 million for the Big Inch and $65 million for the Little Big Inch.[19]

Work began in August 1942, and the first petroleum was shipped from Longview to Norris City, Illinois, in February of the following year. The last phase, taking the oil to Linden, was ready for use in December. It was one of the most impressive engineering accomplishments of the war. Pipelines carried a minuscule portion of all American petroleum prior to the war; by the time the fighting ended, they accounted for almost half the total.[20]

Even before the war ended industry and government representatives met to discuss the matter of ownership and operation of the pipelines during peacetime. As early as the spring of 1943 private petroleum interests raised the possibility of a purchase of the lines. Under terms of the Cole Act the government was required to cease operation of all emergency pipeline facilities within a year of the end of the fighting, so this was no mere academic exercise.[21]

Within a year several industry leaders, the most prominent being T. E. Swigart, president of Shell Pipe Line Corp., had stated publicly that the pipelines would hardly be competitive with tankers, implying the industry would have little incentive to acquire them. Contesting this view was Secretary of Commerce Jesse Jones and several petroleum company executives then working in government agencies.[22] The controversy raged into 1945, with each side marshaling statistics to prove its conclusions.[23]

Most students of the subject agreed that the pipelines would be profitable were they converted to the transmission of natural gas. There was more natural gas available in the Southwest than could be economically used; the gas obtained as a by-product of oil drilling traditionally was burned at the site simply to get rid of it. Yet there was a growing and profitable market in the upper Midwest and Northeast. It appeared that conversion was the most sensible option, but this was opposed by the petroleum and coal interests, who feared natural gas would replace their fuels. The National Coal Association joined with the United Mine Workers in recommending the lines be closed down completely and mothballed for possible future military use. As a leading scholar of the subject concluded, "The whole affair was a classic clash of interest groups."[24]

Jockeying for business and political position followed. By mid-1947 the War Assets Administration (WAA) and the Army-Navy Petroleum Board, both of which earlier favored the disposal of the lines to petroleum interests, had shifted ground, and were willing to reconsider conversion to natural gas. Tennessee Gas Transmission was awarded temporary operation of the lines, while bids were opened to others in the industry.

Belmont understood the pipeline situation better than most on Wall Street, and soon led the Dillon Read effort to obtain the business. At the time, the WAA was still insisting the pipelines be used to transport petroleum, so as to make them available for this purpose in case of another war. A group of Texas businessmen interested in natural gas hoped to purchase the lines and convert them to natural gas. One of their number, E. Holley Poe, came to New York to seek the assistance of an investment banker.

This was where Dillon Read entered the scene. Poe went there, and was directed to Belmont. When asked why he had selected Dillon Read rather than some other investment bank, Poe shrugged his shoulders, and as Belmont later recalled, replied that someone had told him about the firm. "D-R has always been one of the biggest houses down here for underwriting natural gas corporation issues. In fact, before the war, in 1935, it had handled a private placement for $16 million of Northern Natural Gas bonds, selling them to insurance companies."[25]

Belmont studied the situation and told Poe nothing could be done unless and until the WAA changed its mind about the pipelines being used only for petroleum transportation. Unable to obtain satisfactory bids, the WAA soon turned the matter over to Congress, which after a brief debate agreed the lines could be used for any purpose so long as the government had a call on their services during periods of national emergency for twenty years. Bidders would be required to make a good faith payment of $100,000 on filing and another $5 million upon taking temporary possession. The bidders then would have nine months in which to present a satisfactory proposal.

With Wadsworth's assistance, Belmont promptly organized the Texas Eastern Transmission Co. (TETCO), which received its charter on January 30, 1947, and was established with the explicit purpose of bidding for the two pipelines. He then tried to procure funds from several banks and insurance companies, but they refused to come in unless he first raised $1.5 million, a substantial amount of which was to come from Dillon Read itself. Reluctantly he agreed; among TETCO's initial owners, who raised $1,350,000 were Texans—Poe, Everett De Golyer, and Herman and George Brown, the last named Houston construction men who were to receive important contracts from TETCO. The new company's attorneys, Vinson, Elkins, Weims, and Francis, provided $27,000. Dillon Read took a $317,000 interest, quite a sizable amount of money for a firm which always insisted on using other people's money in its deals.[26] Bollard, who had faith in the project, came in for $19,800. Another $150,000 arrived from the sale of common shares to syndicate members—150,000 shares at the price of $1 a share. Dillon Read then raised another $4 million from Manufacturers Trust, which also provided a $3 million construction loan.[27] On February 10, 1947, TETCO bid $143,127,000, nearly twice the highest bid made earlier, and $12 million more than the next highest of the six bids. Belmont later recalled how such an odd sum was arrived at:[28]

We went to Washington and spent the night trying to put together the bid for the next morning. We went through the potential profits and losses, the costs of natural gas, marketing arrangements, requirements to convert the line from petroleum to natural gas, contracting, problems with public service commissions, etc. Each of us wrote down what each thought the bid was going to be. I came up with the figure of $135,000,000. Finally we came up with $143,000,000 and then some bright guy said, "Well we ought to have some kind of an odd amount. Suppose somebody else also bid that amount." So we came up with $143,127,000. [This practice was sometimes known as "putting a tail on a deal."] We did it just by the seat of our pants, that's all it was.

We were scared to death that the bid would be lost through a technicality. You had to put it in a post office box in the post office in Washington by 10:00 that next morning or something like that. So we went to the post office and had our pictures taken on the steps in front of the clock with the envelope in our hands. Then we went in and shoved it into the box. Our attorney knew the Postmaster General and got us permission to sit up in the gallery and watch the boxes to see whether anyone got anywhere near

it or not! Everything worked out fine. That's a long way to tell
you how we got the award.

During the next nine months Belmont had to arrange for the
management of the company and obtain the additional $134.5
million-plus funds needed for reconstruction, operation, redemption of short-term loans, and miscellaneous expenses. The total
would come to $150.6 million. Recounting the experience to a re-
porter later that year, Belmont said:[29]

> Some of them risked their whole careers, their firm's reputa-
> tions—not to mention their own money. I personally handled the
> thing for D-R for about seven months. I didn't do anything else.
> I had to go and see the banks and the insurance people and raise
> $120 million. I had to arrange for the engineering surveys, geo-
> logical studies; I had to go down to Washington and see the gov-
> ernment people; I was talking on the long distance phone as much
> as 10 hours a day. And I wasn't different from the rest of us who
> were working on it. . . . I think it is a damn wonderful thing, and
> personally I'm damn proud of it.

On November 10, 1947, Dillon Read brought its financial package to market. First, the common shares were split on the basis
of seven new shares for each old one. Then the capitalization was
increased to 6 million shares. With this in place, the firm started
to structure the offerings. There was $120 million of an authorized
$300 million of Texas Eastern 3½ percent 25-year bonds which
were placed with twelve insurance companies, ranging from Metropolitan Life and Prudential which took $36 million each to New
England Mutual, which came in for $1.5 million. Simultaneously a
selling syndicate composed of 154 underwriters offered 3,564,000
shares of common at $9.50 a share, which fetched another
$33,858,000, bringing the total before deductions to $153,858,000.
Finally, Dillon Read arranged a $10 million line of credit with three
New York banks. Nothing is known of Dillon Read's profits on the
underwriting, but it was a sizable owner of TETCO common, acquired at a price of 14 cents a share, which rose to $9.50.[30]

It was the largest single corporate deal since the market crash
of 1929, and it went off without a hitch. On November 14, Dillon

Read dispatched a check for $143,027,000 to the Treasurer of the United States, completing the payment, which because of its price elicited comparisons to the Dodge purchase of twenty-two years earlier.[31] Unlike the Dodge deal, the TETCO operation carried risks. Dillon Read made its bid when it had no company, and only the pledge for the initial $5.1 million.

The Texas Eastern deal burnished Dillon Read's image as a major force in the industry and strengthened its credibility in the natural gas and petroleum industries. Needless to say, it also made Belmont a prominent figure within the Wall Street community. Other financings would follow, including several for TETCO, the first of which was a $30 million 5⅕ percent 20-year debenture the following December. During the next twenty-five years Dillon Read would bring to market over $1.7 billion in TETCO debt and equity, and another $1.2 billion for other pipeline companies.[32]

The aggregate figures indicate the scope of Dillon Read's business in those first postwar years. In 1946 the firm managed eighteen offerings, of which eleven were utilities or natural gas and oil pipelines. Of the twenty underwritings the following year, thirteen were in those categories, with the biggest deals by far for gas transmission companies.

The firm expanded once again, and, prompted by the need for additional space, in 1949 moved from Nassau Street to new offices at 46 William Street. It was not a new building, and while the facade was impressive in the massive style that signified corporate stability, taken as a whole the new quarters hardly were awe-inspiring. This was not a significant factor in this period, since so few clients ever came to the offices to conduct business.

This, then, was the kind of operation Dillon Read had become toward the end of the 1940s. As always, power went to performance. The new business atmosphere thrust forth new leadership. McCain remained the president, while Douglas Dillon was chairman. The former lacked the requisite talents to become an important investment banker. Douglas Dillon may have possessed the talents, but he was disinclined to continue a career in the field. As a result Clarence Dillon's dream of a dynasty would not be realized. Instead, Brandi and Belmont would emerge as the key figures at Dillon Read in the 1950s. While they would leave their own imprints on the firm, they would never be able to move entirely from under the long shadow cast by the retired Clarence Dillon.

·13·

The Brandi-Belmont
Era: At Home

(1948–1962)

The financial arena was both prosperous and stable during the immediate post–World War II decade. Most important, there were rules pertaining to ethics and business practices that most there accepted. Bankers and their clients appreciated this and for the most part acted within fairly well defined constraints.

It was the kind of atmosphere in which Dillon Read's bankers performed well. In this period the firm had strategies for winning new business while maintaining the old and the personnel capable of performing well for both, and was prepared to innovate within the prudent constraints established and monitored by Clarence Dillon. If the Dillon-Forrestal era of the 1920s was the firm's Golden Age, the 1950s and part of the 1960s, during which Fred Brandi and August Belmont led the firm, comprised its Silver Age.

With all of this stability and optimism there were significant changes brewing on the investment banking scene, which taken together altered some perceptions and policies during the immediate postwar years. They seemed portentous, stirring debate and prompting talk of an end to the old order. In fact these were relatively minor compared with what was to be in the 1970s and 1980s. Yet they did offer hints of what was to come.

237

One of these changes involved the always thorny issue of competitive bidding. Another concerned a Justice Department antitrust suit filed against seventeen investment banks including Dillon Read, and the Investment Bankers' Association, which soon was known as "Club Seventeen." (The seventeen firms, in order of citation were: Morgan Stanley, Kuhn Loeb, Smith Barney, Lehman Brothers, Glore Forgan, Kidder Peabody, Goldman Sachs, White Weld, Eastman Dillon, Drexel, First Boston, Dillon Read, Blyth, Harriman Ripley, Stone & Webster, Harris Hall, and Union Securities.)

The two issues were related, in that at the very heart of both was the nature of the investment banking relationship. As has been seen, Dillon Read cultivated clients assiduously, and along with other investment banks sought trainees who by background and through contacts would be able to bring in new business. This was not unusual; recall that the first business Clarence Dillon did for William A. Read & Co. was for William Horlick, to whom he had been introduced by mutual friends, and the first underwriting he handled was for Armin Schlesinger's Newport Mining. By themselves such connections would not suffice, since friendship usually counted for little when it came to the raising of large sums of money in the competitive business world. Familial and social affinities might open doors, however, and this is what was needed as a first step.

Such was the circumstance with Peter Flanigan, who arrived at Dillon Read in 1947 with a Princeton degree after service in the Navy during World War II. He was the son of Manufacturers Hanover Trust chairman Horace Flanigan, and his mother was a member of the Busch family, which controlled Anheuser-Busch. Flanigan started out, as did most young associates, preparing spread sheets under Wilbur DuBois's wary eye, a rather tedious and boring exercise later performed by computers, but then considered an ideal training ground.

After a year and a half of this, Flanigan learned that the government required the services of financial analysts to assist with the implementation of the Marshall Plan. In March 1949 he took a leave of absence from the firm to work for the government in London. This was Flanigan's initial experience with public service, to which he would return on several occasions. The experience broadened his vision, and in the process Flanigan came into contact with many individuals with whom he would have dealings later on. On returning to Dillon Read in September of 1951, Flanigan learned from a college friend that his father, who controlled Briggs Manufacturing, wanted to sell it. Would Dillon Read assist in the effort? Flanigan would and did. Together with Brandi he studied the matter, and soon perceived a natural fit between Briggs and Chrysler, for which it was a prime supplier. "It was a difficult negotiation which Brandi handled with great skill," Flanigan recalled. This was followed by underwritings for Anheuser-Busch, which with Flanigan's efforts became a Dillon Read client. Flanigan's contacts were instrumental in getting this business, but the firm kept them because of its ability to meet their requirements.

Dillon Read and other old-line investment banks considered such affiliations not only appropriate, but preferable to the more impersonal competitive bidding supported by those banks which lacked such connections.

Traditional investment bank-client affiliations, in which the bank helped develop financial strategies, would remain intact for those firms with strong relations with their bankers. In 1952, banker George Whitney recalled what business had been like prior to competitive bidding:[1]

It is an interesting fact that the greatest companies by way of size, that had the biggest issues, were frequently those that came most constantly in the old days to the same banker; and the reason was, of course, that it was worth the while of the banker to keep constantly in contact. Like anybody who holds a defensive line, if he is alert you can never break through because he is always manning the defensive line and it takes heavier forces to break through, just as in military affairs. You find that, for example, in that long period that ended with these public sealed bidding regulations. For example, Kuhn, Loeb & Co. would always be on the job with the Pennsylvania. Therefore it would be terribly difficult for anybody competitively to get in. Just as Dillon, Read & Co. would always be on the job with the North American Company, a great public utility holding company, and would make it very difficult for somebody else to break that. Also J. P. Morgan & Co. up to 1930 would be always on the job with respect to the Telephone Company.

The rules were changing, and so were the relationships. Under competitive bidding the corporation or government would decide how much money was required and the form of the offering, and then put it out for bids. The underwriter was responsible for the syndication and distribution of the issue, and little more. Relationships and detailed knowledge of the client were not the prime requirement in competitive bidding. Rather, bankers had to rely more upon their abilities to outbid others, their leadership in syndication, and placement powers. All of these were present earlier, but now they would become paramount.

In 1926 the Interstate Commerce Commission had required competitive bidding on the sale by railroads of equipment trust certificates. During the 1930s, two non–Wall Street banks, Chicago-based Halsey Stuart and Cleveland's Otis & Co., attempted to gain government support for enforced competitive bidding. There was some talk of including the requirement in the Public Utilities Holding Company Act, but nothing came of it. In 1938, however, the SEC adopted a rule aimed at preventing excessive fees for utilities underwritings, a rule which was vigorously opposed by leaders at the Investment Bankers' Association, including Ralph Bollard. Unimpressed, the SEC went on to announce Rule U-50 in 1941, which required competitive bidding with few exceptions on all issues offered by registered holding companies.[2] The rule was subsequently broadened, and the practice spread to other segments of the market. Ultimately all bond issues for utilities and railroads had to be sold by competitive bidding practices.[3]

Clearly to the degree they had clients in these industries such a change was bound to affect all investment banks. Halsey Stuart, which was experienced in competitive bidding, became a more prominent firm. Kuhn Loeb, which previously had avoided the equities underwriting area, now entered it on a trial basis. Dillon Read would be more deeply affected than most, since it was one of the premier firms serving the electric utility industry.

Even before U-50 the bankers knew their profit margins would be lower under competitive bidding, and there was a greater tendency for the larger ones to develop retail operations, distributing issues they had underwritten, thus increasing profits while diminishing the roles of selling syndicates. Some banks, among them Morgan Stanley, reorganized as partnerships in order to qualify for NYSE membership, hoping to develop a specialized brokerage business to augment and complement underwriting operations. In 1944 Kuhn Loeb underwrote its first stock issue, signaling its intention to become active in this market. These banks actively and aggressively sought new business. The cake of custom was crumbling. Old ties were being strained, and from then on the pace would quicken.

None of this sat well with Dillon Read. Along with other old-line investment banks the firm carefully distinguished between transactional and relationship-oriented banks. Transaction-positioned banks would seek as many deals as they could handle, becoming larger with ever greater capital and placement capabilities. The more underwritings managed, the larger the banks would become, and as the banks became larger, they could direct more transactions.

Relationship-oriented banking was long-term, sophisticated, and to a degree personal, while transactional banking by necessity was short-term and impersonal. Dillon Read was the quintessential relationship operation, having exclusive relations with a smaller group of companies which appreciated expert and efficient treatment.[4] The partners thought of themselves as financial advisors to corporations and governments, assisting in the development of financial plans as well as purchasing their paper. Such banking was centered on solving problems for clients, not simply bidding for business, on the assumption that while proficient in their own businesses, clients required the expertise firms like Dillon Read possessed. The firm would function as consultant, called in on a more or less regular basis. It would not seek business in a hostile fashion. This was not unusual, but rather the way most of the old-line investment banks operated. John Haskell, who arrived at Dillon Read in 1958, recalled what the business was like in that period.

In those days, there was no marketing. Dillon Read had a syndicate partner, and I think we had one salesman. What you did was to create the deals. You bought the deals, and then you syndicated them. The actual selling was done by the Merrill Lynches and the brokerage firms or the Salomons in the case of bond trading, but you didn't do any selling. That was just dirtying your hands. The tradition—it's very much in the U.K. tradition.

They would do an underwriting. They would create the financing. The would use their capital to underwrite the deal. But the brokers would do the selling. They would never do any selling. And that's the way Morgan Stanley operated, it's the way Dillon Read operated, and Kuhn, Loeb operated—there were no sales forces at all.

It was in tune with what Otto Kahn proclaimed before the Pecora Committee in 1933. "It has long been our policy and our effort to get our clients, not by chasing after them, not by praising our own wares, but by an attempt to establish a reputation which would make clients feel that if they have a problem of a financial nature, Dr. Kuhn, Loeb & Co. is a pretty good doctor to go to." Kahn continued:[5]

A railroad . . . would come to us and would say: "We have such and such a problem to solve, being a problem of a financial nature. We would like to get your advice as to the best kind of security to issue for that purpose—and by the best kind of security, I mean a security which on the one hand gives to the railroad the most useful instrument, not only for immediate purposes, but for long term purposes, and gives to the public the greatest possible protection without tying up the railroad unduly and beyond what is safe for it." So he says: "Will you tell us what is the best kind of instrument for that purpose? Shall it be a mortgage bond? Should it be a debenture? Should it be a convertible bond? Should it be preferred stock? Should it be an equity? We would like you to look into it and tell us. Here are the facts and figures. Go through them."

At first this strategy seemed both prudent and capable of being implemented. By remaining as it was, Dillon Read did not have to assume the expenses of taking on large numbers of additional personnel in sales, research, and money management areas, which traditionally were low-margin operations. Indeed, Dillon Read was one of the most profitable investment banks when measured in terms of return on capital. In 1945, the firm had only $2.1 million in invested capital, but was third in the number of total issues managed for the period from 1938 to 1946, and for most of the years was one of the top three firms in the industry in managerships.[6]

DILLON READ UNDERWRITINGS OF PUBLICLY OFFERED
ISSUES, 1938–1946
(figures in millions of dollars)

Year	Managerships	Rank	Participations	Rank
1938	161.7	3	42.7	10
1939	220.3	1	47.0	6
1940	181.3	3	64.9	4
1941	235.1	1	39.7	6
1942	66.7	2	14.8	8
1943	20.4	12	12.7	22
1944	132.0	6	21.8	29
1945	247.7	4	78.8	11
1946	190.3	1	58.5	17

SOURCE: Justice Department material prepared for use in U.S. v. Henry S. Morgan et al.

Inclination and tradition also led the firm to oppose competitive bidding. Thus it opposed industry support for compulsory sealed competitive bidding for security issues, knowing perhaps such accord would be impossible to achieve.[7]

Dillon Read's position was complicated by the nature of its business. There were three categories of underwritings, and its niche in each was different from what it was in the others. Acting as manager or agent on negotiated issues, Dillon Read had been among the industry's top three firms in terms of dollar volume from 1935 to 1949, when it accounted for 6.5 percent of the business. When it came to competitive bids the picture changed sharply. Dillon Read managed or comanaged only seventeen such public issues in this period, positioning it in sixteenth place with 2.6 percent of this category of underwritings. Overall, for the fifteen-year period from 1935 to 1949, Dillon Read was seventh in dollar volume and eleventh in number of public sealed bidding issues managed. During the same period it was first in dollar volume of agency private placements.[8]

By 1950 Dillon Read, overall, ranked twelfth in syndicate volume, below such assertive firms as Halsey Stuart, Merrill Lynch, Blyth, and Salomon Brothers. Dillon Read was one of the leaders in private placements, handling such substantial deals as a $125 million financing for Trans-Arabian Pipeline in 1947, and the sale of $756 million of debt for Reynolds Metals from 1951 through 1966.

LEADING AMERICAN SYNDICATORS, 1950

(figures in millions of dollars)

Firm	Amount
1. Halsey Stuart	723
2. Morgan Stanley	644
3. First Boston	555
4. Merrill Lynch, Pierce, Fenner & Beane	338
5. Kidder Peabody	289
6. Blyth	265
7. Lehman Brothers	232
8. White Weld	210
9. Union Securities	182
10. Stone & Webster	169
11. Salomon Brothers & Hutzler	145
12. Dillon Read	120
13. Harriman Ripley	102
14. Kuhn Loeb	97
15. Glore Forgan	79
16. Equitable Securities	50
17. Drexel	40

SOURCE: U.S. v. Henry S. Morgan et al., "Reply Opening Statement," March 29, 1951.

While public offerings for 1950 came to $120 million, private placements were $177 million.[9]

Dillon Read's high profitability and low ranking were not unusual; as noted, private placements were becoming increasingly popular. Nor was Dillon Read alone in cultivating this business and meeting the demands of institutions, insurance companies in particular. From 1942 to 1946, by far the majority of the approximately $4 billion of private placements were taken by insurance companies in direct negotiations with the issuers. In 1946, almost two-thirds of all industrial bonds and notes with maturities of over five years were issued not through dealers in securities after registration under the rules of the Securities Act, but through private placement with limited numbers of financial institutions, or were placed with commercial banks.[10] The proportion of private placements increased gradually afterwards, as Wall Street banks and clients became more oriented in this direction.

With the arrival of competitive bidding under U-50, Dillon Read lost some important clients. It had been the banker for Union Electric, the utility company that serviced the St. Louis area. From 1933 to 1941, it had underwritten $214 million of Union Electric's paper, most of it in the form of debt. Since Dillon Read would not bid competitively on their bonds the firm was also overlooked when Union Electric tried to sell equity and other noncompetitive paper. As a result, its position within the industry for this category of business declined. Yet this alone did not tell the entire story. Dillon Read remained a major force in the area of noncompetitive bidding, or relationship banking, which was by far the more profitable aspect of the business. According to Flanigan, it had become transparently clear that the inevitable result of competitive bidding would be to transform underwriting into a low-margin business. "And Dillon Read had never been interested in high-volume, low-margin businesses." Such a decision meant Dillon Read would forgo size for profitability. By rejecting competitive bidding the firm would also refuse potential clients.

> I think we had a selective list of clients. We never had as many clients as people thought we had. But we had enough. And we were a small institutional house for selling the product which we could develop. The great bulk of the product was sold then through a syndicate. And when you put Merrill Lynch and the other big wire houses in your equity deals, you put Salomon and these other fellows in your debt deals and they could do the selling so you didn't have to have a sales department.

Dillon Read remained one of the leading firms in negotiated public offerings and private placements, but had little business in areas in which competitive bidding was required.

The company continued to take pride in its status as a special bracket house years after it really had fallen from that position. This became a matter of some sensitivity at the firm and occasionally resulted in lost business. For example, when informed it would have to accept the role as one of several comanagers in the 1956 initial underwriting for Ford Motors, and not be a lead bank, Dillon Read opted out of the deal.[11]

Dillon Read also refused to consider the kind of diversification of activities seen at Morgan Stanley and Kuhn Loeb. Indeed, on

March 12, 1945, the firm reverted to the corporate form. Now NYSE membership became impossible. Other members of the Old Guard were going in one direction, and Dillon Read in the other.

The other significant development of the period, the antitrust case filed on October 30, 1947, was one of the most celebrated and baffling in the history of such litigation. Specifically, Attorney General Tom Clark charged that the seventeen companies had violated the Sherman Anti-Trust Act by entering into a conspiracy in restraint of trade. "It is the Government's purpose in this suit," he said, "to correct long-standing restrictive practices in the investment banking field, developed and followed by these 17 important firms, so as to strengthen and produce competition among this group and generally in the investment banking industry."[12]

The government's case rested on what was known as the "triple concept." The first was the unwillingness of the bankers to poach on the preserves of others, which is to say they voluntarily refrained from competing with one another. Then there was the "historical position," the practice of permitting banks to join in syndicates based upon past practice, which of course made it difficult for newcomers to enter the business. Finally, there was reciprocity, the custom of each house repaying participations in the syndicates of others by allowing them to join those they organized. This, too, would operate to exclude the others.

Clark observed that the cited firms had handled approximately 69 percent of the value of underwritings since 1938, and since all were based in New York, they had concentrated investment banking power in the city.

The complaint asked for specific relief. First, Clark wanted to prevent investment banks from "occupying the dual function of advisor to an issuer and purchaser for resale of the securities of the same issuer." If he had his way those in the purchase syndicate could no longer function in the sellers syndicate, not only for that particular issue, but for all from the same firm or government body; "each defendant banking firm [shall] be required to elect which of these two types of business it will conduct for a particular issuer and to stay out of the business not elected for that issuer." In addition each of the defendants would be enjoined from participating in purchase syndicates organized by the others. The banks would be forbidden to place any of its officers on the boards of companies for which they acted as underwriters.

MAJOR UNDERWRITERS, 1938–1947
(figures in millions of dollars)

Firm	Total Issues Managed	Percentage
Morgan Stanley	3,362.4	16.1
First Boston	2,726.0	13.1
Dillon Read	1,486.1	7.1
Kuhn Loeb	1,380.1	6.6
Blyth	902.2	4.3
Smith Barney	804.0	3.9
Lehman Brothers	640.3	3.1
Harriman Ripley	618.3	3.0
Glore Forgan	418.7	2.0
Kidder Peabody	392.9	1.9

SOURCE: *U.S. v. Morgan et al.*, "Copy of Complaint," p. 49.

There were other objectives, but these, clearly aimed at greater regulation of the business and an "opening" to other non–Wall Street firms, were the salient ones. Should the government win the case on all points, the result would be a fractionalized and radically altered business environment, the most revolutionary transformation since the early New Deal days.

Perhaps such allegations and changes would have been supportable during the 1920s, but the business had changed dramatically since then, as had concentration. Consider that National City and Chase Securities each had more capital in 1929 than *all* seventeen indicted firms.[13] In essence, it was a Rooseveltian protest against Coolidge-era practices filed during the Truman Administration based upon legislation passed in the Benjamin Harrison Administration.

This is not to suggest that by then the New Deal was antique or the law outmoded, but the conditions which brought some of the securities legislation into being and the reform impulse generated by the New Deal were long gone, and the nature of investment banking was altered. The charges derived more directly from the TNEC probe of the late 1930s and the anti–Wall Street arguments of Otis & Co., Hayden Stone, and several others than the reality and the specific situation in 1947.

Then, too, there was the matter of the selection of the defendants, which ran in size from Morgan Stanley to Drexel. The list included companies which had transacted little business with one another, and even involved the Investment Bankers' Association, on the presumption that it had assisted the banks in their operations.[14] From the roster it would appear the group had been chosen more by virtue of opposition to competitive bidding, and their Old Guard status, than any other factor.

This would explain the omission of Halsey Stuart, then a major industry force. Merrill Lynch and Salomon Brothers participated in syndicates organized by defendants, and neither firm, each larger than some defendants, was cited. Blyth may have been included because Charles E. Mitchell of National City joined it in 1935, while Harris Hall was an outgrowth of Harris Forbes, which once had been a powerful organization.

The action did not come as a surprise. There had been talk of such a filing for at least eight years, and each of the firms had known of Clark's attitudes and activities for the past year. The previous April attorneys for the seventeen firms had filed a memorandum responding to charges that corresponded to those filed, indicating they were in communication with the Justice Department on the matter for more than half a year.

Virtually all of the larger firms protested their inclusion and pointed out weaknesses in the allegations. Hours after the filing Dillon Read sent the following statement to *The Wall Street Journal* and financial columnist Leslie Gould.[15]

> The charge of lack of competition in the investment banking business is not in accord with the facts. The business is essentially competitive. In fact, Dillon, Read & Co. owes its existence and present position to such competition. Dillon, Read & Co. has always competed actively for business and has never been prevented from negotiating or bidding on any piece of business by reason of restrictive agreement or arrangement with anyone.
>
> Dillon, Read & Co. has never been a party to any agreement or arrangement designed to prevent any other investment banking firm from competing for any piece of business.

The trial began on November 28, 1950, before sixty-two-year-old Judge Harold Medina. One of the nation's most distinguished jurists, Medina was born in Brooklyn of Mexican parents, had attended Princeton, and gone on to Columbia Law School, from which he graduated in 1912. He entered private practice and headed his own firm while teaching part-time at Columbia. Medina had been named to the federal bench in 1947, and before undertaking the Club Seventeen case had presided over the trial of eleven Communist party officials which resulted in their conviction and incarceration for violations of the Smith Act, which made it a crime to "advocate, abet, advise, or teach . . . overthrowing any government of the United States by force or violence."[16]

From the first Medina was troubled by several aspects of the government's presentation, and was quick to show irritation. He found the decision to cite these specific seventeen firms puzzling. How was the number selected? After hearing testimony for three months he confessed, "I have never understood how they picked the seventeen," to which George Whitney of the house of Morgan replied, "They picked them because those are the people who have been the most energetic and resourceful and tended to have most managing and underwriting business . . . just as if you were to pick the 17 most successful, or attempted to pick the 17 men you thought were the most successful lawyers in New York and said, 'Well, if we can prosecute and knock them down, then doubtless all the other lawyers will fall in line.' " Medina was skeptical, remarking, "And get more business." Whitney persisted, however, in claiming it was their success which did them in.[17]

Several of the defendants took the Whitney approach: First Boston replied: "The suit is discriminatory in that the 17 firms named include only a portion of those which occupy a position of importance in the industry. . . . The Attorney General thus seeks to impose a penalty on an arbitrarily selected group of firms who have emerged, as a result of competition, as among those capable of success in the underwriting of securities."[18]

Finally, there was the nature of the Complaint, which was riddled with errors. For example, the government contended that the modern syndicate method of distributing securities "was invented by the defendants and their predecessors in 1915," when in fact the first buying syndicates appeared in 1813 and Jay Cooke's selling syndicates of the late 1860s were not substantially different from those of the 1940s.[19]

Medina criticized the government for the shoddiness of the preparation. He questioned the naming of the IBA as a defendant, and the government was compelled to drop its charges against that organization. Was mere opposition to sealed bidding evidence of criminal action as the government alleged? Medina thought not. "It positively shocks me that men who openly press their views on public bodies in the open should be accused of wrongdoing," he observed, and later told a government attorney that while he could discern criminality in "sneaky, furtive lobbying," there was nothing wrong in "coming right out in the open where everyone can see who the man is, that he is frankly furthering his own economic interest—that seems different to me, and that is a thing that I just bristle up at every time you get down to it."[20]

On one occasion Dillon Read attorney Matthew Correa of the firm of Cahill, Gordon, Zachry & Reindel referred to a government exhibit, a solicitation letter from First Boston to Columbus & Southern Ohio Electric, a client of Dillon Read. Not only had the government erred in claiming that the letter was sent to Dillon Read and was confused regarding its meaning, but the government's subsequent denial that the letter constituted evidence irritated Medina. "If this is not competition," he said, "I am an Eskimo."[21] On another occasion Medina chided government attorney Henry Stebbins. In his argument Stebbins erroneously stated that a letter McCain actually sent while president of United Light & Power was dispatched while he was CEO of Dillon Read, and because of this he completely misunderstood the nature of one episode. When this was pointed out to him, Stebbins made the mistake of trying to cover up his error. Glaring with moustache bristling at the hapless attorney, Medina roared, "When it was pointed out to you that instead he [McCain] was president of the issuer, instead of admitting that you were wrong about it, you said, 'Well, it means the same thing as it would have meant if it had been sent to the man at Dillon, Read & Co.,' and that is perfectly absurd."[22]

As the trial wore on the government was obliged to either abandon or modify its charges, and Medina often criticized flaws in the preparation. In spite of this, the trial was the most extensive study of the investment banking business in modern times. Ultimately, the government's case rested on the reasons why companies selected the same lead underwriter time and again. As the defendants suggested, it was because good service prompted ad-

ditional business. The Justice Department's attempts to show col-
lusion or pressure simply could not be supported. And when this
failed, the other two legs of the case also collapsed.

In his decision Medina opined that each of the defendant firms
conducted business in similar ways, as was the case in any industry.
"But each has followed its own course," he wrote, "formulated its
own policies, and competed for business in the manner deemed by
it to be most effective."

The proceeding ended in a complete victory for the defendants.
Medina charged the government with having created a "fictional
foundation" for its case. He dismissed the complaint, doing so with
prejudice, an unusual step which virtually assured the government
would not appeal the ruling.[23]

Unfortunately for historians, Dillon Read's operations were not
a critical issue at the trial, and so contemporary documented evidence on the firm is thin. Of the partners, only Karl Behr appeared
to offer testimony. Behr made his depositions, none of which were
read into evidence. He presented the picture of a small, uncomplicated operation, which was of little value in terms of the case,
but he did manage to reveal some aspects of the firm. After observing that Dillon Read had abandoned its small private banking
business in 1934, and Egly headed the syndication efforts, Behr
was asked about other departments.[24]

Q. Do you have a buying department?
A. No, sir.
Q. Do you have a trading department?
A. No, sir.
Q. Do you have a statistical department?
A. Not as such, I would not say we have today a statistical
    department.

Behr testified that Dillon Read considered new business at
meetings which took place on most weekdays. Full assent of all
vice presidents was needed before business would be accepted, but
the practice was to accept business if the vice president involved
was an expert in that area. Brandi and Belmont, for example,
occupied that position in pipelines, while Brandi was responsible
for several oil companies, most notably Union Oil of California and

Superior Oil. Harry Egly was directly involved with a great many utility financings.

Behr also offered examples of what Dillon Read meant by relationship-oriented banking. He told the court of the time the CEO of American Chain arrived to discuss a problem he was having on one project. It seemed the cable provided for a bridge in the Detroit area had cracked, and the firm was being sued by the contractor. Behr, who held an undergraduate degree from Yale and was not a lawyer, was nonetheless asked his opinion. "Just from a pure business angle, do you think we ought to settle this thing for X hundreds of thousands of dollars; is that too much for us to pay, etc?" the executive asked. What he wanted was Behr's insights based on experience in business, and not a legal opinion, which is what one could expect from relationship-investment bankers.[25]

> And those are the sort of discussions that I had that were different than, I think, most investment bankers would have with a client. It had nothing to do with the issuing of securities at all. At times some of these people would come in and say they were considering making such and such a type of product, did I think it fitted with their business. And at times they would come in and say, "We are thinking of acquiring such and such a company, do you think that would be a sound thing for us to do?" And at times I would point out that the products made by that company did not fit their selling organization at all, they were in conflict with it, and could not be absorbed in their selling, and all kinds of things of that nature; questions on patents, they would come in and ask innumerable questions.

When Behr denied Dillon Read had attempted to dominate companies for which it performed investment banking functions, Medina agreed, and noted the government's evidence was "far from impressive." Indeed, Dillon Read placed representatives on a smaller percentage of boards of companies for which it performed investment banking services than any of the other defendants except Stone & Webster.[26]

Behr stated that all of these additional services, for which Dillon Read did not charge, would have to be suspended if competitive bidding became the rule. The profits from competitive bidding were so small as to require barebones operations, which would force all but the largest investment banks from the business and result in unwise underwritings. "I think it would harm, in the long run, the issuer, and I think it will harm the investor, and I think the investment banker will be harmed."[27]

The antitrust charges, however flimsy, did have their impact. From the day the brief was filed to the handing down of the Medina decision on September 22, 1953, the entire investment banking industry operated under a cloud, fearful of the impact of its actions upon its very survival. The timidity born of the Depression was reinforced by the threat of government action, dampening all thought of bold and novel action. One can easily imagine the thoughts running through Clarence Dillon's mind, the comparisons he might have drawn between the Pecora hearings and the trial, and his relief when the ordeal ended.

Having said this, it should be noted that while both were unpleasant episodes, the Pecora investigations and the antitrust trial were quite different in both tone and significance. The times were strikingly dissimilar. The Pecora hearings had been conducted when the very existence of capitalism was in doubt; the antitrust proceeding came when business was good and getting even better. If Dillon Read's conventional business was being eroded by competitive bidding, new opportunities presented themselves on a fairly regular basis.

These changes on the investment banking scene occurred against the backdrop of a startlingly strong economy. The post–World War II conversion to a peacetime status had gone more smoothly than virtually all the experts had thought possible. By late 1947, the automobile industry was operating at a higher rate than in 1929. Paperboard production, then considered a crucial economic indicator, broke records each year from 1945 to 1948. The construction industry showed similar progress; housing starts increased each year from 1945 through 1950, and by the end of this span there were twice as many starts as in 1929. "Wherever one looked, the U.S. was splitting its breeches," commented *Time* on January 14, 1948. "In mushrooming Houston, millionaires were so common nobody paid them much attention."

American consumers, who had suffered during the Depression

and could not purchase much in the way of goods during the war, went on a massive spending spree, which sparked a boom in capital investment. Gross private investment had been $7.1 billion in 1944, the last full year of the war; in 1950 it reached $51.8 billion, more than three times what it had been in 1929. New industries and products, from television to ballpoint pens, generated interest in business. In 1945 there were 3 million enterprises of various sizes in the United States, the same as in 1929; their number reached 4 million in 1950.[28]

Even so, the securities markets did not yet reflect the growing economy. Both individual and institutional investors remained wary of stocks, while corporate underwritings were far lower than all of this economic activity might indicate would have been. The major reason was the high degree of liquidity corporations found themselves in, as a result of caution in the Depression years and large profits during the war. Studying this situation in 1961, a government task force concluded that corporate capital requirements were financed chiefly through recourse to internal sources. Retail profits in the postwar period to that time came to $139 billion and depreciation was another $204 billion. Some $76 billion came from trade credits extended by other firms and by current accruals in excess of payments. This left $149 billion to be raised from banks and other institutional lenders, and from the sale of securities.[29]

Nonetheless, the situation was changing. During the late 1940s Merrill Lynch, Pierce, Fenner & Beane aggressively and successfully sought new accounts and strove to interest small investors in securities. The institutional market, dominated by trusts, corporate accounts, banks, and insurance companies, was about to undergo major long-term transformations. As a result of contract negotiations in 1950 between General Motors and the United Auto Workers, a new pension plan was established which permitted the purchase of stocks and corporate bonds. Other plans followed, increasing the demand for such paper.[30] In time they would enlarge the market for private placements, with more pension funds and other institutions prepared to contract for the purchase of larger blocks of bonds prior to underwriting. In 1951 Keith Funston took over as NYSE president, and almost immediately embarked upon a crusade for "People's Capitalism," with the slogan, "Own Your Share of America."

NET CHANGES IN OUTSTANDING CORPORATE SECURITIES,
1945–1958
(figures in billions of dollars)

| Year | Total | Net Changes in Outstanding Securities | |
		Bonds	Stocks
1945	− 573	−1,038	464
1946	2,226	1,114	1,111
1947	4,191	3,005	1,186
1948	5,818	4,725	1,093
1949	4,592	3,285	1,307
1950	3,469	2,004	1,465
1951	5,886	3,583	2,306
1952	7,383	4,942	2,441
1953	6,688	4,757	1,932
1954	5,602	3,799	1,802
1955	6,081	4,188	1,893
1956	7,158	4,611	2,548
1957	9,739	7,026	2,713
1958	7,977	5,850	2,127

SOURCE: United States, *Historical Statistics of the United States* (1975), II, 1005.

In its own way, Dillon Read created a virtual revolution in the financing of petroleum exploration. The petroleum industry, which, as has been seen, had long been Brandi's particular preserve, performed well. Union Oil of California had used Dillon Read's services for the first time in a 1922 bond offering and, for more than half a century, regularly employed the firm for financial assistance. After the war, Union Oil embarked upon an ambitious exploration program which required large amounts of capital that, given its balance sheet, could not be raised in the conventional fashion. So Brandi devised a clever financing scheme. First, he organized a company that he called Nassau Associates as a subsidiary of Dillon Read. Nassau would hire petroleum engineers to obtain estimates of the production in a producing Union Oil field. The company then estimated what the value of petroleum would be over the life of the field. Taking into consideration the discounted price of future earnings, Nassau would contract to purchase a portion of the oil production from Union Oil.

Nassau then would create two companies, called "A" and "B." The "A" securities were, in effect, if not actual, form, bonds, because they had a first call on all income. Since the investors in "A" paper had the petroleum engineer's report on the potential for the field, the only real risks involved the price of petroleum and market conditions, and the possibility that the reserves simply might not be there. The "B" investors retained ownership plus the generous depletion allowances of the period, which translated into large tax breaks. Moreover, the "B" securities could receive substantial leveraged profits if output was more than anticipated. In some deals the purchaser of the "A" would receive "B" securities as a sweetener, somewhat in the same manner that the purchasers of bonds in the 1920s received common stock as an extra inducement.

The next step was to sell the production contract to an investor, usually an insurance company, Metropolitan Life being one of the first. Dillon Read generally retained a quarter ownership in both the "A" and "B" companies, and would sell the remaining interest to investors. Other similar deals followed. For example, in late December 1949, Nassau purchased a 30 percent interest in a 30,000-acre natural gas field in the Carthage area of Panola County, Texas.[31] It was a highly profitable business, which catapulted Brandi into a major leadership role at the firm.

August Belmont thought that Brandi also originated the concept of purchase and leasebacks. If not, he was certainly one of the first to create innovative applications for this technique. In 1956, he organized the first of what eventually would become seven companies that arranged the sale of a Union Oil office building and other facilities, which Union Oil would then rent or lease, obtaining cash needed for operations as well as a business write-off of the rents for tax benefits. These companies were owned by Dillon Read partners, associates, and institutions favored by the firm, and financed by funds borrowed from several banks, including Manufacturers, which as noted was headed by Horace Flanigan, also a Union Oil director.

The deal proved profitable for all concerned. Brandi used the technique to raise funds for other Dillon Read clients. In addition to sales and leasebacks on structures, he sold Texaco service stations for leaseback purposes. Brandi became Union Oil's most important financial advisor, and soon was named to the company's board.

Other Dillon Read bankers entered the field. August Belmont created some twists of his own. He located a client who owned a natural gas field and had a large bank loan outstanding that required repayment. Belmont organized three companies—"A," "B," and "C." The gas reserves were behind the "A" bonds, facilities went into "B" bonds, and the "C" stock had ownership rights, received dividends on whatever remained, and benefited from depreciation charges.[32] Through Nassau-controlled Sabine Natural Gas & Products, Dillon Read purchased a 30 percent interest in a plant that processed the gas produced from its leasehold, which became a "B" portion of the Sabine deal.[33]

Another Brandi innovation in leasebacks came in the form of a financing for tankers and office buildings to be leased to Union Oil. Dillon Read created a company for the Union Oil business known as Barracuda Tanker Corp., owned by twenty-seven individuals associated with Dillon Read. Barracuda would purchase tankers that would be leased to Union Oil. The partners contributed a total of $20,000, with the rest of the funding financed with a $51 million loan granted by Metropolitan Life to an intermediary company. The tankers were constructed in 1958 and 1959, and immediately chartered to Union Oil.

The particulars became public when in 1961 Dillon Read sold $120 million worth of debentures for Union Oil, and disclosed the identities of the seven leasing companies. The *Wall Street Journal* put a team of reporters on the story, and one of the first steps in their investigation was to set up an appointment with Brandi. When it was suggested that since he was on the Union Oil board there might be a conflict of interest, Brandi, who together with his wife and son had shared in Barracuda, retorted that this wasn't so, since Union Oil benefited from the arrangement. Not only were the lease terms "less than the going rate," but the firm realized tax advantages by entering into the leases. Union Oil Chairman Reese Taylor agreed, asserting that all negotiations with Barracuda were conducted at arm's length.[34]

In June two stockholder suits were filed against Dillon Read, Union Oil, and several officials at both concerns. Alleging conflicts of interest, the shareholders asked the courts to require Dillon Read to make restitution for losses sustained by the company. Brandi said the suit was "without merit," and indicated that Dillon Read was prepared to contest all charges.[35]

While there was no evidence Union Oil had sustained losses, such cases were bound to be dragged out and result in costly legal fees, and whatever the resolution the publicity was bound to be harmful to Dillon Read, even though Barracuda was a separate entity. Accordingly, on December 12 the seven companies, including Barracuda, agreed to pay Union Oil $200,000, with the stipulation that by so doing they were not conceding that any wrongdoing was involved.[36]

While those Dillon Read partners involved with the Union Oil leaseback companies were embarrassed, this did not mean the technique itself was unwise, uneconomical, or disadvantageous to any party. Dillon Read would structure similar deals for other companies, and the practice became fairly common for several others in the financial-services industry.

Brandi and Belmont were to the Dillon Read of this period what Clarence Dillon and Forrestal had been in the 1920s, namely the leaders at the firm. Brandi excelled in his segment of investment banking and the conceiving of new vehicles, while Belmont also performed in these areas, and in addition had a primary role in running the bank.[37] Douglas Dillon was there as well, and served as chairman, but was not very active. He was becoming increasingly interested in politics, and was disposed to permit others to lead the firm. Clarence Dillon, by virtue of his holdings in the firm, was still the ultimate source of power at Dillon Read.

As for McCain, he had experienced problems with his health in late 1949, and soon was diagnosed as having Parkinson's disease. He came less frequently to the office until late 1951, when he was unable to do so at all. McCain resigned the presidency as of December 31 of that year, though remaining as a director. The selection of his replacement did not require much consideration. Even before McCain resigned it was known Brandi would succeed him.

In 1952 President-elect Eisenhower appointed Douglas Dillon ambassador to France. From then on Dillon would devote far more time to public service than to banking, though he would reappear at the firm between assignments. He resigned his chairmanship at Dillon Read and left the office vacant, presumably awaiting his return. In 1960, John F. Kennedy was elected President, and he asked Dillon to serve as his Secretary of the Treasury. This appointment required him to dispose of his ownership shares, which reverted to family trusts.

When it became apparent that the younger Dillon would not return to the firm, what had for years been a form of interim arrangement became more permanent. Brandi became chairman and Belmont was named to the presidency. This de jure resolution of what had been a de facto situation for years brought about no consequential change at Dillon Read. In investment banking power always went to those who had the ability to produce business, and Belmont's star rose throughout the 1950s. Thus though the Brandi-Belmont regime was "officially" installed in 1962, it had long since begun with the generation of underwritings and related operations in the natural gas and petroleum businesses more than a decade earlier.[38]

Brandi, Belmont, and others at the firm appreciated that the investment banking industry was evolving, slowly in the 1950s but at an accelerating pace. The changing times required alterations in strategies, innovations in tactics, a flexibility and willingness to come to accept modifications. Yet Clarence Dillon refused to come to terms with the new dispensation. Without his assent or acquiescence, little was possible. The result was a gradual erosion of industry position, which the partners seemed willing to accept so long as their remuneration remained satisfactory. How long this would be so in the increasingly aggressive investment banking position would be the most important question facing the firm during the next two decades.

·14·

The Brandi-Belmont Era: Abroad

(1963–1967)

In retrospect the 1950s and much of the 1960s seem a golden era for American business, and for commercial and investment banking in particular. Never before or since were the nation's businessmen so confident, their prospects so pleasing, their reputations so elevated. Almost the entire Western and developing world seemed to crave American expertise and capital, and Wall Street was prepared to offer both.

In some ways it was similar to the situation after World War I, when American banks made a massive push into foreign markets. Recall that Clarence Dillon had been alert to the opportunity to provide banking services to a variety of governmental and corporate clients in Europe, South America, and to a lesser degree, Japan. But it would be a mistake to consider the two periods analogous. The American role in reconstructing Europe and Asia after World War II was far more complex than had been the case after World War I.

Indeed, apart from political risks, international banking in the 1920s had been relatively uncomplicated and unchanged from what had gone before. An investment banker conversant with foreign markets in 1914 would have been equally comfortable in them in

1924. Even though its power was diminished London was still considered a mighty financial center. The gold standard remained intact. The trans-Atlantic brotherhood of bankers hadn't been altered much.

World War II brought greater modifications in these areas. One of the most obvious differences was the paramount role played by the United States. During the 1920s Great Britain and France considered themselves equal to America in terms of power and prestige, and certainly capable of playing independent roles in diplomacy. Such was not the case in the late 1940s and 1950s. Washington had become the political capital and nerve center of the West, while New York had become the world's financial hub, with no close rivals.

There were yet other differences between the situations at the close of each world war. While American business became more global in the 1920s, a sizable portion of the American people and their leaders thought it possible to return to isolationism and withdraw from a world about which they were disillusioned. This was not so after World War II, when President Harry Truman signaled his intention to utilize American political power in Europe and Asia. As had been the case after World War I, Washington actively and openly encouraged American business to expand overseas.

Following the Bretton Woods Conference of 1944, the dollar was tied to gold, and all other currencies were pegged to the dollar, which meant that to all intents and purposes, the West and much of the rest of the world were on a dollar standard. The International Monetary Fund and the International Bank for Reconstruction and Development were established; among their goals was the prevention of the kind of disequilibrium that had threatened world stability in the late 1920s and was a major cause of the Great Depression. Both institutions were to be dominated by American representatives.

It was the beginning of the American Imperium, the dawn of the American Century. A confident, exuberant, and interventionist America had taken center stage on the global arena.

One manifestation of this was the demand for dollars and dollar credits which was being heard in virtually every capital market; another was the export of American banking services. American capital markets historically had been more efficient and open than those in every European country, and this was another meaningful factor in the years after Bretton Woods. Clients long accustomed to dealing with banks in their own countries were now attracted by the speed and efficiency of the Americans.

Even so, American bankers would have to work hard to gain new markets, and considering the altered business scene, a knowledge of what had gone before, while useful, was of limited utility. Rather, firms interested in going abroad would have to study matters afresh and then decide how best to capitalize upon new opportunities.

Few American investment banks had as much experience with European underwritings as Dillon Read. Of course the bankers who had led Dillon Read in the expansionist 1920s—Dillon, Forrestal, Eberstadt, Draper, Mathey, and Fiske—had departed the scene, which meant that their successors possessed a tradition but not the experience that went with it. True, the firm maintained a strong exposure to the Canadian market, but it had virtually nothing to do with other parts of the world in the 1930s and the wartime years.

Just as Fred Brandi and August Belmont had become the principal figures in the domestic market with their imaginative financings in petroleum and natural gas, so Brandi and Ted Wadsworth would lead the firm into new areas in overseas financing, many of which were quite different from the kinds of deals Dillon and Eberstadt had entered into in the 1920s. Brandi was the key figure in this period, unquestionably the strongest Dillon Read personality since the late 1930s, when Forrestal had occupied that niche. In some respects Brandi was even more pivotal, because Dillon was not less a presence than he had been in the 1930s. Brandi succeeded even though he lacked the kind of educational background and social connections so common in the elite American banking fraternity of the period. (Though his family had become prominent in Germany, this counted for little on Wall Street, and may even have been a liability.) Brandi overcame these obstacles through talent and performance.

In recognition of this, and of the fact that Douglas Dillon would be gone for quite a few years, Brandi assumed the chairmanship in 1963, a position that Douglas had resigned ten years earlier. Belmont was named to succeed Brandi as president, while Wadsworth was to be executive vice president.[1]

The hallmark of the Brandi era was conservatism combined with careful innovation and expansion of traditional business—and hewing to the wishes of Clarence Dillon. Like Dillon and Forrestal, Brandi stressed and fostered strong client relationships, which by then had become a Dillon Read hallmark.

Brandi was determined to meet perceived client requirements through cautious forays into formerly ignored areas, innovating when necessary to accomplish a goal. The most striking example of this came in 1960, when California sought Dillon Read's assistance in connection with its proposed $1.75 billion bond issue to help fund the state's water program. After studying the situation the firm recommended that the state issue general obligation bonds which had some of the characteristics of revenue bonds. The assignment required working closely with consulting engineers and attorneys. The offering went well, and two years later Dillon Read was back in California working on the second phase of the project.[2]

Evidence of Dillon Read's conservatism may be seen in its reasons for finally purchasing a seat on the NYSE in 1963.[3] The membership did not mean Dillon Read expected to develop a retail business, even though many of its historic rivals had moved in that direction. Rather, the seat enabled the firm to perform brokerage services for clients in the secondary market when these were called for. More important, Dillon Read traditionally maintained large client balances in banks, these coming from bond coupons and the like. These ran into the millions of dollars at any given time. In order to obtain such deposits banks would place orders for stock purchases and sales with the depository agent. Now that Dillon Read was an NYSE member it could expect such business, which Belmont suggested could come to hundreds of thousands of dollars a year.

Even so, Dillon drew the line when it came to the matter of the firm trading for its own account. This was far too speculative for his taste, and so Dillon Read remained away from this increasingly lucrative area. Trading on the NYSE was the first new activity Dillon Read had entered since the Great Depression. Not only did brokerage services prove to be as profitable as Belmont had hoped, but by 1965 it provided the firm with almost a third of its income.

The more imaginative side of Dillon Read was evident in the developments of the "A-B-C" structure for Union Oil and the concept's application elsewhere in the origination of the notion of induced revenues as in the Triborough financings, and Belmont's sophisticated efforts in the Texas Eastern Transmission underwriting. Of course the firm continued with its conventional business, more difficult than before in the age of competitive bidding, but Brandi concentrated on convincing both established and new clients of the firm's ability to come up with imaginative solutions to its problems. This was true in the foreign areas as well as domestically.

Reentry into the overseas markets came slowly, and was made under Brandi's aegis. In the early 1950s Dillon Read and the Deutsche Bank assisted Texaco in its purchase of Deutsche Erdol, which began as the first postwar unfriendly tender offer. Dillon Read also led the way in opening the American capital markets to Japanese governments and companies. Wadsworth made several trips to Japan in the mid-1950s before other banks realized the strength of the Japanese recovery. In 1957 Dillon Read handled a private placement of a $12 million bond issue for Alaska Lumber & Pulp, a subsidiary of Japanese-owned Alaska Pulp, the proceeds used for the construction of a pulp mill near Sitka, the first Japanese credit offering sold in the United States after the war, and made possible by Dillon Read's prewar Japanese connections. This was when such ventures appeared risky, and other American banks rejected the business. To place the issue Dillon Read had to offer a high interest rate and a sinking fund, and even so could not sell long-term paper—it was a nine-year maturity. The issue was a success, and opened the way for other Japanese offerings.[4]

In 1960 DuBois, Wadsworth, and senior associate Richard Yancey traveled to Tokyo seeking additional business.[5] The trip was a success. Dillon Read's 1961 financing for Nippon Telegraph & Telephone was the first public offering outside of Japan for a Japanese government guaranteed security since the 1930s. Dillon Read became one of Hitachi Ltd.'s bankers. In 1962, it arranged the first international placement of a convertible debenture for the electronics company; this was also the first time a Japanese issuer had sold this kind of security overseas. It was followed in 1963 by a Hitachi common stock underwriting in the United States, and in 1969 Hitachi sold another $30 million in convertible debentures through a Dillon Read syndicate.[6]

In this way Dillon Read established itself one of the leading banks for Japanese companies to consult on matters pertaining to American capital markets. In addition to Hitachi, Wadsworth handled underwritings for such clients as Dai Nippon and Mitsubishi Reynolds Aluminum, and managed a $100 million offering for the Japan Development Bank.

All of this was accomplished without a Japanese office, which meant Wadsworth had to spend a good deal of time flying back and forth to Tokyo when trips there took several days of travel time. Dillon Read did not open a Japanese bureau because it shied from such expansion, and in this period Japan seemed secondary to developments in Europe, and, for a while, Africa.

The initial African business derived from the work of another partner, Kingman Douglass, one of Anne Dillon's cousins, who had formed a business and personal relationship with the legendary South African industrialist Charles Engelhard, and Harry Oppenheimer, that country's most powerful businessman. Douglass was one of the few prominent Dillon Read executives who had not been trained at the firm. After graduating from Yale in 1918 he entered the Army, rising to the rank of captain. Douglass joined R. G. Dun & Co. after the war, rose to become general manager of the Chicago office, and left in 1930 to become a senior partner at the brokerage house of A. O. Slaughter & Co. He remained there until 1941, when he accepted the presidency of Allied Railway Equipment Co. Douglass reentered the Army during World War II, and was a colonel when discharged in 1946. He then became instrumental in the establishment of the Central Intelligence Agency, and served as its deputy director for a few months. In 1952 he came to Dillon Read as a vice president.[7]

It was through Douglass that Dillon Read obtained its initial underwritings from the Republic of South Africa and the Federation of Rhodesia and Nyasaland, the former in 1950, the latter in 1958. It was also in 1958 that Dillon Read brought to market the American-South African Investment Company (ASA), the first post–World War II closed-end trust specializing in the securities of a single country and a single industry (mining), which also marked the reentry of Dillon Read into this kind of activity. ASA started out as a $35 million operation whose assets eventually rose to more than $800 million. Brandi and Douglass went on the board, and in the years that followed other business was generated from such contacts.[8]

Dillon Read would soon have representation in Europe, with one person, John Haskell, operating out of Paris. After graduating from West Point and serving in the Army, Haskell had attended and graduated from Harvard's Graduate School of Business. He then traveled to Europe, and found employment in London, Paris, and Geneva in the summer and autumn of that year.

In those years few American firms had permanent offices in Europe, so Haskell's opportunities were he to remain in Europe, which was his intention, were limited. Given his knowledge of European business practices, he decided that business reputation and prior history would be the key to operating in this environment. Discussing such matters with European contacts and studying the subject, Haskell concluded that only a handful of American banks qualified, and Dillon Read was one of these. He joined the firm in November 1958.

Haskell was hired into the firm as a trainee by Ted Wadsworth and began by working under several partners—DuBois, Belmont, and others—performing routine work on underwritings. The closest he came to foreign business in the first year was an assignment to work out bond yields on a technical study of the viability of a tunnel under the English Channel, for which Dillon Read had received an assignment through Flanigan.

Douglass approached Haskell in 1960 and asked whether he would be interested in representing the firm in Europe, from a headquarters in Paris. Since this was what he had hoped for from the first, Haskell leaped at the opportunity. Douglass was pleased, and told him that all that remained was to win approval from Clarence Dillon.

Haskell traveled to Far Hills to meet Dillon and discuss plans and strategies. As it turned out Dillon completely misunderstood Haskell's reasons for going to Paris, thinking he was to settle affairs at the family's personal estate at Haut-Brion. Anxious and nervous, Haskell did not try to disabuse Dillon, but returned to New York where he was assured everything was fine. He set out for Paris the following February to restart the operations that had been closed since shortly after the outbreak of World War II and established an office for the firm at 16 place Vendôme.

Haskell started by poring over the roster of prewar European underwritings. The $30 million 1927 Dillon Read underwriting for Milan interested him. He thought perhaps that city would be the best place to start. An aggressive new mayor eager to raise funds for municipal development had taken command there, and he granted Haskell an interview. Haskell observed that Dillon Read had prewar ties to Milan, and a civil servant who worked in the accounting office not only remembered the 1927 transaction but was able to locate the documents relating to it. Out of that initial contact came negotiations for a debt offering, discussions for which began in 1961.

Living out of his suitcase for more than two years, Haskell hopped from one capital to another, obtaining dollars for nations, municipalities, and companies. There was a 1963 $12 million private placement for the Kingdom of Norway, $100 million for Portugal raised over several years, and, also in 1963, Dillon Read underwrote a $20 million debt issue for Milan.[9]

Though the only Dillon Read executive permanently situated in Europe, Haskell could always call on the expertise of the home office when required. Brandi, Flanigan, and others would arrive when their talents and experience were needed. On the Portuguese underwriting, for example, Flanigan flew to Lisbon and spent four days with Haskell putting the deal together.

Selling the new offerings proved no problem. American institutions had become familiar with the foreign debt issues, most of which paid a higher rate than equivalent American paper. From 1957 to 1962 $3.7 billion in American capital went to purchase foreign securities, and most of it went to Europe. This attracted other banks to the Continent. Morgan Stanley and Kuhn Loeb were strong players from the start, and the competition for business intensified.

It wasn't long before European demand for dollar financings affected the American economy, pushing interest rates higher and leading to warnings of trouble ahead. Moreover, there had developed a net balance-of-payments deficit resulting from overseas military expenditures and government assistance programs in addition to those foreign borrowings in the American capital markets.[10] From his perch in Washington Treasury Secretary Douglas Dillon warned that "our balance of payments problem limits the amount of long-term capital which we can prudently supply to others." There was some talk of dollar devaluation and other means of rectifying the situation, along with veiled warnings that unless foreigners cut back on their borrowings and eased pressures on the domestic markets stringent actions would be undertaken.[11]

The European governments got the message. In 1961 and 1962 they prepaid approximately $700 million of indebtedness to the United States, and in the latter year Germany paid in advance $450 million for military equipment to be delivered later on. The Treasury sold $700 million in bonds denominated in Swiss francs and Italian lira but paid for in dollars by Europeans. Even so, the dollar outflow continued, placing pressures on American interest rates and raising fears of recession.

The Kennedy Administration recommended a tax cut, but feared part of the money would find its way into foreign markets. There was an accelerated public works program, and both stimulated the economy. But not enough. In July 1963, Kennedy announced the imposition of a 1 percent Interest Equalization Tax (IET) on all foreign securities sold in the United States, exempting Japan and Canada from its provisions. The IET clearly was directed at the Europeans. In addition the Federal Reserve increased the discount rate from 3 to 3½ percent. Taken in its entirety, the program was designed to attract American lenders to the domestic market and turn them away from European securities. Douglas Dillon recalled, "We hoped that it would stimulate foreigners to develop their own capital markets."[12]

Haskell was dismayed, though not surprised, by the IET. "I thought my world was going to end and I'd better get on the next plane and go back to New York." The Milan deal had been filed the week before, so it was "grandfathered," and would not be affected by the IET. Brandi had come over to lend the authority of his office to the underwriting, while Yancey, now a partner, was there to help in putting together the prospectus. They decided to attempt to market most of the offering in Europe, and found there were many institutions prepared to purchase the bonds with their excess dollars.

The IET thus accelerated the growth of the Eurobond market. American businesses now conducted an increasing part of their borrowings in this market, which meant more business for Dillon

Read and work for Haskell, who became a partner in 1964. Simultaneously his office was designated Dillon, Read Overseas Corporation (DROC).[13] By then the American presence was larger than ever. In 1964, 11 American banks had 181 branches outside the United States, holding nearly $7 billion in assets, this being three times what it had been four years earlier. By 1970, 79 American banks had 536 branches overseas, with assets of more than $52 billion.[14]

Others at the firm, operating from New York, were involved with the financing of overseas business. Flanigan and Wadsworth were particularly concerned with such matters, working initially through the Export-Import Bank, a government corporation organized in 1934 to facilitate foreign trade by making or guaranteeing private loans. The bank was rechartered and its operations expanded in 1945, when it seemed the logical vehicle to help finance loans to Europe.[15]

Even before Haskell learned of and then helped meet the European demand for American paper, Dillon Read moved to enter that market through the Export-Import Bank. In 1959 Flanigan traveled through Europe, selling the bank's portfolio of loans to investors there and then repatriating the money back to the United States. Other business followed. In 1962 the bank wanted to raise $100 million for loans, and given the situation in the American money markets decided to try to market its paper in Europe. Dillon Read and Kuhn Loeb were awarded the underwriting, and in July Flanigan set off for a circuit of European capitals to arrange for placement of participation certificates with a 5½ percent coupon, which were sold to institutional investors in denominations of $250,000.[16] Other placements followed, and in the 1960s the selling of such loans to European investors became a significant part of Dillon Read's business.

The American trade picture started to change toward the end of the 1960s. From a $6.8 billion surplus in 1964 it dropped to $399 million in 1969. This was not so much the result of a failure of exports to advance, which indeed they did, rising from $25.5 billion to $36.4 billion, but rather a dramatic increase in imports, which went from $18.7 billion to $35.8 billion.[17] Washington and the American business community interpreted these statistics as signifying weakness in the American industrial sector, to be corrected by major assistance to those companies in the export sector. Aircraft, especially jet passenger planes, were among the nation's major export items, and exports of these in particular seemed in need of assistance. Ordinarily the problem could be taken care of by expansion of the lending facilities of the Export-Import Bank, and in 1968 Congress did extend that institution's lending ceiling from $9 billion to $13.5 billion. There were unmistakable signs, however, that due to fiscal pressures caused by President Lyndon Johnson's social programs and the Vietnam War additional increases were unlikely and cutbacks might be made the following year.[18]

The search for supplemental support began in the mid-1960s, when a tightening in the credit markets made it difficult for foreign airliners to finance purchases of American jet passenger planes. The Export-Import Bank entered the picture to offer assistance, but within a year it became apparent that that institution's resources were becoming strained.[19] Now the Bankers' Association for Foreign Trade (BAFT) discussed the possibilities of creating some agency to assist the Export-Import Bank in its work, and such concepts were approved by the White House, the State and Treasury departments, the Federal Reserve, and other governmental agencies. In the spring of 1967 James W. Bergford, a senior vice president at Chase Manhattan who had become one of the central figures in the discussions, approached Dillon Read, asking it to undertake a new study of the possibilities. Out of this came the concept of a private export finance corporation (PEFCO).

Under the Dillon Read plan, drawn up in April 1968 by a team headed by Wadsworth, PEFCO would sell its bonds to the public (meaning large domestic and foreign institutions) secured by export loans in its portfolio that were guaranteed by the Export-Import Bank and exempt from the IET. Funds raised in this manner would be loaned to foreign purchasers of American goods, such as a foreign airline wanting to purchase planes from Boeing, Douglas, or Lockheed. American banks would be responsible for introducing foreign borrowers to PEFCO. In the case of those airlines, PEFCO would take care of medium-term and long-term needs, while the banks would provide short-term borrowings.

According to the Dillon Read proposal, PEFCO might easily expand into a $1.5 billion operation by 1972 and double that by the early 1980s. It seemed a reasonable solution to part of the foreign trade problems, but there were some flaws, one of which was antitrust constraints. Because the organization and operation of PEFCO inevitably involved some degree of association among banks and exporters who were competitors or potential competitors, compliance with the federal antitrust laws presented difficulties. Assurances were given that under terms of the Dillon Read plan the Justice Department would not take action, but nothing could be done until after the presidential and congressional elections.[20]

The PEFCO proposal appealed to incoming President Richard Nixon, and was endorsed by the Export-Import Bank after some alterations. Now PEFCO would handle middle-range obligations, while the Export-Import Bank took care of longer maturities. PEFCO was incorporated in 1970. Sixty-six banks that were members of the BAFT Committee on PEFCO had previously contributed $800,000 to cover the organizational and development costs.[21]

PEFCO really got started when it successfully raised $14 million of equity capital in 1971. While concentrating on aircraft orders, in time PEFCO arranged financings for a wide variety of projects, running from atomic installations in the Republic of Korea to telecommunications systems in Brazil and cement plants in Honduras.[22] In the next eighteen years it made export loans of more than $5 billion, and Dillon Read was one of the lead underwriters that raised funds in the bond market to enable PEFCO to make these loans.[23]

This activity demanded a reconsideration of the overseas business. One problem was that of simple geography. London now experienced a surge of growth. No other banking community, not even New York, had its experience in international finance, which now was in greater demand than ever. "They have everything but the money," said one American banker, "and every banker knows that money comes to people who know how to handle it."[24]

London's growth came at the expense of New York. In 1963 some 73 percent of international bonds were floated in New York; in 1964 the share had fallen to 55 percent. There was some stabilization by 1968, but by then New York's share of international underwritings had declined further.[25] Dillon Read considered relocating its European operations as early as 1966, and moved DROC from Paris to London in 1971.

The experience at PEFCO was not Dillon Read's first exposure

272   THE LIFE AND TIMES OF DILLON READ

to the financing of jets, an area in which it generated considerable
expertise. Indeed, Brandi's most dramatic deal pitted him as a key
member of a consortium against the man who was perhaps the
century's most flamboyant and controversial businessman, Howard
Hughes, a major player in several industries that ranged from
motion pictures to aviation. It, too, involved jet aircraft and took
place at the dawn of the jet age.

Two of Hughes's prime holdings, Hughes Tool Company
(TOOLCO) and Hughes Aircraft Company, were throwing off tremendous profits that he used to finance his other interests, including Radio-Keith-Orpheum. In part because he was interested
in aviation, but also to avoid taxes, Hughes ordered TOOLCO to
start accumulating shares of Trans World Airlines, particularly
when its price dipped. By the mid-1950s he owned more than 75
percent of the stock and was the dominant force at TWA for two
decades, helping develop the Lockheed Constellation for use by
the airline. Hughes never held office at the company, but through
subservient directors had complete control. Everyone at the company knew he had the ultimate power and made all of the important
decisions, sometimes with a shrewdness based upon a wide knowledge of the business, often in a manner that seemed bewildering
and frivolous.

By then it had become evident to all in the industry that the
jet age had arrived, and airlines that were hoping to be competitive
in the long-distance passenger business would have to convert to
the new models. Britain's de Havilland was first, introducing the
Comet in 1952. It proved to have design flaws, was unsafe, and
all but killed that country's chances in the jet age. Several
additional models were being created, the two most important
American entries being the proposed Boeing 707 and the Douglas
DC-8. The 707, which was a converted military jet, made its first
flight in 1954, and its virtues soom became obvious. The same was
so for the DC-8. Others were also making bids, and one of these,
the Convair 600 (later known as the 880), made by a subsidiary of
General Dynamics, seemed quite promising.

Hughes now committed a monumental blunder. Miscalculating
the swiftness with which the market was developing, TWA ear-
marked $50 million for twenty-five Lockheed 1649 Constellations,
not jet but turboprop aircraft which the 707s and DC-8s would
soon render obsolete on long-range highly traveled routes. Then

arch-rival Pan American World Airways ordered twenty 707s and twenty-five DC-8s. Hughes now realized this would not do; he would have to move into jets. Attracted by both the Boeing and Convair planes, and knowing the prestige that would come to the airline first in the field with jets, he had nonetheless decided to split the initial order between turboprops and jets. TOOLCO placed deposits on thirty-three Boeing 707s and 30 Convairs, the bill for which would be $315 million for the planes, another $90 million for engines, for a total of $405 million.[26]

TWA then fell into bad times. Profits were sliding; after eight years in the black TWA lost $2.3 million in 1956. It was then that financial vice president A. V. Leslie informed Hughes that the firm would not be able to pay for the jets until 1958 at the earliest. A $70 million stock offering helped somewhat, but the losses continued; there was another $2.3 million loss in 1957. In 1955 TWA common had reached a high of 35½; the 1957 low was 9¼. The company lost nearly $12.8 million the first half of 1958, and seemed headed toward insolvency.[27] In July Hughes tried to obtain from Equitable Life and Irving Trust an extension of a $12 million loan. They agreed on condition he arrange long-term financing for that $405 million needed to finance TWA's entry into the jet age.

In July Hughes placed a new president in charge of operations. While an able executive, Charles S. Thomas had no airline experience other than that acquired while Secretary of the Navy. By ruthless cost cutting he managed to cut losses to a slender $700,000 for the year.[28]

Now Hughes scrambled to obtain funds to pay for his ambitious expansion program. In October he engaged First Boston to formulate a financing plan. Within two months First Boston's Chairman, George Woods, was prepared to relinquish the assignment, irate at Hughes's unwillingness to sit down with him for a face-to-face meeting. It was at this point that Brandi entered the picture.

Brandi had met Hughes on several occasions, but had never done business with him. He doubtless knew Hughes's reputation and the general nature of the problems at TWA. He also would have understood what was happening in the aircraft industry. The conversion to jets would require billions of dollars of financing, and any banker who obtained that business was bound to do well for his firm.

His back to the wall, Hughes seemed almost contrite. He invited Brandi to generate a financial plan but told him that in the past he had tried to work with Lazard Frères and Lehman Brothers, and while nothing had come of these discussions he felt he owed them something for their efforts. Would Brandi include the two banks in the project? He would and did, and with this began Dillon Read's strange contest with Howard Hughes, the kind of bailout that recalled Clarence Dillon's workout for Goodyear forty years earlier. In its own way the TWA effort was as elegant and difficult.

With Brandi the lead figure, the three investment banking firms came up with two alternative plans. The first, the so-called Dillon Read plan, contemplated TWA's purchasing jets from TOOLCO both with funds raised through senior borrowings from insurance companies and commercial banks and also with funds from substantial subordinated borrowings from TOOLCO. Hughes rejected this plan in favor of the second, the formation of Hughes Aircraft Leasing Corporation (HALCO), which would not require TWA to rely upon its shaky credit for loans. Rather, the key borrower would be the solvent Hughes Tool. Given its good credit rating, TOOLCO would borrow the needed funds and use them to purchase the planes, which then would be leased to the airline. Not only was this possible, said Brandi, but the $20–$40 million a year in depreciation costs would be applied against TOOLCO's profits, and so lower its tax liabilities. The plan, known as "third party leasing," was not new, but never before was it used on so large a scale. It was a sophisticated program, which, however, was opposed by Thomas and TWA's creditors. So the HALCO plan was abandoned.[29]

Some other method was required, and quickly; already the first of the 707s had arrived, and Hughes had to resort to expensive short-term borrowing to pay for it. The planes soon would be arriving at the rate of three or four a month, and there appeared no way TWA could raise funds for the purchases. Desperate, Hughes canceled ten of the Convairs and shifted delivery rights to six 707s to Pan Am.

Even so, there were some positive elements in the picture. Those jets that entered serrvice were highly profitable, so that in 1959 TWA posted a profit of $9.4 million. Now Hughes was in a paradoxical position. While the increased deliveries resulted in higher profits, the more jets that TWA obtained, the higher its debt and the more pressures that would be brought to bear on payments. In effect, the airline was posting higher profits while falling deeper into debt. How long could this continue? The answer came in March 1960, when, as earnings faltered due to the combination of greater competition and the onset of a recession, the bankers decided to halt TWA's credit. The airline owed $150 million in short-term loans, in addition to the $300 million or so required to pay for additional jets, and Hughes had no way of raising that kind of money.[30]

At this point Thomas asserted himself. Dillon Read representatives were recalled in April, and in a two-day meeting the board and the bankers cobbled a new version of the Dillon Read proposal. In the final arrangement of the loan package, which would not be completed and agreed to until December, $265 million was raised. A group of eight commercial banks headed by Irving Trust was assembled by Brandi and Wadsworth to provide TWA with about $70 million of equipment mortgage sinking fund notes due in 1972. Another $90 million of equipment mortgage serial notes due 1961–1964 would come from Equitable Life and Metropolitan Life. And an additional $100 million was lent by TOOLCO for which TOOLCO received interim subordinated notes. In May 1961, TWA would repay these interim notes by issuing income debentures with common stock warrants through a public offering.[31]

In return for these loans the financial institutions wanted Hughes's agreement not to interfere with the airline's operations for the term of the loans, and moreover, Hughes had to place his TWA shares in a ten-year voting trust to be controlled by representatives of the lenders. Thomas informed Hughes that if the terms were not accepted he would resign. Hughes had until July 22 to decide what to do.[32]

Hughes could not forbear interfering in company affairs. In the midst of the tense negotiations over the terms of the loans and the conditions of the voting trust, he was attempting to arrange a merger between TWA and Northeast Airlines. Worn down and offended, Thomas resigned on July 28. The banks and insurance companies promptly informed Hughes that unless he placed his shares in the voting trust they had required, they would foreclose on their loans and seize the airline. He was given a deadline: September 1. Hughes thrashed around seeking assistance, but then September 1 came and went with no action.

In this period Hughes came up with a proposal of his own. General Dynamics' largest shareholder, Henry Crown, had been persuaded to help raise $135.5 million in exchange for orders for twenty-three Convair 880s and 990s. All the money was to come from the sale of TWA debentures, the underwriting to be handled by Merrill Lynch. Market conditions turned poor, however, and the offering was withdrawn. Nothing was left to do but contact Brandi and inform him of acceptance of the Dillon Read plan.

Metropolitan Life and Equitable Life selected the two trustees who would represent the creditors—former U.S. Steel chairman Irving Olds and former Ford Motor chairman Ernest Breech. TOOLCO sent its executive vice president, Raymond Holliday. With this, Hughes lost control of TWA.[33]

One of the nation's most respected businessmen, Breech was perceived as the central figure in the new leadership. He was offered the top job at TWA, but refused it because of his age. By the time of the next board meeting he had selected a new CEO, Charles Tillinghast, a Bendix vice president. Tillinghast faced problems of creating a new management team when the economy was poor and heavy charges were eating into TWA's meager reserves. In 1961, the airline would lose $14.8 million, almost as much as had been earned the previous two years. Hughes watched from the sidelines, angered at what he considered unwise moves on the part of management and chafing at restrictions. TOOLCO's profits were rising, and he had those funds from the Dillon Read bailout program. It appeared he was preparing to seek command once again.

His expected move came soon after. Through intermediaries, in early June 1961 Hughes offered to invest $100 million in TWA if the voting trust was dissolved. In addition, if TWA would purchase thirteen Convair 990s owned by TOOLCO and an additional eight 880s at cost, that firm would invest in an additional $11.2 million in the airline's debentures.[34]

As much to bar such a move as anything else, Brandi and Cahill Gordon attorney John Sonnett recommended to the board that it sue Hughes to prevent TOOLCO from regaining control of TWA. Accordingly, on June 30, 1961, the airline filed a $115 million suit against Hughes and TOOLCO, alleging that TWA had been obliged to purchase all of its airplanes from TOOLCO, and that this constituted a violation of the antitrust acts. After some sparring Hughes responded in February 1962 with a $366 million counter-suit, in which TOOLCO alleged the trustees had obtained control of TWA illegally.[35]

With this began another chapter in the bizarre career of Howard Hughes. By now a recluse, Hughes refused to appear in court. He ignored the judge's demands that he give testimony, inviting a contempt of court charge. On May 3, 1963, Hughes was found to be in "deliberate and wilful" default and the TOOLCO counter-suit was dismissed with prejudice, which meant it could not be refiled.[36]

This left the TWA suit against Hughes. There were interminable legal delays, during which the airline recovered and did quite well. TWA earned $19.7 million in 1963, $37 million the following year, and moved $50 million in 1965, when the common stock rose to a high of 71⅝, going on to 101 in 1976. Hughes sold before then, disposing of his 6.5 million shares on May 3, 1966. After deductions for underwriting fees, he netted over $546 million. Then, in 1967, TOOLCO was found guilty, and TWA was awarded $138 million, a decision which was overthrown by the Supreme Court in 1973. Thus ended one of the most celebrated private antitrust cases in American history.[37] TWA had also filed a state lawsuit against Hughes and TOOLCO in Delaware in 1962, alleging that Hughes had delayed TWA's introduction of jet aircraft for his own benefit to the detriment of the airline. After fifteen more years of litigation, including a six-week trial in 1985, a $50 million judgment in TWA's favor was ultimately paid by TOOLCO in 1988.

There were no true losers in this case, though all involved underwent considerable anguish. Hughes received a measure of vindication, and TWA was able to remain out of his hands.

Dillon Read profited by becoming the airline's investment bank. The 1960 underwriting was followed by other financings every few years. Through 1981, Dillon Read was involved in financings amounting to over $2.2 billion worth of notes, loan certificates, and stock for TWA.[38] Included in this sum was a record $900 million financing that took place in 1967, of which $425 million was new money, the rest renegotiation of outstanding loans. It was the first time since 1947 that TWA had been able to borrow money without placing a mortgage on its properties, this being the measure of the success brought about by Tillinghast and Brandi.[39]

Several of the offerings required Dillon Read to exercise imagination and develop new financing concepts. In the fall of 1968, for example, TWA had to generate $70 million to help pay the $100 million cost for ten aircraft due to be delivered in mid-1970, and in addition had on order forty-seven other planes to come in during the next few years. By then the airline industry had become accustomed to third-party leasing for equipment purchases, while most other needs were financed by privately placed loans. After conferring with TWA's treasurer, Malcolm T. Hopkins, Yancey, who was now working on TWA financing, determined that neither approach would be appropriate for this situation. Third-party leasing was complicated and the institutional private lenders had just about as much in the way of aircraft loans as they could absorb. Yancey concluded that the best way to approach the situation would be to attempt to sell loan certificates publicly. After receiving the necessary approval from the SEC and the Internal Revenue Service Dillon Read came out with a $70 million public offering of paper with a 10 percent coupon. Under the terms of the financing, First National City would purchase the planes for $100 million and lease them to TWA for a fifteen-year period. At the end of the term the bank would own the planes, while TWA had the right to purchase them at fair market value. There were benefits for all involved. While the bank provided only $30 million of its own money it was to receive the full benefits of the 7 percent investment tax credit and accelerated depreciation permitted by the IRS. This suited TWA, which lacked the kind of profits that would make such write-offs valuable. As for the purchasers of the bonds, they received high-yielding paper guaranteed by TWA and secured by the equipment and the lease. "We broke the ground, and we would expect other airlines to follow," said Hopkins. "But most important, by showing that you can finance the debt part of the lease through the public, we have added a whole new dimension to leasing."[40]

Innovative, yes, but not in many more areas than this. Dillon

Read provided excellent service of this type to an increasingly smaller client base, when other firms were plunging boldly into new areas. The Dillon Read partners persisted in asserting that they were quite content to continue performing services in the traditional manner. But was that enough?

·15·

Decline and Transition

(1965–1971)

In the late 1960s Dillon Read experienced a marked decline in its relative position on Wall Street. Income rose as did remuneration, but did not keep pace with the rest of the industry. For a while, however, the increased revenues masked the firm's comparative erosion.

Though in many ways it continued to be creative and original in packaging old business in new ways, the firm was slow to follow secular trends within the industry. As competitors rushed to finance burgeoning high technology companies and help assemble conglomerate corporations, Dillon Read remained content with retaining its traditional business. To be sure, the firm made some concessions to those and other changes taking place on the corporate scene, but its leaders were reluctant to innovate, and generally averse to any significant departures in their business. For instance, Dillon Read was not preparing for the period when trading would assume greater significance. Nor was it interested in accumulating capital through the retention of earnings, or obtaining it by selling equity in the business. It was in this period that "story" stocks became the vogue, companies in such industries as nursing homes, pollution control, oceanics, leisure, and telecommunications—Dillon Read scorned them all.

The firm's continued reluctance to make a strong effort in competitive bidding was another problem, especially since an expanding amount of underwritings was done that way. In a world of increasingly rough-and-tumble rivalry in investment banking, Dillon Read was resolutely a firm of gentlemen bankers, seemingly determined to preserve its style even as it lost accounts.

Upstart firms such as Merrill Lynch and Salomon Brothers and rejuvenated older ones, including Lazard Frères, began taking substantial business away from the less aggressive firms. Old, durable ties between bankers and clients were loosening, as the nation's corporations were becoming increasingly transaction-oriented. The time was not so distant when a client would inform a caller from an old-line house that "You are *an* investment banker, not *our* investment banker." Maintaining relationships in such an environment would be most difficult for even the most entrenched houses. "The face of Wall Street is changing," lamented Goldman Sachs co-CEO John Whitehead shortly before resigning to accept a post in Washington. "Our clients no longer look to us as wise advisors, as they once did. Now the emphasis is on transactional business rather than advisory business."[1]

So both the players and the rules were changing. Talents and abilities vital in the past were becoming irrelevant, as American finance underwent what was perhaps its most drastic alteration in history.

The transformation of the playing field must have perplexed the Dillon Read partners, accustomed as they had been to conducting business in the Clarence Dillon fashion. They saw the rise of those firms utilizing new techniques, and not only getting away with it but profiting enormously in the process, while the old-line conservative firms languished. The partners and associates should have realized that some of the rising banks were not brazen parvenu but rather led by individuals who appreciated the nature of change, and as a result, profited greatly.

The challenges were there every day, and in some ways the symbolism was striking. For example, in 1963 Lehman, Blyth, Eastman Dillon, and Bear Stearns won the competition for a $30 million bond issue for an old Dillon Read client, Union Electric.

Dillon Read had not even bid on the Union Electric issue. There had been a time when Dillon Read listed on its client roster Bank of America, Monsanto, and American Telephone & Telegraph. By the end of the decade all would be gone.

It was a serious matter, but like all such phenomena occurred in such a piecemeal fashion that some of the firm's leaders scarcely realized what was happening. For example, one day in late 1967, not long after John Haskell had returned from Europe and was starting out in the domestic business, Fred Brandi took him to Winston-Salem to visit one of Dillon Read's clients, R. J. Reynolds. Actually, Dillon Read hadn't underwritten anything for the giant tobacco firm since 1948, but Brandi, as was traditional, was going to pay a courtesy call. Haskell recalls a strangely pleasant evening, as he and Brandi dined and played a few rubbers of bridge with Chairman A. H. Galloway and his wife. As the evening ended, Brandi seemed quite pleased. "Well," he said to Haskell, "I think we did very well."

Haskell was puzzled, however, and with good reason. The next day Brandi, his work apparently done, went home, leaving Haskell to call on the Reynolds treasurer, C. F. Benbow. After an exchange of pleasantries Haskell politely asked Benbow whether there was anything happening at the firm that required his assistance, only to be flatly informed that Reynolds was currently engaged in a stock buy-back program, which was being handled by Morgan Stanley. Haskell recalls his shock upon recognizing that while Brandi had simply assumed Reynolds was once and for all a Dillon Read client, it actually had retained another, more aggressive banker. The story is emblematic of what was happening to Dillon Read; its business was slowly slipping away.

Another of the changes transforming the industry concerned its very essence, namely what was required of those individuals who hoped to become investment bankers. The prerequisites when Brandi appeared at Dillon Read and Belmont at Bonbright before World War II had been the same as they had been when William A. Read had arrived at Vermilye & Co. seventy years earlier. The neophyte had to be intelligent, hard-working, possess social graces, and if at all possible, have friends or relatives in positions to provide him with the opportunity to bring in business. Lacking this, the would-be banker had to possess the imagination to develop new concepts to entice clients to employ their services.

As has been seen, Dillon brought the Schlesinger account to William A. Read & Co., and Flanigan was able to deliver the Briggs and Anheuser-Busch underwritings. By themselves these would not have been enough to provide both men with successful and satisfying careers, but they did give them a start, an opportunity to show what they could do. Brandi and before him William A. Read had lacked those connections, but each man in his own way had been able to provide clients with expertise and creative underwritings and concepts.

While connections and friendships remained important in this period, as did the "old school tie," Wall Street was being flooded by a new generation of bankers. They arrived from the familiar graduate schools, but their undergraduate training often was at public colleges with decidedly blue-collar images. They were not aristocrats, but bore greater resemblance to William A. Read insofar as backgrounds were concerned. If members of the traditional white-shoe crowd were still in prominent positions there were unmistakable signs of scuffing around the insoles. First Boston had started to lose its Yale image and Morgan could no longer accurately be described as a Princeton firm. Jews and southern and eastern European Catholics didn't have to settle for second-line concerns and accept the old rule that they could not become members of the prestigious clubs. They were followed by blacks, Hispanics, and Asians, who a generation earlier could not have aspired to posts at the investment banks and were now found there in increasing numbers.

The need for capital was also becoming more evident. Recall that in the 1920s Clarence Dillon, like his contemporaries at other investment banks, had operated on low capital in high-profit deals. Such remained the firm's approach in the decades that followed. By 1960, when Dillon Read ranked only 120th in capital among investment banks, it was not yet viewed as a cause for concern. Brains, after all, not brawn, were what it took to be successful, and Dillon Read's bankers were still men of exalted status, highly regarded in the business of finance.[2] The firm simply was not prepared to retain capital or expand in any meaningful manner to meet its competition.

Dillon Read's conservatism may be explained in large part by its continued mistaken assumption of being a special bracket firm when such was no longer the case, which implied no changes were needed, and also by the particular preferences and skills of its personnel. Then there was the tacitly lingering influence of Clarence Dillon, who still had ownership control of the business. Taken together, this implied a rejection of structural change within the firm. For example, trading activities were traditionally denigrated as risky, and block trading in particular seemed downright offensive. Yet institutional trading activity was increasing sharply in the 1960s, accounting for 3 percent of NYSE volume in 1963 and 14 percent in 1969. This was a well-paying business, since in a period of fixed commissions the earnings from handling a trade of 20,000 shares was 200 times that of a 100-share trade. Jay Perry of Salomon Brothers, Will Weinstein of Oppenheimer, and Robert Mnuchin of Goldman Sachs, all brash, irreverent young men, would compete head-on in this market, making fortunes for their firms. "I'm basically a risk-taker," Perry told a reporter. "Taking risks turns me on. It gets me nervous. It starts my adrenaline." To which CEO Billy Salomon nodded assent: "We'll buy anything."[3]

Imagine how Clarence Dillon might have reacted to such talk! Dillon Read had steadfastly refused to enter the trading arena, even after it purchased an NYSE seat. It was not until 1969 that Dillon Read made its first, modest foray into trading, when it created Dillon Read Municipals, in order to make a secondary market in these bonds.

Other investment banks similar in style and objectives to Dillon Read proved better able to adapt to the changing market environment. The outstanding example in this area was Lazard Frères, which was recast under the leadership of André Meyer. A partner in that firm's Paris office, Meyer had fled to America as a Jewish refugee in 1940. He took a post in the New York branch, soon rose to become its head, and then began the process of transformation. Not unlike Dillon, Meyer looked upon retail brokerage as undignified, and so closed all Lazard's retail branches and dismissed its customers' men. Under Meyer not only would Lazard not take part in selling syndicates, but it generally declined to participate with others in underwriting syndicates, preferring to go it alone. The mature and more cautious Clarence Dillon doubtless would have approved of such behavior, but even though he had managed some of the more renowned merchant banking activities during the 1920s, he would not have permitted Dillon Read to take Meyer's next step, which was into merchant banking. Meyer transformed Lazard into one of the premier firms in this area, and did so by expanding its capital, having partners share in risks and so become more entrepreneurial, but also without expanding personnel on a wholesale basis.[4]

So even had Dillon Read the desire to enter new fields and make significant alterations in company policy, it lacked the management as well as the mandate to carry it out. Some important newcomers had arrived in the 1950s, but while still associates and junior to the established leaders, they were very much in the old mold. Yancey and Haskell were among the younger group as were Nicholas F. Brady and Arthur B. Treman, Jr., close friends who had attended Harvard Business School together, and who had arrived at Dillon Read in 1954.

Born in 1930, Brady was the grandson of the same James Cox Brady who had helped organize Maxwell Motor Company, turned it over to Walter Chrysler, and later served as intermediary when Dillon sold Dodge to Chrysler. He grew up in an atmosphere of easy affluence at the 4,300-acre family estate known as Hamilton Farms in New Jersey. Handsome, self-confident, and personable, Brady was a prominent sportsman even when quite young, and as a student at Yale, from which he graduated in 1952, captained the squash team. By his own admission Brady was a poor student, obliged to content himself with "Gentleman's C's," this as much due to his affliction with dyslexia as anything else. "Even though I graduated from college," he later remarked, "I had the reading ability of a seventh-grade student." This was an exaggeration, to be sure, and Brady worked to overcome his problem through a summer course in reading. It helped, but Brady still tired quickly when obliged to read, and found he functioned best when called upon to listen and speak rather than read.[5]

Brady also became interested in investments while a student. This was not unusual; among his Yale classmates were John Barry Ryan, Moreau D. Brown, William Donaldson, Dan Lufkin, and George Herbert Walker III, all of whom were destined for Wall Street careers, forming what was called "The Yale Mafia." It was not unimportant that Brady played what were then still largely deemed patrician sports, golf and tennis, and when viewed against the backdrop of the family's estate appeared the very model of a country squire. Indeed, his family had long been concerned with horses, both in breeding and racing. Brady became a member of the Jockey Club, and in 1974, its chairman.

For a while the Brady clan possessed a seemingly congenital knack for investing wisely. One of Brady's associates put it this way: Anthony Nicholas Brady had "caught the electricity curve," and James Cox Brady had "caught the automobile curve." Nick's father, James Brady, Sr., was a prominent figure in racing circles and associated in ventures with the Rockefellers, du Ponts, and Mellons.[6] He headed a family firm known as Brady Securities & Realty, which made investments in several companies. The firm performed well, even though James Brady, unlike his forebears, missed many of the more spectacular curves which appeared during his business career—chemicals, aircraft, computers, and electronics, among others. In the 1950s, James Brady became involved in several microwave and related ventures, none of which worked out favorably. He also controlled and was chairman of Purolator, the New Jersey–based leading independent manufacturer of oil filters. Even though inheritance taxes and the dispersion of assets to many heirs had shrunk and dispersed the family fortune, the Brady clan was one of New Jersey's largest private landowners, and quite wealthy.

Upon graduation from Yale Brady entered Harvard Business School, where the tough discipline came as a shock after his relatively leisurely approach to academics at Yale. Even before completing his studies Brady had decided to enter investment banking. It was only natural for him to consider Dillon Read; it was there that his family connections would do him the most immediate good. August Belmont was one of his neighbors, who recalled that "I'd known him since he was a kid."[7] Clarence and Douglas Dillon also lived nearby; "His father was a very good friend of mine," recalled Douglas, and Brady's move to Dillon Read was not altogether unexpected. After graduation, at Dillon's urging, he applied for and obtained a post at the firm.[8]

According to August Belmont, Clarence Dillon had originally thought that employing Brady would be a mistake. In the summer of 1954, Belmont visited Dillon at his winter home in Jamaica, and told him of the firm's new associates. "You shouldn't have hired Brady," Dillon complained, "because Brady will never stay there, he's got too much money. You're never going to be able to hang on to him."⁹

One reason for such a conclusion was that Brady possessed the kind of support network which, as has been seen, was conventional in this business, where getting past the receptionist is the first step in obtaining clients. As Paul Cameron, CEO at Purolator, put it, "Success is often a matter of getting the right patrons," and through family attachments Brady possessed them. James Brady was close to Paul Mellon, patriarch of one of Pittsburgh's most distinguished families, and Ogden Phipps, whose fortune arose from the Carnegie interests, and whose family controlled Bessemer Securities. Brady associates were sprinkled over the corporate map, some getting there through involvement with Brady concerns. For example, Cameron started out attempting to resuscitate several Brady ventures in electronics.¹⁰ Such individuals would provide business and use their influence for Dillon Read during the Brady years. Of course this was very much in the firm's culture. Clarence Dillon had his Harvard, Milwaukee, and Washington associates at his side in the 1920s, and now Brady drew upon his. All of this redounded to the benefit of the firm. "The real source of business at Dillon was Brady," a competitor remarked later on. "The loyal corporate clients stemmed purely from Nick's tremendous connections."¹¹

Brady pursued other interests while at Dillon Read. Shortly after arriving he became involved with Richard Scudder of the *Newark Daily News* in developing a technology to recycle newsprint. Needing capital, he borrowed $2 million from the Phippses, procured an additional $12 million from the Prudential, and organized the Garden State Paper Company, which proved successful, and later was merged into Media General. Brady took a seat on the board, which was in keeping with investment banking industry practices. He also served on the boards of ASA, Georgia International, Doubleday, and Josten.

As with all newcomers, Brady started out by generating and checking statistics for bond underwriting, doing so under the guidance of Wilbur DuBois. Like others before him, Brady found the work mournfully dull and tedious. But he stayed the course, and received assignments in investment banking. As it turned out, he possessed all the social and temperamental requisites for success in that arena.

As juniors, Brady, Haskell, and other newcomers observed Brandi and Belmont and the men of their generation and assumed they would be taking their places someday, and probably engage in the same kind of deals. There were some signal successes for them to learn from: the merger of Union Oil when it acquired Pure Oil bore the Brandi-Belmont imprimatur, and the firm also was instrumental in the corporate marriages of Hess Oil & Chemical and Amerada, International Telephone & Telegraph and Grinnell, R. J. Reynolds and McLean Industries, and Studebaker and Worthington. Even though Dillon Read was not a major player in the mergers and acquisitions area, these were substantial deals.

What Brandi's private views on the matter of expansion and entry into new businesses were cannot be known, but there was no doubt regarding Dillon's position. From his Far Hills citadel Dillon Read's éminence grise sent the word: the firm would continue to avoid risk, and to him, all of these changes were hazardous.

This situation presented challenges. Brandi and his partners had to come to terms with the fundamental reality that the transformation of investment banking was accelerating and that only perceptive and decisive investment bankers would be able to prosper in the increasingly complex environment. Yet these veterans could not bring themselves to confront Dillon on such matters; while no longer present at the firm, absentee owner Dillon was feared and respected. Both Brandi and Belmont were nearing the age of retirement. They had performed well at the old business and did little to adjust to the new dispensation. Brandi and Belmont were fortunate in having come to leadership posts when a clear though unwritten code existed to guide behavior, in an atmosphere where their talents could have full play. Neither man had any intention of creating a stir at that point in his career.

Indeed, Brandi and Belmont had been superb bankers, gentleman bankers of the old school who had thrived in the kind of business climate that prevailed in the immediate postwar world. A story, probably apocryphal but illustrative of the way such men thought and acted, is told of a business meeting between Brandi and Meyer, who were cut from the same cloth. After having had some earlier negotiations regarding a deal, the two men met to arrange for its conclusion. "It looks gray outside, doesn't it?" remarked Meyer, peering at the sky. "Yes. I think today is might rain," replied Brandi. "Well, is there anything else we ought to talk about?" concluded Meyer, apparently signaling, without directly referring to it, that the arrangement they had struck was acceptable.[12]

The world was passing such men by. A faster-paced, more irreverent mood was rapidly developing in American finance, which showed itself in many ways.

In the early summer of 1970 Brandi and Belmont set about planning the succession at Dillon Read. Brandi had reached the age of sixty-five. He was willing, and according to some, even eager to remain, but he wanted it on his own terms, and so engaged in a typically cryptic conversation on the matter with Clarence Dillon. "I think it's probably time for me to retire, Mr. Dillon," said Brandi one evening, to which Dillon replied, "I think that's a good idea, Fred."[13] That was that. Brandi departed to pursue other interests; his would be a retirement from Dillon Read, but not from his profession.[14] Among these concerns was American–South African Investment Co. Its CEO, the fabled Charles Engelhard, died in March 1971, and Brandi succeeded him as president. Brandi also retained an office at Dillon Read, and his work on corporate boards kept him quite occupied.

Despite the fall-off in business toward the end of his tenure at Dillon Read, Brandi could look back with considerable satisfaction on a brilliant career. He had become an effective banker when first-generation German-Americans were widely viewed in America with some suspicion, making his accomplishments all the more impressive.[15] On the eve of retirement Brandi displayed the continuing sharpness of his vision on foreign affairs, as he discussed a wide range of subjects relating to the future of investment banking. "The currencies of the EEC will get closer together in interchangeability as the ecomomies of the six member nations become more inter-related," he suggested. Brandi predicted Japan would be a formidable competitor in the future, at a time when that country's economic miracle had barely surfaced. He didn't think Japan would be able to sustain its growth for long, however. "Accordingly, Japan may export capital to build industrial facilities in countries were labor is cheap, such as Korea and Hong Kong." As for the domestic economy, "I do not think that we shall ever be able to return to low interest rates and moderate wage progression."[16]

In fact, the American economy was troubled, as were the securities markets. The Dow had peaked at just below 1000 in December 1968, and then declined steadily, winding up at the 630 level a year and a half later. While only perceptible in retrospect, the great bull market of the post–World War II period had ended, and a more difficult period, marked by inflation, economic dislocation, stagnation, deregulation, and a gigantic restructuring of American business, was about to begin. The skeleton of a global economy, the barest outlines of which were discernible in the 1960s, was now perceptible. For all of American history world power had been centered on those countries bordering the Atlantic Ocean. Now the Pacific Age was dawning. Brandi had seen it coming, and now Dillon Read would require a new leader with the same ability to perceive the possibilities of the future and the capability to act in ways to capitalize upon the possibilities offered.

Of course Brandi's musings regarding the future could not fully anticipate the tumultuous economic developments of the 1970s. Some of the signs were already there, however. In 1968, the budget deficit had come to $27.7 billion, the highest since World War II, putting pressures on interest rates. There was a glut of dollars on the world scene, as Americans spent and invested at record levels overseas. In January 1969, the gold reserve had fallen below $12 billion, as foreigners converted their unwanted dollars to gold, and this continued into the following year, as well as what seemed to be dangerous inflation. Brandi was leaving Dillon Read at almost precisely the time when the milieu in which he had performed so well was fading.

Even so, there was confidence regarding the transfer of power and optimism about the firm's future. The possible line of succession had been well known for many years. First consideration would be given Douglas Dillon who, had he wanted to, might have succeeded Brandi, since this had been his father's design all along. Douglas had disposed of his ownership shares by selling them back to Clarence on becoming Secretary of the Treasury, but this would have signified nothing considering the elder Dillon's power.

Sixty-one years old and physically and mentally fit, Douglas

Dillon appeared to go out of his way to avoid reinstatement. In 1967, he had become president of US&FS, and two years later was elevated to the chairmanship, but these titles were almost completely honorary in nature. Douglas also joined the board of Chase Manhattan Bank, which under terms of the Glass-Steagall Banking Act foreclosed on the possibility of becoming associated with any investment bank. Now deeply involved in educational and charitable work, he showed no interest in assuming a role at the family firm.[17] Whether his continuing lack of interest in taking up his father's mantle came as a major disappointment to Clarence Dillon is not known, but Douglas was certain he did not relish another stint in investment banking, later telling a reporter flatly that he "didn't want to return to that sort of work."[18] Likewise, there was no chance of August Belmont taking the post, though he too might have had it for the asking. Two years older than Dillon, Belmont was also looking forward to retirement, though prepared to remain at the firm to assist the new CEO.

Dillon Read was still a small company, so there was little doubt who was on the short list of candidates for the chairmanship and presidency. In the end it appeared to come down to Brady, Ted Wadsworth, and Peter Flanigan. Under ordinary circumstances Flanigan might have had the edge. Not only had he brought in new business, but Flanigan had developed into a skillful banker, conversant with all areas of the industry. His interests in a public career, however, which led him to take leaves of absence to engage in governmental activities, all but eliminated him from consideration. In any case, Flanigan was in Washington in 1969, serving as assistant to President Nixon, and showed no intention of rejoining the firm in the immediate future. "Peter is certainly the kind of guy we would consider to head this firm someday," said Belmont, but Flanigan would not return until early 1975.[19]

After due consideration, Brandi, Belmont, and the Dillons decided upon Brady as the next CEO. Indeed, the reason Clarence Dillon was willing to see Brandi leave was because he felt Brady's time had arrived. Brandi and Belmont notified Brady of the selection a full year before they were scheduled to retire. This would enable Brady to join Brandi on the older partner's many visits to clients, so key external relationships would be assured that a smooth transfer of power would take place within the firm.[20]

Wadsworth, then fifty-nine years old, a seasoned veteran who had the respect of everyone at the firm, was to have become chairman of the board. As it happened he died suddenly of a massive heart attack on June 2, 1970, which necessitated another change in the firm's top management. Because Brandi was now adamant regarding his retirement, Brady approached Belmont regarding the prospect of his staying on as chairman. Belmont was reluctant to do so, but accepted on condition it not be for very long. Still, it was important to have a second, active member of the firm in a position to help Brady with general administrative responsibilities, and so as Brady assumed the presidency, Bud Treman was promoted to executive vice president.[21]

Brady's major task was to carve out a position for himself which would enable him to make the necessary changes without disrupting the essential collegiality of his cohort group in the firm. The role of chairman at an investment bank was not quite the same as that of the chief executive or operating officer of a corporation, and his authority derived more from earned respect from peers than the power to make demands and give orders. In such a structure the chairman was to provide leadership, a sense of direction, and in some cases, a vision and strategy. This had been the case with Brandi, and remained so at most investment banks in the 1970s. Dillon Read was not about to break new ground in this regard.

There were no rigid job descriptions at Dillon Read, no strict separation of duties, no hard-and-fast lines demarcating the area of concern of any partner. Each man had his own clients, interests, and concerns. As has been noted, investment banks were more like law firms than corporations, in that whether or not they were partnerships, the top individuals functioned as such. They were prepared to take on virtually any client in any industry, and for any kind of underwriting. Brandi could move easily from a deal for a California oil company to government underwritings in any part of Europe. In time, however, they came to specialize, Brandi in petroleum and Belmont in gas pipelines, for example. It was the way business had been conducted in the days of William A. Read, Clarence Dillon, and James Forrestal. This much hadn't been modified.

Brady recognized this, knew changes were needed, and was

prepared to act. Shortly before taking office he spoke with Douglas Dillon of his feelings regarding the firm's future. Dillon recalled, "Nick came to me and said, 'The string is running out. You just can't continue on a name and what you did in the past.' His great contrubution was to see the thing in the large." If adjustment to new realities were to be made Dillon's assistance would be needed.[22]

In September 1971, Douglas Dillon resigned his position on the Chase Manhattan board, repurchased his shares in Dillon Read, and assumed the post of chairman of the executive committee.[23] These were significant moves in more than one way. Douglas refused to return unless his father agreed to retire completely from Dillon Read activities, which he did. There would be occasional telephone calls for information, but not counsel.

This completed the team for the new dispensation. Dillon did not intend to assume a position of active leadership. Rather, he was there to protect the family interests and make certain the generational transition went smoothly. Yet his presence was of critical significance. Dillon was available for advice, to open doors, and to provide a sense of continuity, all of which he did.[24]

The passing of authority to a new generation took place in a manner reflective of the Brandi technique of conducting business. He came to work as usual on Thursday, December 31, and remained until 5:00 P.M., the normal closing time. All but Brandi and Brady and a secretary had left early for New Year's Eve celebrations. Brady brought in a bottle of champagne for some private toasts, after which the firm's leaders, past and future, went home. The Brady era had begun in a quiet, traditional, perfectly gentlemanly fashion.

· 16 ·

Caution in an Era
of Change

(1972–1980)

Nick Brady was a natural successor to Fred Brandi as Dillon
Read's CEO. To the manor born, he was a true country gentleman, with all the elegance and status expected of a traditional
Dillon Read banker. With Brady in charge the firm could cling to
its reputation as one of the grand old banks in an age of upstarts.
As one writer put it, Brady's "gracious manner . . . lets him serve
wax paper wrapped roast beef sandwiches at his boardroom table
as if it were a champagne hunt breakfast."[1]

Brady's major task was to adapt Dillon Read to the changing
realities of investment banking without sacrificing its essentially
conservative legacy, which meant satisfying Clarence Dillon that
there would be no "imprudent" changes in the business. The firm's
slowness in meeting the mounting competitive challenges of the
period had to be addressed. The glory days of Dillon were long
over, and the leading members of the firm realized that while
Brandi and August Belmont had led Dillon Read into several lucrative areas, many opportunities for growth had been bypassed.
Since the 1950s Dillon Read had played the conventional game as
well as might be expected, and while it had tended to ignore some
opportunities, this was to a large degree the way Clarence Dillon

wanted it. None of the bankers seemed to find this unacceptable or even a matter for serious debate and discussion. On the other hand, there was no great sense of urgency. Even though the business was not expanding, remuneration for the firm's principals was quite high.

Brady's orientation to the business of investment banking was traditonal, which helps explain much of what followed. His skills were primarily directed to the acquisition of new investment banking business and deals. Brady excelled at the kind of relationship banking which had characterized Dillon Read since its beginnings. He was highly regarded for the meticulous care he afforded clients. Between 1976 and 1980, 20 to 30 percent of the firm's investment banking business would derive from new clients, many of these brought in by Brady, while approximately 70 percent came from familiar old ones.

Brady's strengths and weaknesses as a leader were two sides of the same coin. He was (as he indeed characterized himself) a tactically oriented thinker, a man who liked to analyze all the elements of a problem. "The devil lies in the details. It's a Clarence Dillon style, of overwhelming the detail. You've got to do the pick-and-shovel work to find where the devil might lie. And it gives you a tremendous edge."[2] Such was fairly typical of the Brady approach, more micro than macro, geared to performing delicate tasks superbly. Yet he did not have such a personal love of detail to grapple with it on a day-to-day basis, and left the work of managing the detail to others. "Nick absolutely hated to manage," said one of his associates. "He was quite competent to make broad policy decisions, but he disliked like crazy sitting around tables at meetings with diverse inputs."[3] On his part, Brady always claimed this was necessary in order to achieve results. "The essence of trying to make progress is to separate the details from the important things and act on the important things," was the way he put it years later.[4] This inclination toward hands-off management took many forms, the most striking being an alteration in the firm's structure, which resulted in delegating as much of the day-to-day decision making as possible.

Despite his apparent dislike of meetings, his manner of conducting them won the admiration of many of his colleagues. Typically, Brady would do more listening than talking, conveying a sense of calm and thoughtful deliberation. John Haskell remarked that Brady "listens to all of us, contributes, synthesizes and comes up with the idea that puts into practical terms where we are headed."[5]

By 1974 Brady had reshaped the firm so that each of eight managing directors had a wide degree of latitude in his activities.[6] Under his leadership alterations in administration designed to make the firm more efficient were put into place. With Brandi, for example, there had been no formal reporting procedures. This was changed. In time it would become routine for department heads and other officers to prepare annual reports on activities, client relationships, and associated matters, which would be distributed and then discussed at a weekend meeting in early January, when allocations of capital for the forthcoming year would also be determined.

Because of these predilections Brady relied heavily on Arthur Treman, who became his second in command and handled many administrative matters. Like Brandi and Belmont before them, Treman and Brady were a team. But there were differences. Brandi and Belmont each concentrated on a specialty, while covering a wide range of business at a time when the industry was relatively stable. By then there was a clear need for a greater degree of functional specialization. Brady would bring in new business, functioning as the firm's spokesman, and preserve and burnish the firm's image, while Treman performed the day-to-day tasks required of a chief operating officer. In a firm the size of Dillon Read it was an effective division of labor. In the parlance of the day, Brady was the rainmaker, while Treman would cultivate and then harvest the crops.

Treman, who had a passion for supervision Brady lacked, made the system work, but also contributed to virtually every other aspect of the firm's business. A bachelor and workaholic, he was regularly seen in the office late at night and during weekends. He took a direct interest in the training of newcomers, made business assignments, bore obligations for a wide variety of activities, and was usually the only person at the firm who knew all of what was happening at any given time. In addition, he had direct oversight of the investment banking area, which he had taken charge of in 1965. Treman carried out all the functions of an investment banker, including the generation of new business, and he was successor to Brandi and Belmont as the firm's expert in the area of natural gas. As such he testified before congressional committees on pipeline projects, providing the firm with a new cachet in this industry.

As a rainmaker in his own right, Treman was responsible for bringing in one of the more important new accounts, Adolph Coors Co. It was an example of Dillon Read at its best as a typical relationship banker, transforming goodwill into business for the firm. The Colorado-based brewery was experiencing accelerating growth in the 1970s, and for the first time in its history needed outside advice regarding financings. Because Treman had formed a business and then personal relationship with Joseph Coors when both men investigated a potential investment opportunity, it was only natural for the latter to turn to him when, in 1975, Coors needed financial advice. Treman led Dillon Read in bringing Coors public.[7]

Brady and Treman formed a capable executive team in administering the firm, but strategically they left Dillon Read to run in conventional channels when Wall Street was undergoing an expansionary and innovative upheaval. There were several reasons for this, quite aside from the inclination of the firm's management, which can be characterized as an abiding preference for small-scale, albeit profitable operations over the rapid growth and often wrenching change which characterized the era's more glamorous firms. But even were it otherwise—had Brady desired to create a new atmosphere at Dillon Read—he was constrained by the living legacy of Clarence Dillon. Dillon had once been willing to cede authority to James Forrestal, who after all was a colleague, and Fred Brandi was one of his protégés. August Belmont had been the bearer of one of the most distinguished names on Wall Street as well as a superb banker in his own right. Neither Brandi nor Belmont was much younger than Dillon. Nick Brady, on the other hand, was a comparative youngster, of an entirely new generation, much the junior of even Douglas Dillon. For this reason he had to approach the senior Dillon on an entirely different level than his predecessors. What Forrestal could do before informing Dillon and Brandi and Belmont might do afterwards, Brady might shrink from considering. In other words, Brady had an implied mandate to be cautious, which he may not have felt he could challenge, even when the situation on Wall Street might well have called for boldness.

Brady also maintained a number of significant, time-consuming interests outside the firm. A few months after assuming the helm he became chairman of Purolator, and during the next decade led that oil filter company into a variety of new businesses, including courier and armored car services. He remained at the Jockey Club as well, work which absorbed several hours of his time per week. In addition, he became seriously involved with New Jersey Republican politics. In 1969, he served as finance chairman for the unsuccessful gubernatorial bid of Raymond Bateman, and in 1980 he would cochair the New Jersey for George Bush Committee, thus annealing ties with the future President, whom he had known since they summered together in Kennebunkport, Maine. (It was Brady who, at the convention that summer, made the official announcement of his state's unanimous support for Bush's vice presidential nomination.) He also labored for the candidacy and then election of New Jersey gubernatorial candidate Thomas Kean. All this activity seemed natural enough at the time; investment bankers often became involved in such varied enterprises. Recall that Clarence Dillon engaged in the manufacture of phenol prior to World War I, doing so with William A. Read's approval if not blessing. Besides, as Brady would later assert, such seasoning served investment bankers well, since it enabled them to better understand corporate problems and prospects. As for the Jockey Club, his efforts there lent the firm stature and opened the door to new business.

In their time Dillon and Forrestal had performed public service, and Peter Flanigan was an assistant to President Nixon in the White House, dealing with domestic and international economic matters. The tradition would continue to the 1980s, when eminent bankers such as Lehman Brothers' Peter Peterson worked on the Brandt Commission, which concentrated on third world problems and crusaded for a balanced budget, while Lazard Frères' Felix Rohatyn chaired New York's Municipal Assistance Corporation and became a spokesman for many causes. During his tenure as head of Dillon Read, Brady was to chair or serve on seven presidential commissions which dealt with issues ranging from Central American politics to government pay scales to management of the defense program. He is perhaps best known for the last of these commissions, the Presidential Task Force on Market Mechanisms, also known as the Brady Commission, which analyzed the reasons for the stock market crash of October 1987 and suggested reforms to prevent its recurrence.[8]

At other times such avocations for a Wall Street CEO would have been not only acceptable, but even desirable. In the 1970s, however, they proved distracting when multiple challenges had to be addressed. Acquisition of new clients remained a paramount goal, but economic and political developments would oblige Dillon Read at least to consider entering other areas previously ignored or rejected. And there would be increasing demands for administrative skills to plan and manage the firm's growth in the even more turbulent era which was to come in the 1980s.

To appreciate this, recall that the investment banking environment underwent a series of convulsions during the 1970s. These began in 1971, when President Nixon took the nation off the gold bullion standard, imposed restrictions on imports, instituted wage and price controls, and cut the budget. Taken together with the lingering effects of the disruptive political events of the late 1960s, particularly the divisive Vietnam War, these moves seemed in keeping with a general awareness that after only two decades "the American Century" was coming to a close. Then, in the mid-1970s, economic dislocations already caused by war and poor fiscal management were exacerbated by the Watergate scandal, hostilities in the Middle East, the international oil crisis, and "stagflation." In addition financial deregulation, the continuing revolution in the technologies of communication and computation, and political uncertainties contributed to gyrating exchange and interest rates.[9]

The tumultuous environment presented both problems and opportunities which demanded sharp and timely responses from the nation's investment banking community. Bankers no longer had the luxury of time, which is to say movements which once took weeks to develop were telescoped into days, and then hours and even minutes. Clients needed more services. The old distinction between the origination of an underwriting and its distribution, which seemed sensible enough earlier, now appeared needlessly cumbersome and archaic. Bond trading, once an adjunct to underwriting, was becoming potentially more profitable as price movements became more abrupt.

BOND YIELDS AND INTEREST RATES, 1965–1975

Year	Corporate Bonds Aaa	Baa	High Grade Municipals	Federal Funds Rate
1965	4.49	4.87	3.27	4.07
1966	5.13	5.67	3.82	5.11
1967	5.51	6.23	3.98	4.22
1968	6.18	6.94	4.51	5.66
1969	7.03	7.81	5.81	8.20
1970	8.04	9.11	6.51	7.18
1971	7.39	8.56	5.70	4.66
1972	7.21	8.16	5.27	4.43
1973	7.44	8.24	5.18	8.73
1974	8.57	9.50	6.09	10.50
1975	8.83	10.61	6.89	5.83

SOURCE: *1985 Economic Report of the President*, p. 311.

The bond markets had been dull during the 1950s and most of the 1960s. In those years there was a gentle upward move, with yields on Aaa rated bonds rising from 2.96 percent in 1952 to 4.49 percent in 1965. It was possible for an intermediate-term bond to trade at the same price for more than a month, and such vehicles did not interest traders. This suited Dillon Read, which was not overly concerned with the secondary markets, concentrating as it did on raising money for its corporate clients.

The situation started to change in the second half of the 1960s, and the markets became positively feverish in the 1970s. Trading activities accelerated, and Dillon Read's leadership felt it could no longer delay entry into this newly exciting arena.

The sharply altered condition of the economy and markets demanded responses. Wall Street banks were being driven in one of two directions. Some would attempt to meet the challenges by expanding operations. The most striking example of this came at Salomon Brothers, which throughout its history had viewed itself as a rough-and-tumble distribution and trading house. In the mid-1970s its leaders, Billy Salomon and John Gutfreund, decided to enter investment banking. Felix Rohatyn noted this development with interest. "They have the competence and the capital, but they may have to buy the three-piece suit."[10] So they did. Salomon started hiring new personnel, concentrating on proven veterans at other banks and for the first time making a concerted effort to recruit at the top business schools. "In 1977 we set our sights on expanding market share," remarked Terry Connally, one of the newcomers. "We said okay, we'll drive a truck through into the *Fortune 500* and we got trememdous support from the firm." Within five years Salomon had performed services for 88 of those 500 corporations.[11]

Another response to the new market forces came from those firms opting for a more intense specialization on one aspect of the industry, preferably requiring highly sophisticated knowledge which would translate into high margin business. A few firms considered transforming themselves into "boutiques," small operations staffed by cadres of accomplished bankers prepared to perform specialized services for a limited number of select clients. As noted, Lazard Frères was the prototypical boutique. By the 1970s it was concentrating even more than earlier on functioning as advisor to a select roster of clients, and there was talk on the Street that the firm might leave all forms of underwriting, and focus on marketing its expertise.

Of the two different forms of reactions, the latter was much more in the Dillon Read tradition. Concentration on those highly profitable low-risk value-added deals, requiring a great deal of brainpower but little capital, must have tempted the senior members of the firm, since this approach was so much in their blood.

While all of this was transpiring, Dillon Read's relative position in the industry declined. John Mullin, who came to Dillon Read from the Wharton School in 1969, was one of a number of Dillon Read partners who recognized the problems. "It was increasingly apparent that we were losing position on Wall Street," he said. "We were not invited into as many syndicates."

Yet to most within the firm there was no cause for anxiety. Remuneration remained high, and the work was pleasant. As before, the Dillon Read bankers divided two-thirds of the annual profits among them, the other third going to the Dillon ownership interests. They were as well compensated as their counterparts at some of the more aggressive firms.[12] Even so, given the changes on Wall Street itself, there was no way of avoiding the conclusion that the time would come when Dillon Read's management could no longer assume it could survive without coming to terms with the altered investment banking environment. There was an erosion of the client base which was not fully compensated for by new accounts.

Through most of the 1970s Mullin and others of the younger generation were convinced that Dillon Read's conservatism was justified, even though it meant forgoing business when other firms were resorting to highly aggressive tactics and were diversifying their services rapidly to win new business. "We don't want to be the storm troopers of Wall Street," said Fritz Hobbs, who began with the firm in 1972.[13]

With no groundswell from the ranks and always aware of Clarence Dillon's influence, Brady proceeded cautiously in this new environment. Nonetheless, he recognized that new business mandated some expansion. Brady sought to invigorate the firm by bringing in talent from outside. Frederick Cook, who had arrived from Congoleum Corp., supervised all marketing efforts, while Stephen Anbinder, formerly of Scudder, Stevens & Clark, was placed in charge of trading of debt securities. Charles P. "Pat" Durkin, Jr., who previously had been at ITT, moved into mergers and acquisitions, a field Dillon Read had tended to ignore after Flanigan had left for Washington. By 1975 the firm had doubled in personnel from what it had been in the late 1960s. As a result expenses were rising rapidly, due in part to the arrival of new personnel but also to the increased costs of conducting the business.

With all of this expansion, Dillon Read did not enlarge the scope of its business sufficiently to compete along a broad front. Whenever the partners weighed the benefits of growth they also considered the problems such change would bring, not only to the business practices, profits, and image, but to maneuverability and to an extent, client services. Large-scale investments in personnel and facilities meant the firm would be compelled to take risks to cover its fixed costs. "You must avoid being driven by your overhead," commented Rohatyn. "Once you are big, it is impossible to become small again."[14] Such an approach also meshed with Brady's tactical strengths and stated objectives. "We don't strive for bigness," he told a reporter. "What we strive for is quality."[15] What this translated into was an acceptance of the status quo. For years, observed former managing director Robert Gerard, the firm had refused to consider any significant alteration in its objectives. "Dillon Read's management didn't pay attention to lost market share [in underwritings]. No one saw fit to gear up like Salomon, Goldman Sachs, or Smith Barney." When transformation finally did come, said Gerard, it arrived as almost an afterthought. "Expansion and contraction were *ad hoc*. The firm has always reacted to change rather than planned for it."[16]

And what of Clarence Dillon? As far as the firm was concerned, he was very much alive and well, maintaining his interest in developments. He took pains to compliment Brady on his stewardship, noting at one point that "1976 was as good a year as he could remember," as indeed it was, as the firm posted record earnings.[17]

One measure of how much the world had changed in the twentieth century is the swiftness with which modern celebrities are forgotten. Back in 1951, during the Medina trial, Dillon Read's chief counsel, Matthew Correa of Cahill, Gordon, Zachry & Reindel, had sketched a history of the firm since the early years of the century. In his summation, Correa described how Clarence Dillon had assumed command after William A. Read's death, noted the advent of the new generation of partners in the 1920s, and highlighted in particular James Forrestal's banking and governmental career. "These men," Correa proclaimed, "by reason of their experience, were able to make a real contribution to the companies they served." Judge Medina nodded in solemn agreement.[18] It was almost a eulogy of once great investment bankers. That was the way it was reported in the newspapers the following day. The *New York Times* wrote, "The Dillon, Read executives [Correa] referred to were James A. Forrestal and Clarence L. Dillon, both deceased."[19]

Of course Forrestal's death was known to virtually every literate American. Clarence Dillon had been so long away from public scrutiny that the reporter, perhaps rushing to meet a deadline, might have justifiably assumed he, too, had died. Yet Dillon was a healthy sixty-nine years old at the time of the trial, elderly perhaps by the standards of the day, but still vigorous and active, notwithstanding that he had last made headlines in the America of Franklin Roosevelt and Babe Ruth. One wonders whether Clarence Dillon saw this item in *The Times*, and if so was amused or chagrined by it.

He continued to intervene at the firm. Brandi and Belmont heard from him regularly. So did others. William Esrey, for example, recalled that as a young investment banker he received what must have been somewhat disconcerting telephone calls from Dillon who, after reading one or another item in the newspapers concerning Dillon Read, wanted details. Dillon was the gruff but disembodied presence, literally wired to the firm, always asking questions, only to hang up without so much as a good-bye once he had the information. More often than not he telephoned to express concern that Dillon Read was assuming undue risk, or that it was wrong to accept anything less than a special bracket position in a tombstone advertisement.[20] Such calls were to be taken seriously; the Dillon family, after all, had a controlling stake in the ownership.

Occasionally there would be a dinner for new "partners" or vice presidents at Far Hills, and then the young people would meet for the first and only time the legendary banker behind the voice, the true power at Dillon Read, which while not present remained its guiding force. Even while not knowing him very well, the senior members of the firm seemed to imagine how he might react to one or another of their actions.

Dillon died in 1979 at the age of ninety-six, when he was almost completely forgotten outside of the firm. He is not even mentioned in any of the major histories of the Great Bull Market of the 1920s. Rather, Clarence had been relegated to a position in history as "the financier father of Douglas Dillon," one of the nation's more distinguished treasury secretaries and ambassadors.

Even in death Clarence Dillon still cast a long shadow over William Street, and it was in this shadow that Brady would have to govern, as he considered alternative methods of meeting the new institutional challenges. Would there be growth or retrenchment? Would Dillon Read become a version of Lazard Frères or would it try to compete with Salomon, Morgan Stanley, Goldman Sachs, and their like? This was the major stategic question Brady faced. As it turned out, a concern for traditional investment banking services alone could not carry the firm, and prompted Dillon Read to enter trading, at least to the degree that constraints on capital and risk permitted.

The development of a trading operation was bound to create a degree of tension at the firm, since such activities were so out of character for Dillon Read. Most long-established Wall Street investment banks have one of two personalities: that of an investment banking or of a trading operation, and the predilection can be seen in the kinds of leadership the different firms have had.

Unlike bankers, traders didn't require relatives, friends, and classmates to be effective, and they often seemed to share a delight in trampling on traditions. In contrast, investment bankers were noted for their probity, diplomatic skills, and network of relationships, which perhaps helps explain why so many of them entered government service at high levels. They have long time frames, working slowly with clients, planning for years and even decades ahead, while traders focused on the moment, the price, and where it might be headed in seconds and minutes.

Underwriters act for clients, in that they attempt to raise funds for clients, while traders are principals, risking the firm's money. Underwriters do not require enormous amounts of capital, which is why Dillon Read was able to divide profits so munificently. Capital is the lifeblood of traders, and houses which wanted to participate in that field had to possess capital and have the will to risk it. Moreover, they would have to assume major risks. In other words, the two occupations demanded different personalities, outlooks, perceptions, capital, and talents.

There were aspects of trading which bothered more than a few old-line investment bankers, who held an enduring conviction that underwriting and consultation were practices of gentlemen who raised funds for American business and enabled corporations to become more productive and remunerative. Trading, on the other hand, was regarded as a sterile pursuit, a search for profits from the exchange of paper rather than the creation of goods and services. Of course, clients who had purchased bonds from a salesman increasingly insisted the firm make a market in that security, so that if and when the purchaser wanted to sell, quotes could be obtained. For all of its expansion, Salomon, for example, remained a characteristic trading house, founded by traders and salesmen who passed down leadership to other traders and salesmen. At such firms investment banking, while quite significant, was secondary to trading and sales.

For more than half a century Dillon Read had been the archetypal investment bank, a private provider of advice, the intermediary between the clients which required funds and the institutions which provided them, noted for probity and a sense of mission.[21] The Dillon Read bankers were underwriters and consultants, and well aware of the differences between their activities and those of traders. By virtue of background, training, ideology, and appearance, Brady was the quintessential traditional investment banker, the kind who had led the Street almost since its inception. "Brady is a patrician—the old white shoe mold of banker, from a time when bankers didn't mix with traders, who were the immigrant class of the time," reflected Salomon's CEO John Gutfreund. "Then it took a generation to be purified."[22]

As Dillon Read responded to its clients' wishes, Brady recognized that trading was a lucrative enterprise as well as an increasingly necessary ancillary function to underwriting. But to move into trading in a serious way would require a change in attitude. Brady later recalled, "We had always maintained the fiction that you can price a bond equally well whether you're trading every day or not." Now this would have to end.[23] Yet there was more to it than that. "We had to get closer to the markets," Brady explained when discussing the situation in which the firm found itself. "We really had only one and a half businesses—corporate underwriting and financial advice."[24] This is to say that while Dillon Read had a strong "buying" operation, it lacked its counterpart in the "selling" area. As before, the firm concentrated on working out deals for clients and left the distribution and trading of securities to others.

Among other things, the decision to expand trading activities meant additional professionals would have to be recruited. William Esrey arrived from AT&T after graduating from Denison College and receiving a Harvard MBA. In addition to his other activities he served as a combination treasurer and controller. In effect, Esrey took charge of the Dillon Read back office, having prime responsibility for that area just as Treman led in investment banking. In time he also assumed overall responsibility for trading.[25]

Esrey recalls the nervousness exhibited by the older investment bankers regarding the newcomers in trading and sales. Some of them would have been just as pleased to remain at their old tasks, but they realized that to do so not only would mean forgoing large profits, but losing clients.[26] They looked askance at traders like W. Harvey Mell, who was recruited by Brady along with five other traders from Legg Mason. Mell emerged as one of the firm's more important traders, and earned substantial sums for the firm from trading in municipal securities. He went on to become responsible for building the corporate bond department and attempted to get Dillon Read more involved in sales and trading.

It was quite a new situation for the company. John Mullin remembers his first impressions of Mell, who had arrived only a few months earlier. To Mullin, who had gone into corporate finance, Mell seemed significantly different from the bankers. "I wouldn't say Harvey was a 'barroom brawler,' exactly," recalled Mullin, "but he was certainly much more aggressive than anyone else at the firm in those days." He was a decided asset, but was never to become an integral part of the firm. Though Mell became an officer, he departed within a few years. Indeed, in this period the pattern was for traders *not* to become officers of the firm. Made to feel like second-class citizens, most departed Dillon Read within a few years of their hiring. The firm remained committed to relationship banking, with trading viewed as a secondary operation, and this remained reflected in the composition of the leadership.

Dillon Read first expanded activities in municipal bond trading, followed by corporates, then Government National Mortgage Association certificates ("Ginnie Maes"), and finally opened a small unit for stocks, when in 1977 the firm was able to woo John Durand from William Witter and Patrick Burke from Edwards & Hanley. In 1979, the firm gathered together all of its trading activities in governments into Dillon Read Government Securities (DRGS), capitalized at $3 million, which was organized as a wholly owned limited liability subsidiary, to be managed by James P. Morgan. When Brady took over, the company had twelve professionals in debt sales, trading, and syndication; by 1979 there were forty in these spheres.[27]

In retrospect we can see that Dillon Read was making its move into trading when the capital markets were being transformed by yet another environmental change: the gathering forces of deregulation. By the mid-1970s regulatory concepts dating back to the New Deal were fast unraveling. The first major modification in this regard came in the area of stock commissions. Brokerage firms that were not members of the NYSE started trading listed stocks in what came to be known as the "Third Market," and also challenged the legality of NYSE Rule 394, which obliged member firms to deal in listed shares only on the floor. Then the SEC entered the picture, ruling that starting on April 1, 1971, commissions could be negotiated on trades of more than $500,000, and the figure would be lowered in stages, culminating in fully negotiated commissions on May 1, 1975. The reaction on the Street was almost uniformly melancholy. "This industry isn't ready for competitive rates," asserted veteran banker I. W. "Tubby" Burnham just prior to their advent. "The effect would be disastrous. I don't think the Exchange would survive six months."[28]

Dillon Read was not directly affected, of course, since it did not have a large equity business. But the indirect ramifications were significant. Under the pressure of deregulation the industry as a whole was beginning to evolve rapidly, as small discount brokerage houses contested the large wire houses for customers. The latter then sought additional areas of opportunity to make up for lost commission earnings. This took them more heavily into areas in which Dillon Read competed.

The new atmosphere stimulated those firms which had positioned themselves by virtue of capital and inclination to grow rapidly. Several observers were predicting the wholesale disappearance of scores of banks in this new highly competitive environment. And so they were. In 1972, there were more than 600 NYSE member firms doing a public business. During the next six years 240 of them either had been absorbed through mergers or had failed.[29]

These dislocations were a consequence not simply of the new problems and possibilities presented by deregulation, but also by an increasingly volatile climate on the interest rate front. A condition which in the first half of the 1970s seemed unstable became almost chaotic by the end of the decade.

This situation impacted directly upon Dillon Read's emerging trading operations, which at first had been quite profitable but now were becoming troubled. In 1976 the trading units had contributed close to $7 million in profits, with governments performing best. Losses were posted in both the corporate and equity sides in 1977, with much more red ink shown the following year. In 1979 there was a major failure in the Ginnie Mae area. Relative to its low level of capital, the firm had extended itself far more than was prudent. In this instance, Dillon Read suffered losses when in-

BOND YIELDS AND INTEREST RATES, 1976–1980

Year	Corporate Bonds Aaa	Baa	High Grade Municipals	Federal Funds Rate
1976	8.43	9.75	6.49	5.04
1977	8.02	8.97	5.56	5.54
1978	8.73	9.49	5.90	7.93
1979	9.63	10.69	6.39	11.19
1980	11.94	13.67	8.51	13.36

SOURCE: *1985 Economic Report of the President*, p. 310.

terest rates moved sharply. Also, there was great concern that financially troubled counterparts might default on their Ginnie Mae trades with Dillon Read. Although the ultimate losses were negligible, there were several tense months. This only added to the growing lack of confidence in this new and untested part of the company.[30]

In late summer of 1979, Dillon Read decided to withdraw from the Ginnie Mae market. The problem was finding the best way to do so. By then the firm's investment bankers had become reluctant to entrust the matter of unwinding the portfolio to the same traders who had taken the positions.

In the wake of the Ginnie Mae calamity Dillon Read looked outside for help, a concession to its weaknesses in that area. Luis Mendez, formerly a managing director in charge of all trading activity at Morgan Stanley, was brought in as a consultant, and later made an officer. Mendez's arrival in June indicated just how far Dillon Read had come as far as personnel was concerned. A Cuban-American law student, he had fled Cuba for America in 1962, impoverished and without friends. With his Latin accent and volatile temper Mendez contrasted sharply both in appearance and style with the Ivy League types who dominated Dillon Read's management. Where they tended to be subdued, he was flamboyant. Even so, he was no parvenu in the industry. His presence in what had become widely considered one of the most exclusive clubs on the Street illustrated how much the industry had changed and how Dillon Read must.

Mendez soon learned not only that the Dillon Read traders had performed badly, but that they had overextended themselves with some shaky deals. The firm's top management understood this clearly, and to make certain its capital remained intact and above legal limits, Brady, Haskell, Treman, and Douglas Dillon pledged several million dollars in securities among them, to be drawn upon if necessary. (Within two years this guarantee was no longer needed, and so the agreement was dissolved.)

Treman, Mullin, and Mendez succeeded in extricating the firm from its position. By October 2 these men and their assistants had substantially liquidated the portfolio and settled accounts. Dillon Read did succeed in terminating its Ginnie Mae operation, but not before suffering more than $3.6 million in losses that year, a serious blow for a firm of its size, but one which could have been far more serious had it not been for the success of the Treman-Mullin-Mendez collaboration.[31]

Less than a week later, on October 6, 1979, Federal Reserve Board chairman Paul Volcker announced that thenceforth he would ignore interest rates and concentrate on controlling the money supply, doing so to "curb speculative excesses in the financial, foreign exchange, and commodity markets, and thereby . . . dampen inflationary forces."[32] The Fed also raised the discount rate from 11 to 12 percent. This was followed by hikes in the prime rate, all of which was translated into higher interest rates and sharply lower bond prices.

Volcker's announcement and the actions that followed sent tremors through Wall Street, and shook Dillon Read's remaining trading activities. The unstable condition hurt other aspects of the firm's business. "During 1979, private placement activity in general was lower than in the prior two years, particularly in the industrial sector," the company related. "The primary reasons for the lower volume of private financing were the high level of interest rates prevailing in the private market, especially in the closing months of the year, and the relatively wide spread in interest rates between the public and private markets for higher-rated issuers."[33]

Soon afterwards a similar experience befell and scarred the European operations. By 1971 it had become increasingly evident that London's renaissance as a financial center would be permanent. Dillon Read Overseas Corp. moved its offices from Paris to London.[34] Evan Galbraith had been hired in 1975 from Bankers Trust International to become chairman, bringing along Dmitri de

Gunzberg. Danforth Starr arrived from the New York office to help restructure the firm. Under their leadership DROC made a small but significant mark in the European markets.[35]

In 1981 Galbraith left Dillon Read to become American ambassador to France, to be succeeded by Lorenzo Weisman, who had arrived at the New York office in 1973. It wasn't long before the London branch experienced the same kind of dismal trading experience that had befallen the New York office in 1979. Mendez had put together a seven-man trading team by recruiting seasoned traders from Europe, Canada, and the United States, and their results were dismal. By early summer the losses would reach the $1 million level and climbing, prompting a wholesale dismissal of the trading team. "We had people who were totally unreliable," said Weisman, who went on to call for a far-reaching reconsideration of the firm's trading operations.[36]

In the meantime, Brady involved himself with restructuring the firm's domestic investment banking operations. By 1980 Dillon Read was able to state that its organizational approach of assigning teams of generalists to clients had been supplemented "in recent years . . . by the formation of a number of specialist functional groups" in such areas as energy and natural resources, mergers and acquisitions, private placements, pollution control, and utility financing.[37] In this and other ways the firm was responding to the transformed industry conditions. The personnel changes continued as well. Worn out by the ordeal of the past two years and ill, Treman was to leave in 1981, and other departures followed.

While still viewed by some as epitomizing the old Wall Street Establishment, Dillon Read was making an attempt to come to terms with the rapidly changing world of investment banking, with mixed results. Even so, the vision for the firm's future was clear enough. Amidst the ongoing scramble of so many Wall Street firms for unbounded volume growth, Brady's concerns remained on profitability rather than size. "There is a real role for the retail firms and there's a role for those of us that specialize in problem solving," he explained. As he and his partners looked toward the future, they were determined that Dillon Read would remain in the latter category.[38] The rationale was expressed this way in the 1979 Annual Report:

While Dillon Read's growth in recent years has been impressive, we do not necessarily aspire to be at or near the top in such quantitative measures as capital, revenues, or number of employees. We do aspire, however, to be the first in the quality of investment banking services rendered to our clients.

A more focused strategy would be crucial to Dillon Read's survival, because as the 1970s came to a close, changes within the industry began to accelerate, forcing those firms which had not grown into huge, multipurpose service companies either to specialize in those areas in which they had a comparative advantage or to leave the arena.

The choices facing Dillon Read in mid-decade remained as the industry was about to move into the 1980s. At the most general level of strategy there still was that basic choice. The Ginnie Mae debacle notwithstanding, Dillon Read would have to decide whether it would move into such high-volume low-margin liquid capital markets as government bonds, trading, and brokerage services, or concentrate instead on such smaller but higher-margin areas such as corporate restructurings and the financing of start-ups. And as before, tradition and proclivities dictated the latter path for Dillon Read. But it had become evident during the past few years that even such concentration would require additional capital, especially if the firm was to enter several fields in which several banks had done well and which were part of the old Dillon Read tradition, such as merchant banking. Would the risk-averse Dillon Read bankers be willing to participate in deals they recommended to clients? The need for capital and a willingness to accept greater risks were two of the major issues to be confronted in the coming decade.

· 17 ·

Reformation

(1981–1983)

Given a relatively static business environment, Dillon Read might have continued on in the early 1980s as it had under Brandi and Belmont and during the early Brady years. Clarence Dillon's conservative values could have been honored and practiced. But those changes which convulsed the industry in the 1970s did not abate. Rather, they quickened.

Consider the trends in the industry. During the 1970s most leading Wall Street investment banks, along with many upstarts as well, were seeking ways to enlarge their capital bases in the rapidly expanding financial markets. By the end of the decade the Street's leaders were concerned not only about competition from within but also from the Japanese and European giants which were beginning to make their presences felt in New York. In response, many firms began to plan to enter all fields involving money. The clearest manifestation of these sentiments was the rapid transformation of some of the most prominent banks into multiservice "financial supermarkets" and the abrupt disappearance of others through mergers and combinations. A few of them would incorporate and sell parts of their equity to the public, thus raising funds and providing partners with a means of cashing in their holdings.

One dramatic example of this phenomenon was the growth of Shearson Loeb Rhoades, the second-largest investment brokerage in 1980 (after Merrill Lynch), which was the end product of the mergers of eight major and midsize houses during the preceding decade. In 1981 Shearson was acquired by American Express, which later would engulf Lehman Brothers, whose earlier acquisition had been the prestigious house of Kuhn Loeb. On the other hand, Bache & Co., which had become Bache Halsey Stuart Shields, went from being the industry's second-largest concern in 1970 to twelfth position. This made Bache the object of several suitors, including the Belzberg family, Beneficial Finance, Transamerica, Prudential Insurance, and even Baldwin-United, which was being transformed from a piano manufacturer into a financial services company. In the end it was Prudential that won the bidding race, a development it was later to regret. Then Salomon Brothers was acquired by Phibro Corp., the parent of the giant Phillips Brothers, the world's leading commodity trader. (Salomon's superior skills and more powerful culture eventually made it the dominant force in the merged company.) Others would follow. Equitable Life would capture Donaldson Lufkin & Jenrette. Merrill Lynch would take over A. G. Becker. Bear Stearns went public, and was followed by L. F. Rothschild Unterberg Towbin.

Concomitant with this explosion of restructurings was the gradual erosion of the barrier established between investment banking and commercial banking by the Glass-Steagall Banking Act, as each type of institution attempted to enter the other's areas under the more laissez-faire regulatory environment of the 1980s. Such powerhouses as Citibank and BankAmerica purchased discount brokers, while large Japanese and European banks established securities operations in New York.

Not unexpectedly, Dillon Read was one of those firms that became the subject of acquisition rumors. While growing, the trading operation was small when set beside those of the aforementioned firms, and had been weakened as a result of the 1979 Ginnie Mae debacle. Dillon Read lacked a research department, had no equity business, and lacked capital and marketing power in its fixed income operations. It was not deemed a major player, but it had some assets that were still quite impressive. Dillon Read remained profitable. Its client base and personnel were respected, its bankers had solid reputations, and of no small importance was the fact that Dillon Read possessed one of the most esteemed nameplates in an industry where goodwill is viewed almost as a tangible asset. "They have a sought-after competence that would nicely complement a Paine Webber, an E. F. Hutton, or a Bache," one banker speculated in early 1979.[1]

That Dillon Read could not be acquired without the consent of the Dillon family was obvious, and Clarence Dillon hadn't the slightest intention of parting with what he still considered the crown jewel of his holdings. With Dillon's death in 1979 it appeared possible that a sale might be made.

The sale of shares to partners was not deemed a matter of great consequence. "The time came when they [the partners] wanted some shares, so they could take part in growth, and so we just sold them to them," was Douglas Dillon's recollection of how it happened. The price was based upon asset value, with the understanding that any repurchase would also be made on the same basis. Still, no disposition of the company could be made without the Dillons' permission.[2]

Now head of the clan, Douglas Dillon was more than ready to sell. Moreover, he had a generous attitude toward who might make the purchase. From the first Dillon made it clear that the bank's leaders, and not he, would make the decision. In other words, Dillon would permit those most affected by the change to decide what it would be. Too, he was willing to sell at book value, meaning he would not insist on being paid for goodwill, including that incalculable value of the firm's name. This was an extraordinary gesture for a Wall Streeter, an indication perhaps of Dillon's willingness to reward his associates for their service. Through various trusts which had controlling interest, Douglas Dillon could decide the company's future. His analysis of Dillon Read's needs and his own position were in complete alignment.[3]

We decided to sell for a very good reason. It became obvious at that time the situation had changed dramatically on Wall Street and you needed substantially more capital if you were going to function there.

Dillon was concerned with acquiring capital for expanded operations. Leaders at the firm preferred not to merge with any of several Wall Street firms which might have been interested. Dillon noted that an alternative would have been for the firm to make a public offering of shares, "but we didn't particularly want to do that." So Brady began to cast about for an appropriate buyer.

Several interested shoppers surfaced in a strong market. One was Credit Suisse White Weld, whose chairman, John Craven, suggested that the acquisition of Dillon Read made sense. Others there disagreed, and in the end CSWW turned to First Boston. Donaldson Lufkin & Jenrette also became interested, and there was a personal element as well, as Donaldson, Lufkin, and Brady had been classmates at Yale. Any possibility there was for a merger was dashed when it became obvious that DLJ intended to be the senior partner in such an arrangement, while the Dillon Read partners were determined to maintain their operational independence. Finally, there was the potential of a sale to insiders at the firm, though this was unlikely. The older partners, who were raised in an atmosphere of avoiding risk, were loath to take so entrepreneurial a role, while some of the younger ones, who had a desire to become owners, lacked the capital. As it happened a group of the latter, including Mendez and Gerard, was prepared to make a bid for ownership, but this faltered. In part as a result of this failure, Mendez began to contemplate his departure, which occurred the following year, when he was replaced at the trading desk by Dick Bianco.[4]

The beginning of a change came in 1980. Both Clarence and Douglas Dillon had a business and personal relationship with Marcus Wallenberg, the doyen of Sweden's most powerful family. Wallenberg's Skandinaviska Enskilda Banken had organized the Scandinavian Securities Corp., which was to provide investment banking services to its Scandinavian clients. Scandinavian Securities was performing badly, and Wallenberg was seeking outside assistance in a way so as to preserve the bank's image. Eugene Black, formerly president of the World Bank, was on Scandinavian Securities' board, and he suggested that Wallenberg approach Douglas Dillon on the matter. Dillon referred Wallenberg to Brady, who arranged for the bank to purchase an interest in Dillon Read and for Scandinavian Securities to merge with Dillon Read. In exchange for this merger plus $5 million Enskilda received $2.5 million in demand notes, 5 percent of Dillon Read voting common stock, and another 15 percent in the form of nonvoting shares. Wallenberg apparently was not interested in acquiring control of Dillon Read. Rather, this was an investment and indication that the two institutions would work together in the future.

Brady did not have to look very far to find the eventual purchaser; in fact, one surfaced quickly. During Peter Flanigan's most recent tour in Washington he had become friendly with George Shultz, who had been Secretary of Labor and then Secretary of the Treasury in the Nixon administration. Upon leaving government service Shultz became president of the Bechtel Group, the San Francisco–based construction firm and the nation's fifth-largest privately owned company.

By any measure Bechtel was a giant in its field. Founded by Warren Bechtel who at the turn of the century had used his mules to help construct railroads in the Far West, Bechtel had become one of the world's major construction firms, responsible for such structures as the Hoover Dam and the Oakland Bay Bridge, the latter a project for which Dillon Read had arranged financing. Through its construction activities and involvement with petroleum and natural gas projects, Bechtel had earned enormous sums in the 1970s and was in need of advice as how best to invest it. In 1981 the firm would complete $11.4 billion in projects, and would end the year with a backlog of over $10 billion, with contracts to construct nuclear power plants in Washington and Texas, projects for oil fields in Alaska and Saudi Arabia, and a copper and gold mine in Papua, New Guinea, among other projects. Stephen Bechtel, the group's chairman, was reputed to have a personal financial worth of around $200 million, while his father's came to three-quarters of a billion dollars.[5]

Bechtel's need for large-scale financing grew along with its order book. Because of this the company had established Bechtel Financial Services, a subsidiary that acted as an intermediary between the construction operations and a group of banks utilized to raise funds. That Bechtel needed further assistance in this area was obvious to all at headquarters. Given such an arm, the firm might be able to design, finance, build, and operate projects without recourse to outside assistance. If Bechtel was to be self-contained and control all aspects of any deal, the reasoning went, it would require greater support in the financial area.

In addition there was a more immediate need for such an affiliation. Bechtel had a family investment arm, known as Sequoia Ventures, which had a tax problem regarding some offshore funds it wanted to repatriate and was seeking advice on how best to accomplish the task. Starting in 1978, it sought an investment bank which might be acquired to provide such services.

Flanigan introduced Shultz to Brady, and the two men quickly became friends. Brady already had met the Bechtels, having socialized with them on trips to the West Coast. From these contacts he had concluded that Bechtel's top management had the right motives to purchase ownership control of Dillon Read, and that the "fit" made sense.

There was another, personal dimension to the situation. Freed from control by Clarence Dillon and given Douglas Dillon's willingness to divest the company, for the first time since taking command Brady had a free hand in operating the firm. Shultz, who felt comfortable with economists and bankers, saw the value of having Dillon Read as an advisor in Bechtel's financial dealings.[6] The relationship started simply enough. In 1979, Dillon Read engineered Bechtel's acquisition of Dual Drilling and its purchase, in conjunction with Hanna Mining, of WellTech, Inc., and there was talk of more business to follow.

Meanwhile Douglas Dillon was becoming increasingly concerned with selling, and for good reason: by 1981 Dillon Read had become a troubled concern. While surviving the 1979 debacle, business continued to decline in 1980. London was a problem, while the situation was even worse in the United States, where the firm was beginning to lose some of its corporate clients. To cap things off there was an accelerating departure of middle management to other firms, along with the imminent departure of Treman and others.

By then Shultz had concluded that Dillon Read could provide Bechtel and Sequoia with much-needed expertise, and he recommended its purchase. The plan was for Sequoia to purchase the Dillon interests, which would give it control of the firm, the balance held by Dillon Read management and Enskilda. The Bechtels were to be "passive but interested proprietors."

On April 29, 1981, Bechtel announced it had acquired a controlling interest in Dillon Read, in effect replacing the Dillon holdings. Stephen Bechtel told reporters the price was around $25 million. Shultz, Willis Slusser, and Steven White, also of Bechtel, would join Wallenberg on the expanded eighteen-member Dillon Read board.[7]

The intention was for Dillon Read to serve some of Bechtel's investment banking and investment requirements while continuing its own business as an autonomous investment bank. As Brady explained, the sale to Bechtel was a logical and safe response to the "revolution going on in the Street. This alliance allows us to come up with our [own] plans and act on them." Shultz confirmed that Bechtel had no intention of interfering in the way Dillon Read was managed, that had he thought significant changes were in order he would not have recommended the purchase. The Bechtel approach, he told reporters, was for "the present Dillon Read people to keep managing it." Shultz had a clear vision of how Dillon Read would fit in with Bechtel. "Here is Wall Street, growing into larger and larger and more conglomerate-type firms doing all manner of things," he noted. "That's an exciting trend." Even so, this was not a route he wanted to pursue. "At the same time there is going to be room for the relatively small, high-powered firms doing investment banking things, concentrating on personal, high-level service."[8]

The acquisition of Dillon Read by Bechtel was somewhat unusual. In most instances in which investment banks were acquired the purchasers hoped to expand into investment banking as a natural addition to financial services operations already in place, becoming an industry powerhouse on the model of a Merrill Lynch. Bechtel entertained no such notions regarding Dillon Read, which would continue in the future as it had in the past, but would devote special attention to Bechtel interests. In the latter regard, all agreed that Brady would personally handle Bechtel's business dealings with the firm, thus leaving the rest of the firm's bankers to pursue other, independent business. Douglas Dillon considered the sale as fortunate as it was fortuitous. "Bechtel seemed sent from heaven, because they were willing to buy, they were willing to put in a lot of extra money over and above what they initially invested, and they were willing to let it run essentially the same

way."[9] Conversely, the thinking went, Dillon Read could recip-
rocate by producing investment opportunities and assisting in finance. As Dillon Read partner Charles Ballard later explained,
"[Bechtel] was a big project builder, [and] they had a tremendous
visibility in electric utilities—anything in regard to construction—
so our common interest would be in the electric utilities and the
like." Flanigan put it simply: "We would bring business to them
and they would bring business to us." So the union at least seemed
reasonable, if not ideal. Bechtel's chief financial officer, Cordell
Hull, was prepared to be patient and seemed sanguine regarding
prospects. "Like all marriages," he said, "it takes time to decide
what you should be doing together."

The acquisition required Dillon Read to rethink its problems
and possibilities. Shortly after the deal was struck Bechtel's management asked the firm to create a study group to draw up a set
of goals and the means to realize them, something it had never
done before. "We had been a seat-of-the-pants effort," Mullin conceded, "focusing more on each year at a time."[10] This was very
much in the Brady practice. But this was not in tune with Bechtel's
approach, which was long term and also involved much larger
commitments of capital than those traditional at Dillon Read.

While both sides entered the arrangement enthusiastically,
they did so with some basic misunderstandings. Bechtel was an
aggressive firm and thought Dillon Read was the same. Shultz
hoped the bankers would seek investment opportunities, into which
Bechtel would pour capital. To further this aim Bechtel provided
the firm's partners with a $5 million investment line to encourage
them in this direction. But this was not the Dillon Read way; the
firm was not accustomed to or equipped for going into the field
seeking investment opportunities of this kind.

In May 1981 Brady and the other senior partners called in a
group of the younger partners, or managing directors, including
Fritz Hobbs, Dick Bianco, Bob Gerard, Garrett Kirk, and John
Mullin, and constituted them as a task force which was to set forth
an agenda for the next few years. In effect, they were being asked
to assess more systematically than had ever been done before
precisely where Dillon Read should position itself. At the same
time Brady commissioned a study group from Stanford University-
based SRI International to explore the firm's options.

The task force, known as "The Business Planning Group," presented its report on July 15. Its message was direct and simple: "We can no longer continue to attempt to be all things to all people."[11] In surveying the industry, the task force members perceived a spectrum that ran from full-service firms that believed they could do everything (Merrill Lynch) through those that concentrated on the retail business (E. F. Hutton) and the wholesale side (Salomon) to merchant bankers (Lazard Frères) and venture capital specialists (New Court). As they saw it, Dillon Read was somewhere in the middle, neither big nor small, skilled and established in relationship banking but a minor force in other areas.

That said, there were three options for Dillon Read to explore. The firm might expand its efforts in distribution and trading, even while concentrating on traditional investment banking, or it might cut back on everything else but investment banking, in this way reducing overhead. Finally, Dillon Read might attempt to move in another direction, improving investment banking and marketing, but devoting resources to the development of merchant banking, expanding into equities, venture capital money management, and perhaps risk arbitrage.

The younger partners opted for the third path, which implied major expansion into specialized businesses. "We believe our competitive thrust should be in two areas—idea-oriented transactions and efforts toward obtaining the general investment banking business (including management positions) of companies which have a basis for dissatisfaction with their existing banker."

The implication was that Dillon Read would focus on high-value-added activities. Concentration would be upon such activities as mergers and acquisitions, asset management, and "entrepreneurial financings," suggesting a greater stress on merchant banking. In addition the firm might weigh promising new opportunities, such as leveraged buyouts, real estate, and risk arbitrage.

Personnel indeed was a key element in the program. The goals were ambitious, and no one then at Dillon Read possessed the requisite skills and experience in these new areas. Dillon Read would have to attract individuals from other banks who not only had these qualities, but in addition would conform to the firm's demands for ethical, meticulous, client-oriented standards. Moreover, the firm would have to improve upon its traditional ways of indoctrinating new associates.

> Today the training of our associates is almost strictly confined to techniques of financial analysis. Little attention is devoted to understanding the environment in which we operate, selling our products or the process of developing ideas. Indeed, signs of initiative, independence and aggressiveness had in the past been viewed by some as a liability in an associate's early years at the firm.

Fresh thinking was required at all levels of the firm. Under the heading of new business, the study group hoped to generate additional transactional underwritings, and move more forcefully into equity financing. In the future Dillon Read would have to devote more attention to smaller companies which were growing more rapidly than the corporate giants and often had more need of advisory services. The method of achieving these goals seemed drastic by the traditional standards of the firm. There was talk of retraining "senior and middle management thought processes" and lowering the ratio of junior to senior people, meaning the orientation would be toward senior personnel, and that advancement could be quite rapid. Dillon Read stressed this point in a 1987 brochure, entitled: "Opportunities for Entry-Level Associates."

> Both the size and structure of our firm ensure that Associates have direct access and accountability to senior bankers. Further, it is Dillon Read policy to encourage Associates to assume as much responsibility as possible, consistent with our attitude of rewarding initiative and performance. Our small size dictates that projects be staffed economically—usually no more than three professionals, with Associates reporting directly to Managing Directors in many cases.

There also was a call for more teamwork. The investment banking side of Dillon Read had little structure, with each partner taking care of little else but his own clients. The younger partners were especially concerned about this. "While important long-term business objectives are frequently set, the officers responsible for carrying out such objectives frequently eschew such responsibilities in favor of pursuing projects of their own choosing." This too had to change.

SRI came to somewhat the same conclusions regarding the nature of the firm, but did offer some additional and useful observations. In SRI's opinion Dillon Read was not equipped by virtue of personnel, capital, or inclination to compete with the special bracket firms for fixed-income financing business with the Fortune 100 companies. In addition, the firm had several glaring internal problems of morale arising from a lack of unity in management's direction and goals. Perhaps most damning was SRI's observation that Dillon Read's personnel found it to be "a nice place to work, rather than an exciting and demanding place to work."[12]

The consultants had surveyed the senior partners to assess their agendas, and learned that while three-quarters of them advocated a larger effort in the area of mergers and acquisitions, only one-third were interested in venture capital, and fewer than one-quarter believed the firm should gear its efforts toward Fortune 100 firms. Half of them opposed investment management as not relevant to the firm's operations. The survey revealed a sharp division on the delicate matter of the trading operation; one-third of the partners wanted to shrink or eliminate that part of the business, while the same number wished to increase emphasis on trading. A similar division existed on equity underwriting; a quarter of the partners wanted to reduce the business, while a like percentage wanted more underwritings.

In all, the SRI survey presented a portrait of a group of senior partners reluctant to enter new areas or attempt major changes, who believed they could not hope to compete with the larger firms for clients. By contrast, the firm's own Business Planning Group appeared more eager for change and expansion. Thus, there was something of a generational gap at the firm with which Brady would have to deal. In any case, the younger partners were hardly rash. The Business Planning Group took care to stress prudence in reform. The firm should strive, it wrote, "to maintain fixed income issuing and trading activities in both corporate and public finance sectors—*but only if clear profitability can be achieved* [emphasis added]."

Both groups—that is, the more senior and junior partners alike—concurred on one key element: the firm's ultimate objective ought not to be growth for its own sake, but rather growth to enhance profitability. In this important respect, Clarence Dillon's legacy remained very much intact. One goal presented by the Business Planning Group was for a return on the firm's equity of at least 20 percent. Among other things, this meant that revenue per professional, which worked out to $192,000 in 1980, would have to be increased to around $400,000. This was another point upon which all agreed, which would seem to indicate that Dillon Read would have to develop clearer focus on its priorities and enter selected new areas.

The Bechtel purchase and the study group reports were only the first of several critical developments that year. The departure of Treman would leave a large gap at the firm. More than anyone else he had been responsible for the operations at Dillon Read, and had literally worn himself out in the company's service. Now Brady needed someone not only to replace him but also to bring fresh vision and energy to the implementation of the agenda worked out by the junior partners and conditionally accepted by the seniors. Treman's successor would not only take over day-to-day management of the various units but would also be charged with implementing the new strategy. Brady would continue to take care of his own clients and concentrate on the investment banking operations. Much of the rest of the company, including the additional operations to be initiated, would be placed in the hands of the incoming chief operating officer, who, given the job description, was bound to become Dillon Read's next leader.

By the late summer of 1981, the Dillon Read managing directors had come to acknowledge that none of them possessed both the requisite expertise and inclination to assume the kind of managerial leadership role the Business Planning Group had envisaged. Whatever misgivings some of the veterans may have had about doing so, there was little doubt that the firm would have to look outside to find what amounted to a chief managing partner, someone who would "fit in" with Dillon Read's style, tradition, and culture, even as he would be expected to cultivate new areas of business that the firm had either avoided or overlooked.[13] In the meantime Pat Durkin, John Mullin, and Luis Mendez would perform as a management committee, while Brady searched for a candidate. Steve Bechtel and Shultz were told of the probe, which they found surprising. Even then they did not appreciate the seriousness of the problems at Dillon Read, and saw no need for a new leader.

The exploration was not lengthy. It was in September when fifty-one-year-old John Birkelund came aboard as president and chief operating officer.

By dint of his experiences Birkelund did not fit the conventional Dillon Read profile, but his pedigree was true to form. He had graduated from Princeton in 1952 with a major in International Studies, intending a career in diplomacy or law. First Birkelund joined the Navy, and after training as an officer in Naval Intelligence was dispatched to Berlin, where among other duties he was responsible for screening many of the East German refugees who were streaming across the border in that pre-Wall era. While there Birkelund was able to cultivate friendships with many influential Europeans, including Edmund Stinnes, who later would introduce him to the Rothschilds.

Upon separation from the Navy, Birkelund considered several opportunities at Wall Street investment banks. There was a very strong suggestion that he consider returning to school to obtain an M.B.A. Rejecting this, he joined the management consulting firm of Booz, Allen & Hamilton in Chicago as its first trainee. Birkelund had been there only six months when Stinnes contacted him with an offer of a position in New York with the Rothschilds. In 1956, he went to their Amsterdam Overseas Corporation, which in 1967 spun off its venture capital and corporate finance operations into a new company called New Court Securities Corporation, owned jointly by the Rothschild banks in Paris and London, Pierson Heldring Pierson in Amsterdam, and New Court's American management.

Birkelund was a cofounder of New Court, and would shortly become its chief executive. "A very exciting company," he recalls, New Court developed an important role in venture capital, leveraged buyouts, institutional investment management, corporate finance for smaller companies, and various transatlantic transactions. Under Birkelund's leadership, subsequently strengthened by the recruitment of Charles Lea, New Court became one of the nation's leading and fastest-growing venture capital firms. Among the companies it had spawned and nurtured were Federal Express, Tandem Computer, Monolithic Memories, Amgen, Repligan, and

Cray Research. By 1981 it had become an acknowledged leader in the specialized fields of its choice.

In 1981 the Rothschilds decided to take a more direct role in the management of New Court, which precipitated a personal career crisis for Birkelund. Unwilling to cede authority after so long a successful run, he and Charles Lea decided to leave the firm to establish their own company. The new entity was to be called Concord Partners. Essentially a venture capital fund, Concord was to carry forward many of the activities of New Court, by investing capital provided by limited partners in young, emerging companies and then assisting them in their financing and development requirements.[14]

Even while prepared to proceed with Concord, Birkelund and Lea received offers of posts at several established investment banks. That Dillon Read was one of them was not surprising; Birkelund had a reputation as a talented investment banker whose expertise was in the younger, faster-growing areas the Dillon Read partners had tended to overlook in the past but were now determined to exploit. Moreover, he had considerable managerial skills, which was precisely what the firm needed. Birkelund was no stranger to some of the Dillon Read partners, whom he had met during the course of business. For instance, he and John Haskell had sat on opposite sides of the table in a merger negotiation, and Birkelund had worked with Pat Durkin on a leveraged buyout. It was in fact Durkin who made the initial contact.

Birkelund was not at first interested in joining what he believed to be a traditional investment bank which seemed content to remain so. Then Brady telephoned and requested a meeting, at which he told Birkelund of the firm's plans. After some further discussions Brady presented Birkelund with an offer of a leadership position, which was accepted. What apparently intrigued Birkelund was the opportunity to help shape a bank which was of manageable size and was prepared for change. "Dillon Read was the only firm we thought was interesting and in which we felt we could have a meaningful impact on the same business," Birkelund explained to a reporter. "It's still small enough to be flexible and have a partnership environment."[15]

The "we" included Charles Lea, who also came with the understanding he would have an opportunity to develop the kind of business in venture capital that he had conducted so successfully at New Court. As for Birkelund himself, he saw Dillon Read as an opportunity to re-create much of his work at New Court, with one big exception, and that was that Dillon Read had the investment banking positon, client contacts, and sophistication that New Court did not have.

Even more than Brady's accession, and before that the promotions of Brandi, Belmont, and Forrestal, Birkelund's arrival marked the inauguration of a new era at Dillon Read. With the exception of Charles McCain, who took over after Forrestal left for Washington, the firm had never been headed by an outsider, and even McCain, who had been little more than a caretaker during a relatively quiet period in the industry, had been with Dillon Read for a year before his elevation. By contrast, Birkelund arrived at a firm in the process of seeking a new direction, losing clients, and badly in need of an executive who could provide it with tighter management. It was an investment bank, he thought, which had lost all the advantages of being small, when the industry was in turmoil, evolving rapidly into unexpected and unfamiliar forms.

It is necessary to understand Birkelund's initial impressions of Dillon Read, coming as he did from a background which was in some ways similar but in others quite different from that of Dillon Read's managing partners. He realized that with its small capital base, Dillon Read simply could not compete in the same arena with the much larger houses in many segments of the business. The firm had always been known as a bond underwriter, but as competition forced larger and larger commitments at increasing risk, that role might have to be limited unless additional capital were added. Then, too, Dillon Read's strengths in the energy field mattered less than they once had, since the energy companies that historically had provided it with a good deal of business were troubled by lower prices and tighter margins. Moreover, a program of diversification to compete head-on with the larger firms would not have been feasible given the skills of Dillon Read's existing personnel. Birkelund was also concerned by what he saw as an absence of "capitalist" habits on the part of the managing directors, who, while they had percentages in the Dillon Read compensation fund, neither owned much of the company nor were accustomed to putting their own funds at risk. It was, and had been for years under the conditions of family-dominant ownership, a risk-averse culture.

Finally, Birkelund felt that the firm had been undermanaged, though it may not have appeared that way to the old Dillon Read hands who had lived through what must have seemed to them a growing tendency to bureaucratize in what was still, after all, a very small firm. From an outsider's perspective, however, Dillon Read appeared a tradition-bound loose partnership, a casually coordinated group of colleagues in an age of more efficient, "managerial" firms. What Dillon Read required, Birkelund recalls having told Brady at one point, was more "vertical" management, not to render the firm less collegial so much as to impose greater control over the allocation of resources. For instance, there was little command over how the capital and professional resources of the firm would be committed or how fees were to be set. All this would have to be subjected to a more formal administrative process.

Birkelund also perceived several important assets to go with the liabilities. The most important of these were the close to one hundred experienced and sophisticated investment bankers and a small but highly competent trading organization, all of whom agreed on the need for change and strong management and who were willing and even eager to create the kind of operation the partners had in mind. Years later, Birkelund reflected that had it not been for the high quality and unity of its professionals, the firm might not have made it through the 1980s. And there was the nameplate on the door, Dillon Read, still one of the most venerable names on the Street, a franchise in itself.

Birkelund and Brady explained the new business plan to Shultz and the Bechtel management in December 1981. In it was encapsulated the thinking of the Business Planning Group, the SRI Report, and Birkelund's own vision of where the firm should be headed—or to be more precise, where he wanted to lead it. Dillon Read was to remain small and should not try to become a full-service investment bank. Rather, it would focus its resources in the areas where it had a high probability to excel. To do so profitably, Dillon Read would have to concentrate its efforts on the kinds of high-margin, specialized areas that could capitalize on the expertise of professionals whose strength lay in corporate advisory services, supplemented by additions from without, who would introduce such new functions as investment management, equity research and trading, venture capital and leveraged buyouts, and risk arbitrage. In short, the plan was to superimpose on the investment banking structure an entrepreneurial capitalistic culture. There was a note of caution in the plan; Birkelund would consider becoming involved in these new areas only "if the right personnel could be hired."[16] As he later explained:

> I have believed all my life that you shouldn't try to be in business in areas where you can't structurally and otherwise qualify to be best. That doesn't mean that you will succeed in being number one, but there should be no structural barriers to becoming number one. Obviously, as an underwriter of high-grade bonds we could never be that dominant. We lacked the capital, the scale, and the culture. In fact, we shouldn't be in any commodity-type low-margin, high-volume businesses.

The Bechtel directors agreed, and Brady and Birkelund proceeded to implement the program—which involved no additions to capital, but a substantial change in the attitude toward innovation and risk.

As it happened, Birkelund was left to his own devices more quickly than expected by the changing fortunes of Brady's career. New Jersey Senator Harrison Williams was being tried on criminal charges and forced out of office, and it was already obvious that Brady, who as noted had been prominent in Governor Kean's campaign, would be one of the more prominent choices for the post. At a time when Dillon Read was adjusting to new ownership, a new president, and a new operating plan, the thought of Brady's departure was worrisome. It could not have been a more inopportune moment for Brady to leave, and several partners urged him to remain at the firm during the transition.[17]

Brady did depart for Washington in the spring of 1982, indicating he had no intention of running for the Senate seat during the special election scheduled for that November. In other words, he would return to Dillon Read in January 1983, after eight months in the Senate. The entire senior management of Brady, Treman, and Mendez had gone within months of one another. Birkelund was left to cope with the new situation without their guidance. Quite aside from the authority the change afforded him was an opportunity for him to get to know the managing directors of the firm on a much more direct basis. The result was to confirm in his mind that the people he found there were as good or better than any he knew, including himself, and so if they were that good, then the problem must have been organization.

One of Birkelund's earliest tasks was to preside over the relocation of the business to midtown. Dillon Read had been situated in lower Manhattan for more than a century and a half, and at its William Street location since 1949. A move to more capacious and better organized quarters had been contemplated for years, but had been delayed by inertia, a very favorable lease, and trepidations regarding making so large a capital commitment. The old offices gave Dillon Read an air of boring stodginess and indifference to appearances. The entrance and boardrooms retained an atmosphere of genteel shabbiness redolent of an earlier era, while the back offices were musty and crowded. Lea recalled his first impression of the Dillon Read offices in 1981:

> To get to Dillon Read you found yourself on William Street at a brass-fronted building. There was always a doorman and elevator there, and he got to know you very well. You walked into a small anteroom and took an elevator to the tenth floor. There would be a green carpeted office area, and it was almost like walking into a small bank in the sense that there were the rolltop desks and all that went with that kind of furniture, as well as some very elaborate offices off in the various corners for the very senior partners. And of course the usual touches of the old portraits on the wall. The place had something of a Victorian, musty-dusty feeling about it. When you walked into the offices of Dillon Read you knew you were in place where life was ordered and established and moved at a certain pace.

Relocation had been one of the recommendations made by the Business Planning Group, which felt that enlarged and more modern quarters would be required if the plan was to be implemented. A committee was established to make the search for a suitable new headquarters.

Birkelund himself wanted to move not only in order to enlarge the facilities, but also as a symbol of Dillon Read's new outlook.

The partners also recognized the need to be closer to clients, quite a familiar thought at the time. The exodus from Wall Street to uptown had already begun. Morgan Stanley and First Boston, among others, had made the trek, and Salomon was considering a move.

The search for new quarters resulted in the 1983 relocation to a new $50 million building at 535 Madison Avenue on Fifty-fourth Street, not far from the recently erected AT&T and IBM buildings. Because the firm was to be the major tenant, occupying eleven floors under a fifteen-year lease, the structure would be called the Dillon Read Building.

By the time the move was completed Bechtel and Dillon Read were coming to concede that their corporate marriage had not worked out fully as expected. It became more obvious that the underlying economic outlooks of the two firms had proven quite dissimilar. Dillon Read would not be able to meet all of Bechtel's banking needs, and could not transform itself into what amounted to the financial arm of Bechtel without altering its strategic direction drastically; yet to remain as it was would mean the firm would be of limited utility to the new parent.[18] "They [Bechtel] could spend two years on a project and if they got the project they would make enough money on it to more than justify the time and effort expended," Ballard reflected. "They wanted us to be able to function in the same fashion, and it simply wasn't the way investment banking worked. They wanted us to work with them on projects, but if we did Bechtel literally could have usurped all our banking talent just for one or two projects. That wouldn't do." Peter Flanigan saw yet another side to the matter.

> The Bechtels recognized what I think is a financial truism. The people who have responsibility—the people who benefit from the income statement—should also have responsibility for the balance sheet. That is, if someone is going to benefit from income he had better take his lumps if the balance sheet gets in trouble.

Then, too, the personal element, so important when the marriage occurred, played a role. Shortly after Brady left for the Senate George Shultz resigned from Bechtel to become secretary of state. With this the two architects of the purchase departed the scene, leaving it to others who did not fully share their commitment.

In any case, in the light of the changed business environment and Shultz's exit, by 1983 Bechtel concluded that the Dillon Read investment was a diversion from its main concerns, and was now willing to consider the sale of their interest at a substantial profit. That Bechtel was so fortunate was indicative of a much improved situation at Dillon Read. It was agreed that the partners would be offered the opportunity over time to purchase additional shares in Dillon Read from Bechtel at book value, with the understanding that Bechtel would share in the profit from any subsequent sale of the company to other parties. Everyone benefited from this arrangement, noted Flanigan. "[Bechtel] sold control of the business over a period of time to us. The price at which they sold was obviously considerably in excess of the price at which they bought because the profits in those years were excellent."

Birkelund considered this investment by the partners a major step forward. As noted, when he had arrived he found that they had no thought of investing their own money in the business, and even used outside managers for personal investment advice and assistance. Some partners already had shares, but now more of them became owners of the enterprise for which they worked, and this brought about more than a subtle change in atmosphere, since they now were, in effect, proprietors. By the winter of 1983 the managing directors as a group had become the majority owners of the firm. Sequoia was still involved through its remaining shares, as was Skandinaviska Enskilda Banken, but both as minority partners.[19]

Much had taken place from 1981 to 1983. Bechtel's dilution to minority ownership, the move uptown, the creation and implementation of the new business plan, and Birkelund's arrival, taken together, brought Dillon Read into new areas of opportunity with a fresh approach. Moreover, Birkelund was effecting a quiet revolution in the way Dillon Read was managed.

It was of no minor matter that Brady's continuing presence as head of the firm provided a cushion which both Birkelund and the veteran Dillon Read bankers would appreciate. In the years that passed between Birkelund's arrival and Brady's final departure to the Treasury, Birkelund was able to draw upon Brady's expertise and advice as well as his prestige in his dealings with the veteran Dillon Read partners. It was a smooth transition, a careful grafting of a new CEO on an old culture, preparing it for change while sensitizing the man to its constraints.

There was no question that there would be changes, not the least of which was in the area of managerial style. As has been seen, Brady had been deeply influenced by his apprenticeship under the watchful eye of Wilbur DuBois, and he continued to believe that the devil lies in the details. Brady preferred a casual, ad hoc approach to operations. This would change under Birkelund. All available senior partners in investment banking would meet each Monday morning at 8:00, and while minutes of the meetings were not kept, when the conference ended the partners left with a clearer idea of the business at hand and new prospects. Similar regular meetings were held by other segments of the firm.

Under Brady's aegis partners had been free to set fees for business, not always with an eye to what the competition was charging. On occasion fees were based upon time required, and at other times would be discounted so as to win an account. The partner would discuss the fee with the client, and then bring it back to the firm. Now this, too, changed. Partners would recommend assignments and fees and take them to a fee committee where they would be reviewed—and occasionally rejected because they were inappropriate or inadequately priced. This was no minor reform; it was an important factor in focusing the firm's resources and in widening its profit margins.

Perhaps equally remarkable was a change in the manner by which compensation was determined. Before Birkelund arrived distributions from the compensation fund were set by Brady as CEO, much as had been the case under Clarence Dillon, Forrestal, and Brandi. Again, that was possible to do in a small firm, without the process seeming unduly arbitrary. Larger organizations require more objective criteria for measuring performance, and in time, Birkelund would establish a compensation committee composed of four partners, who applied a somewhat more formal approach in establishing payouts. In addition, before Birkelund's arrival profit participations were determined at the beginning of the year. Initially Birkelund determined that half the share would be set at the beginning of the year, the other half at the end, which to all intents and purposes meant that total compensation was decided upon at the end of the year. Subsequently this became the case.

All of the foregoing reforms were quite a departure for those accustomed to Dillon Read's traditions, but given the broadened nature of the firm, the mandate for change, the altered character of the industry, and even the new physical setting for Dillon Read itself, a tighter organizational structure was clearly required.

It should be noted that the process was not purely opportunistic. The reforms unfolded within the context of an overall strategy. Birkelund had begun by accepting the mandate set down by the partners even before he had arrived. His intention from the start had been for Dillon Read to remain the small, highly professional, innovative, value-added firm it had been in the immediate post–World War II period, though he would adapt it to meet new circumstances and bring it into new areas of business.

The demands of the 1980s were profound, and demanded changes in the investment banking community. These indeed were occurring. Some old-line investment banking firms sought to adapt to capital-intensive market making, and quite a few trading firms had migrated into investment banking. In those institutions where the two coexisted reasonably well, the teams that had formed early in the decade had metamorphosed into well-honed units which usually took on more of the short-term, transactional mentality of trading than the longer-term, relationship mentality of banking.

Unlike Dillon Read a number of the older houses came to be known for their protean abilities to move swiftly with the times and fashions. Many were led by traders; John Gutfreund at Salomon and Alan Greenberg at Bear Stearns were among the more prominent.

How could it have been otherwise, considering the accelerated speed of transactions and the many new trading vehicles which were coming into being, including index options, options on options, and other such esoterica? Down the road were items such as split principal amortizing collars, deferred swaps, superfloat swaps and caps, integrated currency and interest rate swaps, and split risk programs. New instruments appeared on a weekly basis. Merger and acquisitions activity accelerated and became technically more complex. No investment bank hoping to serve clients efficiently could afford to ignore this stream of innovation. Perhaps most important, Wall Street firms and even commercial banks that were establishing their own investment banking operations in a more relaxed regulatory climate were entering into classic merchant banking activities by putting their own capital into deals.

Many new firms with aggressive investment strategies were springing up as well. Irritated with what they perceived as old-fashioned thinking, some of the more talented members of Wall Street went off on their own. First came the family funds—the Bass brothers, the Bronfmans, and the Pritzkers. Next it was Kohlberg, Kravis & Roberts and Forstmann-Little—relatively small units that engaged in a variety of merchant banking activities. Kohlberg Kravis made do with fifteen professionals, and the other boutiques were on the same scale. These were the kind of low-overhead high-valued-added operations envied by some of the larger firms, which had to turn a large profit each day just to cover fixed costs.

The circle had come full around. The descendants of those merchant and private bankers of the early nineteenth century who had become investment bankers and brokers were now returning to merchant and private banking, the kind of lean operation and style which traditionally had been associated with Dillon Read.

·18·

Renaissance

(1983–1989)

John Birkelund is blunt, forceful, and direct, quite different in style from the patrician, oblique Nick Brady, more insistent on structure, and more likely to run meetings than preside over them. He was brought in to be an agent of change, but he has accomplished that by working carefully within the constraints of Dillon Read's culture.

Birkelund wanted the firm to take more risk, and pushed hard in that direction. Yet he also proved sensitive to the firm's relatively traditional banking style. Instead of creating a revolution, Birkelund built from within, capitalizing on Dillon Read's inherent strengths, looking for new business opportunities to build upon the firm's traditional preference for relationship banking. Innovating successfully without upsetting the existing order would mean keeping the firm relatively small, developing new personnel around a stable core of old hands, and seeking profitable niches rather than trying to compete across the board.

In the early 1980s such a strategy may have seemed timid in the brave new world of the financial supermarket. At the close of the decade, however, it turned out to have been a wise strategy. During this period Dillon Read has enjoyed the most vital and profitable years in its history, participating in deals as exciting as those with Goodyear and Dodge had been in the 1920s, restoring important ties to major corporations on the basis of long-term relationships, and entering such new areas of business as venture capital, risk arbitrage, corporate buyouts, and the issuance of equity.

One key modification was to accustom the partners to doing business that required direct investment, which is to say, merchant banking. Dillon Read's risk arbitrage unit was formed in 1982 to invest for the firm's account and those of institutional investors. At about the same time, a venture capital team, called Concord, was organized under Charles Lea, who had come with Birkelund from New Court. Subsequently Dillon Read organized Cord Capital N.V. (1983) to raise capital in Europe, Concord Partners Japan Ltd. (1985) for Japanese investors, and Concord Partners II, which, like the original Concord, was designed for corporate pension funds, insurance companies, and endowment funds. A small organization based in New York and Palo Alto, California, Concord had only ten persons on the team by 1989. Assembling a fund of $180 million from investors, by then Concord and the other venture capital operations had interests in more than forty companies.

Soon after Concord's formation the firm's small equity operation was reorganized, with the expectation that Concord and the Equity Group would collaborate in financing and providing advice for the development of small entrepreneurial businesses. Concord's role was to identify a new firm whose promise merited investment and guidance and to carry it through the development stages, providing it with seed capital and counsel. When the client had matured and required more capital, it would be serviced by the Equity Group, which would arrange for initial underwritings and create a market for its securities. The established concern, now producing and offering its products and services, would be advised all along the way by Dillon Read, which would eventually arrange for debt and convertible securities financings, acquisitions and divestitures, and other appropriate investment banking requirements.[1] In keeping with the new dedication to merchant banking, most of the partners committed their own capital to these enterprises.

Among such endeavors was the firm's support of Nac Re, formed and financed from its inception by Dillon Read, which has become one of the country's larger and more profitable reinsurance companies. Medical Care International, originally a venture investment of the firm, has become one of the fastest-growing entries in the health care industry. Other similar venture-sponsored investment banking undertakings include Associated Natural Gas, Marine Drilling, Viking Office Products, Vintage Petroleum, and Xoma.

Other innovative departures included the 1984 creation of a corporate buyout business called Saratoga Partners, and a second fund three years later, which by 1989 had assembled almost $400 million in capital, broadening Dillon Read's capabilities in the heady arena of high-yield finance. By then the Saratoga partnerships had acquired fifteen companies in leveraged buyout (LBO) transactions, and had concluded the financing for the $400 million LBO of Formica Inc.[2] Similar undertakings abroad resulted in the creation of buyout funds in the United Kingdom, France, and Spain.

The firm expanded into other, complementary, areas. It organized Dillon Read Capital (DRC) under Timothy Dalton, who had been recruited from Oppenheimer. DRC provided investment management services for pension funds and other institutional investors. In its first year, DRC had a list of clients which included Johnson & Johnson, Uniroyal, Alcoa, and Hughes Aircraft, and by 1989, the unit had more than $3 billion under management, handled by a team of ten professionals. Dillon Read International Asset Management (DRIAM) was organized in 1986 to manage foreign portfolios for American institutional clients, and within less than a year had $300 million under management.[3]

All this new activity altered the profile of the Dillon Read banker, who would now have to be able to function as investigator seeking out areas of opportunity, salesman, advisor, nursemaid for young undertakings, and innovative designer of new instruments for clients. Yet it was also important for Dillon Read to maintain its traditional relationships, the bedrock of its business. Birkelund consistently took pains to cast its new activities within the context of Dillon Read's traditional lines of interest. "Venture capital, leveraged buyouts and principal investments are add-ons to our traditional businesses," Birkelund explained, "not a displacement of them."[4] Yet Birkelund was concerned personally to develop new, entrepreneurial enterprises, which Dillon Read could take from concept to realization.

In other words, as the market for financial services changed, Dillon Read was changing with it, sometimes in surprising ways. Consider the reaction to Rule 415, which the SEC promulgated in 1982. This regulation enabled a corporation to register in advance all the securities it intended to sell over the next two-year period. Now a company could offer its securities when market conditions appeared most advantageous, and do so through an underwriter or institution selected at the last moment. The implications were quite clear. Investment banks would have to scramble for the business, as corporations would play one off against the others. "We're moving from the traditional concept of a marrage to one-night stands," ruminated Dain Bosworth's Frederick Friswold, while John Whitehead of Goldman Sachs grumbled that Rule 415 "threatens to sweep away 50 years of investor protection and return the new-issue market to the jungle environment of the 1920s."[5]

This was precisely the kind of ruling that would have horrified Clarence Dillon. But as Birkelund saw it, there was no need for the firm to compete forcefully for this kind of business, which had become increasingly a low-margin function for capital-rich banks. Rather, it would concentrate on the high-margin business, such as corporate restructurings, in which the firm was becoming increasingly involved, and allow others to scramble for competitive, thinly profitable high-grade financings.[6] Thus, Dillon Read was proving adept at adjusting to external events.

Rapid change in the financial markets created an atmosphere of uncertainty in the 1980s, which in somewhat cyclical fashion helped foster a return to relationship banking. Corporations that had reduced their dependency on investment banking advisors were once again perceiving the value of long-term outside financial guidance. Under these circumstances, Dillon Read was able to fortify its relationships with some of its long-standing clients while establishing relationships with new ones.

In such cases, personal ties were always important. A good example of this was General Mills, where Nick Brady had been a major advisor, a role he transferred to Birkelund and John Mullin in the mid-1980s. It helped that Birkelund and General Mills CEO Bruce Atwater had been roommates at Princeton, and that Atwater had originally proposed that Brady seek out Birkelund to join the firm. The two advised General Mills through a far-reaching restructuring program over the next six years, primarily involving divestitures of underperforming and unrelated businesses. These divestitures were required because of the kind of overextended diversification that had hurt the performance of many large corporations in previous decades. Indeed, some of the companies Dillon Read had helped General Mills acquire in the 1960s and 1970s had turned out badly. There were particularly severe problems with the toy and fashion operations which, while profitable, were also cyclical, and harmed the firm's standing with the investment community.[7]

Dillon Read thus enlarged its capacities in what was to become the investment banking industry's biggest business, falling under the general rubric of "restructuring." In the late 1970s there was an acceleration in merger and acquisition activity, including the "hostile" corporate "raids" of such colorful characters as T. Boone Pickens, Carl Icahn, and Irwin Jacobs. The cultivation of the "junk" bond for financing highly leveraged buyouts and the development of networks for placing the bonds quickly accelerated the trend, so that by the mid-1980s, the United States and to a lesser extent Europe were engulfed in a great merger and takeover wave, the likes of which had not been seen since the turn of the century. All of this activity was predicated on the belief (and perhaps in most cases, the reality) that American corporations were underperforming so that the prices of corporate equities did not reflect their underlying values. Through recapitalization, reorganization, divestitures, and better management, true values could be established just as they might be when the unsightly varnish is stripped from fine furniture.

None of this could have been achieved without the cooperation of investment banks able to marshal professional talent, large amounts of capital, and law firms, of course, who were especially important on both sides of hostile takeovers. The combination of brains and money could result in multimillion-dollar fees and profits, and few firms with the capabilities, energy, and resources could resist the allure.

This was one arena in which Dillon Read was well equipped but nonetheless expanded cautiously. In 1981, the firm participated in thirty-three merger and acquisition deals ranging in scope from $3 million to $800 million. The business grew slowly, in part because Dillon Read was reluctant to act as banker for unfriendly takeovers, and more so where there was no demonstrable value added for the client. Furthermore, it would act only for an established client, and not for outsiders and raiders. But even with these self-imposed constraints, merger and acquisition activity became a substantial contributor to profits, as Dillon Read helped its clients, as in the case of General Mills, to organize preemptive restructuring to enhance shareholder values, and was involved in two of the most celebrated restructurings of the decade, Unocal and RJR Nabisco. In the former, Dillon Read helped in successfully defeating a hostile bid, and in the latter it enabled the client's board to realize extraordinary values for the shareholders in what came to be a friendly takeover by Kohlberg Kravis Roberts.

In early 1985 Dillon Read teamed with Goldman Sachs to defend Unocal, the parent of Union Oil of California, which had been a Dillon Read client since 1924, against attempts by T. Boone Pickens to acquire it. Pickens was at the crest of a wave that some called popularity but others described as notoriety. His stern visage appeared on the covers of national magazines. Pickens always claimed he was uncovering shareholder values unrealized by somnolent and irresponsible managements, while his detractors charged he was simply making runs at petroleum companies, obliging them to restructure, and in the end pay him "greenmail," by which he would receive enormous profits. Pickens shot back that all of his tenders were serious and that, if accepted, everyone involved (except the old managements) would benefit.

As with so many of the takeovers during those years, a Pickens raid always resulted in the substitution of debt for equity. To those who engaged in such restructurings, this implied the need for a stricter discipline in the boardrooms, because company managers would be driven to generate sufficient funds to pay interest and principal. Opponents argued that such a financial structure weakened the corporations, focused them on short-term results, and prevented them from engaging in needed research and development.[8]

This was one of the major debates dividing Wall Street in the 1980s. Dillon Read remained the chief exemplar of relationship banking. "Being a gun for hire is not in our nature," said Fritz Hobbs, who was to play a major role in the contest for Unocal. "In a firm like ours, hell, what we're really selling is relationships."[9]

Yet Michael Milken of Drexel Burnham, the acknowledged king of junk bonds, who backed Pickens, was well known for his network of clients who were loyal to him and to whom he was faithful. These differing attitudes were quite common when Wall Street was evolving more rapidly than at any time in memory, and in the midst of the great oil company wars.

By early 1985 it seemed Pickens and others had run out of targets in the petroleum industry. One prime company remained. Unocal had been considered a likely candidate for an unfriendly takeover. The company had good reserves that were not reflected in the price of its stock, then trading in the mid-30s. Thus, it seemed ready to be plucked.

In early July 1984, reports surfaced of share accumulation in Unocal, with interest centering around Standard Oil of Indiana as the acquirer. The rumors persisted, as Unocal's common stock rose and fell in spurts. By late November Unocal was placed on "stock watch" at the proxy firm of D. F. King & Co. Soon after, Nick Brady put in a call to Unocal CEO Fred Hartley. "Fred, you're under accumulation." This much was clear. But who was the accumulator? It might have been any of a half-dozen raiders, and Pickens was one of them. But at the time Pickens was close to the bottom of the list, since he was deeply involved in the battle for another oil company, Phillips Petroleum. At the onset of that contest Pickens had said he was in the fight to the finish. But this was not so. Pickens sold his Phillips Petroleum stake in December for a pretax profit of $75 million, which was a pittance compared to the kind of funds that would be required to purchase Unocal. The estimates began at $3 billion and went up from there.

On February 14, 1985, Pickens announced he had gathered 7.9 percent of Unocal, adding that this was for investment purposes only, and not the prelude to a tender offer. No one really believed this; by month's end Pickens had close to 10 percent of the stock and seemed intent on purchasing more, while Irwin Jacobs—known on the Street as "Irv the Liquidator"—told reporters he had a "substantial stake" in Unocal. In the parlance of the time, Unocal was "in play," and in need of investment guidance.

Dillon Read had been one of the company's advisors for more than sixty years, and so was potentially a natural ally in the struggle. Yet the relationship between Brady and Hartley was not as close as had been Brandi's with the Unocal leaders of his day. The reason had more to do with Hartley's personality than anything else. The Unocal CEO simply didn't like investment bankers, and considered anything but the actual service of underwriting securities gratuitous. Hartley kept his own counsel, and rarely consulted with Dillon Read—or any other banker, for that matter. However, from 1968 Dillon Read had underwritten five debenture issues for Unocal, including a $200 million underwriting in 1976.

Dillon Read received the call for assistance, with Goldman Sachs as its partner in the defense. From the first Hartley made no secret of his intention to run the show himself. Although Brady would be there for consultation, Hobbs would be the point man for Dillon Read, and Goldman Sachs would be represented by senior partner Stephen Friedman and oil merger specialist Peter Sachs.

Unocal took steps to repel Pickens, one of which was a provision providing for staggered elections to the board, and another requiring an 80 percent vote of shares for bylaw changes put forth by anyone seeking to arrange a merger involving Unocal. In addition, the period during which board nominations would be accepted was lengthened. This was done to prevent Pickens from placing his own slate in nomination prior to the forthcoming annual meeting. Undeterred, Pickens continued his purchases; by late March he had 13.6 percent of Unocal's common stock, and indications were that he would continue buying.

Now the tempo picked up. On April 1 Unocal sued Pickens, alleging violations of the Securities Exchange Act. A week later Mesa Partners II's tombstone advertisements appeared. Pickens offered $54 in cash for 64 million shares, which would give Mesa majority ownership. The remainder of the shares would then be purchased with $54 a share in debt securities.[10] The cash was to be raised through the issuance of high-yield bonds through Drexel Burnham, with the understanding that these would be senior to those issued to make the later purchases.

Hobbs and Sachs fashioned a contentious and imaginative response. On April 17, Unocal proposed to purchase almost half of its shares for $72 a share, and to do so only after the Pickens tender was completed. The Unocal tender specifically excluded Mesa Partners II from the offer. Pickens immediately grasped the meaning of the move. If carried out, Unocal would cut its equity by half and would have more than $5.8 billion in additional debt on the books, since Unocal would have to borrow that much for the offer. The price was so high that it would constitute a special dividend to those shareholders who made the tender; given the new capitalization the price of Unocal doubtless would fall sharply when the tender was completed. Of course the shareholders would offer their shares to Unocal, since the price offered by the company was so much higher than that offered by Pickens. By being barred from the offer Pickens would be stuck with his stock, and would suffer more than anyone else during the subsequent decline.

The Unocal offer was structured so that Pickens would be imprudent to attempt to top it. If he did manage in some way to acquire the company, he would be obliged to deal with all the debt that would be created—and repay the loans made to make the purchase. Finally, under the new bylaws, Pickens would not be able to replace more than a third of the board with his nominees.

The plan was presented to Hartley, who seemed genuinely interested and pleased at its elegance. "Who thought up the idea?" he wanted to know. Hobbs recalled, "It was the only compliment I heard him give." In actuality, the concept resulted from a collaboration. Hobbs had the original idea, but it had been elaborated upon so much since then that it really was a group production.[11]

The team had its own fallback position should Pickens manage to gain a majority of the shares. In such an eventuality Unocal would purchase the rest of the shares through the $72 tender. Originally Hobbs and Sachs hoped to swing the deal through a cash offer, but the banks shied from lending the money, fearful of having debt in a company controlled by Pickens. Instead the payment would be in the form of a special debenture, carefully crafted to be senior to any debt Pickens might float after he gained control of the company. Under the circumstances any such new debt would be rated so low that it would require a large interest rate premium—which might easily make Unocal insolvent. And in any restructuring under Chapter 11, the senior debt would receive first consideration. The big question was: Would the courts permit a tender which was not extended to all shareholders?

Pickens appealed to the SEC, which agreed that the exclusionary provision violated the law. In a federal court in Los Angeles on April 29, Judge A. Wallace Tashima ruled otherwise; as far as he could see, nothing prohibited such tenders, but this was not as important as the decision in Delaware, where Unocal was incorporated. On that same day, in a chancery court, Judge Carolyn Berger decided in favor of Pickens. Both sides realized this was a matter that ultimately would be decided in the Delaware courts, and so it appeared that Pickens had won his wager. Now he intended to tender his shares and then come back with an offer for all of Unocal, whose shares he believed would decline sharply. But on May 13 Delaware Supreme Court Justice Andrew G. T. Moore II, after chiding Unocal, decided in the company's favor. The company need not include Pickens in its $72-a-share bid. This meant Unocal might now proceed with its tender offer, after which the price of its stock would collapse, perhaps to around $30 a share, resulting in a $300 million loss for Pickens and his group. On the other hand, if the price declined to such a low level, Pickens well might have opted to renew his bid, and in the end succeed in his takeover.

Now a deal was struck—by Hartley and Pickens, without consultation with Hobbs and Sachs.[12] Pickens would be permitted to tender almost a third of his shares at $72, and the remainder would not be sold for a year, and then only if certain conditions were met. The settlement was announced on May 20, and so the Unocal War ended.

The Unocal War represented a watershed for Dillon Read. In the growing area of battles for corporate control the firm had come against the industry's aggressive new giant, Drexel Burnham, and had triumphed. Morever, Dillon Read had demonstrated that it could play hardball in investment banking's toughest new arena.

While Hobbs was busy on the West Coast with Unocal, Mullin was in New York, helping arrange the largest merger to that time. Again, an old client was involved, R. J. Reynolds, and the merger was to be with Nabisco, out of which would come RJR Nabisco. Reynolds had been a Dillon Read client since before World War II. After the war Brandi and then Haskell handled the account. Later Mullin, and to a lesser extent, Brady, were also involved. With Dillon Read's assistance Reynolds expanded out of its tobacco base into a wide variety of industries—foodstuffs, marine transportation, petroleum, packaging, liquor, and soft drinks, among others. In the process the R. J. Reynolds Tobacco Co. of 1963, which had revenues of $117 million, became the R. J. Reynolds Industries of 1983, a $14 billion behemoth.

In 1984 Reynolds president and CEO Tylee Wilson asked Dillon Read to be on the watch for a major acquisition. Not only did the firm want to expand operations quickly, but its cash flow was so large that the only alternative was a major stock repurchase plan. After a search of the field, Nabisco Brands was targeted as the best "fit."[13] Itself the product of a 1981 merger of Nabisco, Inc., and Standard Brands, Nabisco Brands was a $6 billion firm, with strong positions in cookies, cereals, pet foods, and candies.

At first it did not appear that Nabisco's board would welcome a merger, and that it would have to be a hostile transaction. None-theless Mullin suggested that Wilson set up an appointment with Nabisco's president, Ross Johnson, to see if an amicable marriage could be arranged. Much to Wilson's surprise, Johnson was eager for such an arrangement. Dillon Read's proposal for a share-for-share exchange—this would give a modest premium to the Nabisco shareholders—was accepted as a starting point, as was Mullin's suggestion for a massive stock repurchase program subsequent to the merger. Even so, there were snags. Nabisco backed out, want-ing a larger premium, and then its stock ran up on rumors that other bidders would enter the competition. Fearful of what this might mean, Johnson now acceded to a friendly takeover. The agreement was reached on June 1, 1985. Reynolds would purchase 29 million shares of Nabisco, slightly more than half of those out-standing, for $85 per share, this effective July 2. Then on Septem-ber 10, the merger was completed when Reynolds exchanged 0.34 shares of a new convertible cumulative preferred stock and $42.50 in notes for each of the shares that remained. The total value of the package came to $4.9 billion. Under the terms of the deal Wilson became chairman and CEO of the new RJR Nabisco, while John-son came in as president, COO, and heir-apparent, with the imme-diate duty of merging Nabisco with the various Reynolds food businesses.

This created some problems for Dillon Read. Nabisco had used Lehman Brothers and its successor firms as its investment bank, and Johnson—who was on the board of Shearson Lehman Hutton—felt comfortable with that arrangement. He appreciated the services Dillon Read provided, however, and wanted to maintain a relationship. The result was an ongoing comanagership with Lehman.

During 1986 and 1987 Dillon Read participated in selling off eleven of RJR Nabisco's businesses, including Canada Dry, Sunkist, Heublein, Kentucky Fried Chicken, and Fleishmann's Yeast. Matters seemed fairly stable for the next year. Then, in late October 1988, Mullin was alerted to some startling developments. He had been out to dinner with a client, and arrived home at about midnight. There was an urgent message from Hobbs, who informed him that they had been called to an emergency meeting of the RJR Nabisco board in Atlanta the next day.

The following morning they went to the airport, where the Dillon Read men met Felix Rohatyn and Luis Rinaldini of Lazard Frères, who were going to the same meeting. At that point none of them knew exactly what was happening, but rumors regarding RJR Nabisco had been rife for weeks, and so they were prepared for anything, especially the possibility of restructuring.

When the Dillon Read and Lazard bankers arrived at headquarters they learned that with the help of Shearson Lehman Hutton, Ross Johnson, who had replaced Wilson as CEO in 1986, had made an offer to acquire RJR Nabisco in a leveraged buyout, which he had presented to the board on October 19 at a dinner held the night before the regular board meeting. The price, revealed later on, was $75 a share, which worked out to $17 billion, making it the largest buyout at that time. From the first it seemed evident that this was too low a bid. Wall Street buzzed with rumors that other offers were about to be made, and the Special Committee of the board, headed by Charles Hugel, who was RJR Nabisco's non-executive chairman and CEO of Combustion Engineering, wanted Dillon Read and Lazard to advise the Special Committee on the proposal. The banking team suggested that others might soon come up with a competitive bid, which would have to be considered.

As it turned out this was precisely what happened. After much maneuvering, on October 23 Johnson learned that Kohlberg Kravis planned to make a bid of $90 a share, which he thought would be $78 in cash and $12 in debt.[14] When this bid was received the bankers had to respond to it with another analysis. By early November, the Special Committee announced that it would be interested in receiving other proposals to acquire the company. In addition, Dillon Read and Lazard were instructed by the board to consider other alternatives, such as restructuring, that might realize values in excess of $90.

For more than a month Mullin and Hobbs devoted virtually all of their time and effort to the RJR Nabisco deal, in somewhat the same way that Hobbs had become involved with Unocal. Dillon Read-Lazard teams were organized to analyze the food and tobacco businesses and then developed a program to study the corporation as a whole. Both the Johnson group and KKR were given a deadline of November 18 with which to come up with new offers. On that day, First Boston submitted a proposal and said RJR Nabisco might be worth as much as $105, or even $118, strongly implying it had a client who would make an offer in that area.

First Boston's client turned out to be the Pritzker family and allies, including Harry Gray, the former chairman of United Technologies whose plan was to purchase RJR Nabisco's food business with installment notes that would have to be sold off by the end of the year because of tax law changes. This offer, to be financed solely with paper, was not taken seriously. This became more evident when the group neglected to indicate how it intended to proceed with financing.

To allow additional time for reviewing the bids as well as the First Boston group's proposal, the bidding deadline was further extended to November 29. The Special Committee also instructed its investment bankers to continue studying restructuring options.

Meanwhile the contenders continued to work on their offers. Confusion reigned, and there were two additional rounds of bidding. At first it appeared the Shearson-Johnson group had won, and then it seemed equally clear that KKR had a victory. In the end the Shearson-Johnson group came up with $84 in cash and securities with a face value of $28. In contrast, KKR offered $81 in cash and $28 in securities.[15] Yet it wasn't that simple, since the value of the securities would not necessarily be the same as their face value. There was no simple and clear way to indicate which proposal was better. Rohatyn advised the board, "Both bids are between 108 and 109."[16] After some additional consideration the KKR bid was accepted.

As always, there were other winners. The shareholders reaped tremendous profits, of course, as did the lawyers and investment bankers. So far, it has looked like a good deal; at the end of 1989, RJR Nabisco's balance sheet looked stronger than analysts had predicted.[17]

Such transactions were, needless to say, a risky business. And even Dillon Read's usually conservative approach to risk did not insulate it from making mistakes in the takeover boom. Dillon Read and its new parent company, The Travelers Corporation (which, as discussed below, had acquired the firm in 1986), had a participation in the 1988 deal that provided Campeau Corporation with the bridge financing necessary to acquire Federated Department Stores. Dillon Read's participation in the highly leveraged transaction was relatively minor; First Boston was the leader in the loan. Even so, when Campeau declared bankruptcy on January 15, 1990, Dillon Read and Travelers were left holding some $48 million of Campeau's badly discounted securities.

By then Mullin had become part of the "old guard" at the firm and would soon retire. Newcomers had been fast arriving to fill gaps left by such retirements. From the time of Birkelund's arrival in 1981 to 1989 Dillon Read's total personnel in the United States had risen from 432 to 657, which meant there had been a mass infusion of new blood. Managing directors of the Brady era who stayed on continued to perform well in the Birkelund regime. But in a hotly competitive age locating and then acquiring talented professionals to make Dillon Read a more convincing presence in both old and new areas of concern was of paramount importance. As shakeouts struck many Wall Street banks, several talented bankers departed for Dillon Read. Several bankers came from Lehman Brothers Kuhn Loeb when that firm underwent convolutions. Richard Smith arrived from Kidder Peabody and became a key junk bond trader. In 1989, Neil Benedict left Salomon Brothers and was placed in charge of developing Dillon Read's business in Asia. François de Saint Phalle, arriving from Shearson Lehman Hutton, was given the responsibility for Dillon Read's capital market activities. There had been 76 professionals in corporate and public finance and 66 in marketing in 1981; by 1989, the numbers had grown to 98 and 175 respectively.[18]

The new hires were required to help service an infusion of new clients who were attracted to the firm in the mid- and late 1980s.

DILLON READ NEW PAYS, DOMESTIC CORPORATIONS,
1976–1989

Year	New Pays
1976	28
1977	21
1978	19
1979	38
1980	25
1981	13
1982	24
1983	29
1984	34
1985	34
1986	67
1987	53
1988	56
1989	53

SOURCE: Dillon Read.

A key element used in measuring a firm's progress in this area is "new pays," by which is meant companies and others requiring services who had not been clients previously, but were utilizing the bank's services for the first time.

Throughout this period foreign business was an area of critical concern. Dillon, Read Overseas Corporation continued to perform disappointingly in the early 1980s, though its fortunes began to change in 1984, when DROC entered into a relationship with Pierre Moussa, who had once headed Banque Paribas, one of France's most prestigious financial institutions. When Paribas was nationalized over Moussa's objections, he left to organize the Pallas Group, which was to make investments on an international scale, and Moussa wanted a partner, "a bank of great quality, with a name that is perfectly respected." It was for that reason that Pallas purchased a half-interest in what now became Dillon, Read Ltd., with Moussa coming in as chairman, while Lorenzo Weisman served as president. In effect, Dillon, Read Ltd. was the first investment made by Pallas.[19]

By 1986, however, the arrangement was running into difficulties, principally because Pallas was beginning to make acquisitions in areas which were competitive with those of Dillon, Read Ltd.[20]

In the meantime, Weisman had been conducting discussions with leaders of the Société Général de Belgique, which had been considering ways of entering the investment banking business. As a result, the Belgian company purchased Pallas's 50 percent stake in Dillon, Read Ltd., providing the London firm with a second joint venture partner, a relationship which lasted until 1988, when Dillon Read repurchased the Société Général de Belgique portion. Thereafter, expansion continued apace. Dillon, Read Ltd. joined with Charterhouse Bank Ltd. in the establishment of two funds to engage in the growing field of leveraged buyouts in the United Kingdom and elsewhere in Europe, and with other partners formed a leveraged buyout firm in Spain. Subsequently it formed separate leveraged buyout firms in France and the United Kingdom.

These new affiliations and activities provided Dillon, Read Ltd. with an array of contacts and capabilities it otherwise could not have developed. Dillon, Read Ltd. now entered the Belgian market as one of the more significant American participants. It acted as independent advisor for the French company Moët Hennessey and its successor, LVMH Moët Hennessey, Louis Vuitton, and for Valeo, Alcatel, and others. In addition the firm represented Carlo di Benedetti and a group of European investors in acquiring a Spanish holding company called COFIR, which in a matter of two years became one of the largest capitalized companies in Spain.[21] As part of its overseas expansion Dillon Read established an office in Tokyo in 1989, hoping to re-create the kind of business it had attracted both before and immediately after World War II.

Thus Dillon Read, by the end of the decade, had achieved considerable scope in its activities, but had long abandoned any attempt to become an all-encompassing investment bank. Its strategy was to broaden and deepen those activities where it seemed to have a natural advantage and which were characterized by high margins and relatively modest capital. While other firms were striving for global networks providing every service imaginable to a wide variety of clients, Dillon Read remained wedded to its traditional business augmented by natural outgrowths in related areas of activity. By the time full management ownership was achieved in 1986, Dillon Read was a balanced, rejuvenated enterprise.

At about this time The Travelers Corporation appeared on the scene. More than a year before approaching Dillon Read, Travelers had expressed a strong and growing interest in investment banking. The main question was how this might be achieved, and toward what end.

Other insurance companies were thinking along the same lines. On the face of it Prudential's purchase of Bache & Co. seemed logical enough; Prudential's strategy had envisioned selling insurance and other financial service products through Bache's army of brokers. For a while Travelers considered taking a similar course of action. That approach was soon discarded, as Travelers grew aware of the incompatibility of the two kinds of brokerage operations. Insurance and securities brokers, as Prudential would discover, were quite different in orientation, the former seeking long-term investments in their products, the latter more concerned with transactions which might last a few days or perhaps a year or so. With this vicarious experience in mind, Travelers shifted its attention to firms that had little or no exposure to brokerage, concentrating instead on those in the United States and the United Kingdom which provided creative investment management and investment banking.

Travelers' executives considered several banks, including Lehman Brothers Kuhn Loeb and Kidder Peabody. Thought was also given to purchasing a London-based bank, but that idea too was rejected. Travelers now turned to Dillon Read, which seemed more attractive than the other possibilities. Martin Roenigk, a Travelers' executive involved with acquisitions, liked the fact that Dillon Read "had a solid base domestically" and "was knowledgeable overseas" with "a potential to build fast." It was important, too, that Dillon Read was "a digestible size."[22] Birkelund's moves into asset management were deemed especially relevant.

At the time, Dillon Read's common equity stood at about $75 million and Travelers' was $4.5 billion, so an acquisition was clearly not motivated by the potential impact Dillon Read's profits could make on Travelers' earnings. Where Dillon Read could have an effect was on its prospective parent's investment portfolio. Travelers was concerned with broadening its investment capabilities both domestically and abroad. A firm such as Dillon Read might help manage some of its equity portfolios, identify venture capital and private placement opportunities, and in other ways provide it with needed expertise and a different perspective. Recall that this was a motive that underlay the earlier purchase by Bechtel. But Dillon Read had changed substantially since the Bechtel purchase five years earlier. Now the firm was more competent in this arena.

So Dillon Read's profitability was less relevant than the brain-power Travelers wanted to help manage its assets. The kind of aggressive asset managers who had come to Wall Street in the past decade had gone to smaller firms where there was scope for their talents and few barriers to advancement and recognition. Such professionals were not ordinarily attracted to large insurance companies.

There was opposition on the part of some Dillon Read managing directors to the sale. Some of them, especially those younger ones who had supported Birkelund in the repurchase of majority ownership from Bechtel in 1983, felt betrayed when Birkelund turned around three years later and recommended selling the firm to another company. Even so, despite their enjoyment of their newly acquired independence, the possible marriage intrigued them. They were attracted by the possibility of managing a portion of Travelers' funds, and obtaining support for their venture capital and other existing or prospective specialized investment activities. The older partners, who had purchased shares at book value and now were given the opportunity to sell at what was certain to be a substantial premium, were more enthusiastic about the deal.

Travelers contacted Dillon Read in May 1986, and discussions moved quickly. The matter of price was simplified by the recently concluded General Electric–Kidder Peabody marriage, which established a valuation for such firms of approximately three times book value. The transaction was completed in the summer of 1986. The price was $157.5 million, with an additional $67.5 million in the form of employment contracts.

That both partners remain satisfied with the arrangement cannot be said for most other major merger partners for Wall Street firms in the 1980s. Perhaps the key to success is that Travelers has not tried to manage Dillon Read, leaving it to function by its own internal logic, which was eminently sensible, since the firm remained highly profitable. Dillon Read's management felt it was important for a new owner to permit the firm to set its own priorities and to accept its historical compensation formula, which Travelers did. It was also agreed that Brady and Birkelund would report directly to Chairman Edward H. Budd of Travelers, eliminating layers of staff between parent and subsidiary executive management. And though Dillon Read does not have very high demands for capital, it receives support in those areas where it is important. From Dillon Read's vantage point, it has been a very propitious relationship.

All the while Nick Brady was gradually withdrawing from active participation in the firm. After returning in 1983, he continued to service old clients and seek new ones, leaving management mainly to Birkelund. As before, Brady had outside interests, and increasingly these involved government service. In 1983 Brady served on the National Bipartisan Committee on Central America, and in 1985 he was chairman of the Commission on Executive, Legislative, and Judicial Salaries. Brady shuttled back and forth between New York and Washington, and the focus of his life inevitably shifted. Two years later Birkelund was named co-chief executive officer, a recognition of what had been reality for some time.

After the stock market crash of October 19, 1987, Brady was selected by President Reagan to head a commission to study the subject and report back with recommendations for change to curb market volatility and restore investor confidence. This not only made Brady a household name to everyone even casually following the news that winter, but also brought him into close contact with Secretary of the Treasury James Baker and Vice President George Bush. When Baker resigned to assume leadership of Bush's presidential campaign Reagan nominated Brady as his replacement, a post he assumed on September 15, 1988, whereupon Birkelund became the sole chairman and CEO.

Since the mid-1980s the investment banking community has been undergoing a series of convulsions out of which Dillon Read has emerged largely unscathed. A decade ago it appeared that the firm was going one way while the rest of the industry was going the other, and that Dillon Read had been the loser for it. By 1990 it had become obvious that Dillon Read had not only come through rough times in good shape, but had expanded rationally and profitably. Its business continued to grow. Moreover, Dillon Read's

RETURN ON EQUITY FOR SELECTED INVESTMENT BANKS,
1982–1989
(figures in percent)

Year	Dillon Read	First Boston	Morgan Stanley	Salomon	Shearson
1982	27	47	39	21	33
1983	47	30	27	24	32
1984	20	21	27	9	15
1985	27	28	38	21	9
1986	41	26	32	16	30
1987	17	11	25	4	11
1988	24	16	35	8	5
1989	25	N.A.	27	15	8
Average Return on Equity					
1982–1989	29	26*	31	15	18

* Through 1988 only.
SOURCE: Figures except for Dillon Read are for publicly owned companies. First Boston went private at the end of 1988.

net income and return on shareholder's equity continued to out-perform the industry.[23]

Meanwhile several of the high-flying financiers and firms which had dazzled the investment community for most of the 1980s had come to grief. As more firms disappeared or folded into mergers, more than a dozen arbitrageurs and wheeler-dealers, led by Ivan Boesky, had been indicted, tried, convicted, and jailed. The junk bond market had lost much of its luster, as some highly leveraged companies began to default on interest payments. Drexel Burn-ham, which epitomized the new wave, was reeling from its settle-ment on criminal charges with the federal government. Its star investment banker, Michael Milken, had been forced to depart under indictment, and in 1990 he was convicted of various violations of the securities laws. Even before the stock market crash of Oc-tober 19, 1987, many of the larger investment banking firms were planning for a major contraction, having badly overextended their businesses.

Pursuing a policy of selective growth, Dillon Read was once again moving counter to much of the industry, only this time to its advantage. Within the firm, continuity has been as important as change, as Dillon Read has succeeded in growing its business around the managing directors who were in place when Birkelund was being recruited in 1981. Indeed, fifteen of the seventeen managing directors who were with Dillon Read at that time remained at the firm's core at the end of 1988, when the number of managing directors exceeded forty. In its measured expansion Dillon Read has eschewed adventures that risked skirting ethical boundaries for the sake of quick profits. Relationship banking, which had been considered old-fashioned in the 1970s and early 1980s, was coming back into style. As it entered the 1990s, Dillon Read was an unusual meld of the old with the new, its business in relationship banking flourishing alongside some vital new ventures—a profitable blend of tradition and innovation.

Notes

Preface

1. Howard Gleckman, "The Quiet Crusader," *Business Week*, September 18, 1989, p. 90.
2. Jerry Ritter Interview, January 4, 1989.

Chapter 1

1. Letter from Thomas E. Vermilye to Donald Mackay, December 21, 1891, in Dillon Read files.
2. For a history of the Vermilye family in Europe, see James Riker, *Revised History of Harlem (City of New York), Its Origins and Early Annals* (New York, 1904), pp. 104–6, 647, 652, 661.
3. The Reverend Edward B. Coe, D.D. "A Discourse Commemorative on the Reverend Thomas Edward Vermilye, D.D., LL.D." (New York, 1893).
4. Riker, *Revised History of Harlem*, p. 647.
5. The New York directory for 1830–31 listed Carpenter by home address only, 10 Dutch Street. The 1831–32 directory still had him at Dutch Street, but now identifies him as an accountant, and the same is true for the 1832–33 edition, in which Vermilye is listed by himself as a broker at 42 Wall Street and a home address at 168 Thompson. The following edition, 1833–34, places both men at 42 Wall, while the home addresses had changed, to 160 Wooster for Carpenter and 8 Hamersley for Vermilye. And in this edition, for the first time, is found a listing for Carpenter & Vermilye, at 42 Wall. *Longworth's American Almanac, New York Register and City Directory for the 55th Year of American Independence*

357

(1830–31) (New York, 1831), pp. 172, 176, 486; 1831–32 ed., pp. 193, 681; 1832–33 ed., pp. 167, 168, 619; Thomas E. Vermilye letter to Donald Mackay.

6. Ibid.

7. The Saxon word for misfortune is *broc,* and from this some scholars deduced that a broker was a merchant who had to abandon trade through some commercial misfortune. Others hold that a broker was one who "broke down" large consignments of goods into smaller ones for resale—this is to say, he bought at wholesale and sold at somewhat higher unit prices to retailers. The translation from merchandise to securities would have been relatively simple. John R. Dos Passos, *A Treatise on the Law of Stock-Brokers and Stock-Exchanges* (New York, 1882), p. 1.

8. Business historian N.S.B. Gras describes sedentary merchants as those involved in import, export, and wholesale trade, who were also prepared to engage in retail business, build and lease ships, insure cargoes, provide warehouse facilities, underwrite insurance, arrange for mail deliveries, and even deal in bills of exchange, thus performing banking functions. Some would dabble in manufacturing—soap, candles, distilling, and the like. Gras contends the sedentary merchants evolved from petty capitalists, who were ever on the move seeking opportunities. In contrast, the sedentary merchants remained in one location. The "age of mercantile capitalism" lasted from around the fourteenth to the nineteenth centuries. N.S.B. Gras and Henrietta Larson, *Casebook in American Business History* (New York, 1939), pp. 3–15; N.S.B. Gras, *Business and Capitalism* (New York, 1939), pp. 54–60 passim.

9. Bayrd Still, *Mirror for Gotham* (New York, 1956), p. 79.

10. John Duncan, *Travels Through Part of the United States and Canada* (Glasgow, 1832), I, 27.

11. Allan Nevins, ed., *The Diary of Philip Hone, 1828–1851* (New York, 1927), pp. 202–3.

12. Henry Lanier, *A Century of Banking in New York, 1822–1922* (New York, 1922), pp. 14–15.

13. Henry Hall, ed., *America's Successful Men of Affairs: An Encyclopedia of Contemporaneous Biography* (New York, 1895), I, 693.

14. Quoted in Robert Sobel, *Panic on Wall Street* (New York, 1968), p. 72.

15. New York Stock & Exchange Board, "Book of Minutes B," 1837.

16. George Taylor, *The Transportation Revolution, 1815–1860* (New York, 1951), p. 152; Sereno Pratt, *The Work of Wall Street* (New York, 1903), p. 15; Emerson Fite, *Social and Economic Conditions in the North During the Civil War* (New York, 1910), pp. 155–56.

17. R. C. Michie, *The London and New York Stock Exchanges, 1850–1914* (London, 1987), p. 167.

18. Joseph Hedges, *Commercial Banking and the Stock Market Before 1863* (Baltimore, 1938), p. 36.

19. New York Stock & Exchange Board, "Minutes," January 3, 1842–January 9, 1851.

20. John Doggett, Jr., ed., *Doggett's New York City Directory, 1848–1849* (New York, 1849), pp. 81, 419; United States, "Seventh Census of the United States. Original Returns of the Assistant Marshals, First Series, White and Free Colored Population, Schedule I. Free Inhabitants in 17th Ward, in the County

of New York, State of New York . . . enumerated . . . on September 4, 1850."

21. *New York Assembly Journal*, Albany, 71st Sess., 1848.

22. Thomas Cochran and William Miller, *The Age of Enterprise: A Social History of Industrial America* (New York, 1942), p. 70.

23. Lanier, *A Century of Banking in New York*, p. 213.

24. Ralph Hidy, *The House of Baring in American Trade and Finance* (New York, 1949), p. 411.

25. Hedges, *Commercial Banking . . . Before 1863*, p. 37.

26. Otto C. Lightner, *The History of Business Depressions* (New York, 1922), p. 137.

27. Edward Spann, *The New Metropolis: New York City, 1840–1857* (New York, 1981), pp. 394–95.

28. H. Wilson, comp., *Trow's New York City Directory, 1862–1863* (New York, 1863), p. 892.

Chapter 2

1. United States, Department of Commerce, *Historical Statistics of the United States, Colonial Times to 1970* (Washington, 1975), II, 869.

2. Fritz Redlich, *The Molding of American Banking: Men and Ideas* (New York, 1947–1951), II, 355–57; Henrietta Larson, *Jay Cooke: Private Bankers* (Cambridge, Mass., 1936), pp. 105–8, 125.

3. Larson, pp. 123–24.

4. Vincent Carosso, *Investment Banking in America* (Cambridge, Mass., 1970), pp. 20–22.

5. Ellis P. Oberholtzer, *Jay Cooke: Financier of the Civil War* (New York, 1907), I, 207.

6. Ibid., I, 347.

7. Henry Hall, ed., *America's Successful Men of Affairs: An Encyclopedia of Contemporaneous Biography* (New York, 1895), I, 693.

8. *New York Times*, December 25, 1876; J. A. Humphrey, *Englewood: Its Annals and Reminiscences* (New York, 1899), pp. 85–86.

9. Redlich, *Molding of American Banking*, II, 361.

10. "Vermilye & Co.—William A. Read & Co.—Dillon, Read & Co.," Dillon Read files.

11. Larson, *Jay Cooke*, p. 217.

12. H. C. Fahnestock to Jay Cooke, December 20, 1865, in Oberholtzer, *Jay Cooke*, II, 19.

13. Matthew Hale Smith, *Bulls and Bears of New York* (New York, 1873), p. 412; Letter from Thomas E. Vermilye to Donald Mackay, December 21, 1891, in Dillon Read files.

14. *New York Stock Exchange Directory*, corrected to October 1868, pp. 8, 10, 14.

15. Adaline W. Sterling, *The Book of Englewood* (Englewood, N.J., 1922), pp. 278–79.

16. "Donald Mackay," in *The National Cyclopaedia of American Biography* (New York, 1918), XVI, 429.

17. Redlich, *Molding of American Banking*, II, 366–67; Oberholtzer, *Jay Cooke*, II, 278.

18. W. Worthington Fowler, *Twenty Years of Inside Life on Wall Street* (New York, 1880), pp. 540 ff.

19. Larson, *Jay Cooke*, pp. 410–11.

20. Thomas E. Vermilye to Donald Mackay, December 21, 1891.

21. *The Commercial and Financial Chronicle and Hunt's Merchants' Magazine*, December 30, 1876.

22. Smith, *Bulls and Bears of New York*, pp. 412–13.

23. Vermilye was linked to Richardson, Hill by long-distance telephone, still an oddity at the time, and indicative of a fairly substantial volume of business between the two cities. *The Boston Stock Exchange, With Brief Sketches of Prominent Brokers, Bankers, Banks, and Moneyed Institutions of Boston* (Boston, 1893), unpaginated.

24. R. C. Michie, *The London and New York Stock Exchanges, 1850–1914* (London, 1987), pp. 177, 187.

25. *The Boston Stock Exchange*..

26. "Vermilye & Co.—William A. Read & Co.—Dillon, Read & Co."

27. "Mr. William A. Read, Banker and Bond Expert, Is Dead," *New York Herald*, April 8, 1916.

28. Frank J. Williams, "Rise of New York's Great Investment Houses: No. 3—Dillon, Read & Co.," *New York Evening Post*, October 14, 1926.

29. Clarence Dillon, "Anne's Story." This is an unpaginated typewritten document in the possession of Dillon's daughter, Dorothy Dillon Eweson, and in the Dillon Read files. "Anne's Story" is a memoir and life of Dillon's wife, written late in his life, and presumably was not intended for publication.

30. Ibid.

31. Arthur S. Dewing, *A History of the National Cordage Company* (Cambridge, Mass., 1913), pp. 12–13.

32. John Brooks, *The Takeover Game* (New York, 1987), pp. 38–39.

33. Alfred D. Chandler, Jr., *The Visible Hand: The Managerial Revolution in American Business* (Cambridge, Mass., 1977), pp. 329–30; Thomas R. Navin and Marian V. Sears, "The Rise of a Market for Industrial Securities, 1887–1902," *Business History Review* XXVII (June 1955): 125–26; Naomi Lamoreaux, *The Great Merger Movement in American Business, 1895–1904* (New York, 1985), pp. 87–89.

34. William A. Read v. Donald Mackay, Latham A. Fish, George D. Mackay, George Trowbridge Hollister and Arthur S. Fairchild, Supreme Court, County of New York, March 29, 1905.

35. The Financier Company, *History of the New York Stock Exchange, The New York Stock Exchange Directory* (New York, 1887), p. 56.

36. Vincent Carosso, *The Morgans: Private International Bankers, 1854–1913* (Cambridge, Mass. 1987), p. 351; *The City Record: Official Journal*, December 4, 1896, p. 3509.

37. Robert T. Swaine, *The Cravath Firm and Its Predecessors, 1819–1947* (New York, 1946 ed.), I, 596–98, 646.

38. William A. Read against Donald Mackay, Lathan A. Fish, George D.

Mackay, George Trowbridge Hollister, and Arthur S. Fairchild, Supreme Court, County of New York, *Summons and Complaint*, March 29, 1905.

39. "Security Offerings by Vermilye & Co., 1902 through 1904 and Wm. A. Read & Co., 1905 through 1920." Mss. in the Dillon Read files.

40. *New York Times*, February 10, 1905.

41. *New York Times*, March 12, 1905.

42. *New York Times*, March 24, 1905.

43. *Report on the Fire in the Equitable Building, January 9, 1912* (New York, 1912), p. 29.

44. "Joseph Husband Seaman," in *National Cyclopaedia of American Biography*, XXXVII, 139.

45. "William Mead Lindsley Fiske," in *National Cyclopaedia of American Biography*, XXXVIII, 419.

46. *New York Times*, April 1, 1905.

Chapter 3

1. Robert T. Swaine, *The Cravath Firm and Its Predecessors, 1819–1947* (New York, 1946 ed.), I, 720.

2. John Brooks, *The Takeover Game* (New York, 1987), p. 40.

3. "Underwritings," in Dillon Read files.

4. Frank J. Williams, "Rise of New York's Great Investment Houses: No. 3—Dillon, Read & Co.," *New York Evening Post*, October 14, 1926.

5. Vermilye & Co.—William A. Read & Co.—Dillon, Read & Co., Dillon Read files.

6. "Security Offerings . . . by Wm A. Read & Co." in Dillon Read files.

7. *Report on the Fire in the Equitable Building*, January 9, 1912 (New York, 1912), pp. 9–13.

8. R. W. Martin to Clarence Dillon, November 26, 1913. The reference to industrial enterprises means bonds for industrial companies, which even as late as 1913 were looked upon by some Wall Streeters as speculative.

9. Perhaps the best statement of Read's investment philosophy could be found in his Last Will and Testament, dated February 4, 1916. Directing his executors and trustees, he said:

I authorize and empower them, in their discretion, to retain any bonds, stocks, or other securities which I may leave at the time of my death, and to invest not only in securities in which trustees are authorized by law to invest but also in mortgage bonds of any railroad company in the United States which shall, during a period of at least five years prior to the investment, have paid dividends of not less than four per cent (4%) per annum on an amount of capital stock being not less in amount than fifty percent (50%) of the entire bonded debt of such company; also to invest in the common and preferred stocks of the Minneapolis, St. Paul & Sault Ste. Marie Railway Company, the Atchison, Topeka and Santa Fe Railway Company, the Chicago and North Western Railway Company, and the stocks of the Louisville and Nashville Railroad Company, the New York

Central Railroad Company and the Pennsylvania Railroad Company; also in the guaranteed stocks of railroad companies, notwithstanding that such securities may not be of the description of the securities allowed to trustees by the decisions of the courts or the statutes of the State of New York; giving preference in investments to the purchase of securities which are selling at a price at or below their par value, but in case of the purchase of bonds at a premium my said trustees shall not be required to create a sinking fund from income to repay the amount of any premium so paid.

10. Brooks, *The Takeover Game*, p. 39.
11. R. C. Michie, *London and New York Stock Exchanges, 1850–1914* (London, 1987), p. 226.
12. *Harvard College Class of 1905, Fourth Report, June, 1920* (Norwood, Mass., 1920), p. 251.
13. James C. Young, "Clarence Dillon Became Banker Through Chance," *New York Times*, January 10, 1926; Frank J. Williams, "A New Leader in Finance: Clarence Dillon," *Review of Reviews*, February 1926, p. 148.
14. Young, "Clarence Dillon."
15. Paul Nitze Interview, February 3, 1989; Dorothy Dillon Eweson Interview, February 26, 1988. Michael Forrestal stated that his father told him Dillon was Jewish. Michael Forrestal Interview by Douglas Brinkley, April 27, 1988.
16. Clarence Dillon, "Anne's Story," typescript in the possession of Dorothy Dillon Eweson; Paul Nitze Interview by Charles Murphy, November 4, 1981.
17. Dillon, "Anne's Story."
18. *Academy Weekly*, March 7, 14, May 2, 1901; "Transcripts of Record," 1900–1901.
19. Dorothy Dillon Eweson Interview, February 26, 1988.
20. Dillon, "Anne's Story."
21. *Secretary's First Report, Harvard College Class of 1905* (Cambridge, Mass., 1906), p. 3; *Harvard College Class of 1905, Second Report, June 1911* (Cambridge, Mass., 1911), p. 79.
22. This matter of Dillon's religion has always been a matter of some contention. In 1917 Boleslaw Lapowski wrote a letter to the *New York Times* that was published under the heading "Polish Ambitions: A Yearning for Western Culture, but Not German Culture," which indicated he might have considered himself Catholic. "The Polish nation, from the dawn of history to the present day, has been by its religion, by its habits of life, institutions, and political aims, a nation of Western culture, adding to the growth of that culture and sharing its fruits; it has always leaned toward Rome, not Byzantium." *New York Times*, November 25, 1917.
A 1926 article on Dillon contains this statement: "Mr. Dillon is not as wholly Irish as his surname would indicate. There is Irish in his veins, but it is richly blended with Polish, French, and other strains." "Mr. Dillon: He Thinks Only in Millions," *Liberty*, March 6, 1926, p. 64; in another the author states: "His make-up, his tastes, his versatility are probably explainable by the unusual mixture of blood which has come down to him from his ancestors. This mixture includes French, Irish, Polish, and other European strains." B. C. Forbes, "Clarence Dillon, The Man Who Bought Dodge," *Forbes*, May 15, 1925, p. 164.

In a February 1936 *Fortune* article entitled "Jews in America," we find this: "Dillon of Dillon, Read & Co. is considered a Jew by other Jews but he is not, as his name suggests, an active member of his race nor is the firm considered Jewish by either Jews or non-Jews" (p. 133).

23. Dillon, "Anne's Story."

24. John K. Winkler, "A Billion-Dollar Banker," *The New Yorker*, October 20, 1928, p. 29. According to one source, Dillon also was the only member of his class to own an automobile. "Man with the Purse," *Time*, August 18, 1961, p. 13.

25. Bernard Bailyn, Donald Fleming, Oscar Handlin, and Stephan Thernstrom, *Glimpses of Harvard Past* (Cambridge, Mass., 1986), pp. 141–42. Dillon conferred with Roosevelt in 1936, describing it as a "meeting between two old friends." *New York Herald Tribune*, January 24, 1936.

26. "Clarence Dillon," in *National Cyclopaedia of American Biography* (Clifton, N.J., 1984), LXII, 244; C. Douglas Dillon Interview, October 28, 1987.

27. Dillon, "Anne's Story"; Dorothy Eweson Interview, February 26, 1988.

28. Dillon, "Anne's Story."

29. Forbes, "Clarence Dillon, The Man Who Bought Dodge," p. 165.

30. Paul Nitze Interview, April 10, 1988; Dillon, "Anne's Story."

31. C. Douglas Dillon Interview, October 28, 1987.

32. Dorothy Dillon Eweson Interview, February 26, 1988.

33. Dillon, "Anne's Story."

34. Vermilye & Co.—William A. Read & Co.—Dillon, Read & Co.

35. Williams, "Rise of New York's Great Investment Houses."

36. Dillon, "Anne's Story."

37. Robert Sobel, *Panic on Wall Street* (New York, 1968), pp. 322–49.

38. Paul Nitze believes Dillon learned of the shortages from Morgan banker Edward R. Stettinius, Sr., and the substance was picric acid, also employed in the manufacture of explosives. This account is drawn from "Anne's Story," which was written a half-century after the event. However, there are some inconsistencies. In 1915, for example, Goldman Sachs exhibited some pro-German sentiments, and whether or not it would have joined with Morgan in this venture is problematical.

39. Almost sixty years later Paul Nitze, who became a Dillon Read employee in 1929, recalled a conversation with Dillon during the early summer of that year which illustrates his approach.

I might say a few words about the initial conversation I had with him when I asked him for the letter of introduction. He asked me what I wanted to do with my life. I replied, well, I'd like to be an investment banker. He asked me, "What part of investment banking interests you?" I said the general policy part. He responded, "Here you've walked in, and here I've got these papers before me, what do you think I'm doing?" I didn't know. He said, "I'm going over this advertisement which will appear in the paper tomorrow, advertisement about an issued bond we're selling. And I'm going through to see that all the spelling, addition, punctuation and every word in this advertisement is correct. The reason that I point this out is that if you think that you can do policy without the most minute attention to detail, you've got another thought coming to you. You don't deal with policy unless you're thoroughly the master of detail." [Paul Nitze Interview, April 10, 1988.]

40. Thomas A. Edison to Clarence Dillon, April 21, 1915, in Dillon Read files.
41. Dillon, "Anne's Story."
42. Winkler, "A Billion-Dollar Banker," p. 32.
43. Forbes, "Clarence Dillon: The Man Who Bought Dodge," p. 166. In his memoir, Dillon says that Read's comment was slightly different. "You see that name on the bottom? When we rewrite those papers next year it will be at the top."
44. "Asked to Construe Read Will Clause," *New York Herald*, April 28, 1916. Among his bequests Read left $25,000 to each of his partners. "Last Will and Testament of William A. Read."
45. Duncan Read Interview, February 2, 1988.
46. Paul Nitze Interview, April 10, 1988.

Chapter 4

1. Paul Nitze Interview, January 12, 1982. Nitze added that in the garden of his home in Far Hills, New Jersey, Dillon had a statue of David "drawing a bead on Goliath."
2. Wesley Stanger, Jr., Interview with Charles Murphy, March 11, 1982.
3. Ferdinand Eberstadt to Major George Fielding Eliot, August 7, 1947, in Ferdinand Eberstadt Papers, on deposit at Princeton University.
4. Henry Merritt Interview with Charles Murphy, December 13, 1982.
5. Arnold A. Rogow, *James Forrestal: A Study of Personality, Politics, and Policy* (New York, 1963), p. 66.
6. Henry Merritt Interview, December 13, 1982.
7. Robert Greenhalgh Albion and Robert Howe Connery, *Forrestal and the Navy* (New York, 1962), p. 23.
8. *New York Times*, July 14, 1916; J. P. Morgan to Clarence Dillon, July 14, 1916; American Foreign Securities, Underwriting Statement, July 12, 1916; American Foreign Securities, Second Meeting of Directors.
9. George Edwards, *The Evolution of Finance Capitalism* (New York, 1938), pp. 208–9; William Shultz and M. R. Caine, *Financial Development of the United States* (New York, 1937), pp. 505–6.
10. Alexander Noyes, *The War Period of American Finance* (New York, 1927), pp. 181–84.
11. Ibid., pp. 186–87.
12. Robert Sobel, *Salomon Brothers, 1910–1987* (New York, 1987), p. 18.
13. Thomas Cochran, *The American Business System: An Historical Perspective* (Cambridge, Mass., 1957), p. 91.
14. According to an internal Dillon Read document, "Among those who went into the service and who had been or were to be employees or 'partners' for many years were the following: Messrs. [Edward J.] Bermingham, Bigelow, Charnley, Coney, Dorstewitz, Forrestal, Granstrom, Mathey, Scott, and Shedden." Ver-

milye & Co.—William A. Read & Co.—Dillon, Read & Co., in Dillon Read files.

15. Margaret L. Coit, *Mr. Baruch* (Boston, 1957), p. 176.

16. Bernard Baruch, *Baruch: The Public Years* (New York, 1960), p. 80.

17. Ibid., p. 126; Dorothy Dillon Eweson Interview, February 26, 1988.

18. John K. Winkler, "A Billion-Dollar Banker," *The New Yorker*, October 20, 1928, p. 32. The reference to the "caftan-clad men of his blood" was a veiled reference to Dillon's presumed Jewish background.

19. Grosvenor R. Clarkson, *Industrial America in the World War: The Strategy Behind the Line, 1917–1918* (Boston, 1923), pp. 509–31.

20. Clarence Dillon Diary, April 12, 1919–October 17, 1921, in possession of Dorothy Dillon Eweson. Dillon kept a journal in these years but did not write entries on a regular basis.

21. Dean Mathey, *Fifty Years of Wall Street With Anecdotiana* (Princeton, 1966), p. 56.

22. Later the firm would be renamed Cotton, Franklin, Wright & Gordon and then Cahill, Gordon, Zachry and Reindel.

23. *New York Times*, March 11, 1931; Clarence Dillon Diary, September 11, September 29, November 7, 1919.

24. "Memorandum from A. B. Forbes to Committee Members," May 17, 1917, on deposit in Dillon Read files.

25. *Manchester Guardian*, April 4, 1917, as quoted in Paul Studenski and Herman Krooss, *Financial History of the United States* (New York, 1952), p. 284.

26. United States, Department of Commerce, *Historical Statistics of the United States, 1789–1945* (Washington, D.C., 1949), p. 242.

27. Noyes, *War Period of American Finance*, pp. 286–89; United States, *Historical Statistics*, pp. 143 ff.; Robert Sobel, *The Age of Giant Corporations* (Westport, Conn., 1972), p. 25.

28. Clarkson, *Industrial America in the World War*, pp. 343, 438.

29. Clarence Dillon Diary, July 7, 1919.

30. Quoted in John Brooks, *The Takeover Game* (New York, 1987), p. 40.

31. Clarence Dillon Diary, July 7, 1919.

32. Ibid., July 8, 1919.

33. Ibid., June 26, 1919.

34. Wm. A. Read & Co. Salary Book, 1919–1920, in the possession of Dorothy Dillon Eweson.

35. Hugh Allen, *The House of Goodyear* (Akron, 1936), p. 43; Maurice O'Reilly, *The Goodyear Story* (Elmsford, N.Y., 1983), p. 44; *Moody's Industrial Manual, 1920* (New York, 1921), p. 731.

36. Hugh Allen, *The House of Goodyear* (Cleveland, 1949), pp. 54–55.

37. Ibid., pp. 45–46.

38. "The Goodyear Tire & Rubber Reorganization in Retrospect," in George O. May, *Twenty-Five Years of Accounting Responsibility, 1911–1936* (New York, 1937), p. 306.

39. The following paragraphs, except where otherwise noted, are based on Robert T. Swaine, *The Cravath Firm and Its Predecessors, 1817–1947*, 2 vols. (New York, 1946); and depositions from *F. C. Tomlinson et al. v. Clarence Dillon and The Goodyear Tire and Rubber Company* (February 28, 1927) and *L. T. Weiss v. Leonard Kennedy* (February 1, 1923).

40. May, *Twenty-Five Years of Accounting Responsibility*, pp. 291–92.
41. O'Reilly, *The Goodyear Story*, p. 47.
42. *Moody's Industrials, 1921*, p. 1573.
43. Paul Litchfield, *Industrial Voyage: My Life as an Industrial Lieutenant* (New York, 1954), pp. 194–95.
44. O'Reilly, *The Goodyear Story*, p. 49.
45. Allen, *The House of Goodyear* (1949), p. 55; and Litchfield, *Industrial Voyage*, p. 195.
46. Swaine, *The Cravath Firm*, v, 272–73.
47. Cravath in *Weiss v. Kennedy*, pp. 4, 7.
48. Norman Beasley, *Men Working: The Story of Goodyear Tire & Rubber* (New York, 1931), p. 91.
49. Cravath in *Weiss v. Kennedy*.
50. Edward Willett, who was at Dillon Read in the late 1920s, noted that Forrestal had attended Princeton with Bill Seiberling, Frank Seiberling's son, and that the younger Seiberling went to work at Goodyear in 1920. "It isn't inconceivable," he said, "that he went to Forrestal for help." Edward Willett Interview by Charles Murphy, n.d.
51. Frank J. Williams, "A New Leader in Finance: Clarence Dillon," *Review of Reviews*, February, 1926, p. 148.
52. United States District Court, Southern District of New York, Civ. 43–757, *United States of America v. Henry S. Morgan et al.*, "Deposition of Karl H. Behr," May 4, 1949, p. 7.
53. Brooks, *The Takeover Game*, p. 47.
54. "Record of Addresses to General Sales Meeting Held January 6–7, 1928," in Dillon Read files.
55. United States District Court, New York (Southern District). *Corrected Opinion of Harold R. Medina, United States Circuit Judge, in United States of America v. Henry S. Morgan, Harold Stanley et al., doing business as Morgan Stanley & Co. et al.* (New York, 1954 ed.), Behr Deposition, *U.S. v. Henry S. Morgan et al.*, p. 13.
56. Laura Jereski, "Clarence Dillon: Using Other People's Money," *Forbes*, July 13, 1987, pp. 270, 274.
57. Williams, "A New Leader in Finance," p. 146.
58. Litchfield, *Industrial Voyage*, pp. 195–97.
59. May, *Twenty-Five Years of Accounting Responsibility*, p. 305.
60. Allen, *House of Goodyear* (1936), pp. 46–47.
61. May, *Twenty-Five Years of Accounting Responsibility*, p. 305.
62. Swaine, *The Cravath Firm*, II, 274.
63. O'Reilly, *The Goodyear Story*, p. 53.
64. Swaine, *The Cravath Firm*, II, 277–80.
65. Ibid.
66. "Leonard Kennedy," in *National Cyclopaedia of American Biography*, XXXVI, 401.
67. "There was one other couple that were great friends of ours who was also in Dillon, Read & Co. His name was Leonard Kennedy. He was not in Dillon Read very long, but he was a good friend." Dorothy Dillon Eweson Interview, February 26, 1988.

68. In a deposition in litigation involving his activities with Goodyear, Dillon maintained:

The defendant is informed and believes that A. A. Schlesinger and E. G. Wilmer were stockholders in said Kennedy Company at the time the said contract was entered into; that 45% of the stock in the Kennedy Company was owned by the Nassau Company, an investment corporation whose stock was owned by this defendant and a majority of which was subsequently acquired by his wife, and that all of the stock of the Nassau Company is now held in various trusts for members of his family, which facts this defendant never endeavored to conceal [*Tomlinson v. Dillon*, p. 35].

69. "Security Offerings by Dillon, Read & Co., Years 1921–1927," *New York Herald*, November 12, 1921; *New York Sun*, October 11, 1933. Hayward, who joined the firm in 1916 and would become a partner in 1926, was a Yale graduate who went on to New York Law School and Balliol College, Oxford. During World War I he served as special representative of the State Department in Europe, and was a War Trade Board representative in the Netherlands. That Hayward would speak for Dillon Read on such occasions was clearly appropriate. *New York Herald Tribune*, February 21, 1926.

70. Allen, *The House of Goodyear* (1949), p. 50; "Edward Wilmer, Financier, Dead," *New York Times*, August 25, 1962.

71. This was not at all unusual. Later on Morgan Stanley would be known as a "Princeton firm" while First Boston's top echelon seemed to be drawn primarily from Yale. Samuel L. Hayes III, "Investment Banking: Power Structure in Flux," *Harvard Business Review*, March–April 1971, p. 148.

72. Swaine, *The Cravath Firm*, II, 281.

73. Paul Nitze Interview, February 3, 1989.

74. *New York Times*, January 10, 1922.

Chapter 5

1. *F. C. Tomlinson et al. v. Clarence Dillon and the Goodyear Tire and Rubber Company*, Court of Common Pleas, State of Ohio, County of Summit, "Amended Separate and Special Answer of Clarence Dillon," p. 2.

2. "Suggested General Statement" of Clarence Dillon in testimony before the Senate Banking Committee, 73rd Cong., 1st sess., 1933, in Dillon Read files.

3. For example, in the December 31, 1926, issue of the *New York Times* is this item: "Dillon, Read & Co. has admitted to partnership the following five men, who have been associated with it several years: 'Robert O. Hayward, Henry G. Riter 3d, William S. Charnley, Clifton M. Miller, and Robert E. Christie.' "

4. Harold van B. Cleveland and Thomas F. Huertas, *Citibank, 1812–1970* (New York, 1985), p. 141. The authors refer to National City as a "financial department store."

5. *New York Times*, December 31, 1926.

6. Dorothy Dillon Eweson Interview, February 26, 1988.

Notes

7. United States, *Recent Economic Changes in the United States: Report of the Committee on Recent Economic Changes of the President's Conference on Unemployment* (Washington, D.C., 1929), pp. 93–95.

8. Marriner S. Eccles, *Beckoning Frontiers* (New York, 1951), p. 75; Thomas Cochran and William Miller, *The Age of Enterprise: A Social History of Industrial America* (New York, 1942), pp. 313–15.

9. Robert Sobel, *The Great Bull Market: Wall Street in the 1920s* (New York, 1968), p. 74.

10. Willard L. Thorp, "The Persistence of the Merger Movement," *American Economic Review*, March 1931, Supplemental Issue, XXI, no. 1, p. 85.

11. Marcus Nadler, *Corporate Consolidations and Reorganizations* (New York, 1930), pp. 12–13. Nadler, a perceptive contemporary student of Wall Street, wrote: "From the bankers' viewpoint, there is a powerful incentive to promote consolidation. The banker has access to the capital market which is often indispensable to the accomplishment of a business combination."

12. Samuel Richardson Reid, *Mergers, Managers, and the Economy* (New York, 1968), p. 56.

13. "Amounts of Issues by Dillon, Read & Co. and predecessor by years," Memo prepared for congressional investigation, 1933, in Dillon Read files.

14. United States, *Historical Statistics of the United States* (1975), II, 1006.

15. Clarence Dillon Diary, May 20, 1919.

16. *New York Times*, January 4, 1922.

17. *New York Times*, December 2, 1921; *Iron Age*, December 8, 1921; "Theodore Chadbourne," *National Cyclopaedia of American Biography*, XXX, 308; Mark Reutter, *Sparrows Point: Making Steel—The Rise and Ruin of American Industrial Might* (New York, 1988), pp. 163–64.

18. *New York Times*, January 10, 1922.

19. *New York Times*, May 17–23, 1922.

20. Clarence Dillon Diary, April 15, 1922; *New York Times*, August 2, 1923.

21. *New York Times*, July 7, 1922; *Moody's Industrial Manual, 1922*, p. 568.

22. Clarence Dillon Diary, March 7, 1923.

23. *New York Times*, August 3, 1923.

24. In early April Dillon managed to find time to meet with a group at the Harvard Business School that asked him to help raise funds for research there on the investments business. Specifically, Dillon was asked to raise $5,000 a year for three years. An additional $15,000 per annum would be collected in other cities. "I said I did not think there was any need for such sums as there was no mystery to the investment banking picture and one man could probably collect all the information there was in a year, although it is possible that I did not fully appreciate the scope of their work and it might take more money than I thought." Clarence Dillon Diary, April 5, 1923.

25. William L. Wilson, *Full Faith and Credit: The Story of C.I.T. Financial Corporation, 1908–1975* (New York, 1976), pp. 102–6, 120; security offering, by Dillon, Read & Co. January 1921 through March 1930.

26. Forrestal evidently did not believe this was a prudent policy. He added, "That was the time when the theory of investment in common stocks was not quite so prevalent as it is today—probably it is too prevalent today." Forrestal in *Record of Addresses to General Sales Meeting Held January 6–7, 1928.*

27. In 1929 insiders received reserved shares in a Standard Brands flotation. Among these were Bernard Baruch (4,000), Senator William G. McAdoo (1,000), and Ambassador Norman Davis (500). Former President Calvin Coolidge, the sole of rectitude, was allocated 3,000 on this underwriting. John Brooks, *Once in Golconda: A True Drama of Wall Street, 1920–1938* (New York, 1969), pp. 187–88; United States, Senate, 73rd Cong., 1st sess. *Stock Exchange Practices*, pt. 4, Dillon, Read & Co., October 3–13, 1933, pp. 173–74. Ferdinand Pecora, *Wall Street Under Oath: The Story of Our Modern Money Changers* (New York, 1939), pp. 201–2.

28. Pecora, *Wall Street Under Oath*, pp. 28–30.

29. Ibid., pp. 29–30.

30. Joseph Brandes, *Herbert Hoover and Economic Diplomacy* (Pittsburgh, 1962), p. 15.

31. Theodore J. Grayson, *Investment Trusts: Their Origin, Development, and Operation* (New York, 1928), p. 136.

32. Ibid., pp. 138–39.

33. Hugh Bullock, *The Story of Investment Companies* (New York, 1959), p. 20; Joel Seligman, *The Transformation of Wall Street: A History of the Securities and Exchange Commission and Modern Corporate Finance* (Boston, 1982), p. 223.

34. Securities and Exchange Commission, "Analysis of Questionnaire of United States and Foreign Securities Corporation" (1937), p. 18.

35. Ibid., p. 64; Proctor W. Hansl, *Years of Plunder: A Financial Chronicle of Our Times* (New York, 1935), p. 252; Frederick Lewis Allen, *The Lords of Creation* (London, 1935), pp. 342–43.

36. Hansl, *Years of Plunder*, p. 254.

37. The best source for the flotation and history of US&FS in the 1920s is United States, Senate, 73rd Cong., 1st sess., *Stock Exchange Practices*, pt. 4, Dillon, Read & Co., October 3–13, 1933. Much of what follows regarding US&FS is drawn from testimony during this period, especially that of Clarence Dillon and James Forrestal.

38. The preferred dividends were paid, but U.S. & Foreign did not make a disbursement to holders of the common in that decade. Even so, owners of the common were well rewarded. The shares reached a high of 72 in 1929. Pecora, *Wall Street Under Oath*, p. 210.

39. This matter was raised later at a 1937 SEC investigation, and a document generated by Dillon Read in response to questions posed by the commission is in the Dillon Read files, and is entitled: "Analysis of Questionnaire of United States and Foreign Securities." On page 16 is found this statement: The trust "agreed to subscribe to approximately 25% ($2,700,000) of the $10,800,000 initial issue of capital stock of American and Continental Corporation, and to invest approximately $2,500,000 in the securities of Brooklyn Edison Company, Continental and Commercial Trust and Savings Bank (Chicago), General Electric Company, Central Union Trust Company (New York), and First National Bank (New York)." It should be added, however, that someone at Dillon Read wrote at the bottom of the page of his copy, "Simply without foundation in fact—was of no interest whatever to DR & Co.—nothing to disclose." The commission

probably obtained its information from news stories. See *New York Times*, October 21, 1924.

40. United States, Securities and Exchange Commission, "Summary and Comparative Analysis of Questionnaires of United States and Foreign Securities Corporation and United States and International Securities Corporation," typescript in the possession of Dorothy Dillon Eweson.

41. Ibid., p. 282.

42. *New York Times*, January 1, 1926.

43. At a 1928 meeting, Dillon revealed, "We have an inventory of securities on our balance sheet of approximately $35 million. That is divided between bank stocks, of which we have about 22 percent; railroads, 19 percent; public utilities, 11 percent; industrial stocks, 40 percent; other securities, 5 percent; and bonds, 3 percent. So that today we have about 95 percent—a little over—of our capital invested in equities rather than in bonds. . . ." Dillon in *Record of Addresses to General Sales Meeting Held January 6–7, 1928*.

44. *New York Times* and *New York World*, October 14, 1924; Robert W. Dunn, *American Foreign Investments* (New York, 1926), p. 54; Grayson, *Investment Trusts*, p. 151.

45. Pecora, *Wall Street Under Oath*, pp. 210–12.

46. "Analysis of Questionnaire of United States and Foreign Securities," p. 44.

47. Dean Mathey, *Fifty Years of Wall Street with Anecdotiana* (Princeton, 1966), pp. 14–15.

48. *Moody's Manual of Investments, Utilities*, 1929, pp. 1450–91. When Williams started out with North American in 1924 the value of the outstanding stock was $26 million; by 1929 it was $480 million, and Williams' personal fortune was $680 million. *New York Times*, November 11, 1953.

49. "Analysis of Questionnaire of United States and Foreign Securities," p. 28.

50. Ibid., pp. 42–43. In this instance the SEC appeared to be saying that Dillon Read used US&IS as a dumping ground for what at the time were known as "undigested securities," new issues of stocks and bonds that could not be distributed at the offered prices. Yet Dillon Read did no business in the 1920s with the Pennsylvania Railroad, Southern Pacific, St. Louis-San Francisco, or the Chicago, Rock Island & Pacific. In addition, the Commission's report mangled the name of German Investment & Credit into "German Credit & Investment."

51. Pecora, *Wall Street Under Oath*, pp. 213–14; Vincent Carosso, *Investment Banking in America* (Cambridge, Mass., 1970), pp. 345–46.

Chapter 6

1. Irving Fisher, "Reciprocal Influences Between America and Europe," *Annals of the American Academy of Political and Social Science*, July 1923, p. 171.

2. Max Winkler, "Government Foreign Loans," *Annals of the American Academy of Political and Social Science*, July 1928, p. 3.

3. Quoted in Herbert Feis, *The Diplomacy of the Dollar: First Era, 1919–1932* (Baltimore, 1950), p. 6.

4. Clarence Dillon Diary, April 14, 1919.
5. Dillon, Read & Co., *Record of Addresses to General Sales Meeting Held January 6–7, 1928*, in the possession of Dorothy Dillon Eweson.
6. *New York Times*, September 16, 1921.
7. [London] *Sunday Referee*, June 30, 1929.
8. Carlos Marichal, *A Century of Debt Crises in Latin America* (Princeton, 1989), p. 182.
9. Ibid., p. 254.
10. *Record of Addresses to General Sales Meeting Held January 6–7, 1928*.
11. Ibid.; Marichal, *A Century of Debt Crises in Latin America*, pp. 251–52.
12. Frank J. Williams, "A New Leader in Finance: Clarence Dillon," *Review of Reviews*, February 1926, p. 147; Dillon, Read & Co., "Securities Offerings by Dillon, Read & Co., Years 1921–1927," March 1, 1928.
13. Dillon, Read & Co., Inc.: International Investment Bankers (1977).
14. In 1921 the index for manufacturing (1913 = 100) for the Soviet Union was 23, the United Kingdom 55, France 61, and Germany 75. League of Nations, *Industrialization and Foreign Trade* (New York, 1945), p. 134, as cited in Mira Wilkins, *The Maturing of Multinational Enterprise* (Cambridge, Mass., 1974), p. 51.
15. Clarence Dillon Diary, October 9, 1919.
16. Clarence Dillon Diary, October 9 and October 31, 1919.
17. "Securities Offerings by Dillon, Read & Co., Years 1921–1927"; *New York Times*, January 28, 1928.
18. Harold van B. Cleveland and Thomas F. Huertas, *Citibank, 1812–1970* (New York, 1985), p. 148.
19. The actual figure was 132 billion gold marks, which given the exchange rates of the time worked out to $33 billion. Bascom N. Timmons, *Portrait of an American: Charles G. Dawes* (New York, 1953), p. 216.
20. Charles G. Dawes, *A Journal of Reparations* (London, 1939), pp. 284–91; Timmons, *Dawes*, pp. 215–26; Ferdinand Eberstadt to Robert O. Hayward, October 3, 1927, on deposit at Princeton University.
21. *New York Times*, May 31, 1925.
22. James Forrestal in *Record of Addresses to General Sales Meeting Held January 6–7, 1928*.
23. "Underwritings, 1920–1930," in the Dillon Read files.
24. Theodore J. Grayson, *Investment Trusts: Their Origin, Development, and Operation* (New York, 1928), p. 184.
25. Gustav Stresemann, *Essays and Speeches on Various Subjects* (Freeport, N.Y., 1968 reprint edition), p. 192.
26. William C. McNeil, *American Money and the Weimar Republic* (New York, 1986), p. 71.
27. Ibid., pp. 71–73.
28. Clarence Dillon Diary, December 16, 1924.
29. The issue was a success, Thyssen using the proceeds to consolidate old debts and add to working capital. McNeil, *American Money and the Weimar Republic*, pp. 73–74.
30. James Forrestal comments in *Record of Addresses to General Sales Meeting Held on January 6–7, 1928*.

31. McNeil, *American Money and the Weimar Republic*, p. 73.

32. "Ferdinand Eberstadt," *Fortune*, April 1939, p. 72.

33. Robert C. Perez with Edward F. Willett, *The Will to Win: A Biography of Ferdinand Eberstadt* (Westport, Conn., 1989), pp. 15–29.

34. Ibid., p. 30.

35. *New York Times*, March 2, 1922; Calvin Christman, "Ferdinand Eberstadt and Economic Mobilization for War," Ph.D. dissertation, Ohio State University, 1971, p. 12.

36. "Securities Offerings by Dillon, Read & Co., Years 1921–1930."

37. Robert W. Dunn, *American Foreign Investments* (New York, 1926), pp. 145–47; *New York Times*, July 28, 1925, August 18, 1926.

38. Eric Sutton, ed. and trans., *Gustav Stresemann: His Diaries, Letters, and Papers* (London, 1937), II, 415–17.

39. Christman, "Ferdinand Eberstadt and Economic Mobilization for War," pp. 13–14.

40. Perez, *The Will to Win*, p. 25.

41. Gustav Stresemann, *Stresemann: His Diaries, Letters and Papers* (Bonn, 1931), p. 55.

42. Ferdinand Eberstadt to Clarence Dillon, October 31, 1926, in the possession of Dorothy Dillon Eweson.

43. Ferdinand Eberstadt to Clarence Dillon, November 4, 1926, on deposit at Princeton University.

44. Ferdinand Eberstadt to Robert O. Hayward, October 3, 1927.

45. Ferdinand Eberstadt to James Forrestal, November 24, 1927.

46. Ferdinand Eberstadt to Clarence Dillon, November 20, 1926.

47. Ferdinand Eberstadt to Robert O. Hayward, November 4, 1927.

48. *New York Times*, May 17 and June 26, 1926.

49. James Forrestal in *Record of Addresses to General Sales Meeting Held on January 6–7, 1928*.

50. Feis, *Diplomacy of the Dollar*, pp. 11–14; Cleveland and Huertas, *Citibank*, p. 147.

51. The source for information regarding Dillon's French mission is an unsigned ten-page, single-spaced memorandum in the Dillon Read files.

52. Thomas Lamont to Clarence Dillon, May 14, 1926, in the possession of Dorothy Dillon Eweson.

53. Clarence Dillon to Thomas Lamont, May 26, 1926, in the possession of Dorothy Dillon Eweson.

54. The following episode is related in Ferdinand Eberstadt, "Draft Memorandum," June 29, 1929, in the possession of Dorothy Dillon Eweson.

55. Clarence Dillon to Montague Norman, June 5, 1926, and accompanying memorandum, in possession of Dorothy Dillon Eweson.

56. *New York Times*, January 28, April 20, 1928.

57. Cleveland and Huertas, *Citibank*, p. 146.

58. Ferdinand Eberstadt in *Record of Addresses to General Sales Meeting Held January 6–7, 1928*.

59. Leon Trotzky [*sic*], "Trotzky Calls Dillon Cecil Rhodes of U.S.," *Los Angeles Examiner*, March 31, 1928.

60. Rudolph Hilferding to Clarence Dillon, December 17, 1929, in possession of Dorothy Dillon Eweson.
61. McNeil, *American Money and the Weimar Republic*, p. 259.
62. Ibid., p. 269.

Chapter 7

1. Interview of Tom Blacke by Charles Murphy, June 1983.
2. C. B. Glasscock, *The Gasoline Age* (Indianapolis, 1937), p. 197.
3. Lawrence Seltzer, *A Financial History of the American Automobile Industry* (Boston, 1928), p. 240.
4. Quoted in Richard Crabb, *Birth of a Giant: The Men and Incidents That Gave America the Motorcar* (Philadelphia, 1970), pp. 342–53.
5. Ibid., p. 355.
6. Jerry Heasley, *The Production Figure Book for U.S. Cars* (Osceola, Wis., 1977), pp. 23, 33, 117.
7. *Moody's Manual of Investments, 1925*, p. 2050.
8. Glasscock, *The Gasoline Age*, pp. 197–200; Michael Moritz and Barrett Seaman, *Going for Broke: The Chrysler Story* (New York, 1981), p. 37.
9. Glasscock, *The Gasoline Age*, p. 249.
10. "An Investment Study of a Utility Motor Business," Dodge Brothers, Inc., 1925, p. 4.
11. Franklin K. Sprague, "Main Street Goes Shopping in Wall Street," *Success*, June 1925, p. 16; New York Stock Exchange, Committee on Stock List, "Dodge Brothers, Inc.," 1925, p. 3; Crabb, *Birth of a Giant*, p. 374.
12. Glasscock, *The Gasoline Age*, p. 211.
13. NYSE, "Dodge Brothers," p.4.
14. According to one newspaper report the company was offered to Henry Ford, who wasn't interested. However, this seems unlikely. *Detroit News*, April 1, 1925, as referred to in Seltzer, *Financial History*, p. 241.
15. Dean Mathey, *Fifty Years of Wall Street with Anecdotiana* (Princeton, 1966), p. 13; *New York Times*, November 16, 1967.
16. Clarence Dillon Diary, April 28 and June 5, 1919.
17. Glasscock, *The Gasoline Age*, p. 249.
18. Frederick Haynes memo, June 5, 1925.
19. Seltzer, *Financial History*, p. 223.
20. Alfred D. Chandler, Jr., *Pierre Du Pont and the Making of the Modern Corporation* (New York, 1971), p. 578.
21. Sprague, "Main Street Goes Shopping in Wall Street," p. 16.
22. According to testimony in 1933, in 1930 Dillon Read had capital of $14.7 million. Company records indicate that during the mid-1920s, the capital was around $5 million. United States Senate Committee on Banking and Currency, *Stock Exchange Practices* (Washington, D.C., 1934), pt. 4, pp. 2160–61; transcript in possession of Mrs. Dorothy Dillon Eweson.
23. "Group Agreement—Dodge Brothers Memorandum No. 3," December 9, 1925, in possession of Dorothy Dillon Eweson.
24. As has been noted, investors purchased shares in the trust in the expec-

tation of being cut in on Dillon's deals. This was one of the first examples of how US&FS benefited from the connection with Dillon Read.

Later that year there was some question regarding the precise date the Group assumed ownership of Dodge Brothers. The Dillon Read counsel argued for May 1, but conceded others might conclude it was April 8, when the syndicate was sold its shares on a "when, as, and if" basis. This was of great concern to Group members, since it affected their tax liabilities, though of less interest in terms of understanding the nature of the transaction. In the opinion, the Dillon Read counsel stated, "The Group was formed for the purpose of endeavoring to purchase all or a part of the assets and/or the stock of Dodge Brothers, and to dispose of the same at a profit to the Group." "Group Agreement—Dodge Brothers Memorandum No. 3."

25. *New York Times*, April 4, 1925. Future historian Matthew Josephson, who was a broker at the time, recalled the doubt expressed by several of his colleagues regarding the soundness of the stock, and their belief Dillon Read had obtained a tremendous profit by selling the securities at inflated prices. "In our board room I heard the veteran traders discussing the $37.5 million 'whack' that had gone to the Dillon, Read syndicate, describing it as 'pure water.' " Matthew Josephson, *The Money Lords* (New York, 1972), pp. 18–19.

26. "Dodge Brothers Inc. . . . Originating Profits," document in Dillon Read files.

27. "Group Agreement—Dodge Brothers Memorandum No. 3," December 12, 1925.

28. Ferdinand Pecora, *Wall Street Under Oath: The Story of Our Modern Money Changers* (New York, 1939), p. 49.

29. A. Newton Plummer, *The Great American Swindle, Inc.* (New York, 1932) pp. 258–63.

30. There is no history of National Cash Register, and biographies and special studies are outdated and inadequate. The best source for this period is Stanley C. Allyn, *My Half Century With N.C.R.* (New York, 1967), especially pp. 48–61.

31. Ibid., p. 57. Of course, this was not the case. In the Goodyear refinancing Dillon insisted on ousting Seiberling and putting in his own management team. The two situations were quite different. In addition, one would have expected Allyn to have referred to the Dodge deal as well, since it was the most sensational of the past few years.

32. "Again, Dillon," *Time*, January 11, 1926, p. 27; Behr Deposition in *U.S. v. Henry S. Morgan et al.*, p. 9.

33. *New York Times*, January 5, 1926.

34. *New York Times*, January 2 and 3, 1926. There might have been some substance to this rumor. Shortly before the restructuring negotiations began NCR was accused of patent infringements by Remington Cash Register, a subsidiary of Remington Arms, and a takeover would have obviated legal action. Unsigned memorandum to National Cash Register, February 15, 1926, in the possession of Dorothy Dillon Eweson.

35. *New York Times*, January 4, 5, 1926; [Dayton, Ohio] *Herald*, January 5, 1926.

36. "Amounts of Issues by Dillon Read & Co. and predecessor by Years."

37. *New York Times* and [Philadelphia] *Public Ledger and North American,* January 4, 1926.

38. Frank J. Williams, "A New Leader in Finance: Clarence Dillon," *Review of Reviews,* February 1926, p. 146.

39. Theodore M. Knappen, "Dillon: Wall Street's New Leader," *The Magazine of Wall Street,* January 30, 1926, p. 607.

40. *Hartford Daily Courant,* January 6, 1926.

41. *New York Times,* April 17, 1926.

42. *New York Times,* June 23, 1940.

43. *New York Times,* December 29 and December 30, 1925; *The New York Herald and New York Tribune,* December 29, 1925; *The Japan Advertiser,* December 31, 1925; *Washington Post,* December 30, 1925.

Chapter 8

1. This was the situation in the 1920s, and continues to this day. "So important to some firms is upward progress in the hierarchy that, according to newspaper reports, the managing partner of a well-known house fatally shot himself when he learned that his firm was being denied what he considered its rightful bracket position in an important syndicated issue." Samuel L. Hayes III, "Investment Banking: Power Structure in Flux," *Harvard Business Review,* March–April 1971, p. 142.

2. Robert Lovett Interview by Charles Murphy, n.d.

3. Arthur Krock as quoted in a forthcoming biography of Forrestal by Forrest Pogue and Douglas Brinkley.

4. August Belmont Interview, January 26, 1988.

5. Walter Isaacson and Evan Thomas, *The Wise Men: Six Friends and the World They Made* (New York, 1986), p. 483.

6. Douglas Brinkley Interview, September 9, 1988.

7. "Vermilye & Co.—William A. Read & Co.—Dillon, Read & Co," p. 7.

8. Wesley Stanger, Jr., Interview, January 17, 1989.

9. Ibid.

10. Karl Behr Deposition in U.S. v. Henry S. Morgan et al., p. 4.

11. C. Douglas Dillon Interview, October 28, 1987.

12. Ibid.

13. According to Douglas Dillon, "Dillon Read always paid rather small salaries, and the partners made their money out of percentage. They all made very good money." Ibid.

14. Wesley Stanger, Jr., Interview, January 17, 1989.

15. "Amounts of Issues by Dillon, Read & Co. and predecessor by Years."

16. C. Douglas Dillon Interview, September 21, 1988.

17. United States, 72nd Cong., 1st sess., Hearings before the Committee on Finance, United States Senate, January 4–7, 1932, "Sales of Foreign Bonds or Securities in the United States," pp. 502–6.

18. Richard Crabb, *Birth of a Giant: The Man and Incidents that Gave America the Motorcar* (Philadelphia, 1970), p. 424.

19. Dodge Brothers, "Dodge Brothers Works," 1925, p. 2.

20. Motor Vehicle Manufacturers Association of the United States, Inc., *Automobiles of America* (Detroit, 1974), p. 85.

21. *New York Times*, April 21, 1925; *Wall Street Journal*, April 22, 1925.

22. "Extracts from Mr. E. G. Wilmer's Address to Dillon, Read & Co.'s Sales Organization," April 18, 1925, in Dillon Read files.

23. Wilmer resigned his post at Goodyear on May 18, at which time Paul Litchfield was elevated to the Goodyear presidency. *New York Times*, May 19, 1925.

24. *Time*, March 22, 1926, p. 36.

25. R. P. Thomas, "Style Change and the Automobile Industry During the Roaring Twenties," in L. P. Cain and P. J. Uselding, *Business Enterprise and Economic Change* (Kent, Ohio, 1973), pp. 130–34.

26. E. G. Wilmer, "Address to Dodge Brothers Dealers," January 1927, in Dillon Read files.

27. Wilmer remained a member of the C.I.T. board while serving as Dodge's president. William L. Wilson, *Full Faith and Credit: The Story of C.I.T. Financial Corporation, 1908–1975* (New York, 1976), p. 361.

28. Wilmer, "Address to Dodge Brothers Dealers."

29. "Record of Addresses to General Sales Meeting Held January 6–7, 1928," in Dillon Read file.

30. Michael Moritz and Barrett Seaman, *Going for Broke: The Chrysler Story* (New York, 1981), p. 37.

31. *Detroit Times*, April 14, 1926.

32. C. B. Glasscock, *The Gasoline Age* (Indianapolis, 1937), p. 249.

33. Ed Cray, *Chrome Colossus: General Motors and Its Times* (New York, 1980), p. 258.

34. Alexander Lurkis, *The Power Brink: Con Edison, a Centennial of Electricity* (New York, 1982), pp. 40–41; "The New Deal-Maker at an Old-Guard Firm," *Business Week*, July 12, 1976, p. 46.

35. Moritz and Seaman, *Going for Broke*, p. 26.

36. Walter Chrysler, in collaboration with Boyden Sparkes, *Life of an American Workman* (New York, 1937), pp. 176–90; Theodore F. MacManus and Norman Beasley, *Men, Money, and Motors* (New York, 1929), p. 257.

37. Cray, *Chrome Colossus*, pp. 258–59.

38. Clarence Dillon Diary, February 18–25, 1924.

39. This episode is related in Chrysler, *Life of an American Workman*, pp. 192–95. There is no other source for the events related here.

40. On June 14, 1928, Moody's Investor Services recommended Dodge shareholders accept the offer, writing:

In connection with this same public announcement, earnings of the two companies for the first four months of the year indicated earnings of approximately $1.10 a share on Chrysler corporation common stock for the month of April compared with earnings of approximately $1 a share on Dodge preference stock for the same month. In other words, from the standpoint of current earning-power as well as financial strength, which factors are probably by far the most important in the case of an automobile company, the comparison is quite in favor of Chrysler corporation.

41. *New York Herald Tribune*, July 23, 1928; Arnold A. Rogow, *James Forrestal: A Study of Personality, Politics, and Policy* (New York, 1963), p. 82.
42. *New York Times*, July 31, 1928.
43. Chrysler, *Life of an American Workman*, p. 225. According to another account, the actual words were, "Mr. Dillon, our executives took possession of the plant last night and are operating it this morning. We are grateful but it will not be necessary to call upon your executives," which is not substantially different from Chrysler's saltier version. MacManus and Beasley, *Men, Money, and Motors*, pp. 258–59.
44. *Moody's Manual of Investments, 1927*, p. 49; *Moody's Manual of Investments, 1928*, p. 1134; Moritz and Seaman, *Going for Broke*, pp. 35–36.
45. Arthur Schlesinger, Jr., *The Age of Roosevelt: The Crisis of the Old Order, 1919–1933* (Boston, 1957), p. 157.
46. Crabb, *Birth of a Giant*, p. 426.
47. Chrysler, *Life of an American Workman*, pp. 196–97. If Dillon and Chrysler entertained hard feeling toward one another it could not be seen in their relationships afterwards. Chrysler became a director of American & Foreign Securities, an honorary position that paid $5,000 a year. Since Chrysler rarely attended meetings, it was calculated that he received $1,000 an hour for his services there. This was a petty matter, but one that captured public attention in the antibusiness atmosphere of the 1930s. *New York Times*, February 13, 1937.

Chapter 9

1. Cary Reich, *Financier: The Biography of André Meyer* (New York, 1983), p. 60.
2. Quoted in Robert C. Perez, *The Will to Win: A Biography of Ferdinand Eberstadt* (Westport, Conn., 1989), p. 39.
3. Ibid., pp. 32–33.
4. Ibid., p. 43; Dean Mathey, *Fifty Years of Wall Street with Anecdotiana* (Princeton, 1966). One of Eberstadt's biographers, Calvin Christman, interviewed three people who had worked with the financier throughout his career. All stated he left Dillon Read because of Dillon's reluctance to provide him with a larger percent of the profits. Other sources indicate the sale of his partnership netted Eberstadt between $2 and $3 million. Calvin Christman, "Ferdinand Eberstadt and Economic Mobilization for War," Ph.D. dissertation, Ohio State University, 1971, pp. 17–18.
5. Marcus Gleisser, *The World of Cyrus Eaton* (New York, 1965), pp. 40–41.
6. Ibid., pp. 26, 110; Robert Sobel, *The Great Bull Market: Wall Street in the 1920s* (New York, 1968), p. 115.
7. Barrie A. Wigmore, *The Crash and Its Aftermath* (Westport, Conn., 1985), pp. 93, 118.
8. Robert Sobel, *Panic on Wall Street* (New York, 1968), p. 381.
9. U.S. Senate Subcommittee of Committee on Banking and Currency, *Stock Exchange Practices* (Washington, D.C., 1934), pt. 4, Dillon Read & Co., October 3–13, 1933, p. 192.

10. Wigmore, *The Crash and Its Aftermath*, pp. 204–05.

11. Carlos Marichal, *A Century of Debt Crises in Latin America* (Princeton, 1989), p. 203.

12. Wigmore, *The Crash and Its Aftermath*, pp. 195–96, 205, 288, 291, 668.

13. "Supporting Data for Chart Entitled: Relation of Capital Issues Offered and Managed by Dillon, Read & Co. to Total Capital Issues Offered in the United States," prepared for the Senate Committee on Banking and Currency's 1933 examination of *Stock Exchange Practices*, in Dillon Read files.

14. "Suggested General Statement," text of introductory statement for *Stock Exchange Practices*, p. 2, in Dillon Read files.

15. Paul Nitze Interview, April 10, 1988.

16. John Train, *The New Money Masters* (New York, 1989), p. 189.

17. Paul Nitze Interview, April 10, 1988.

18. "Schedule, Answers to Question No. 14," for *Stock Exchange Practices*, pp. 1–2, in Dillon Read files.

19. "Minutes, Dillon, Read & Co.," August 19, 1929–December 15, 1930, in the possession of Dorothy Dillon Eweson.

20. Ibid., October 3, 1929. Shields, a tough Montanan, was one of Forrestal's closest friends. When Forrestal learned of deals too small for Dillon Read he would turn them over to Shields. Henry Merritt Interview, December 13, 1982.

21. In a memo prepared for Dillon Read when facing congressional investigation, Ivy Lee, at the time considered the nation's premiere public relations expert, wrote, "Now, a trading account, or *pool* account was formed with Dominick & Dominick January 11 and ran until June 22, 1925." "United States & Foreign," memorandum in Dillon Read files.

22. "Schedule, Answers to Question No. 14," for *Stock Exchange Practices*.

23. Document in Dillon Read files.

24. Wigmore, *The Crash and Its Aftermath*, p. 141.

25. "Schedule, Answers to Question No. 14," for *Stock Exchange Practices*.

26. United States, *Historical Statistics of the United States* (1975) I, 126, 224.

27. United States, 73rd Cong., 2nd Sess., Senate, Report No. 1455, "Stock Exchange Practices Report," p. 7; Joel Seligman, *The Transformation of Wall Street: A History of the Securities and Exchange Commission and Modern American Corporate Finance* (Boston, 1982), pp. 1–2.

28. Seligman, *The Transformation of Wall Street*, pp. 1–2.

29. "Suggested General Statement," for *Stock Exchange Practices*.

30. Vincent Carosso, *More than a Century of Investment Banking: The Kidder, Peabody & Co. Story* (New York, 1979), pp. 76–77.

31. Wigmore, *The Crash and Its Aftermath*, pp. 238–39.

32. *New York World Telegram*, December 13, 1933.

33. Wesley Stanger, Jr., Interview, January 17, 1989.

34. The *New York Herald* (European edition of the *New York Herald Tribune*), May 14, 1932.

Chapter 10

1. "Dillon, Read & Co. Association & Corporation, December 31, 1932," in Dillon Read files.

Notes 379

2. William H. Harbaugh, *Lawyer's Lawyer: The Life of John W. Davis* (New York, 1973), pp. 318–19.
3. Vincent Carosso, *Investment Banking in America* (Cambridge, Mass., 1970), p. 323.
4. Joel Seligman, *The Transformation of Wall Street: A History of the Securities and Exchange Commission and Modern Corporate Finance* (Boston, 1982), p. 27. Had Johnson known that from 1906 to 1914 W.M.L. Fiske had served as consul in Chicago for the Peruvian government he doubtless would have raised this issue, but apparently he was not informed of this fact. In any case, Dillon Read had no lead underwriting for that country in the 1920s. Nor did William A. Read & Co. while Fiske was in Peru's employ. "William Mead Lindsley Fiske," *National Cyclopaedia of American Biography*, p. 419.
5. *New York Times*, December 12, 1931.
6. Seligman, *Transformation of Wall Street*, p. 20.
7. Ralph De Bedts, *The New Deal's SEC* (New York, 1964), p. 41; William Leuchtenburg, *Franklin D. Roosevelt and the New Deal* (New York, 1963), pp. 59–60.
8. Harold van B. Cleveland and Thomas F. Huertas, *Citibank, 1812–1970* (New York, 1985), pp. 184–85.
9. *New York Times*, February 25, 27, 28, 1933. That May and June, as Morgan testified and Congress considered securities-related legislation, Mitchell went on trial for criminal acts of tax evasion. He was acquitted on all counts, but the government entered a civil charge and won a judgment of $1.1 million in taxes and penalties. Mitchell appealed the case through the Supreme Court, lost, and made his settlement with the government in 1938. John Kenneth Galbraith, *The Great Crash* (Cambridge, Mass., 1961), pp. 158–59.
10. Ferdinand Pecora, *Wall Street Under Oath* (New York, 1939), p. 5; John Brooks, *Once in Golconda: A True Drama of Wall Street* (New York, 1969), p. 186.
11. U.S. Senate Subcommittee of Committee on Banking and Currency, *Stock Exchange Practices* (Washington, D.C., 1934) pp. 172–75.
12. *New York Times*, May 26, 1933.
13. *New York Times*, May 24, 1933.
14. John T. Flynn, "The Marines Land in Wall Street," *Harpers Magazine*, July 1934, p. 149.
15. Brooks, *Once in Golconda*, p. 191.
16. *New York Times*, March 30, 1933.
17. Joseph Haywood Interview, February 29, 1988.
18. "Confidential: General Memorandum, Based on information given me [Eberstadt] by Striffler in an interview Thursday afternoon, May 4, 1933," dated May 7, 1933. Ferdinand Eberstadt to James Forrestal, June 14, 1933, in the possession of Dorothy Dillon Eweson.
19. Marked-up copies of extracts of testimony, along with responses to Pecora's questions and position papers, are on deposit in the Dillon Read files. Several are marked "Ivy Lee."
20. *New York World Telegram* and *New York Daily News*, both October 3, 1933.
21. U.S. Senate Subcommittee of Committee on Banking and Currency, *Stock Exchange Practices*, pt. 4, Dillon Read & Co., October 3–13, 1933, p. 1671. The

United States Government Printing Office published a transcript of the hearings, but it is an edited version. Dillon Read obtained copies of the original transcript before editing, and these are in the Dillon Read files. Since they are more accurate representations of what actually happened, including as they do off-the-record material, all quotations of testimony are from that source where there is a difference between the two accounts. The unedited transcripts are entitled: "Hearings before the Subcommittee of Committee on Banking and Currency, United States Senate, Banking, Financing and Securities Sales Practices."

22. Ibid. The Dillon-Couzens colloquy is on p. 98 of the transcript.

23. *Stock Exchange Practices*, pt. 4, Dillon Read, pp. 1685–86.

24. The Dillon Read files contain a folder of some four hundred items on the firm's testimony during the investigations in its library.

25. *Christian Science Monitor*, October 5, 1933.

26. *New York World Telegram*, October 5, 1933.

27. Ibid., October 6, 1933.

28. *New York Times*, *Washington Post*, October 3, 1933.

29. *Washington Post*, October 3, 1933.

30. *Stock Exchange Practices*, pt. 4, Dillon Read, p. 1647; *New York World Telegram*, October 4, 1934.

31. *Stock Exchange Practices*, pt. 4, Dillon Read, p. 1658; Harbaugh, *Lawyer's Lawyer*, p. 326.

32. *Washington Evening Star*, October 6, 1933.

33. *Stock Exchange Practices*, pt. 4, Dillon Read, pp. 1647–48; *New York Herald Tribune*, October 6, 1933; *New York Sun* and *New York Times*, October 7, 1933.

34. Seligman, *Transformation of Wall Street*, p. 21; *New York Times*, October 9, 1933.

35. "Investigation: Dillon, Read Probe Draws Senatorial Ire," *Newsweek*, October 21, 1933, p. 22.

36. "The Pecora Hearings," *Newsweek*, October 14, 1933, p. 21.

37. *Stock Exchange Practices*, pt. 4, Dillon Read, p. 1876.

38. "Hearings . . . Banking, Financing and Securities Sales Practices," pp. 635–40.

39. Ibid., p. 1365. Forrestal would be plagued by this for the rest of his life. When a strong anti-Communist as Secretary of Defense, he was attacked vigorously by the pro-Soviet forces. The April 18, 1948, issue of *The Worker Magazine* featured an article by Art Shields entitled "Forrestal Owes You Plenty," with the subheading "Income tax evasion sent Al Capone to prison, but Dillon, Read & Company's man stayed free to join Truman's cabinet and plot profitable war."

40. Ibid., p. 1454.

41. Ibid., pp. 1472–73.

42. Thomas L. Stokes, *Chip Off My Shoulder* (Princeton, 1940), p. 362.

43. Joseph P. Kennedy, *I'm For Roosevelt* (New York, 1936), p. 93.

44. *New York Times*, March 26, 1933; Arthur M. Schlesinger, Jr., *The Coming of the New Deal* (Boston, 1959), p. 439.

Chapter 11

1. United States, *Historical Statistics of the United States* (1975), II, 1104.

2. Ferdinand Pecora, *Wall Street Under Oath: The Story of Our Modern Money Changers* (New York, 1930), pp. 260–62.

3. Samuel O. Rice, "The Investment Bankers Code," *Investment Banking*, September 17, 1934, pp. 300–5; Vincent Carosso, *Investment Banking in America* (Cambridge, Mass., 1979), p. 387.

4. *New York Times*, May 28, 1935.

5. Joel Seligman, *The Transformation of Wall Street: A History of the Securities and Exchange Commission and Modern American Corporate Finance* (Boston, 1982), pp. 111–15.

6. Document in possession of Dorothy Dillon Eweson.

7. *The Federal Reserve Bulletin*, March 1945, p. 254.

8. Wesley Stanger, Jr., Interview, January 17, 1989.

9. C. Douglas Dillon Interview, October 28, 1987.

10. Paul Nitze Interview, November 4, 1981.

11. C. Douglas Dillon Interview, October 28, 1987.

12. "Man with the Purse," *Time*, August 18, 1961, p. 14.

13. John Brooks, *The Takeover Game* (New York, 1987), p. 59.

14. *Historical Statistics of the United States*, II, 1123.

15. John Fowler, Jr., *Revenue Bonds: The Nature, Uses and Distribution of Fully Self-Liquidating Public Loans* (New York, 1938), p. 31.

16. Robert Caro, *The Power Broker: Robert Moses and the Fall of New York* (New York, 1974), pp. 345–46.

17. "August Belmont," in *National Cyclopaedia of American Biography*, Vol. K, 168; Fowler, *Revenue Bonds*, p. 34.

18. John Magrane Interview with Charles Murphy, n.d. Following what then was a Dillon Read tradition, Magrane came to the firm through a familial relationship—he was Ralph Bollard's son-in-law. Wesley Stanger, Jr., Interview, January 17, 1989.

19. *New York Times*, February 1, 1953.

20. *Wall Street Journal*, June 23, 1982.

21. Brooks, *The Takeover Game*, pp. 58–59.

22. United States District Court, New York (Southern District), *Corrected Opinion of Harold R. Medina, United States Circuit Judge, in United States of America v. Henry S. Morgan, Harold Stanley et al. doing business as Morgan Stanley & Co. et al.* (New York, 1954 ed.), pp. 58–63; 88–94; 100–01.

23. *New York Sun*, January 22, 1938; Dillon Read "Partnership Book," 1938–58, in the possession of Dorothy Dillon Eweson.

24. *Historical Statistics of the United States*, I, 595.

25. Malcolm W. H. Peebles, *Evolution of the Gas Industry* (New York, 1980), pp. 55–56.

26. *Wall Street Journal*, April 18, 1940.

27. F. Y. Steiner to Clarence Dillon, November 30, 1937, in the possession of Dorothy Dillon Eweson.

28. Ibid.

29. F. Y. Steiner to Clarence Dillon, November 17, 1937, in the possession of Dorothy Dillon Eweson.

30. "Business Prospects, Dillon Read Paris, December 2, 1937," in the possession of Dorothy Dillon Eweson.

31. Clarence Dillon Diary, in the possession of Dorothy Dillon Eweson.

32. Dillon, "Anne's Story."

33. E. I. Treasure to Clarence Dillon, October 14, 1939, in the possession of Dorothy Dillon Eweson.

34. August Belmont Interview, June 12, 1988; Douglas Dillon Interview, October 28, 1987; "Man with the Purse," p. 13.

35. August Belmont Interview, June 12, 1988; *New York Herald Tribune*, March 17, 1941.

36. "F. H. Brandi, Views in Retrospect & Prospect," p. 18.

37. William O. Douglas, *Democracy and Finance* (New Haven, 1940), pp. 180–82; Carosso, *Investment Banking in America*, p. 383.

38. Seligman, *Transformation of Wall Street*, p. 251.

39. "Dillon Read Underwritings, 1931–1941," document in Dillon Read files.

40. Karl Behr Deposition, *U.S. v. Henry S. Morgan et al.*, pp. 88–91.

41. United States, 76th Cong., 2nd Sess., Hearings Before the Temporary National Economic Committee, Pursuant to Public Resolution No. 113, *Investigation of Concentration of Economic Power* (Washington, D.C., 1940), pt. 24, p. 12629.

42. George Whitney, in *U.S. v. Henry S. Morgan et al.*, "Defendant's Opening—Mr. Whitney," February 20, 1951, p. 3395.

43. *TNEC Hearings*, pt. 24, p. 12630.

44. According to R.G.A. van der Woude, Shell Union's president, "We thought the basis of Dillon, Read was a more acceptable one, and it was logical to do business with our old friends." Ibid., p. 12633. But Dillon Read had conducted only two earlier financings for the Royal Dutch/Shell Group, so they hardly could be considered close.

45. Ibid., pp. 12635–36.

46. Van der Woude testified that "on more than one occasion I pointed out to Dillon Read that we did not look upon them as our permanent banking connection. On two or three occasions I made it quite clear that we considered ourselves entirely free." Ibid., p. 12641.

47. Ibid., pp. 12640, 12924.

48. Ibid., p. 12654.

Chapter 12

1. Paul Nitze Interview, January 12, 1982.

2. Ibid.

3. James Forrestal, *The Forrestal Diaries*, edited by Walter Millis with the collaboration of E. S. Duffield (New York, 1951), p. xxii; Robert H. Connery, *The Navy and the Industrial Mobilization in World War II* (Washington, D.C., 1951), p. 56.

4. Among the honorary pallbearers at his funeral were former President

Hoover, Chief Justice of the Supreme Court Fred Vinson, former Secretaries of State James Byrnes and George Marshall, General Dwight Eisenhower, and from Wall Street, Dillon, Baruch, Eberstadt, Mathey, and Shields. *New York Times,* May 25, 1949.

5. "Partnership Book, 1938–1958," in the possession of Dorothy Dillon Eweson.

6. According to August Belmont, McCain assisted in bringing in underwritings for American Viscose and several other firms. August Belmont Interview, June 12, 1988.

7. *New York Times,* June 23, 1940.

8. *New York Times,* December 14, 1951; Ferdinand Pecora, *Wall Street Under Oath: The Story of Our Modern Money Changers* (New York, 1939), p. 134.

9. U.S. Senate Subcommittee of Committee on Banking and Currency, *Stock Exchange Practices,* pt. 8 (Washington, D.C., 1934), p. 4194.

10. United States, *Historical Statistics of the United States* (1975), I, 135, 224.

11. Charles C. Abbott, *Financing Business During the Transition* (New York, 1946), p. 31.

12. Ibid., p. 101; *New York Times,* January 3, 1943.

13. Robert Sobel, *NYSE: A History of the New York Stock Exchange, 1935–1975* (New York, 1975), p. 127.

14. "Underwritings, 1936–1945," document in Dillon Read files.

15. "August Belmont," *National Cyclopaedia of American Biography,* IV, 212; XI, 499–500; XXXVII, 25–26; Vol. K, 168–69.

16. August Belmont Interview, January 26, 1988.

17. Ibid.

18. Wallace R. Finney and J. B. Adoue, "The 'Big Inch' Pipe Line," *Mining and Metallurgy,* October 1943, p. 442.

19. John W. Frey and H. Chandler Ide, eds., *A History of the Petroleum Administration for War, 1941–1945* (Washington, D.C., 1946), pp. 418–19.

20. Arthur Johnson, *Petroleum Pipelines and Public Policy, 1906–1959* (Cambridge, Mass., 1967), pp. 320–27.

21. United States, 79th Cong., 1st sess., Senate Committee on Military Affairs, *War Emergency Pipe-Line Systems and Other Petroleum Facilities,* Hearings Before the Special Committee Investigating Petroleum Resources and Surplus Property Subcommittee (Washington, D.C., 1945), pp. 251 ff.

22. Finney and Adoue, "The 'Big Inch' Pipe Line," pp. 444–45.

23. For an example of the thinking at the time, consider that in August 1944, Sam G. Spal of the Interstate Commerce Commission assumed a postwar valuation of $60 million for the Big Inch. Allowing an 8 percent return on depreciated investment, he found the cost of moving crude oil from Longview to New York ranged from 16 cents per barrel at full capacity to 25.5 cents at half capacity. Tankers could carry the crude at 18.3 cents per barrel. Sam G. Spal, "War Built Pipe Lines and the Post-War Transportation of Petroleum" (Washington, D.C., 1944), pp. 92–94, as cited in Johnson, *Petroleum Pipelines and Public Policy,* p. 344.

24. Ibid., p. 345.

25. August Belmont Interview, June 12, 1988.

26. Ibid.
27. Johnson, *Petroleum Pipelines and Public Policy*, p. 347; Richard W. Hooley, *Financing the Natural Gas Industry* (New York, 1961), p. 91.
28. August Belmont Interview, June 12, 1988.
29. John Weiss, "The Wall Street Pipe Dream That Paid Off Millions," *P.M.*, November 23, 1947.
30. Hooley, *Financing the Natural Gas Industry*, pp. 92–95.
31. Weiss, "The Wall Street Pipe Dream That Paid Off Millions."
32. "1933–1966, Public Offerings and Private Placements Managed or Co-Managed by Dillon, Read, & Co., Inc.," document in Dillon Read files; Dillon Read, *Annual Review, 1971*, p. 7.

Chapter 13

1. *U.S. v. Henry S. Morgan et al.*, "Defendant's Opening—Mr. Whitney," February 20, 1951, p. 3388.
2. Vincent Carosso, *Investment Banking in America* (Cambridge, Mass., 1970), pp. 437–39.
3. Ibid., pp. 444–46.
4. Among the firm's larger clients during the first two decades after the war would be Black Hills Power & Light, Celanese, CIT, Columbus & Southern Ohio, Copperweld Steel, Hawaiian Electric, National Cash Register, Natural Gas Pipeline, Potomac Electric, Reynolds Metal, Robbins Mills, Southwestern Public Service, Standard Oil of New Jersey, Standard Oil of Indiana, Standard Oil of California, Texaco, Texas Eastern Transmission, Texas Gas Transmission, Trans World Airlines, Union Oil of California, and United Gas. As can be seen from this roster, Dillon Read's corporate clientele included largely utilities, petroleum, natural gas, and pipeline companies.
5. U.S. Senate Subcommittee of Committee on Banking and Currency, *Stock Exchange Practices* (Washington, D.C., 1934), pp. 958–79; Carosso, *Investment Banking in America*, p. 257.
6. "Totals of Participations in Underwritings of Registered Issues and Management of Registered Issues for the years 1938–1946, together with invested capital as of 1945." Document prepared for *U.S. v. Henry S. Morgan et al.*, in Dillon Read files.
7. *Corrected Opinion of Harold Medina in U.S. v. Henry S. Morgan et al.*, p. 94.
8. *U.S. v. Henry S. Morgan et al.*, "Defendants Tables," M-2, 1–2.
9. Dillon Read, *Annual Report, 1971*, p. 6.
10. Of a total of $2.3 billion in industrial bonds underwritten in this period, $824 million were publicly offered. Private placements and term loans constituted $1.5 billion of the total. "Notes on the Statistical Data Contained in the Memoranda to the Attorney General of April 7, 1947," and Allan M. Pope, President of First Boston Corp., to stockholders, November 28, 1947, in Dillon Read files.
11. "The New Deal-Maker at an Old-Guard Firm," *Business Week*, July 12, 1976, p. 47.
12. *U.S. v. Henry S. Morgan et al.* "Complaint," p. 30.

13. Cahill, Gordon, Zachry & Reindel et al., "Memorandum for the Honorable Tom C. Clark, Attorney General of the United States, re: Investment Banking," April 7, 1947, p. 3, in Dillon Read files.

14. *New York Times*, October 31, 1947.

15. Document in the Dillon Read files.

16. Hawthorne Daniel, *Judge Medina* (New York, 1952), p. 5.

17. *U.S. v. Henry S. Morgan et al.*, "Defendants' Opening—Mr. Correa," February 26, 1951, pp. 3650–51.

18. Allan M. Pope to First Boston Stockholders, November 28, 1947.

19. Civil Action No. 43–757. In the District Court of the United States for the Southern District of New York, *U.S. v. Henry S. Morgan et al.*, "Complaint," pp. 2, 10, 20; Carosso, *Investment Banking in America*, p. 52.

20. Carosso, *Investment Banking in America*, p. 473.

21. *New York Times*, February 22, 1951.

22. *U.S. v. Henry S. Morgan et al.*, "Defendants' Opening—Mr. Correa," February 21, 1951, p. 3549.

23. *New York Times*, September 23, 1953.

24. Behr Deposition, U.S. v. Henry S. Morgan et al., p. 13.

25. Ibid., p. 31.

26. *Corrected Opinion of Harold Medina in U.S. v. Henry S. Morgan et al.*, pp. 170–71.

27. Behr Deposition, *U.S. v. Henry S. Morgan et al.*, pp. 30–31.

28. United States, *Historical Statistics of the United States* (1975), I, 911.

29. United States, 87th Cong., 1st sess., Joint Economic Committee, *Variability of Private Investment in Plant and Equipment* (Washington, D.C., 1962), Pt. I, pp. 32, 40–41.

30. Peter F. Drucker, *The Unseen Revolution: How Pension Plan Socialism Came to America* (New York, 1979), pp. 8–11.

31. *Wall Street Journal*, December 22, 1949.

32. August Belmont Interview, June 12, 1988.

33. *New York Times*, December 22, 1949.

34. Edward Cowan, *Oil and Water: The Torrey Canyon Disaster* (Philadelphia, 1968), pp. 21–22; "How Union Oil Director Helped Family, Aides To Profit on Tankers," *Wall Street Journal*, June 13, 1961; "Tanker That Blew Up Provides Insight Into Oil Shipping," *New York Times*, February 15, 1977.

35. *Wall Street Journal*, June 30, 1961.

36. *Wall Street Journal*, December 13, 1962. This was not the end of the story. One of the tankers, *Torrey Canyon*, was wrecked in the English Channel in March 1967, causing the world's greatest oil spill to that time. In December 1976, another Barracuda tanker, *Sansinena*, blew up in Los Angeles harbor. *New York Times*, February 15, 1977.

37. Wesley Stanger, Jr., Interview, January 17, 1989.

38. Their status could be seen in their percentages of profits distributions. While complete records do not exist, one notation indicates that from 1956 through 1958 Brandi's share was 20 percent and Belmont's 10 percent, with the next-largest share being that of DuBois, which was 7 percent. Document in Dillon Read files.

Chapter 14

1. *New York Journal American*, April 23, 1963; *New York Times*, July 12, 1963.
2. "Dillon, Read & Co., Inc., 1962," document in Dillon Read files.
3. *Wall Street Journal*, February 25, 1963.
4. *New York Times*, October 17, 1957.
5. Dillon Read Press Release, January 19, 1960.
6. Dillon, Read & Co., Inc., International Investment Bankers (1977).
7. "[Abner] Kingman Douglass," in *National Cyclopaedia of American Biography*, 58, 710; *New York World Telegram and Sun*, July 15, 1952.
8. C. Douglas Dillon Interview, September 21, 1988.
9. Dillon, Read & Co., Inc., "International Financings," document in Dillon Read files.
10. Jordan Jay Hillman, *The Export-Import Bank at Work* (Westport, Conn., 1982), p. 39.
11. Quoted in Martin Mayer, *The Fate of the Dollar* (New York, 1980), pp. 119–20.
12. Ibid., pp. 121–22.
13. *New York Herald Tribune*, January 15, 1964.
14. Andrew Brimmer and F. R. Dahl, "Growth of American International Banking: Implications for Public Policy," *Journal of Finance*, May 1975, p. 345.
15. David Baron, *The Export-Import Bank: An Economic Analysis* (New York, 1983), pp. 5, 8.
16. *New York Times*, July 20, 1962.
17. United States, *Economic Report of the President, 1982* (Washington, D.C., 1983), p. 346.
18. Howard S. Piquet, *The Export-Import Bank of the United States* (Washington, D.C., 1970), p. 19.
19. "A C.I.T.–Type Operation for the World," *Forbes*, February 1, 1969, p. 22.
20. Ibid., p. 22.
21. *New York Times*, January 8, 1970; Baron, *Export-Import Bank*, p. 16.
22. Hillman, *The Export-Import Bank at Work*, p. 143.
23. Private Export Funding Corporation, *Annual Report, 1989*, p. 3.
24. Anthony Sampson, *The Money Lenders: Bankers in a World of Turmoil* (New York, 1981), p. 110.
25. Michael Moffit, *The World's Money: International Banking from Bretton Woods to the Brink of Insolvency* (New York, 1983), p. 60; R. B. Johnson, *The Economics of the Euro-Market* (New York, 1982), pp. 29–30; Gunter Dufey and Ian Giddy, *The International Money Market* (Englewood Cliffs, N.J., 1978), pp. 214–15.
26. Charles Kelly, Jr., *The Sky's the Limit: The History of the Airlines* (New York, 1963), pp. 180–98; Robert Serling, *Howard Hughes' Airline: An Informal History of TWA* (New York, 1983), p. 236.
27. Kelly, *The Sky's the Limit*, p. 230.

28. David B. Tinnin, *Just About Everybody vs. Howard Hughes* (New York, 1973), p. 41.

29. Ibid., pp. 42–43.

30. Ibid., p. 46.

31. Trans World Airlines, Inc. Prospectus, May 25, 1961; Moody's Investors Service, Inc., *Moody's Transportation Manual*, Supplements, April 12, 1960– January 6, 1961.

32. Serling, *Howard Hughes' Airline*, pp. 248–57.

33. Tinnin, *Just About Everybody vs. Howard Hughes*, pp. 74–78.

34. Serling, *Howard Hughes' Airline*, pp. 268–69.

35. *New York Times*, February 14, 1962.

36. Serling, *Howard Hughes' Airline*, p. 277.

37. Ibid., pp. 274–77.

38. Dillon, Read & Co. Inc., "TWA Financings." Schedule in Dillon Read files.

39. See the advertisement in *Investment Banking and Corporate Financing* (Winter 1968), p. 56.

40. "TWA Discovers How to Make Everybody Happy," *Corporate Financing*, March/April, 1970, p. 11; Trans World Airlines Inc., Plaintiff v. Summa Corporation and William R. Lummis, Delaware Ancillary Administrator of the Estate of Howard R. Hughes, defendants in the Court of Chancery of the State of Delaware in and for New Castle County, Unreported Opinion Submitted October 1, 1985, and Decided, May 15, 1986, in Dillon Read files.

Chapter 15

1. Ken Auletta, *Greed and Glory on Wall Street: The Fall of the House of Lehman* (New York, 1986), p. 141.

2. The ranking was generated by Professor Samuel L. Hayes III, who went on to note, "They [Dillon Read] had a lot more clout than their capital might suggest." *New York Times*, May 6, 1985.

3. Quoted in Chris Welles, *The Last Days of the Club* (New York, 1975), p. 46; "The Toughest Kid in Block Trading," *Business Week*, October 4, 1969, pp. 114–15.

4. John Brooks, *The Takeover Game* (New York, 1987), pp. 70–72; Cary Reich, *Financier: The Biography of André Meyer* (New York, 1983), pp. 230–36.

5. Said Brady, "I don't think it's a heavy dyslexia. It's just something that makes it easier for me to work in a group where there is talking going on rather than reading." Alan Murray, "Treasury Chief Brady, Hardly Quick-Witted, Quickly Tackles Issues," *Wall Street Journal*, April 19, 1989.

6. Arthur Treman Interview, November 30, 1988.

7. Erik Ipsen, "A Kinder, Gentler Treasury Chief," *Institutional Investor*, March 1989, p. 83.

8. "The New Deal-Maker at an Old-Guard Firm," *Business Week*, July 12, 1976, p. 47; John H. Allan, "New Chief of Old-Line Firm," *New York Times*, March 7, 1971. "Just before I went to France his [Brady's] father asked me if I could get him a job, and I said, 'Sure.' " C. Douglas Dillon Interview, September 21, 1988.

9. August Belmont Interview, January 26, 1988.

10. "Brady's Patrons: Contributing Wisdom and Money," *Business Week*, July 12, 1976, p. 49.

11. Howard Gleckman, "The Quiet Crusader," *Business Week*, September 18, 1989, p. 90.

12. Arthur Treman, Jr., Interview, November 30, 1988.

13. Ibid.

14. *Wall Street Journal*, March 10, 1971.

15. What was not generally known outside of the firm was that Brandi's brother had been one of Germany's most decorated submarine commanders during World War II. August Belmont Interview, June 12, 1988.

16. Tristan D'Oelsnitz, "Frederic H. Brandi," "Views in Retrospect and Prospect," *Weekly Bond Buyer for the Capital Market Investor*, March 1, 1971, pp. 18–19, 73.

17. *World Journal Tribune*, February 2, 1967; *Wall Street Journal*, February 2, 1967; *Wall Street Journal*, June 24, 1969.

18. Julie Connelly, "The Statesmen of Dillon Read," *Institutional Investor*, January 1979, p. 40.

19. "Watch Peter Flanigan," *Dun's*, July 1971, p. 72; *New York Times*, January 22, 1975.

20. *Newsday*, June 3, 1970.

21. August Belmont Interview, January 26, 1989.

22. "The New Deal-Maker at an Old-Guard Firm," p. 48.

23. *New York Times*, September 27, 1971; *The Weekly Bond Buyer*, October 4, 1971.

24. Arthur Treman Interview, November 30, 1988.

Chapter 16

1. Moira Johnston, *Takeover: The New Wall Street Warriors: The Men, the Money, the Impact* (New York, 1986), p. 105.

2. "The New Deal-Maker at an Old-Guard Firm," *Business Week*, July 12, 1976, pp. 46, 49.

3. Erik Ipsen, "A Kinder, Gentler Treasury Chief," *Institutional Investor*, March 1989, p. 84.

4. David E. Rosenbaum, "The Treasury's 'Mr. Diffident,' " *New York Times*, November 19, 1989.

5. "Dillon Read Refuses to Play the Game," "*Institutional Investor*, January 1979, p. 42.

6. These directors were: Brady, Douglas Dillon, Arthur Treman, Frederick Cook, Charles P. "Pat" Durkin, William Esrey, John Haskell, and Richard Yancey. *Wall Street Journal*, December 30, 1974. While Douglas Dillon was named a managing director, by then he was no longer regularly involved with the firm's business.

7. Arthur Treman Interview, November 30, 1988.

8. Ipsen, "A Kinder, Gentler Treasury Chief," p. 87.

9. Michael Moffit, *The World's Money: International Banking from Bretton Woods to the Brink of Insolvency* (New York, 1983), pp. 35–40.

10. "A Maverick Pushes into Wall Street's Club," *Business Week*, April 3, 1978, p. 82.

11. Robert Sobel, *Salomon Brothers, 1910–1985* (New York, 1987), p. 124.

12. C. Douglas Dillon Interview, September 21, 1988. Dillon's remarks in this regard jibe with the observations of Dillon Read principals, which I take to be genuine in the absence of hard data.

13. Quoted in Johnston, *Takeover*, p. 108.

14. James Sterngold, "A Comeback for Dillon, Read," *New York Times*, May 6, 1985, p. 6.

15. "The New Deal-Maker at an Old-Guard Firm," pp. 46, 49.

16. Tim Anderson and Stephen Bronte, "The Upheaval at Dillon, Read," *Euromoney*, June 1981, p. 258.

17. Jeannette M. Reddish, "People of the Financial World," *Financial World*, March 12, 1979, p. 44.

18. *U.S. v. Henry S. Morgan, et al.*, "Defendant's Opening—Mr. Correa," p. 3445.

19. *New York Times*, February 21, 1951.

20. William Esrey Interview, October 10, 1988.

21. Ken Auletta, *Greed and Glory on Wall Street: The Fall of the House of Lehman* (New York, 1986), pp. 155–65.

22. Quoted in Connie Bruck, "The Old Boy and the New Boys," *New Yorker*, May 8, 1989, p. 82. On another occasion Gutfreund said, "The world has changed, but Dillon Read continues to be highly reputable." Howard Gleckman, "The Quiet Crusader," *Business Week*, September 18, 1989, p. 90.

23. "The New Deal-Maker at an Old-Guard Firm," p. 48. William A. Read & Co. had conducted trading operations, but Dillon Read, after World War I, had never considered such practices important.

24. Ibid.

25. Arthur Treman, Jr., Interview, December 28, 1988; William Esrey Interview, October 10, 1988.

26. Ibid.

27. Dillon Read, *1972 Annual Review*; *1979 Annual Review*.

28. Chris Welles, *The Last Days of the Club* (New York, 1975), p. 5.

29. Dillon Read, *1977 Annual Review*.

30. Ipsen, "A Kinder, Gentler Treasury Chief," p. 84.

31. Anderson and Bronte, "The Upheaval at Dillon, Read," p. 265.

32. *Wall Street Journal*, October 8, 1979.

33. Dillon Read, *1979 Annual Review*.

34. Anderson and Bronte, "The Upheaval at Dillon, Read," p. 262.

35. "The New Deal-Maker at an Old-Guard Firm," p. 49.

36. Anderson and Bronte, "The Upheaval at Dillon, Read," p. 271.

37. Dillon Read, *1979 Annual Review*.

38. Reddish, "People of the Financial World," p. 44.

Chapter 17

1. "The Statesmen of Dillon Read," *Institutional Investor*, January 1979, p. 45.

2. Tim Anderson and Stephen Bronte, "The Upheaval at Dillon, Read," *Euromoney*, June 1981, p. 266.

3. C. Douglas Dillon Interview, September 21, 1988.

4. Anderson and Bronte, "The Upheaval at Dillon, Read," p. 266.

5. Tim Carrington, *The Year They Sold Wall Street* (New York, 1985), pp. 210–11.

6. Anderson and Bronte, "The Upheaval at Dillon, Read," p. 273.

7. Carrington, *The Year They Sold Wall Street*, p. 211.

8. *Wall Street Journal*, April 30, 1981.

9. C. Douglas Dillon Interview, September 21, 1988.

10. Quoted in Erik Ipsen, "A Kinder, Gentler Treasury Chief," *Institutional Investor*, March 1989, p. 84.

11. Unless otherwise indicated, all material on this topic is derived from "Report of the Business Planning Group," July 15, 1981, in the Dillon Read files.

12. The material in this section is based on SRI International, "A Business Direction for Dillon, Read & Co., Inc.," November 1981.

13. Arthur Treman thought the fact Dillon Read had to seek a new leader from the outside a "terrible, terrible comment on the firm." Ipsen, "A Kinder, Gentler Treasury Chief," p. 84.

14. Dillon Read, *1981 Annual Review*, p. 6.

15. *New York Times*, September 28, 1981.

16. This material derives from a two-page memo, entitled, "DILLON, READ & CO. INC. Elements of a Three-Year Program," on deposit in Dillon Read files.

17. On the other hand, Peter Flanigan, the partner with the most government service, urged Brady to approach Governor Kean and place himself in contention to fill the vacancy.

18. Anderson and Bronte, "The Upheaval at Dillon, Read," p. 273.

19. In the *1983 Annual Review* can be found this item: "Following a transaction with our major shareholder early in the year, management now holds a majority of the capital of the firm for the first time in our recent history. At the same time we are gratified that Sequoia Ventures, Inc. and Skandinaviska Enskilda Banken remain as important shareholders and partners." The process was completed in 1986, when Sequoia sold its last shares to the partners, and except for the minor holding by the Enskilda Bank, Dillon Read was wholly owned by the partners.

Chapter 18

1. Dillon Read, *1983 Annual Review*.

2. Dillon Read, *1989 Annual Review*.

3. Ibid.

4. *Wall Street Journal*, September 24, 1985.

5. Quoted in Neil Osborn, "The Furor Over Shelf Registration," *Institutional Investor*, June 1982, pp. 61–71.

6. Dillon Read, *1982 Annual Review*.

7. *Wall Street Journal*, March 27, 1985.

8. Moira Johnston, *Takeover: The New Wall Street Warriors: The Men, the Money, the Impact* (New York, 1986), p. 48.

9. Ibid., p. 108.

10. *Wall Street Journal*, April 1, 1985.

11. Johnston, *Takeover*, p. 169.

12. Ibid., p. 172.

13. Bryan Burroughs and John Helyar, *Barbarians at the Gate: The Fall of RJR Nabisco* (New York, 1990), pp. 64–65.

14. Ross Johnson, "They Cleaned Our Clock," *Fortune*, January 2, 1989, p. 72.

15. Ibid., p. 73; Proxy Statement, RJR Nabisco, April 5, 1989; p. 40; John Mullin of Dillon Read to Board of Directors, RJR Nabisco, November 30, 1989; Lazard Frères to Board of Directors, RJR Nabisco, November 30, 1989.

16. Burroughs and Helyar, *Barbarians at the Gate*, p. 497.

17. *New York Times*, February 6, 1990, reported that while RJR had reported a predictable loss as a result of the costs associated with the buyout, its cash flow for the year had been $647 million, "more than had been expected at the time of the buyout."

18. Dillon Read, *1981 and 1989 Annual Reviews*.

19. Ibid., p. 12.

20. Dillon, Read Ltd., *Annual Review 1985*.

21. *Annual Review 1987*, p. 7, 22.

22. Martin Roenigk Interview, January 10, 1989. Roenigk noted that Dillon Read might have been targeted sooner, but it was believed the partners had no desire to sell.

23. *New York Times*, June 26, 1989.

Selected Bibliography

Abbott, Charles C. *Financing Business During the Transition*. New York. 1946.

Albion, Robert Greenhalgh, and Connery, Robert Howe. *Forrestal and the Navy*. New York. 1962.

Allen, Frederick Lewis. *The Lords of Creation*. London. 1935.

Allen, Hugh. *The House of Goodyear*. Akron. 1936.

———. *The House of Goodyear*. Cleveland. 1949.

Allyn, Stanley C. *My Half Century With N.C.R.*. New York. 1967.

Anon. *Report on the Fire in the Equitable Building, January 9, 1912*. New York. 1909.

Auerbach, Joseph, and Hayes, Samuel L. III. *Investment Banking and Diligence*. Boston. 1986.

Auletta, Ken, *Greed and Glory on Wall Street: The Fall of the House of Lehman*. New York. 1986.

Bailyn, Bernard, Fleming, Donald, Handlin, Oscar, and Thernstrom, Stephan. *Glimpses of Harvard Past*. Cambridge. 1986.

Barnard, Harry. *Independent Man: The Life of Senator James Couzens*. New York. 1958.

Baron, David. *The Export-Import Bank: An Economic Analysis*. New York. 1983.

Barron, Clarence, and Martin, Joseph G. *The Boston Stock Exchange, With Brief Sketches of Prominent Brokers, Bankers, Banks, and Moneyed Institutions of Boston*. Boston. 1893.

Baruch, Bernard. *Baruch: The Public Years.* New York. 1960.

Beasley, Norman. *Men Working: The Story of Goodyear Tire & Rubber.* New York. 1931.

Brandeis, Louis. *Other People's Money, and How the Bankers Use It.* New York. 1932.

Brandes, Joseph. *Herbert Hoover and Economic Diplomacy.* Pittsburgh. 1962.

Brooks, John. *Once in Golconda: A True Drama of Wall Street, 1920–1938.* New York. 1969.

———. *The Takeover Game.* New York. 1987.

Burroughs, Bryan, and Helyar, John. *Barbarians at the Gate: The Fall of RJR Nabisco.* New York. 1990.

Cain, L. P., and Uselding, P. J. *Business Enterprise and Economic Change.* Kent, Ohio. 1973.

Caro, Robert. *The Power Broker: Robert Moses and the Fall of New York.* New York. 1974.

Carosso, Vincent. *Investment Banking in America.* Cambridge, Mass. 1970.

———. *More than a Century of Investment Banking: The Kidder, Peabody & Co. Story.* New York. 1979.

———. *The Morgans: Private International Bankers, 1854–1913.* Cambridge, Mass. 1987.

Carrington, Tim. *The Year They Sold Wall Street.* New York. 1985.

Catton, Bruce. *War Lords of Washington.* New York. 1948.

Chandler, Alfred D., Jr., *Pierre Du Pont and the Making of the Modern Corporation.* New York. 1971.

Chapman, Stanley. *The Visible Hand: The Managerial Revolution in American Business.* Cambridge, Mass. 1977.

———. *The Rise of Merchant Banking.* London. 1984.

Chevalier, Michel. *Letters from North America.* New York. 1930 ed.

Christman, Calvin. "Ferdinand Eberstadt and Economic Mobilization for War." Ph.D. dissertation, Ohio State University. 1971.

Chrysler, Walter, in collaboration with Boyden Sparkes. *Life of an American Workman.* New York. 1937.

Clarkson, Grosvenor R. *Industrial America in the World War: The Strategy Behind the Line, 1917–1918.* Boston. 1923.

Cleveland, Harold van B., and Huertas, Thomas F. *Citibank, 1812–1970.* New York. 1985.

Cochran, Thomas. *The American Business System: An Historical Perspective.* Cambridge, Mass. 1957.

———, and Miller, William. *The Age of Enterprise: A Social History of Industrial America.* New York. 1942.

Coit, Margaret L. *Mr. Baruch.* Boston. 1957.

Connery, Robert H. *The Navy and the Industrial Mobilization in World War II.* Washington. 1951.

Cowan, Edward. *Oil and Water: The Torrey Canyon Disaster.* Philadelphia. 1968.

Crabb, Richard. *Birth of a Giant: The Men and Incidents that Gave America the Motorcar.* Philadelphia. 1970.

Cray, Ed. *Chrome Colossus: General Motors and Its Times.* New York. 1980.

Crowell, Benedict, and Wilson, Robert. *How America Went to War: The Giant Hand.* New Haven. 1921.

Daniel, Hawthorne. *Judge Medina.* New York. 1952.

Dawes, Charles G. *A Journal of Reparations.* London. 1939.

De Bedts, Ralph. *The New Deal's SEC.* New York. 1964.

Dewing, Arthur S. *Corporate Promotion and Reorganizations.* Cambridge, Mass. 1924.

———. *A History of the National Cordage Company.* Cambridge, Mass. 1913.

Dos Passos, John R. *A Treatise on the Law of Stock-Brokers and Stock-Exchanges.* New York. 1882.

Douglas, William O. *Democracy and Finance.* New Haven. 1940.

Drucker, Peter F. *Adventures of a Bystander.* New York. 1979.

———. *The Unseen Revolution: How Pension Plan Socialism Came to America.* New York. 1979.

Dufey, Gunter, and Giddy, Ian. *The International Money Market.* Englewood Cliffs, N.J. 1978.

Duncan, John. *Travels Through Part of the United States and Canada.* Glasgow. 1832. 2 vols.

Dunn, Robert W. *American Foreign Investments.* New York. 1926.

Eccles, Marriner S. *Beckoning Frontiers.* New York. 1951.

Edwards, George. *Evolution of Finance Capitalism.* New York. 1938.

Eyck, Erich. *A History of the Weimar Republic.* Cambridge, Mass. 1963.

Feis, Herbert. *The Diplomacy of the Dollar: First Era, 1919–1932.* Baltimore. 1950.

Ferris, Paul. *The Master Bankers.* New York. 1984.

Finance and Industry. *The New York Stock Exchange.* New York. 1886.

Financier Company. *History of the New York Stock Exchange, The New York Stock Exchange Directory.* New York. 1887.

Fisher, Irving. "Reciprocal Influences Between America and Europe." *Annals of the American Academy of Political and Social Sciences.* July 1923.

Fite, Emerson. *Social and Economic Conditions in the North During the Civil War.* New York. 1910.

Forrestal, James. *The Forrestal Diaries* (edited by Walter Millis with the collaboration of E. S. Duffield). New York. 1951.

Fowler, John, Jr. *Revenue Bonds: The Nature, Uses and Distribution of Fully Self-Liquidating Public Loans.* New York. 1938.
Frey, John W., and Ide, H. Chandler, eds. *A History of the Petroleum Administration for War, 1941–1945.* Washington, D.C. 1946.
Galbraith, John Kenneth. *The Great Crash.* Cambridge, Mass. 1961.
Gleisser, Marcus. *The World of Cyrus Eaton.* New York. 1965.
Gras, N. S. B. *Business and Capitalism.* New York. 1939.
———, and Larson, Henrietta. *Casebook in American Business History.* New York. 1939.
Grayson, Theodore J. *Investment Trusts: Their Origin, Development, and Operation.* New York. 1928.
Hall, Henry, ed. *America's Successful Men of Affairs: An Encyclopedia of Contemporaneous Biography.* New York. 1895.
Hammond, Paul. *Organizing for Defense: The American Military Establishment in the Twentieth Century.* Princeton. 1965.
Hansl, Proctor W. *Years of Plunder: A Financial Chronicle of Our Times.* New York. 1935.
Harbaugh, William H. *Lawyer's Lawyer: The Life of John W. Davis.* New York. 1973.
Hayes, Samuel L., III. "Investment Banking: Power Structure in Flux." *Harvard Business Review.* March-April 1971.
———. "The Transformation of Investment Banking." *Harvard Business Review.* January-February 1979.
Heasley, Jerry. *The Production Figure Book for U.S. Cars.* Osceola, Wis. 1977.
Hedges, Joseph. *Commercial Banking and the Stock Market Before 1863.* Baltimore. 1938.
Hidy, Ralph. *The House of Baring in American Trade and Finance.* New York. 1949.
Hillman, Jordan Jay. *The Export-Import Bank at Work.* Westport, Conn. 1982.
Hoffman, Paul. *The Dealmakers.* New York. 1980.
Hooley, Richard W. *Financing the Natural Gas Industry.* New York. 1961.
Humphrey, J. A. *Englewood: Its Annals and Reminiscences.* New York. 1899.
Hunt, Bishop Carleton, ed. *Twenty-Five Years of Accounting Responsibility, 1911–1936.* New York. 1937.
Isaacson, Walter, and Thomas, Evan. *The Wise Men: Six Friends and the World They Made.* New York. 1986.
Janeway, Eliot. *The Struggle for Survival.* New Haven. 1951.
Johnson, Arthur. *Petroleum Pipelines and Public Policy, 1906–1959.* Cambridge, Mass. 1967.
Johnson, R. B. *The Economics of the Euro-Market.* New York. 1982.

Johnston, Moira. *Takeover: The New Wall Street Warriors: The Men, the Money, the Impact.* New York. 1986.

Josephson, Matthew. *The Money Lords.* New York. 1972.

Kelly, Charles, Jr. *The Sky's the Limit: The History of the Airlines.* New York. 1963.

Kennedy, Joseph. *I'm For Roosevelt.* New York. 1936.

Kuczynski, Robert R. *Banker Profits from German Loans.* Washington. 1932.

Kuhn, Arthur J. *GM Passes Ford, 1918–1938: Designing the General Motors Performance-Control System.* University Park, Pa. 1986.

Lamoreaux, Naomi. *The Great Merger Movement in American Business, 1895–1904.* New York. 1985.

Lampert, Hope. *Till Death Do Us Part.* New York. 1983.

Lanier, Henry. *A Century of Banking in New York, 1822–1922.* New York. 1922.

Larson, Henrietta. *Fay Cooke: Private Banker.* Cambridge, Mass. 1936.

Leuchtenburg, William. *Franklin D. Roosevelt and the New Deal.* New York. 1963.

Litchfield, Paul. *Industrial Voyage: My Life as an Industrial Lieutenant.* New York. 1954.

Lurkis, Alexander. *The Power Brink: Con Edison, a Centennial of Electricity.* New York. 1982.

MacManus, Theodore F., and Beasley, Norman. *Men, Money, and Motors.* New York. 1929.

McNeil, William C. *American Money and the Weimar Republic.* New York. 1986.

Marcus, Kenneth Karl. *The National Government and the Natural Gas Industry.* New York. 1979.

Marichal, Carlos. *A Century of Debt Crises in Latin America.* Princeton. 1989.

Martin, James Stewart. *All Honorable Men.* Boston. 1950.

Martin, Joseph G. *Seventy-Five Years' History of the Boston Stock Market: From January 1, 1798 to January 1, 1871.* Boston. 1871.

Mathey, Dean. *Fifty Years of Wall Street with Anecdotiana.* Princeton. 1966.

May, George S. *A Most Unique Machine: The Michigan Origins of the American Automobile Industry.* Detroit. 1975.

Mayer, Martin. *The Fate of the Dollar.* New York. 1980.

Michie, R. C. *The London and New York Stock Exchanges, 1850–1914.* London. 1987.

Moffit, Michael. *The World's Money: International Banking from Bretton Woods to the Brink of Insolvency.* New York. 1983.

Moody, John. *The Masters of Capital.* New Haven. 1921.

Moritz, Michael, and Seaman, Barrett. *Going for Broke: The Chrysler Story.* New York. 1981.

Motor Vehicle Manufacturers Association of the United States, Inc. *Automobiles of America.* Detroit. 1974.

Nadler, Marcus. *Corporate Consolidations and Reorganizations.* New York. 1930.

Navin, Thomas R., and Sears, Marian V. "The Rise of a Market for Industrial Securities, 1887–1902." *Business History Review,* XXVII (June 1955), 105–38.

Nelson, Ralph. *Merger Movements in American History: 1895–1956.* Princeton. 1959.

Neuner, Edward J. *The Natural Gas Industry.* Norman, Okla. 1960.

Nevins, Allan, ed. *The Diary of Philip Hone, 1828–1851.* New York. 1927.

North, Douglass. *The Economic Growth of the United States. 1790–1860.* New York. 1960.

Oberholtzer, Ellis P. *Jay Cooke: Financier of the Civil War.* New York. 1907.

O'Reilly, Maurice. *The Goodyear Story.* Elmsford, N.Y. 1983.

Pecora, Ferdinand. *Wall Street Under Oath: The Story of Our Modern Money Changers.* New York. 1939.

Peebles, Malcolm W. H. *Evolution of the Gas Industry.* New York. 1980.

Perez, Robert C., with Edward F. Willett. *The Will to Win: A Biography of Ferdinand Eberstadt.* Westport, Conn. 1989.

Pickens, T. Boone. *Boone.* New York. 1987.

Piquet, Howard S. *The Export-Import Bank of the United States.* Washington, D.C. 1970.

Plummer, A. Newton. *The Great American Swindle, Inc.* New York. 1932.

Porter, Kenneth Wiggins. *John Jacob Astor.* 2 vols. Cambridge, Mass. 1931.

Pratt, Sereno. *The Work of Wall Street.* New York. 1903.

Pusey, Merlo. *Charles Evans Hughes.* 2 vols. New York. 1952.

Ramo, Simon. *The Business of Science: Winning and Losing in the High-Tech Age.* New York. 1988.

Redlich, Fritz. *The Molding of American Banking: Men and Ideas.* 2 vols. New York. 1947–1951.

Reich, Cary. *Financier: The Biography of André Meyer.* New York. 1983.

Reid, Samuel Richardson. *Mergers, Managers, and the Economy.* New York. 1968.

Reutter, Mark. *Sparrows Point: Making Steel—The Rise and Ruin of American Industrial Might.* New York. 1988.

Riker, James. *Revised History of Harlem (City of New York), Its Origins and Early Annals.* New York. 1904.

Rogow, Arnold A. *James Forrestal: A Study of Personality, Politics, and Policy.* New York. 1963.

Sampson, Anthony. *The Money Lenders: Bankers in a World of Turmoil.* New York. 1981.

Schlesinger, Arthur, Jr. *The Age of Roosevelt: The Crisis of the Old Order, 1919–1933.* Boston. 1957.

———. *The Age of Roosevelt: The Coming of the New Deal.* Boston. 1959.

Schwartzchild, Leopold. *World in Trance: From Versailles to Pearl Harbor.* New York. 1942.

Seigfried, André. "The Passing of England's Economic Hegemony." *Foreign Affairs.* July 1928.

Seligman, Joel. *The Transformation of Wall Street: A History of the Securities and Exchange Commission and Modern American Corporate Finance.* Boston. 1982.

Seltzer, Lawrence. *A Financial History of the American Automobile Industry.* Boston. 1928.

Serling, Robert. *Howard Hughes' Airline: An Informal History of TWA.* New York. 1983.

Shultz, William, and M. R. Caine. *Financial Development of the United States.* New York. 1937.

Smith, Matthew Hale. *Bulls and Bears of New York.* New York. 1873.

Sobel, Robert. *The Age of Giant Corporations.* Westport, Conn. 1972.

———. *The Great Bull Market: Wall Street in the 1920s.* New York. 1968.

———. *NYSE: A History of the New York Stock Exchange, 1935–1975.* New York. 1975.

———. *Panic on Wall Street.* New York. 1968.

———. *Salomon Brothers, 1910–1985.* New York. 1987.

Spann, Edward. *The New Metropolis: New York City, 1840–1857.* New York. 1981.

Sterling, Adaline W. *The Book of Englewood.* Englewood, N.J. 1922.

Still, Bayrd. *Mirror for Gotham.* New York. 1956.

Stokes, Thomas L. *Chip Off My Shoulder.* Princeton. 1940.

Stresemann, Gustav. *Essays and Speeches on Various Subjects.* Freeport, N.Y. 1968 reprint edition.

Studenski, Paul, and Krooss, Herman. *Financial History of the United States.* New York. 1952.

Sullivan, Mark. *Our Times.* New York. 1933.

Sutton, Anthony. *Wall Street and the Rise of Hitler.* Seal Beach, Calif. 1976.

Sutton, Eric, ed. and trans. *Gustave Stresemann: His Diaries, Letters and Papers.* London. 1937.

Swaine, Robert T. *The Cravath Firm and Its Predecessors, 1819–1947.* 2 vols. New York. 1946 ed.

Taylor, George. *The Transportation Revolution, 1815–1860.* New York. 1951.

Thorp, Willard A. "The Persistence of the Merger Movement." *American Economic Review.* XXI, no. 1. March 1931.

Timmons, Bascom N. *Portrait of an American: Charles G. Dawes.* New York. 1953.

Tinnin, David B. *Just About Everybody vs. Howard Hughes.* New York. 1973.

Train, John. *The New Money Masters.* New York. 1989.

United States, Department of Commerce. Bureau of Foreign and Domestic Commerce. *American Direct Investments in Foreign Countries* [by Paul Dickens]. Washington, D.C. 1930.

———. *Historical Statistics of the United States, 1789–1945.* Washington, D.C. 1949.

———. *Historical Statistics of the United States, Colonial Times to 1970.* 2 vols. Washington, D.C. 1975.

———. *Recent Economic Changes in the United States: Report of the Committee on Recent Economic Changes of the President's Conference on Unemployment.* Washington, D.C. 1929.

———. 72nd Congress, 1st sess. Senate. Committee on Finance. Hearings. *Sales of Foreign Bonds or Securities in the United States.* Washington, D.C., 1932.

———. 73rd Congress, 1st sess. Senate. Committee on Banking and Currency. *Stock Exchange Practices.* pt. 4, Dillon, Read & Co. October 3–13, 1933. Washington, D.C. 1934.

———. 73rd Congress, 2nd sess. Senate. Report No. 1455. *Stock Exchange Practices Report.* Washington, D.C. 1934.

———. 76th Congress, 2nd sess. Hearings Before the Temporary National Economic Committee, Pursuant to Public Resolution No. 113. *Investigation of Concentration of Economic Power.* Washington, D.C. 1940.

———. 79th Congress, 1st sess. Senate Committee on Military Affairs. Hearings Before the Special Committee Investigating Petroleum Resources and Surplus Property Subcommittee. *War Emergency Pipe-Line Systems and Other Petroleum Facilities.* Washington, D.C. 1945.

———. 87th Congress, 1st sess. Joint Economic Committee. *Variability of Private Investment in Plant and Equipment.* Washington, D.C. 1962.

United States District Court, New York (Southern District). *Corrected Opinion of Harold R. Medina, United States Circuit Judge, in United States of America v. Henry S. Morgan, Harold Stanley, et al. doing business as Morgan Stanley & Co. et al.* New York. 1954 ed.

Walker, James. *The Epic of American Industry.* New York. 1957.

Wechsberg, Joseph. *The Merchant Bankers.* Boston. 1966.

Welles, Chris. *The Last Days of the Club.* New York. 1975.

Wesser, Robert S. *Charles Evans Hughes: Politics and Reform in New York, 1905–1910.* New York. 1967.

Wigmore, Barrie A. *The Crash and Its Aftermath.* Westport, Conn. 1985.

Wilkins, Mira. *The Maturing of Multinational Enterprise.* Cambridge, Mass. 1974.

Wilson, William L. *Full Faith and Credit: The Story of C.I.T. Financial Corporation, 1908–1975.* New York. 1976.

Winkler, Max. "Government Foreign Loans." *Annals of the American Academy of Political and Social Science.* July 1928.

Wojahn, Ellen. *Playing by Different Rules.* New York. 1988.

Wycoff, Richard D. *Wall Street Ventures and Adventures Through Forty Years.* New York. 1930.

INTERVIEWS

Transcripts of interviews have been deposited at the Dillon Read library. In addition to the transcripts there have been conversations with several of the interviewees, either in person or by telephone, for which there are no transcripts. These conversations include August Belmont, John P. Birkelund, Nicholas F. Brady, and C. Douglas Dillon.

Charles A. Ballard	October 5, 1988
August Belmont	January 26, June 12, 1988
James H. Brandi	February 24, 1988, July 18, 1989
Douglas Brinkley	November 28, 1988
Alan Curtis	January 17, 1989
Timothy Dalton	January 23, 1989
C. Douglas Dillon	October 28, 1987, September 21, 1988
Charles P. (Pat) Durkin	October 21, 1988
William Esrey	October 10, 1988
Dorothy Dillon Eweson	February 26, 1988
Peter M. Flanigan	January 21, 1988, September 1, 1988
John Haskell, Jr.	July 5, 1988, February 10, May 24, 1989
Joseph Haywood	February 29, 1988
Franklin W. (Fritz) Hobbs, IV	October 10, 1988
Charles Lea	January 17, February 10, 1989
Luis Mendez	January 23, 1989
John H. Mullin, III	October 5, 1988, March 3, 1989

David W. Niemiec	February 23, 1988
Paul H. Nitze	April 10, 1988, February 3, 1989
Robert C. Perez	September 13, 1988
Duncan H. Read	February 2, 1988
Jerry Ritter	January 4, 1989
Martin Roenigk	January 10, 1989
Wesley Stanger, Jr.	January 17, 1989
Arthur B. Treman, Jr.	November 30, December 28, 1988
Lorenzo D. Weisman	January 23, 1989
Edward (Ned) Whitney	January 24, May 24, 1989
Richard Yancey	August 16, 1988
Philip M. Young	February 21, 1989

In addition, I have benefited from other interviews, including several conducted by Charles Murphy in the early 1980s, when he was conducting research for a biography of James Forrestal, provided by Professor Douglas Brinkley of Hofstra University, who with Forrest Pogue assumed direction of the project on Murphy's death. Professor Brinkley also shared with me an interview he conducted with Michael Forrestal on April 27, 1988. The Murphy interviews include:

Tom Blacke	June 1983
Robert Votett	no date
John Magrane	no date
Henry Merritt	December 13, 1982
Paul Nitze	January 12, 1982
Edward F. Willett	no date

Index

403